EXEMPLARITY IN
GLOBAL POLITICS

Bristol Studies in International Theory

Series Editors: **Felix Berenskötter**, Kings College London, UK, **Neta C. Crawford**, University of Oxford, UK, and **Stefano Guzzini**, European University Institute, Italy.

This series provides a platform for theoretically innovative scholarship that advances our understanding of the world and formulates new visions of, and solutions for, world politics. Guided by an open mind about what innovation entails, and against the backdrop of various intellectual turns, interrogations of established paradigms, and a world facing complex political challenges, books in the series provoke and deepen theoretical conversations in the field of International Relations.

Also available in the series:

Benevolence in International Relations
by **Frédéric Ramel**

International Theory at the Margins
by **Nicholas Greenwood Onuf**

Broken Solidarities
by **Felix Anderl**

Care and the Pluriverse
by **Maggie FitzGerald**

Praxis as a Perspective on International Politics
edited by **Gunther Hellmann** and **Jens Steffek**

The Civil Condition in World Politics
edited by **Vassilios Paipais**

Snapshots from Home
by **Karin M. Fierke**

What in the World?
edited by **Mathias Albert** and **Tobias Werron**

The Idea of Civilization and the Making of the Global Order
by **Andrew Linklater**

Find out more at:
bristoluniversitypress.co.uk/
bristol-studies-in-international-theory

EXEMPLARITY IN GLOBAL POLITICS

Edited by
Dorothy Noyes and Tobias Wille

First published in Great Britain in 2025 by

Bristol University Press
University of Bristol
1-9 Old Park Hill
Bristol
BS2 8BB
UK
t: +44 (0)117 374 6645
e: bup-info@bristol.ac.uk

Details of international sales and distribution partners are available at bristoluniversitypress.co.uk

Editorial selection and matter © the Editors 2025; individual chapters © their respective authors 2025

The digital PDF and EPUB versions of this title are available open access and distributed under the terms of the Creative Commons Attribution 4.0 International licence (https://creativecommons.org/licenses/by/4.0/) which permits adaptation, alteration, reproduction, and distribution without further permission provided the original work is attributed.

DOI: 10.51952/9781529248050

British Library Cataloguing in Publication Data
A catalogue record for this book is available from the British Library

ISBN 978-1-5292-4804-3 paperback
ISBN 978-1-5292-4806-7 ePub
ISBN 978-1-5292-4805-0 OA PDF

The right of Dorothy Noyes and Tobias Wille to be identified as editors of this work has been asserted by them in accordance with the Copyright, Designs and Patents Act 1988.

All rights reserved: no part of this publication may be reproduced, stored in a retrieval system, or transmitted in any form or by any means, electronic, mechanical, photocopying, recording, or otherwise without the prior permission of Bristol University Press.

Every reasonable effort has been made to obtain permission to reproduce copyrighted material. If, however, anyone knows of an oversight, please contact the publisher.

The statements and opinions contained within this publication are solely those of the editors and contributors and not of the University of Bristol or Bristol University Press. The University of Bristol and Bristol University Press disclaim responsibility for any injury to persons or property resulting from any material published in this publication.

Bristol University Press works to counter discrimination on grounds of gender, race, disability, age and sexuality.

Cover design: blu inc
Front cover image: Kehinde Wiley, Napoleon Leading the Army Over the Alps, 2005. © Kehinde Wiley. Collection of the Brooklyn Museum

Contents

Notes on Contributors   vii
Acknowledgments   ix

PART I   Introduction

1. Theorizing Exemplarity for Global Politics   3
   Dorothy Noyes and Tobias Wille
2. From Performance to Uptake: A Process Model of Exemplarity   23
   Dorothy Noyes and Tobias Wille

PART II   Individuals and Inspiration

3. Gandhi's Exemplarity   49
   Ramachandra Guha
4. Tyrannicides, Tyrants, and Emperors: Exemplarity in the Graeco-Roman World   60
   Fritz Graf
5. The Child Greta: The Exemplar as Embodied Future   73
   Kyrre Kverndokk

PART III   The Complexities of Uptake

6. The Truths of Suffering and Injustice: Confucian Exemplarity in the History of Exemplar-Prisoners   91
   Ying Zhang
7. The Exemplary Normativity of International Precedents   110
   Christopher Daase and Tobias Wille
8. Exemplarity in Global Resistance: Beyond Epics and Romanticism   127
   Iratxe Perea Ozerin

PART IV   Exemplary Orders

9. Exemplarity and Hierarchy   145
   Ayşe Zarakol

| 10 | The Violence of the Exemplar: The French Civilizing Mission in French and Algerian Memories, 1918–Present
Guillaume Wadia | 164 |
| 11 | Prototyping Events: Creating Child-Oriented Methods of Disaster Preparedness
Chika Watanabe | 180 |

PART V Trajectories

12	The Soft Power of a Small Country: Self-Perceptions of the Netherlands as a Model for Europe and the World *Robin de Bruin*	199
13	Exemplary Appropriation: Holocaust Remembrance Practices in Post-Communist Europe *Jelena Subotić*	218
14	From Exemplarity to Farce? The Career of Cold War Threshold Crossings *Dorothy Noyes*	235

PART VI Thinking with Examples

15	Salient Examples in Flawed Reasoning about International Politics *Jack Snyder*	263
16	The Disciplinary Exemplarity of the Concert of Europe *Jennifer Mitzen*	273
17	Conclusion: The Fragility and Persistence of Examples *Dorothy Noyes and Tobias Wille*	286

Index   296

Notes on Contributors

Christopher Daase is Professor of International Relations at Goethe University Frankfurt and Deputy Director of the Peace Research Institute Frankfurt (Germany).

Robin de Bruin is Senior Lecturer in Modern European History at the University of Amsterdam (Netherlands).

Fritz Graf is Professor Emeritus of Classics at the Ohio State University (US).

Ramachandra Guha is a historian and biographer based in Bengaluru (India).

Kyrre Kverndokk is Professor of Cultural Studies at the University of Bergen (Norway).

Jennifer Mitzen is Professor of Political Science at the Ohio State University (US).

Dorothy Noyes is Professor of Folklore and Director of the Mershon Center for International Security Studies at the Ohio State University (US).

Iratxe Perea Ozerin is Associate Professor of International Relations at University of the Basque Country (Spain).

Jack Snyder is Professor of International Relations at Columbia University (US).

Jelena Subotić is Associate Professor of Political Science at Georgia State University (US).

Guillaume Wadia is Assistant Professor of History at Ahmedabad University (India).

Chika Watanabe is Senior Lecturer in Social Anthropology at the University of Manchester (UK).

Tobias Wille is Assistant Professor of International Security at Goethe University Frankfurt (Germany) and John F. Kennedy Memorial Fellow at Harvard University (US).

Ayşe Zarakol is Professor of International Relations at the University of Cambridge (UK).

Ying Zhang is Professor of Chinese History at Leiden University (Netherlands).

Acknowledgments

The patience and goodwill of many went into the production of this book. Interdisciplinary and international collaboration are challenging at the best of times, which the COVID-19 pandemic and its aftermath was not. They are especially challenging around the effort to bring a new scholarly object into being. Not even the editors knew entirely what they had in mind when they began convening conversations on exemplarity, but the convergence of approaches and assumptions from our contributors brought the phenomenon gradually into focus. We are grateful to our busy authors for sticking with us.

We cannot name all of the colleagues who offered insight into the emerging project, but extend special thanks to the series editors of Bristol Studies in International Theory – Felix Berenskötter, Neta C. Crawford, and Stefano Guzzini – as well as the anonymous reviewers. In addition, further participants at the 2020 Mershon Center conference 'Exemplarity: Performance, Influence, and Friction in Political Innovation' and in panels at the International Studies Association Conference in 2019, 2021, and 2022 were important interlocutors: these included Wendy Hesford, Hye Yun Kang, Maria Mälksoo, Iver Neumann, Wayne Sandholtz, Sebastian Schindler, Robbie Shilliam, Srdjan Vucetic, and Maja Zehfuss.

The conference and the open-access publication of the volume were generously supported by the Ohio State University Mershon Center for International Security Studies, the Research Center Normative Orders at Goethe University Frankfurt, and the Hessian Ministry of Higher Education, Research and the Arts through the LOEWE project 'ConTrust: Trust in Conflict.' In addition, Dorothy Noyes thanks the Mershon Center, the Ohio State University College of Arts and Sciences, the Lichtenberg-Kolleg of the University of Göttingen, the Research Center Normative Orders, and the Center for Advanced Studies in the Humanities of Goethe University Frankfurt for supporting essential intervals of research leave. Tobias Wille thanks the Research Center Normative Orders as well as the Minda de Gunzburg Center for European Studies at Harvard University for fellowships that supported parts of his work on this volume.

The labor of research assistants Theo Glaeser, Frederik Hermle, Chandler l'Hommedieu, and Sophie Peter was essential to the production of the volume. Finally, we extend our warm thanks to Stephen Wenham, Zoë Forbes, Lee-Ann Ashcroft, and the staff of Bristol University Press for their commitment and patient support.

PART I

Introduction

1

Theorizing Exemplarity for Global Politics

Dorothy Noyes and Tobias Wille

Nothing brings a prince so much consideration as great undertakings and giving extraordinary examples of himself.
Niccolò Machiavelli, *Il Principe*, 1975 [1532], 176

The rule must be abstracted from the deed, ... against which others may test their own talent, letting it serve them as a model not for *copying* but for *emulation*.[1]
Immanuel Kant, *Critique of the Power of Judgment*, 2000 [1790], 188

Be the change you want to see in the world.
Social movement maxim

Ten days after Vladimir Putin launched his invasion of Ukraine, the *New York Times* published an editorial, headlined 'Zelensky's Heroic Resistance Is an Example to the World.'[2] After the 2014 Russian intervention in the Donbas and takeover of Crimea, Ukraine had not been expected to withstand a full-fledged Russian assault, but it was pushing back with surprising success. Its media-savvy president Volodymyr Zelensky, striding among his soldiers in combat fatigues, made a striking contrast to Putin, sleek

---

[1] In keeping with our language later in the essay, we have modified the translation of *Nachahmung* from the published 'imitation' to the also permissible 'emulation.'
[2] *The New York Times.* '"I Want Peace" Zelensky's Heroic Resistance Is an Example for the Word.' March 4, 2022, Online: https://www.nytimes.com/2022/03/04/opinion/ukraine-russia-war-biden.html (accessed October 27, 2023).

and remote in his Kremlin fastness. Zelensky further surprised the West by boldly remapping the geopolitical divide: Ukraine was not a Russian satellite but the West's own last redoubt: 'The fate of not only our state is being decided, but also what Europe will be like.'[3] Zelensky did not play the suppliant outsider, but asserted Ukraine's Europeanness as a self-evident claim to European support.

Western media were quick to take up the cue, calling the invasion 'the biggest attack on a European state since World War Two.'[4] They snapped up images and anecdotes: the Snake Island border guards defying the flagship Moskva; Zelensky unshaven and grim in his bunker; Ukrainian farmers towing abandoned Russian tanks with their tractors; Ukrainian schoolgirls learning how to handle rifles for civil defense. Ordinary Ukrainians were seen everywhere, asserting the national claim to centrality in a global struggle: one woman told an MSNBC interviewer, 'The world is under attack, but only Ukrainians are fighting.'[5]

As Ukrainians captioned their struggle as one for democracy, freedom, and the right to a home, Western leaders and publics responded empathetically. An official reported to the *Washington Post* that a video call between Zelensky and European leaders 'was extremely, extremely emotional … He was essentially saying: "Look, we are here dying for European ideals".'[6]

Within their own society, Ukrainians drew strength from national examples of threat and resistance: the anti-Bolshevik insurgent Nestor Makhno, the Euromaidan protests that became the 2014 Revolution of Dignity, even the television satire 'Servant of the People' in which the actor Zelensky had played the president before assuming the actual office. But in calling for Western support, Zelensky cited and channeled their own examples: Winston Churchill to the British, Pearl Harbor and 9/11 to the Americans, Guernica to the Spanish. Western commentators found other resonant analogies, likening the Jewish Zelensky to David against Goliath.

These, however, were examples from the past, and in the present it was Ukraine that was standing up to invasion and sacrificing lives to assert freedom, national sovereignty, and democratic rule. It was now Ukraine

---

[3] *The Guardian*. 'The Guardian View on Putin's War in Ukraine.' February 24, 2022, Online: https://www.theguardian.com/commentisfree/2022/feb/24/the-guardian-view-on-putins-war-in-ukraine-a-bleak-new-beginning (accessed December 8, 2023).

[4] Reuters. 'Missiles Rain Down Around Ukraine.' February 22, 2022, Online: https://www.reuters.com/world/europe/putin-orders-military-operations-ukraine-demands-kyiv-forces-surrender-2022-02-24/ (accessed October 27, 2023).

[5] Rachel Maddow Show. MSNBC. March 4, 2020.

[6] *The Washington Post*. 'Historic Sanctions on Russia Had Roots in Emotional Appeal from Zelensky.' February 27, 2022, Online: https://www.washingtonpost.com/business/2022/02/27/russia-ukraine-sanctions-swift-central-bank/ (accessed October 27, 2023).

setting the example to a West in crisis. *The Times* affirmed: '[Zelensky] has first shown Ukrainians who they want to be, and then reminded Europeans of who we used to know we were.'[7] *The Washington Post* concluded sadly, 'We need to be worthy of Ukrainians' respect.'[8] For once, the media establishment was not at odds with the populace, left or right. Ukrainian flags popped up on Western façades; blue and yellow memes blanketed the internet. Diverse appropriations claimed the Ukrainian example. In the US, frustrated young men donned T-shirts proclaiming 'I need ammunition, not a ride'; the gun lobby pointed to the invasion as evidence of the need for an armed populace; Zelensky appeared along liberal icons like Anthony Fauci and Ruth Bader Ginsburg as the face of a votive candle.

Zelensky's challenge, 'Do prove that you are indeed Europeans,' a startling inversion of the liberal status hierarchy, evoked active responses at every scale of action and degree of commitment, from the silly to the transformational. Emmanuel Macron paraded through the Élysée Palace in a hoodie, Germany announced a *Zeitenwende* from its postwar pacifism, and the long-neutral states of Finland and Sweden applied for NATO membership. Suddenly, after the long, muddy years of postsocialism and neoliberal globalization, there was a line in the sand.

The convergence of the West around the shining Ukrainian example was foreseeably ephemeral. A long, costly struggle makes any performance hard to sustain and disperses its audience around other interests, established affinities, and new crises. Still, the consequences of that first exemplary moment have been multifarious, serious, and durable. A structurally weak actor on the geopolitical stage exerted a remarkable, if hard to measure, influence on global politics.

This book sets out to illuminate the exemplary gestures that abound in global politics: not only Ukraine's resistance, but John Paul II's visit to Poland, the elevation of the Goddess of Democracy in Tiananmen Square, the 9/11 terrorist attacks, Greta Thunberg's school strike, and many others. Powerful embodied performances of conduct invite evaluation and emulation, sometimes setting in motion a process of cultural transmission that we name exemplarity. Compressed into days or stretched across centuries, a cycle of this process comprises four analytical stages. A social actor offers a surprising *performance* of conduct to an audience of significant others. Struck by its transgressive character, aesthetic impact, historical resonance, risky

---

[7] *The Times*. 'We All Buy into Zelensky's Brand Ukraine.' February 28, 2022, Online: https://www.thetimes.co.uk/article/we-all-buy-into-zelenskys-brand-ukraine-cczzj8zzf (accessed December 8, 2023).

[8] *The Washington Post*. 'Character Is Contagious: Look What Ukraine Has Inspired.' February 28, 2022, Online: https://www.washingtonpost.com/opinions/2022/02/28/ukraine-inspires-west/ (accessed December 8, 2023).

commitment, or other features, some of these others share the performance more widely, through both simple reports and fuller representations. This *amplification* enables the performance to circulate through various communicative networks and to persist across time and space. New actors encountering the performance and its representations engage in collective reflection and *judgment*. Through this, they turn the performance into an example, even while disagreeing over its import and meaning. Some may elevate the initial actor as a general exemplar. *Citation* and *emulation* follow, concluding the cycle and sometimes setting new examples in turn.

As we show, this cultural process has social force: as a component of general cultural competence, exemplarity can be harnessed by both established and aspiring political actors. While many performances are rightly dismissed as empty gestures, and genuinely costly efforts may fall flat, the potential force of example is such that both world leaders and social movement organizers rely on it as a primary resource for political mobilization, and a wide range of cultural traditions recognize it explicitly as a principle of social order. Moreover, in situations of turmoil and crisis, actors look for examples to guide their actions and make sense of what is happening. The ability of examples to vault across gaps in time, space, and ideology distinguishes exemplarity as a unique social phenomenon and makes it a topic of special importance for international theory.

In this introduction we point out the lexical complexity and commonsense formulations that have impeded analytical recognition of exemplarity as an integrated and dynamic process. We furthermore situate exemplarity among other modes of cultural transmission: rule, procedure, practice, and representation. We then discuss what an engagement with exemplarity can contribute to international theory before, finally, laying out the chapters of the volume as instantiating how an understanding of exemplarity can illuminate a wide range of issue spaces in global politics.

From concept bundle to mechanism

In extracting concepts from social life, academics are doomed to imprecision. 'Natural' language develops *ad hoc*, with competing, cohabiting, and overlapping vocabularies for shared experiences. Authorities of all kinds propose concepts to govern this disorder, but concepts released into the wild of social life branch out in turn, recombining into multiple, sometimes contradictory applications. Already in classical Latin, *exemplum* could mean 'sample; example; precedent; warning; punishment; portrait; copy' (Morwood 1994), and derivatives in modern Western languages have elaborated these meanings. Major research agendas in the humanities and social sciences have crystallized around three of them: the rhetorical analysis of examples as *samples* claimed to represent a whole or population

(Fleming 2009; Lyons 2014); the epistemological analysis of examples as *cases* that render some abstraction visible or, conversely, invite abstraction from their particulars (Flyvbjerg 2001; Højer and Bandak 2015); and the ethical analysis of examples as *models* of conduct proffered for emulation (Ferrara 2008; Gomá Lanzón 2019; McNay 2019; Evans 2023).

This last meaning in particular pushes 'example' into the territory of what ethicists call 'thick concepts,' in which fact and value are inseparable. But more than that, these three base meanings are not separable in practice. Contemporary critical theorists are quick to notice the implicit normativity of apparently casual illustrations or putatively representative samples. Conversely, a model for action is not taken up if it neither offers a striking picture nor resonates with the experience of its intended emulators. This complexity of social process engenders both multivocality and multiplication in terminology. To take only English, we have *example* with grammatical derivatives such as *exemplary*, *exemplify*; the back formation *exemplar*; the etymological doublet *sample*; formulaic phrases like *setting an example* or *exemplary sentence*; historical synonyms including *pattern*, *paradigm*, *model*; attempted specifications such as *precedent*, *watershed moment*, *role model*, *demonstration effect*; and so on. In contrast to the concept cluster – the network of distinctly named concepts that structures a particular discourse (Berenskoetter 2017) – we might call this messy lexical overlap a concept bundle. Instead of seeking to disentangle its elements, we take their multi-millennial coexistence to be evidence of an underlying phenomenon that connects them, which we propose to call 'exemplarity.'

Example is accordingly different in kind from sovereignty, freedom, democracy, or other core concepts of international theory. Though thick and multivocal, it is not 'essentially contested' (Gallie 1955–56), a 'keyword' (Williams 1976), or 'basic' (Koselleck 2011). Although it plays a role in a variety of ideological formations, social debate does not coalesce around it,[9] nor has it excited sustained scholarly attention as a social phenomenon (see Lyons 2014, x).

The status of example in modernity and in the liberal international order is particularly confusing. As Reinhart Koselleck argues, the classical understanding of history as a reservoir of examples to guide the present lost its sway in the mid-18th century with the consolidation of modern conceptions of time and change (1985 [1979]). But the concept bundle did not disappear or even decline in usage, embedded as it was in pedagogic, pastoral, and penal discourses shaped by the Church tradition of *imitatio*

---

[9] One exception is in democratic Spain, where an influential formulation of exemplarity by José Ortega y Gasset has informed an enduring debate over elite privilege and political responsibility (Noyes 2022).

Christi as well as in prestige arenas influenced by classical republicanism's culture of competitive emulation. Both traditions – the call for the masses to follow good examples and the urging of elite individuals to set new ones – inform global politics along with every other domain of modernity. In modern Western cultures, the idiom of exemplarity is what Raymond Williams (1977, 122) calls a residual element: not an isolated archaic survival but an older formulation that remains 'an effective element of the present' and may indeed lend important support to dominant narratives and institutions, as evidenced in the idiom of 'leading by example' so central to both Anglo-American and European Union foreign policy thinking. Hiding in plain sight, exemplarity has not called for scrutiny and yet it is everywhere. To dig beneath the common sense of example and postulate something real behind it is therefore to engage in what Guzzini (2013) categorizes as 'empirical theorizing,' working inductively from the observation of social phenomena to identify social mechanisms. Exemplarity lends itself to comparative projects as a descriptive term, not least because a global range of traditions recognize and name elements of the exemplary process (Evans 2023). We aim to place exemplarity within the universe of 'empirical mechanisms' (Guzzini 2013) that, at different scales and foci of analysis, can be seen to sustain social life. More precisely, we situate it as a mode of cultural transmission, interacting with but different from rule, procedure, practice, and representation. We posit that exemplarity is of special significance for global politics, insofar as it is capable of connecting actors across distance and discontinuity: of time, geography, culture, and social position.

A mode of cultural transmission

To call exemplarity a mode of transmission is to assert that it transports cultural objects, that is, recognizable, isolable patterns of behavior at various scales and degrees of organization, across temporal, geographic, cultural and social distance (Urban 2001). To clarify what we mean by this, it will be helpful to contrast exemplarity with other modes of cultural transmission that are regularly studied and extensively theorized in International Relations (IR).

The most easily recognized mode of transmission is the *rule*, which we encounter in the social world as commandment, law, norm, precept, and so on. Rules are general principles, made explicit and publicly available, that call for particular application. disciplining what happens in situ. Rules play a prominent role in international theory, called on to explain both actor behavior and the reproduction and transformation of international order. One such debate concerns how international law can bind states in the absence of a central authority that could enforce compliance (Goldsmith and Posner 2005). Norms, understood as 'a standard of appropriate behavior for actors with a given identity' (Finnemore and Sikkink 1998) have also extensively been studied. The transmission they facilitate has been described in the simplest model as compliance, but also more substantively as socialization and – most recently – as diffusion and translation (Acharya 2004; Checkel 2005; Zimmermann 2017).

A more embedded mode of transmission is the *procedure*, as inscribed in plans, blueprints, or protocols. Procedures are pre-designed, explicit systems for prescribing, coordinating, shaping, and governing particular actions and sequences as components of a broader operation. In the eyes of institutionalists, such procedures configure the agency of organizations and give continuity to social and political life (March and Olson 1984). They also explain why organizations often behave in seemingly inefficient or outright contradictory ways. One prominent formulation of this idea in IR can be found in Graham Allison's (1971) account of the Cuban Missile Crisis, where standard operating procedures explain why the US in a crisis situation did not act as a rational actor model would predict. More recently, technological advance has transformed procedure. With the transition from mere automation to algorithms and artificial intelligence, procedure is no longer associated with inertia but with radical disruption and change, even if effected under the radar of actor attention (Ansorge 2016).

Both rule and procedure, at different scales of abstraction, provide general guidance for particular instantiation. The remaining modes circulate differently, from instance to instance, even though mass reproductive technologies assist their movement. Of these, *practice* has received most recent attention in IR (Adler and Pouliot 2011; Bueger and Gadinger 2015; for an overview, see Wille 2018). Practice and similar concepts such as habit and routine (Mitzen 2006; Hopf 2010; Ejdus 2018) refer to patterns of quotidian, untheorized and generally inarticulate behavior that are learned and reproduced through interaction and observation. While critical theorists emphasize the unthinking reproduction of ideology through the formation and transmission of habitus (Pouliot 2010; see Schindler and Wille 2015), pragmatists focus more on the conscious and active transmission through peripheral participation in a community of practitioners (Adler 2008; Bicchi 2022) and adaptation to new circumstances through play and experimentation (Bueger and Edmunds 2021). Recently, IR theorists have also drawn on the notion of ritual to capture heightened, semiotically rich practices that unfold in a well-defined sequence and thus may be formalized into procedure, extrapolated into rule, and enhanced by representation (Kustermans et al 2021; Mälksoo 2021).

Representation denotes a cultural form presented at a remove from direct social action, instead inviting reflection. Representation implies a higher degree of organization, framing, and conscious design than does practice: representation has an aesthetic, or attention-grabbing, dimension that assists its transmission and reproduction. Such transmission moves even across gaps of time and space, for like rule and procedure, but unlike practice, a representation, once made, is free of its maker. Most strictly identified with domains such as art, play, religion, or scholarship, representation also impinges on instrumental life through everyday narrative and metaphor, décor, documentation, the circulation of news, and so on. In IR, cultural representations have been studied by discourse analysts (Der Derian 1987; Neumann 1999) as a mode in which culture is reproduced and transformed. Recent scholarship has placed a particular emphasis on popular culture (Nexon and Neumann 2006; Dittmer and Bos 2019) and visual representations (Bleiker 2018). With so many channels, however, representation is a chaotic and contingent mode of transmission compared to rule, procedure, or even practice. As they circulate, representations cluster and remix in complex networks, furnishing social actors with imaginaries and repertoires for making sense and orienting action.

Where does *exemplarity* fit in? Unlike rule and procedure, exemplarity does not transmit a general and abstract form, but proceeds by linking particular instances to each other in a temporal sequence. In this eschewal of general forms, exemplarity is similar to practice and representation. In contrast to these other two modes, however, exemplarity is founded in action, in Arendt's sense (1998 [1958]). It is neither everyday labor nor purposeful work towards a clear goal. The example begins as a gesture through which an actor intervenes in the spacetime of social life to realign its actors and elements. The gesture may be metaphorical – cutting ties, standing fast, leading the way – but it most powerfully inspires uptake when the social action is embodied in literal gesture that excites bodily identification in the immediate audience and lends itself to secondary representations that can travel far afield from the moment. Indeed, the outward and visible form of an exemplary gesture – the shout to the Russian warship – can be readily replicated. Exemplarity in the fullest sense, however, implies the concurrent transmission and uptake of the gesture's attitudinal core: defiance, humility, renunciation. The exemplary gesture is often understood to point to something – a future state, a past example, or, sometimes, an eternal reality. In this sense exemplarity furnishes matter for extrapolation into general rules and procedures. The affective power of the example, however, comes from its uniqueness: its life as a salient moment in time. The example is a deed, with a before and an after. Moreover, a deed has a doer. A powerful example redounds upon its agent, and the agent thereby is often reified as an exemplar: a saint, a monster, founding fathers.[10]

---

[10] Some contributors to this volume, most explicitly Watanabe (Chapter 11), challenge the idea that every example requires a prominent exemplar who appears as its original

We have presented the four modes of transmission as ideal types. In our theorizing, they themselves become representations, elegant models that create an image of the social world before our inner eye. In social reality they intersect and blend, forming complex constellations. All will inform the repertoires of actors. They are nonetheless distinguishable, as can be seen when the cultural object of 'greeting' jumps from one mode to another. The everyday social *practice* of exchanging greetings is one of several cultural forms that cement social interaction into customary obligation: gift-giving, mutual aid, the exchange of marriage partners, and so on. Together, these practices can be abstracted into *rules*: the scholarly concept of reciprocity, the religious precept 'Thou shalt love thy neighbor as thyself,' the civil rights movement's demand for respect and inclusion. The practice of greeting may enter *representation* as a meaningful device that moves from text to text, as when Fellini's film *La dolce vita* builds on Dante's *Vita nuova* to suggest, through a failed greeting exchange, that the character Marcello has moved beyond the pale of salvation (Bondanella 2002). Greeting can also be converted into *procedure*, as in diplomatic protocol or indeed the employee script for welcoming customers in retail franchises. But in a new context, where the normality of practice and procedure does not exist, gesture can be raised to *exemplarity*, as when Richard Nixon and Zhou Enlai shook hands on the Beijing airport tarmac in 1972.

Why exemplarity matters for international theory: relationality, change, and agency

As an ambitious interdisciplinary enterprise, this volume combines a wide range of perspectives from the humanities and the social sciences. An inductive approach to 'empirical theorizing,' as practiced in the ethnographic disciplines, allows for cogent description, comparison, and analysis of the social phenomenon of exemplarity. We also attempt 'ontological theorizing,' striving to participate in a new and more precise articulation of the theoretical building blocks with which we make sense of global politics (see Guzzini 2013). Specifically, we intend the work presented in this volume to advance the debate on three interrelated themes in international theory: the constitutive role of relations, the dynamism of continuity and change, and the question of agency.

---

author and protagonist. The sovereign agent is central to the articulation of exemplarity in Western modernity, and some other religious and philosophical traditions focus on the individual exemplar (for example, Zhang, Chapter 6, this volume), but we do not view the elevation of the performer's personhood as essential to the exemplary process.

Along with social and political theory generally, international theory has embraced the turn from a structural and entity-based framework to *relational and processual perspectives* highlighting the perpetual co-constitution and reconstitution of social life (Jackson and Nexon 1999; McCourt 2016). We expect that many reified agents, norms, and narratives of global politics can be traced back to the social negotiations from which they were abstracted, when gestural performances of conduct were amplified, judged, cited, and emulated: the exemplary process. Against this background, we posit that examples are relational in at least two important respects. First, their very status as examples cannot be decided by a single actor, whether the author of the exemplary deed or the observer and interpreter. As we will argue in detail in the next chapter, at every stage of the process that leads from the performance of an example to its uptake, a complex web of relations between actors determines not only the 'success' of an example as a social force, but its very meaning and relevance. Second, as Noyes shows in Chapter 14 on Cold War threshold crossings, examples and their associated exemplars are constituted by their interactions as they cite and emulate, but also avoid, eclipse, and overwrite each other. Unlike the continuous fabric of social practice, they form a loose network that provides tight links between some acts and events while elsewhere bridging great distances without noticeable impact.

What emerges is thus a highly dynamic account of global politics that incorporates elements of *continuity* with a complex rendering of *social change*. The exemplary process operates across a socio-temporal network that by its nature can never be closed down and thus necessarily contains a transformative element, even as it continually throws off reifications. Exemplarity thus implies a complex interplay of continuity, as actors refer to the reified examples of past conduct, and change, as these examples are assessed, revised, and repurposed for new application. Even in its most repressive invocations, exemplarity is future-oriented. Actors propose examples to attract attention and intervene in a present social trajectory, even launch a phase shift. If other actors take up an example, supporting, deflecting, appropriating, reforming, or resisting it, it becomes a dynamic force that opens new avenues for future development while closing off others. The citation of historic examples does not contradict this dynamism; instead, it may mask and mediate it. To invoke some long-enshrined exemplar is of course the time-honored strategy for representing even radical change as 'conservative,' sanctified by tradition or eternity. It is no less common for actors committed to progress, liberal or revolutionary, to claim harbinger exemplars from the past in celebrating the deeds of the present. Attached to a particular community or purpose, the harbinger can lend focus and legitimacy to a transition, opening a narrative of which the present moment can be cast as the turning point, when past becomes future.

Moreover, the relative autonomy of the processes of cultural transmission has the potential to disrupt reified structures and narratives, as cultural objects continue their movements largely independent of grand principles. Each of the five modes of transmission inflects the reproduction and transformation of social order in its own fashion. Practice is the ground of social order, sustaining continuity even as it absorbs new elements and effects incremental transformation. Rules and procedures constitute deliberate interventions in social life, and while they are intended to stabilize practice, their institution can itself be disruptive and is often fraught with unintended consequences. Conflicting and overlapping jurisdictions create their own dynamism. Moreover, the accumulation of rules and procedures over time may create its own disruptions, as the legacy of one intervention comes into conflict with a successor regime. Representations, being fixed and situated at one remove from social life, are both less and more continuous. Different genres and traditions will coexist and recombine; a formulation may go out of fashion and be rediscovered in a different place and century.

Exemplarity's relation to order differs from these other modes by its inextricability from *agency*, that is, from the ability of specific actors to affect the course of events. Actors with command of a stage and means of amplification can most easily propose examples, but exemplarity is more than mechanical reproduction: transmission requires active judgment, citation, and emulation by other actors. In this way, political exemplarity inflects the individual prestige of leaders, states, and movements as well as the relations among them. This uptake creates opportunities for creative appropriation and contestation by aspiring and marginal actors (Abrahamsson and Dányi 2019; Braun, Schindler, and Wille 2019; Perea Ozerin, Chapter 8, this volume; Pingeot and Pouliot 2024). A skillful seizing of the stage may win amplification as news, becoming available for wider uptake. Giving public form in historical time to the energy and volition of actors, exemplarity confirms or transforms the distribution of social power. Exemplarity thus plays a key role in reproducing global political life – or at any rate our perception of global political life – not as a well-ordered society or self-regulating system, but as an amalgam of interrelated, contingent human actions over time.

Getting a grip on exemplarity

Our project has evolved toward a systematic account of exemplarity from a kaleidoscopic initial stocktaking followed by gradual mutual accommodation across disciplines and case studies. Beginning at the Annual Convention of the International Studies Association in Toronto in 2019, we recruited an array of scholars – political scientists, historians, anthropologists, folklorists, and classicists – to collectively think about examples and their uptake. At the end of February 2020, just as the COVID-19 pandemic was about to seize hold, we held the conference 'Exemplarity: Performance, Influence, and Friction in Political Innovation,' at the Mershon Center for International Security Studies at the Ohio State University; the conversation then continued in email exchanges, video calls, and eventual further conference panels. The framework presented in Chapter 2 and the contributions that follow reflect the results of this intense transdisciplinary engagement. While the chapters draw on distinct disciplinary methods and work through specific disciplinary concerns, they all incorporate insights from our collective discussions, illuminate aspects of the general process we posit, and confirm its applicability to empirical cases across periods, social contexts, cultural frameworks, and scales of action. Each chapter addresses multiple phases of the exemplary process, and the chapters speak to one another across many dimensions. Our chapter groupings alternate familiar contexts of exemplarity with pieces pointing to new areas for research.

Individuals and inspiration

We begin with the globally most familiar conception of the exemplar: the charismatic individual whose example inspires others to virtuous conduct. In Chapter 3, historian Ramachandra Guha makes a compelling case for retaining this figure at the core of the phenomenon, while rejecting the conversion of such figures into plaster statues embodying eternal truths. His essay, drawn from a speech presented at a 2011 United Nations commemoration of the International Day of Non-Violence, offers a passionate recapitulation of Mohandas Gandhi's political innovations, each spearheaded by a startling performance; their influence on major developments of the 20th century; and the even greater urgency of their reflective uptake in the current world situation. Some exemplars prove their value over the long term.

Classicist Fritz Graf takes up the question of demand in Chapter 4. Athenian democracy, perpetually threatened with oligarchic takeover, developed an 'exemplarity template' intended to prepare individual citizens to defend the city against tyranny. The individual exemplar was amplified through artistic means ranging from sculptural elevation at the heart of the agora to symposium songs facilitating 'indoctrination through inebriation.' The exemplarity of the tyrannicide was deemed so important to regime stability that actually existing cases, both historic and recent, underwent considerable narrative revision in order to reaffirm the template.

In the midst of climate collapse, legitimation belongs to the precarious future rather than the glorious past. In Chapter 5, folklorist Kyrre Kverndokk shows how Greta Thunberg presented herself in the category of childhood to invert the normal temporality of exemplarity and of history *tout court*.

Prophesying a future in which possibilities shut down rather than open up, she positions herself as the last example that can be followed.

Also raised in these three chapters is the relationship of the individual to the collective. Gandhi's use of commitment oaths for his followers in the first satyagraha evinces his recognition that a long-term effort would require the ongoing participation of a large number of people. The Athenian artistic apparatus that raised a mortal exemplar among the gods enticed individual citizens to imagine themselves in the tyrannicide's role. Thunberg has attempted to reject the machinery of contemporary celebrity, but it has not rejected her, and the person-to-person logic of social media influencing has encouraged individuals to take up her example. Still, difficult collective efforts, whether to transform the status quo or, as in the case of Athens, preserve it, are too easily reduced to the individuals who first give them face. As the sample elevated to represent the collective, the reified exemplar may be scapegoated, used to discredit the movement, or expected to carry its burden alone. The concentration of attention on one person may leave other potential exemplars and their innovations out in the cold, as has been noted of Thunberg's visibility in contrast to her counterparts in the global South, who in one much-reported instance were actually cropped out of the picture. Guha's call for reflective humility from all participants in the exemplary process must push against the overwhelming force of the current media of amplification, which raise individuals to superhuman heights, typically followed by an all-too-human crash from the pedestal.

The complexities of uptake

Both popular narrative and scholarly analysis often reduce the intertwined stages of the exemplary process, to a mechanical operation: the indoctrination of an ideal, citation of a precedent, copying of a model. Our second cluster of chapters demonstrates the need for closer scrutiny. Historian Ying Zhang responds in Chapter 6 to stereotypes of top-down cultural authority in the Chinese Confucian tradition as well as liberal assertions of democratic resistance by tracing the long-term interaction of elite and popular communication around Chinese exemplars, whether literati imprisoned by Ming emperors or Dr Li Wenliang, early hero of the COVID-19 pandemic. The verbal and visual arts of exemplarity have generated a space of exchange for critical reflection, affective empathy, and spiritual veneration that can be utilized by state propaganda but does not allow it to dominate.

Moving from domestic to international politics, Christopher Daase and Tobias Wille ask in Chapter 7 why justifications of the international use of force so often cite precedents, despite their lack of binding force in international law. Drawing on Arendt's political rereading of Kant's argument that aesthetic judgment emerges from reflection on unique examples, the authors propose that precedent actions carry 'exemplary normativity.' In a context of uncertainty or crisis, where both rule and established consensus are lacking, precedents are of vital importance as points of reference to orient action through reflective judgment.

Working with feminist and postcolonial critiques of International Relations theory, Iratxe Perea Ozerin puts forward in Chapter 8 both the power and the limitations of exemplarity as a framework for learning from the past. Working against institutions and outside of them, global resistance movements often turn to earlier exemplars of success and failure for insight and inspiration. Their quest is, however, severely constrained by biases and gaps in the historical record. So spectacular a success as the Haitian Revolution, active in outreach to colonized neighbors who might follow its example, was not only materially punished but, as best as possible, shut down as an available narrative by the colonial powers. On the other hand, the unshowy everyday tactics of 19th-century women's movements failed to command the attention their successes deserved, confirming the exclusionary logic of a politics of appearances in which the incumbent exemplars tend to retain their preeminence over time at the expense of potentially superior alternatives.

Exemplary orders

While exemplarity has proven to be a valuable mechanism both for legitimating and for challenging a variety of social orders, IR theorist Ayşe Zarakol helps us in Chapter 9 to understand why the Western-led liberal international order has been particularly insistent on the importance of 'leading by example.' In practice, Zarakol argues, exemplars are typically raised from the ranks of the aspirants. Exemplarity, on her account, is the mechanism that mediates between an ideology of equality and a hierarchical structure. The early liberal order, with its 'Standard of Civilization' for entry into international society, was such a configuration, and it enabled countries such as Turkey and Japan to claim exemplary regional leadership, though not to cross the threshold into full membership. These exemplars responded to and sustained a Western promise of inclusion, while undermining the putative symmetry among sovereign nations.

In Chapter 10, historian Guillaume Wadia examines the postcolonial aftermath of such exemplary hierarchies. The French claim to offer a universal example allowed it to impose its *mission civilisatrice* on Algeria and other colonies, providing an idiom for the national ambitions of natives and reassuring European settlers of their legitimacy. After independence, the many layers of the French model were simultaneously repudiated, appropriated, and unconsciously reproduced among Algerians. This ongoing violence of example had its counterpart among the former colonizers, where old habits continue to shape the treatment of the immigrant population and a never fully examined discourse of exemplarity has been reappropriated for reactionary politics.

Anthropologist Chika Watanabe points in Chapter 11 to a shift in the global exemplary order, with as yet unclear implications: the rise of design thinking, in which prototypes, adapted to particular situations through participatory iteration, replace the rigid templates that justified their imposition through universalist claims. Her trans-Pacific case study examines a disaster-preparedness intervention developed by a Japanese NGO as it is implemented in Chile. This example is productive by virtue of its very incompleteness, demanding creative adaptation in its uptake. Significantly, like the climate activism of Greta Thunberg, this NGO focuses on children, the actors not yet stiffened into conformity with reified exemplars, as the target of intervention. In both cases, as agency is pushed towards the emulators, we might wonder about the abdication of the institutional exemplars. The origin of prototyping in consumer capitalism, specifically as a Western innovation in product design, also merits examination.

Trajectories

This chapter cluster addresses the late careers of well-established exemplars. In Chapter 12, historian Robin de Bruin shows how the Dutch conception of itself as a 'model colonizer' became unviable in the wake of postwar decolonization, necessitating a new understanding of the role of the Netherlands in the world. An exemplary self-consciousness of this small country as *primus inter pares* among its great-power neighbors was retained by reconceiving the Netherlands as a 'guide country' for the rising European Union. While different political factions argue over the content of this exemplarity, historians are divided as to whether the claim is psychological compensation for the loss of empire, or stems from the longer internationalist tradition of a nation that is both commercial and evangelical.

IR scholar Jelena Subotić takes us in Chapter 13 to the other, Eastern end of the European Union, where its aspiring and new members were required to engage in Holocaust remembrance as the exemplary performance of the self-critical commitment to human rights that is the hallmark of Europe's own claim to global exemplarity. These states indeed adopted the Western commemorative repertoires, but in many cases repurposed them to elevate the suffering of national majorities under Communist rule. As the demographic and democratic weight of Poland, Hungary, and other new members imposed itself on European institutions, their revision became available to right-wing parties in Western Europe. This reversal of victim status between Jews and the 'national' ethnicity thus indexes an emergent reversal of European political geography, in which Eastern innovations are providing exemplars for Western emulation.

In Chapter 14, folklorist Dorothy Noyes considers the apparent banalization of exemplarity as media spectacle. Mapping the transmission network of post-World War II threshold crossings, when a political leader steps for the first time onto enemy territory, from their high water mark in the era of détente to the diplomacy of the first Trump administration, she identifies the obvious argument for exemplary decadence: as spectacle pulls ahead of the lower-level diplomatic work that can ensure its performative force, it fails even as performance in the moment. Nonetheless, the very diffusion and dispersal of this exemplary tradition made it available to once-peripheral actors and facilitated the confidence of the Republic of Korea and the United Arab Emirates in claiming protagonism on the global stage.

Thinking with examples

Jack Snyder and Jennifer Mitzen carry us into a specific zone of exemplary reflexivity: the overlap between academic analysis and policy formulation in international relations. Snyder in Chapter 15 emphasizes the limitations of exemplarity as a resource for decision-making. Drawing on research from political psychology and cognitive science, he observes that leaders under pressure resort to the most salient examples from their own generational formation and the cultural surround, leading to mechanical, epistemically deficient revisitings of Munich, Pearl Harbor, and Vietnam. The emotional and symbolic relevance of such examples overrides logical consideration of their applicability. Even where normative rather than practical examples are in question, they suggest an invariant rule that distracts thinkers from the particular situation. The elevation of a prior example thus makes the practical and ethical error of neglecting the complexity of the case at hand.

In Chapter 16, however, Jennifer Mitzen reminds us that certain founding examples seem doomed to stay with us for all eternity – at least the little eternity of IR theorizing. Just as the Peloponnesian War provided the case from which the general rules of realism are extrapolated and revised (Lebow 2001), so the Concert of Europe and its preceding Congress of Vienna exemplify great-power management and subsequent conceptions of global governance. But as she shows, the centrality of the Concert example makes it difficult for the academic discipline of IR and the adjacent policy discourse to integrate new insights from historical work that highlights such themes as the role of women, non-state actors, and transnational capital at the Congress. The reified Congress and Concert thus become a mechanism that stabilizes the academic field of IR and possibly also international politics, at the cost of drawing arbitrary boundaries and excluding relevant perspectives. In the current political moment, when the authority of both academic experts and foreign policy professionals is under pressure, it remains to be seen whether this stabilizing effect can be sustained.

The editors conclude the volume by resituating the chapters in the historicity of both individual examples and exemplarity itself, an exercise that brings us to the implications of the current political moment. The destabilization of the liberal international order, interacting with technological transformation, has energized the proliferation of examples while severely damaging the conditions for their transformative uptake. International theorists and political actors alike are reckoning with the loss of faith in dominant examples. Recognizing exemplarity as a networked process, depending on multiple agencies at each stage, helps us to understand why modern exemplarity, with its insistence on the individual performer-exemplar as the source of progress, is losing force in the current moment. We hope this understanding will help open the way to more collaborative practical models of political transformation.

References

Abrahamsson, Sebastian, and Endre Dányi. 2019. 'Becoming Stronger by Becoming Weaker: The Hunger Strike as a Mode of Doing Politics.' *Journal of International Relations and Development* 22 (4): 882–898.

Acharya, Amitav. 2004. 'How Ideas Spread: Whose Norms Matter? Norm Localization and Institutional Change in Asian Regionalism.' *International Organization* 58 (2): 239–275.

Adler, Emanuel. 2008. 'The Spread of Security Communities: Communities of Practice, Self-Restraint, and NATO's Post-Cold War Transformation.' *European Journal of International Relations* 14 (2): 195–230.

Adler, Emanuel, and Vincent Pouliot. 2011. 'International Practices.' *International Theory* 3 (1): 1–36.

Allison, Graham T. 1971. *Essence of Decision. Explaining the Cuban Missile Crisis*. Little, Brown and Company.

Ansorge, Josef Teboho. 2016. *Identify and Sort. How Digital Power Changed World Politics*. Oxford University Press.

Arendt, Hannah. 1998 [1958]. *The Human Condition*. 2nd ed. University of Chicago Press.

Berenskoetter, Felix. 2017. 'Approaches to Concept Analysis.' *Millennium: Journal of International Studies* 45 (2): 151–173.

Bicchi, Federica. 2022. 'Communities of Practice and What They Can Do for International Relations.' *Review of International Studies* 48 (1): 24–43.

Bleiker, Roland, ed. 2018. *Visual Global Politics*. Routledge.

Bondanella, Peter E. 2002. *The Films of Federico Fellini*. Cambridge University Press.

Braun, Benjamin, Sebastian Schindler, and Tobias Wille. 2019. 'Rethinking Agency in International Relations: Performativity, Performances, and Actor-Networks.' *Journal of International Relations and Development* 22 (1): 787–807.

Bueger, Christian, and Timothy Edmunds. 2021. 'Pragmatic Ordering: Informality, Experimentation, and the Maritime Security Agenda.' *Review of International Studies* 47 (2): 171–191.

Bueger, Christian, and Frank Gadinger. 2015. 'The Play of International Practice.' *International Studies Quarterly* 59 (3): 449–460.

Checkel, Jeffrey T. 2005. 'International Institutions and Socialization in Europe: Introduction and Framework.' *International Organization* 59 (4): 801–826.

Der Derian, James. 1987. *On Diplomacy: A Genealogy of Western Estrangement*. Blackwell.

Dittmer, Jason, and Daniel Bos. 2019. *Popular Culture, Geopolitics, and Identity*. 2nd ed. Rowman & Littlefield.

Ejdus, Filip. 2018. 'Critical Situations, Fundamental Questions and Ontological Insecurity in World Politics.' *Journal of International Relations and Development* 21 (4): 883–908.

Evans, Nicholas H.A. 2023. 'Exemplars.' In *The Cambridge Handbook for the Anthropology of Ethics*, edited by James Laidlaw. Cambridge University Press.

Ferrara, Alessandro. 2008. *The Force of the Example: Explorations in the Paradigm of Judgment*. Columbia University Press.

Finnemore, Martha, and Kathryn Sikkink. 1998. 'International Norm Dynamics and Political Change.' *International Organization* 52 (4): 887–917.

Fleming, Paul. 2009. *Exemplarity and Mediocrity: The Art of the Average from Bourgeois Tragedy to Realism*. Stanford University Press.

Flyvbjerg, Bent. 2001. *Making Social Science Matter: Why Social Inquiry Fails and How it Can Succeed Again*. Cambridge University Press.

Gallie, W.B. 1955–1956. 'Essentially Contested Concepts.' *Proceedings of the Aristotelian Society* 56: 167–198.

Goldsmith, Jack L., and Eric A. Posner. 2005. *The Limits of International Law*. Oxford University Press.

Gomá Lanzón, Javier. 2019. *Ejemplaridad Pública*. 2nd ed. Taurus.

Guzzini, Stefano. 2013. 'The End of International Relations Theory: Stages of Reflexivity and Modes of Theorizing.' *European Journal of International Relations* 19 (3): 521–541.

Højer, Lars, and Andreas Bandak, eds. 2015. *The Power of Example: Anthropological Explorations in Persuasion, Evocation and Imitation*. Supplement issue of the *Journal of the Royal Anthropological Institute*.

Hopf, Ted. 2010. 'The Logic of Habit in International Relations.' *European Journal of International Relations* 16 (4): 539–561.

Jackson, Patrick Thaddeus, and Daniel H. Nexon. 1999. 'Relations Before States: Substance, Process and the Study of World Politics.' *European Journal of International Relations* 5 (3): 291–332.

Kant, Immanuel. 2000 [1790]. *Critique of the Power of Judgment*. Cambridge University Press.

Koselleck, Reinhart. 1985 [1979]. 'Historia magistra vitae: The Dissolution of the Topos into the Perspective of a Modernized Historical Process.' In *Futures Past: On the Semantics of Historical Time*, translated by Keith Tribe. MIT Press.

Koselleck, Rainer. 2011. 'Introduction and Prefaces to the Geschichtliche Grundbegriffe,' translated by Michaela Richter. *Contributions to the History of Concepts* 6 (1): 1–37.

Kustermans, Jorg, Ted Svensson, Julia Costa López, Tracey Blasenheim, and Alvina Hoffmann. 2021. 'Ritual and Authority in World Politics.' *Cambridge Review of International Affairs* 35 (1): 2–30.

Lebow, Richard N. 2001. 'Thucydides the Constructivist.' *American Political Science Review* 95 (3): 547–560.

Lyons, John D. 2014. *Exemplum: The Rhetoric of Example in Early Modern France and Italy*. Princeton University Press.

Machiavelli, Niccolò. 1975 [1532]. *Il Principe*. Rizzoli.

Mälksoo, Maria. 2021. 'A Ritual Approach to Deterrence: I Am, Therefore I Deter.' *European Journal of International Relations* 27 (1): 53–78.

March, James G., and Johan P. Olsen. 1984. 'The New Institutionalism: Organizational Factors in Political Life.' *American Political Science Review* 78 (3): 734–749.

McCourt, David M. 2016. 'Practice Theory and Relationalism as the New Constructivism.' *International Studies Quarterly* 60 (3): 475–485.

McNay, Lois. 2019. 'The Politics of Exemplarity: Ferrara on the Disclosure of New Political Worlds.' *Philosophy & Social Criticism* 45 (2): 127–145.

Mitzen, Jennifer. 2006. 'Ontological Security in World Politics: State Identity and the Security Dilemma.' *European Journal of International Relations* 12 (3): 341–370.

Morwood, James. 1994. *The Pocket Oxford Latin Dictionary*. Oxford University Press.

Neumann, Iver B. 1999. *Uses of the Other. The 'East' in European Identity Formation*. University of Minnesota Press.

Nexon, Daniel H., and Iver B. Neumann, eds. 2006. *Harry Potter and International Relations*. Rowman & Littlefield.

Noyes, Dorothy. 2022. 'Corrupted Exemplars: Exhortation and Legitimation in Contemporary Spanish Politics.' Paper presented at IKOS (Department of Cultural Studies and Oriental Languages), University of Oslo. April 28, 2022.

Pingeot, Lou, and Vincent Pouliot. 2024. 'Agency Is Positionally Distributed: Practice Theory and (Post)Colonial Structures.' *International Studies Quarterly* 68 (2): 1–9.

Pouliot, Vincent. 2010. *International Security in Practice. The Politics of NATO-Russia Diplomacy*. Cambridge University Press.

Schindler, Sebastian, and Tobias Wille. 2015. 'Change in and through Practice: Pierre Bourdieu, Vincent Pouliot, and the End of the Cold War.' *International Theory* 7 (2): 330–359.

Urban, Greg. 2001. *Metaculture: How Culture Moves Through the World.* University of Minnesota Press.

Wille, Tobias. 2018. 'Practice Turn in International Relations.' In *Oxford Bibliographies in International Relations*, edited by Patrick James. Oxford University Press.

Williams, Raymond. 1976. *Keywords: A Vocabulary of Culture and Society.* Croom Helm.

Williams, Raymond. 1977. *Marxism and Literature.* Oxford University Press.

Zimmermann, Lisbeth. 2017. *Global Norms with a Local Face? Rule-of-Law Promotion and Norm Transition.* Cambridge University Press.

2

From Performance to Uptake: A Process Model of Exemplarity

Dorothy Noyes and Tobias Wille

German Chancellor Willy Brandt, on a 1970 state visit to Poland to sign the treaty that will recognize the postwar border settlement, unexpectedly falls to his knees before the memorial to the victims of the Warsaw Ghetto uprising. American football player Colin Kaepernick, before a routine game in 2016, drops to one knee as the national anthem begins and remains there until it is concluded.

Each act was immediately amplified and immediately controversial. The photo of Brandt's *Kniefall* eventually became the icon of a turning point in Germany's approach to the world as it began to reckon with the Nazi past. Kaepernick's gesture of solidarity with #BlackLivesMatter protesters, taken up by other players and in due course endorsed by Nike, circulated across US and global sport and incited ferocious backlash as a supposed display of disrespect – and Kaepernick never played for the NFL again.

Despite limited direct consequences for either act, both were widely understood as potent examples that called for reflection and uptake. Cited in argument and emulated in new performance, they were read backwards and forwards for the precedents they revised and the futures they implied. Whether emanating from a national leader whose moves before the cameras ought to reinforce state power, or from a racialized player-worker authorized to act only within the limits of the game prescribed, such gestures compel attention by transgressing the bounds of expectations and performing other possibilities.

In Chapter 1, we posited that exemplarity is a mode of cultural transmission. Performances such as Brandt's *Kniefall* and Kaepernick's taking a knee cite and emulate past examples, becoming in turn points of reference for future judgment, citation, and emulation. They create new nodes in a spatiotemporal network of cultural objects and thus contribute to both order and transformation in the social world. *But how do examples do this? And under what conditions can it happen?* In this chapter, we will take a first step towards answering these questions by proposing a model of exemplarity that emphasizes its relational and dynamic character as founded in social action.

Exemplarity as process: a dynamic model

To structure our enquiry into the dynamics of exemplarity, we propose a process model (see Figure 2.1). It depicts the ideal-typical spiraling path by which a successful example 'takes' and becomes a cultural object in circulation. We assume that the full sequence occurs in some empirical cases, but that is by no means inevitable. Rather, at every stage of the model we ask about the conditions under which we can expect an example to find resonance and move on to the next stage. The model is thus an idealization of a complex social process to formulate theoretical propositions and guide empirical enquiry.

The following sections define each stage, highlighting the features that distinguish exemplarity from other modes of cultural transmission. We also posit the accumulating felicity conditions that either propel or hinder a given example. We then discuss the relationship between exemplarity and power, before concluding with a brief reflection on our positionality as researchers.

Performance

Opening this chapter with Brandt and Kaepernick, we have introduced the example as a public act with a tightly associated actor, who may thereby achieve the status of exemplar.[1] It is appropriate, then, to understand the career of the example as taking off from performance. To be sure, not every example begins in public, and many acts deemed exemplary are the opposite of showy. But the heroic private renunciation sets no example until history hears of it, and the gesture of humility is still a gesture. Exemplarity begins with the calling of attention. In contrast to rules, procedures, and practices, the example either begins or is reconstructed as a singular performance in time that stands out from the social flow and invites evaluation.[2] It

---

[1] Some contributors to this volume play with the idea that there can be examples without exemplars. We do not rule out this possibility, but note that at least in the idiom of liberal exemplarity that dominates Western discourse, the heroic individual figures prominently as protagonist and author of the example.

[2] We derive our account of performance from Dell Hymes (1981) and Richard Bauman (1984), who in their studies of oral verbal art define performance as 'the assumption of responsibility before an audience for a display of communicative competence.'

Figure 2.1: The spiral model of exemplarity

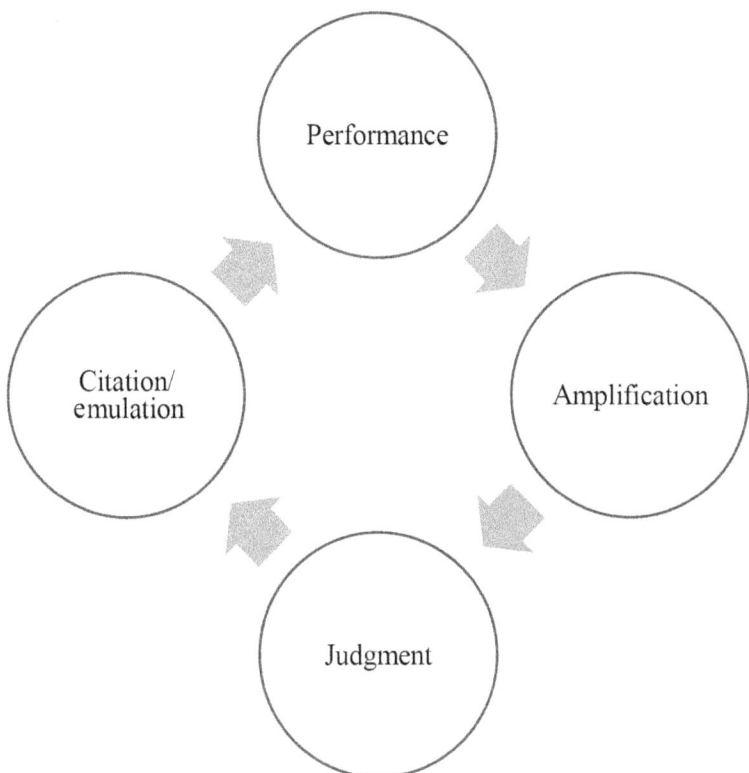

manipulates expectations of the actor, the action, or the situation in ways that are aesthetically, affectively, and cognitively striking; it surprises. In this respect it becomes not just action but an act.

The example gives graspable form to inchoate impulse. The English word *model*, the German *Vorbild*, the Romance *exemplaire*, and the social movement term *prefiguration*, among many other members of the concept bundle, evoke sculptural or pictorial representation. Whether inaugurating a series (Wagner-Pacifici 2017) or a multiform network of action, exemplary performances are characterized by excess, a gratuitousness that points beyond the situation and calls for interpretation and judgment (Bataille 1985 [1933]). The example asserts itself before an audience as something that cannot be ignored.

There is a wide literature on the 'felicity conditions' under which a performance can have tangible effects (Austin 1962; Butler 1997; Buzan, Wæver, and de Wilde 1998). Recognizing the complexity and contingency of interacting conditions, in this volume we probe the theses that a performance of conduct is more likely to be taken up as an example when it, first, puts the actor's reputation and/or body at risk; second, finds a platform that reaches a large, heterogeneous audience; third, competently reinterprets the relevant cultural repertoires of the context, and, fourth, violates expectations, breaking out of the flow of regular conduct. As we will see, these conditions affect not only the immediate resonance of the performance, but also how well it proceeds through the further stages of amplification, judgment, and citation/emulation.

First, the act implicates the actor. We assume that examples take on special force when they commit the body, individual or collective, to a dangerous course: kneeling, breaking a barrier, withdrawing, opening a door, lighting a flame. Performed before witnesses, such acts cannot be taken back. The embodied gesture moves beyond its performer. It materializes social risk and distributes it among the audience by forcing affective response: fear, discomfort, awe, tenderness, horror.

Second, the audience must be there, and the composition of the audience affects the scale and complexity of uptake. One who would set an example seeks a platform commanding wide attention, and this would seem to make exemplarity yet another privilege of power. The great powers of post-Napoleonic Europe had the resources to create an extraordinary stage for themselves in the Congress of Vienna (Mitzen 2013; Chapter 16, this volume), with music and festive décor to give aesthetic form to political transformation. It is important to remember, however, that the stage was temporary and the circumstances unprecedented. The many varieties of 'theatre state' (Geertz 1980) plow enormous resources into their self-staging, and, as seen before, established actors of even the most liberal tendency imagine themselves to be natural exemplars. Once created, a powerful representational apparatus may sustain itself by recruiting exemplars, as Graf (Chapter 4, this volume) describes for ancient Athens.

But this very power to schedule, script, sacralize, and convene a public for performance can perversely undermine its efficacy. At best, sanctioned normative performance elevates itself into ritual: meaningful, aesthetically powerful, stabilizing, and seemingly agentless (Aalberts et al 2020; Mälksoo 2021). Their expectations confirmed by repetition, audiences stop paying attention, and ritual is sooner or later numbed into routine.

The occasions, however, remain, and this creates the opportunity for 'détournement' (Debord 1994 [1967]) or 'hijacking' (Dayan and Katz 1992). Brandt's acquiescence to the wreath-laying ritual was significant as a diplomatic move, but the unexpected Kniefall became the global example. Kaepernick's disruption of the national anthem turned ritual into example still more dramatically, as he seized protagonism in a sphere outside his purview as a sports player.

The power and centrality of a platform are of special value for social movement exemplarity, both for the prestige accruing to a disruptor and, obviously, for the relative ease of amplification. Perea Ozerin (Chapter 8, this volume) notes the importance of remote examples for social movements in constrained media environments. Examples recovered from a chance source are better than nothing, but the opportunity to emulate a globally available example can provide both an alibi in situ and a sense of momentum for protesters at risk. Failing access to the most powerful stages, unauthorized actors will often seize on what is both ready to hand and existentially central: their own bodies, disruptively assembled in sit-ins, marches, and traffic blockades.

Powerful examples gain force in dialogue with ritual, as when Sadat's assassins chose the anniversary of his victory as their moment (Noyes, Chapter 14, this volume), Greta Thunberg launched her demand for immediate action at the doorway of the Swedish Parliament (Kverndokk, Chapter 5, this volume), and Zelensky crashed into the slow pavane of NATO procedure with his eloquent impatience. To disrupt a ritual compellingly, however, requires command of the relevant cultural repertoires: we see this in Sadat's Abrahamic invocations, Thunberg's self-presentation as a child, and Zelensky's citation of Western exemplars. Zarakol (Chapter 9, this volume) demonstrates that newcomers and aspirants are especially called upon to demonstrate competence in established repertoires. These actors are expected to follow the example of the center, converted for their use into rule, procedure, or practice. But the very novelty of their participation creates opportunities for canny performers, and the center may also be hoist by the petard of its own examples (Wadia, Chapter 10, this volume).

For above all, and this is our fourth felicity condition, an example must surprise. Unlike practice, habit, and routine, it disrupts the regular flow of social life and commands attention. To be clear, surprise is not bewilderment. An idiosyncratic gesture that comes out of nowhere does not become an example. Rather, as shown earlier, the example must be interpretable in relation to available cultural repertoires. More immediately, the example stands out within a particular flow of conduct and expectations: it plays off its context to propose a change of direction.

Amplification

In small-scale societies, performance is itself a primary medium for the transmission of cultural objects, whether songs or examples. Even in large-scale ones, the impact of presence in an exemplary moment can be indelible, above all for those imbricated with the actor – those belonging to a whole of which the actor will be taken as a sample. Kaepernick's teammates, presented with a choice for the future, and the NFL executives and sponsors who provided his platform, had their lives changed in the very moment of his taking the knee: his example was something they had to reckon with. On the other hand, even during the sacralized ritual of singing the anthem, some in the stadium were surely distracted by a text message or a tugging child, and others saw the strange gesture and shrugged it off.

To be taken up as societal examples, performances of conduct must be amplified by other actors. Calling attention to a performance beyond its immediate time and place entails representation: reducing and fixing a situated act into a form that can circulate widely and remain available for reactivation. Exemplarity thus here intersects with another mode of social transmission. Amplification takes myriad forms, the more the better for the purposes of uptake: live streaming, a paragraph of description in an ambassador's dispatch, a praise song, a broadside print, a biopic, a monument. Each medium and genre will inflect the performance with its own conventions and their legacy of associations, so that interpretation and judgment already begin in the act of representation itself. This may domesticate the example's disruptive force: consider the reduction of Rosa Parks' carefully planned action to the instinctive response of a tired worker, or the sweetening of Martin Luther King's politics in dominant US representations of the Civil Rights Movement. Conversely, audiences recognize the positionality of amplifiers, and assess the work of a state broadcaster or court painter differently from that of a revolutionary satirist. Despite these reciprocal constraints, a powerful gesture forces both representer and audience to take it into account: it pushes through genre into event and resists full interpretive capture.

With the force of the example behind it and new contexts in front of it, the representation itself can inflect but not determine reception. Even the most controlled media and vehicles of amplification must release the example into the wild of social life. The amplifier detaches the example from the control of the performer and surrenders control of it in turn.

The skill of the amplifier makes a difference. A compelling, well-placed representation may pull a marginal performance into central view. The survival, in 1816, of 15 men on a raft cut adrift from the sinking ship *Méduse* off the coast of Senegal became known through a memoir by the ship's doctor, published in Paris. The memoir denounced the incompetence and negligence of the French royalist officers, but it was the painting by the abolitionist sympathizer Théodore Géricault, exhibited at the Paris Salon in 1819, that highlighted the heroism of the conscripted African Jean-Charles, turning him into an exemplar for French citizens under a corrupt regime and, in later centuries, for colonized subjects and refugees striving to rise up from bare life (Noyes 2020).

Once captured in representation, the example is transmissible across wider social spaces: it can leap contexts, missing some and hitting others. Its uptake is also optional, in contrast to the mandatory following of rules. Thus the example's transmission network is more irregular, less determined, and more episodic than the networks created by rules, procedures, and practices; we might call it a network laid over a meshwork.

While conceived here as a stage in the spiraling process through which examples proliferate, amplification itself unfolds over time. Disruptive performances are newsworthy and will circulate through whatever media the society relies on, whether dispersed in gossip or monopolizing state broadcasts. The effects of the vehicle are especially clear in social media, which fosters instantaneous amplification of all kinds of performance – someone is bound to be interested – but by the same token through sheer volume can easily drown out the performances that lack powerful sponsorship. After an initial moment of attention, amplification of most performances is likely to become spottier, and some potential examples may simply vanish. Others remain in plain sight but stop drawing notice.

Judgment

The amplification of an attention-catching act makes it an example *of* something, that is, a case: its import and meaning demand consideration. In both Brandt's Kniefall and Kaepernick's taking a knee, the departure from norms associated with their social roles demanded attention and discussion. The German weekly *Der Spiegel* immediately captioned the Chancellor's image on its cover with the central question: 'Should Brandt have knelt?'[3] Debate in both instances reflected prior stances within the field of relevance, sometimes overriding the mere evidence. Despite Kaepernick's well-publicized Christian belief, the familiarity of kneeling in prayer to the majority-Christian audience of US football, and Kaepernick's immediate explanation of his action as a call for reflection, taking a knee was nonetheless framed in right-wing quarters as an act of disrespect and defiance towards the US military. Such an interpretive move, however, did not compel everyone, and despite the headwinds against it the anthem protest won support not just from individual emulators but also from a significant number of team owners, sponsors, and members of the public in and beyond American football.

So what is the case a case of? Is taking a knee a case of deference to a higher authority, disrespect toward the national anthem, or humility in the face of past national wrongs? This question can only be answered in a context of collective debate and negotiation. By means of such debate, examples play a major role in the naming of social phenomena as well as their redefinition over time. As Hannah Arendt (1992, 84–85) pointed out, many political concepts are derived from examples – first there is Napoleon, then 'Bonapartism.' Importantly, however, agreement on Napoleon's exemplarity does not preclude intense disagreement on the character and value of Bonapartism.

---

[3] Der Spiegel, December 14, 1970; see Rauer (2006, 259).

But judgment is not purely or even primarily intellectual; its verbalizations are often after-the-fact rationalizations. Kant (2000 [1790]) writes of exemplarity as reflective judgment, derived from particular experience rather than general rule, and as such proper to the aesthetic realm. To his reflective encounter with a rose, which generates a conception of beauty, we would add the affective encounter – in which the nose is as much engaged as the eye – that processes the experience of the rose as embodied. All the more is such complexity inherent in the judgment of social performance, where awe, disgust, horror, or tenderness inevitably and instantaneously inflect conscious assessment.

Judgment often draws on and reconfigures existing identifications. If an example is taken to be a sample of some social grouping, or a harbinger of one emerging, its relevance as case is more easily established. An example has an initial, though not a finite, constituency; already its amplifiers judge it to be relevant to an audience of potential actors, and its performer has typically shaped it for that purpose. Brandt, possessing the 'two bodies' of an individual who is also a representative of the state (Rauer 2006), had his relevance to Germany predetermined. Kaepernick, not so defined, was identified in different ways: proposing himself as a sample of a possible new America, read on the right as a sample of Black youth or Black radicalism. In addition, his individual predicament highlighted the conditions under which all American football players labor. Kaepernick was relevant to multiple audiences and his gesture could be deployed in a range of arguments.

Performers and amplifiers of course try to stage the example in a way to preempt interpretation and guide uptake. But, as Watanabe (Chapter 11, this volume) argues, too much definition and prescription affords no agency to the judges of a model's utility for their own circumstances and thus cuts off the exemplary process. Conversely, the very mystery of a gesture under the right conditions may provoke an interpretive storm that affirms its exemplarity and transmits it to the future (Noyes 2015). We propose the thesis that an example is most likely to be taken up when its relevance as sample is clear, but its application as case is not. Mitzen (Chapter 16, this volume) shows that the indisputably consequential Concert of Europe remains what Claude Lévi-Strauss (1963, 89) called 'good to think with': it can be revisited and re-examined from multiple lenses to reveal new dimensions of social order and generate new prescriptions as well as critique. Indeed, the planning theorist Bent Flyvbjerg (2001) advocates grounding social science in such exemplary case studies, arguing that immersion in the contingencies and complexity of successive cases produces a 'feel for the game' that is more generative than the effort to discover law-like regularities at a more abstract level. By the same token, the cases adjudicated in popular culture, such as celebrity scandals, are not simple occasions for condemnation or defense but opportunities for serious ethical questions to be focalized, aired, and considered among individuals sharing a lifeworld.

A promising example, felicitously interpreted, can launch a new category. Social movement actors, needing to innovate within local settings, tend to scan widely for models and participate in their amplification and interpretation; in so doing they can define new social wholes (Perea Ozerin, Chapter 8, this volume). The global spread of #BlackLivesMatter protest, not least through the example of toppling dominant exemplars, established a new transverse solidarity within which all activists of color can be understood as samples. Other efforts to claim participation in a common whole are less successful, as when 1968-era Occitan cultural activists sought to redefine their region as an internal colony of France, which might therefore take example by the successful Algerian War of Independence. Finally, the effort to claim exemplary status for a putative global whole can be denied by other samples thereof, as when in the 1970s non-Western feminists, who understood themselves as allied with anticolonial, indigenous, and class struggles, rejected the amplification of middle-class US liberal feminism as a template for their own activism (Olcott 2017).

Citation

Examples gain practical relevance when they are cited in political controversies and thus connected to other persons, deeds, or situations. The dynamics of citation are obvious in the realm of law and politics, where referencing past decisions as precedents is an important argumentation strategy (Daase and Wille, Chapter 7, this volume; Duxbury 2008; Schauer 2008). Beyond the confines of formal argumentation, however, effective performers draw on their 'intertextual encyclopedia' (Eco 1984) in search of examples that will resonate with an audience. Audiences with divergent encyclopedias and concerns will then invoke their own examples and exemplars in the course of collective judgment.

A special case of citation is the resort to what Victor Turner (1974) called 'root paradigms': sacralized examples treated as foundational to a social group and deeply rooted in its cultural imaginary. Turner understood these paradigms to assert psychological control as actors respond to structural crisis, but we can also recognize more opportunistic mobilizations of events like the Boston Tea Party, the Battle of Kosovo, or the Battle of Karbala to win legitimacy and adherents for controversial initiatives. Either way, their invocation offers a measure of ontological security by giving actors and audiences a firmer sense of their place in a complex and uncertain world (Mitzen 2006; Subotić 2016; Ejdus 2018). Similar to these performative citations are the interpretive citations of 'paradigmatic examples' to warn or predict (Breiner 2024). The Weimar Republic is inevitably invoked in contemporary debates over democratic fragility, and the example of Hitler serves to highlight the worst-case scenario when an elected leader shows authoritarian tendencies. The force of such analogies decays through overuse (Lebow and Norman 2024) and their citation may be challenged for both legal and emotional reasons. As the case from which the international legal category of genocide was extrapolated, the Holocaust cannot be invoked without consequences; as a case elevated to sacred example through a dense network of cultural amplifications and judgments, it is surrounded with discursive prohibitions.

Citations can fail both through overuse that renders them banal and through disproportionate application, when they are too trivial or too heavily freighted for the problem at hand. A felicitous citation will balance surprise with relevance, often by invoking a historically distant model that is also a sample of the entity currently in crisis. Brandt's Kniefall was read backwards as part of a chain of revisions of Germany's stance towards the world: Henry IV's submission in the snow before the Pope; Bismarck's inverse declaration that Germany would never again go to Canossa; Brandt's new reversal, implicitly acknowledging that the global public had the power to excommunicate Germany (Rauer 2006). Kaepernick's act also evoked priors of Black athletes, notably the Black Power salutes of John Carlos and Tommie Smith at the 1968 Olympic Games in Mexico City, as well as the examples of Muhammad Ali, Kareem Abdul-Jabbar, and others (Webber 2025). With the force of these activist citations, however, the subtlety of Kaepernick's revision was soon largely ignored by both critics and supporters. Instead of being situated within a lineage of Christian nonviolence and humility, another possible locus of citation, he was decisively aligned, and came to align himself, with a more militantly progressive approach, valid in its own right but less amenable to political coalition-building. Social movement activists similarly must toe a challenging line between the excavation of alternative exemplary lineages, capable of exciting new adherents, and citations that might compel the establishment that must ultimately be won over (see Perea Ozerin, Chapter 8, this volume).

Where a relevant precedent has gone awry, actors may struggle to avoid citation: later Middle East peace initiatives danced around the example of Anwar el-Sadat and the Camp David Accords (Noyes, Chapter 14, this volume). When the stakes are high, however, even a clumsy citation can be powerful, as shown in Chapter 1's discussion of Zelensky's mirrorings to different national audiences in his pleas for military support. Rudimentary as they were, these citations brought home the broader performance of Ukraine as a sample of Europe and the liberal order and its struggle as a case of defense of democracy, both drawing on the Western model and becoming a model in turn.

Ultimately, the assessment of import is a comparative problem – one case put against others. Examples respond to one another in a spatiotemporal network thickened by implicit and explicit mutual citation (Noyes, Chapter 14, this volume). The spiraling process of exemplarity thus concludes its first circle with a citation that itself is a performance and that – depending on its reception – might become an example in its own right. Citation thus marks both the end of an episode of cultural transmission in which a form has been transposed and transformed, as well as the potential beginning of a new episode.

Emulation

Standing out of the regular flow of conduct, having been amplified and publicly assessed, cited and compared with other instances, the example calls for emulation. Indeed, if imitation is the sincerest form of flattery, then emulation of an example is the most committed form of its citation. To emulate an example acknowledges its force but need not imply submission to the exemplar nor even alignment with the exemplar's project. The Latin word *aemulus* in fact meant a rival, and up through the early modern period the concept of emulation was understood in Europe as interpersonal competitive rivalry, the stance of an aspirant seeking parity or preeminence over an established actor. For Machiavelli (1975 [1532]) in the domain of politics and for Giorgio Vasari (1966–1987 [1550]) in the domain of the arts, an example was something to surpass. Machiavelli describes how princely prestige depends on achieving something 'sanza esempio,' unexampled and thus able to monopolize attention – a principle internalized by later leaders from Napoleon to Donald Trump. Vasari, interested in the logic of artistic progress, provides a global analysis of how the Renaissance came into being through the network of mutual observation and borrowing among Italian artists, each seeking, with each commission, to outdo the latest extraordinary work by a rival. Renaissance thinkers also highlighted the dangers of emulation: Shakespeare responded to the crisis of aristocratic factionalism in the Elizabethan court with *Troilus and Cressida*, a play staging one-upmanship among the Greek heroes as jeopardizing victory in the Trojan War (Mallin 1990).

Although the semantics of emulation have evolved in the direction of imitation, subtle thinkers continue to recognize its competitive and destabilizing effects on social order. Thorstein Veblen (2009 [1899]) theorized the dynamism of class society though 'pecuniary emulation' driving aspirants to consume at the level of the next rank above them, and Pierre Bourdieu's (1984) analysis of class 'distinction' similarly demonstrates how the push of elites to stay ahead of their emulators drives changes in taste. In the sphere of statecraft, Ivan Krastev and Stephen Holmes (2019) understand emulation as imitation within hierarchy, but nonetheless driven by a logic of competitive aspiration. Taking a clue from Jacques Derrida (1982), we may deepen their argument by positing that pure repetition is impossible: in every iteration, a prior instance is recontextualized, and reconciliation with the putative original must be deferred. Jelena Subotić (Chapter 13, this volume) makes a compelling case for the import of this dynamism, showing how Eastern Europeans, constrained to emulate the example of Western memory culture, transform its application into nationalist examples that are now destabilizing the liberal core of Western norms.

While emulation requires commitment and often comes at a high cost, citation is comparatively cheap. Once it had crystallized as the paradigmatic example of perpetrator apology, Brandt's Kniefall was cited by Bosnians against the Serbs, Chinese against the Japanese, Italians against the Slovenes, and Chileans against their government, as a standard that was not being met (Rauer 2006). Germany, having already paid the price, was able to follow its own example, as in its 1997 apology at Guernica, which cited the Kniefall as a precedent (Rauer 2006). Picasso's extraordinary, celebrated amplification of the 1937 bombing also surely affected the calculus of this apology, with the force of the example overriding the cost of association with it. Kaepernick's act was personally costly but performatively straightforward, lending itself to wide, transparent emulation. Despite the risks for NFL players, high school athletes, and others, it spread like wildfire both in the US and internationally. Indeed, once performed, the easy replicability of both the context and the action forced all racialized players to make a choice, for as other samples of Kaepernick's class they were marked whether they took a knee or did not. In basketball, a sport with a different demographic, the gesture soon became dominant, as influential players took it up, and White players emulated Black ones.

The political counter to such contagious examples is of course to 'make an example' of the transgressor and thus deter emulation. While this may no longer serve as a dominant mechanism of social control, as described by Michael Foucault (1977) for the early modern period with its spectacles of punishment, it has persisted especially in the control of marginalized actors aspiring to inclusion. The de facto blacklisting of Kaepernick from the NFL could not but serve as warning to others. Social media has facilitated a new wave of making examples from below as a weapon against the powerful, as in the #MeToo movement, although this trend has evoked a forceful backlash against the presumed excesses of 'cancel culture.' The need to make an example of a dangerous transgressor is equally important in international relations, where debates over sanctions and intervention are heavily influenced by concern over precedent (Daase and Wille, Chapter 7, this volume): consider the Western anxiety that the 2022 Russian invasion of Ukraine might give China permission to invade Taiwan. (China's retort denied the exemplary relationship by refusing to accept Taiwan as a sample of the ensemble of sovereign nations.)

When successful examples offer models for action, simple necessity may drive emulation. With international institutions such as the World Health Organization weak and mistrusted, the COVID-19 pandemic left states scrambling for policy models from both past epidemics and the actions of allies and rivals. Initial good outcomes elevated countries such as New Zealand, Vietnam, and Sweden into exemplary visibility and prompted intensive debates over whose policies might successfully be adopted. Identity and reputation quickly entered the calculus, however, jumping easily across political scales: in March 2020, a US Republican governor facing a rapid rise in death rates angrily rejected urgings to impose a lockdown by announcing, 'Mississippi's never going to be China.'[4] Alignments around powerful exemplars, both states and persons, do often become more symbolic than pragmatic, and may promote more passive identification than active revision and adaptation. Here is where exemplarity comes up against both the logic of mass politics and the ease of social media. It is unclear how many young male fans of Elon Musk will found their own startups, or how many of the young women who signed Gordon Brown's 'I am Malala' petition to the Pakistani government are living in countries under fundamentalist rule (Hesford 2013).

Accordingly, the contributions to this volume paint a complex picture of the emulation of examples in which functional necessity is only one factor among many. Engaging with the literature on state formation and international order, Ayşe Zarakol's (2011; see also Chapter 9, this volume) study of national humiliation considers the consequences of hypercorrection towards Western models. Raymond Kuo (2021) shows how the prestige of 'core alliances' provokes emulation by peripheral countries that might be better served by other arrangements. Pushing back against Eurocentric claims to exemplarity in both politics and scholarship, Chin-Hao Huang and David Kang (2022) argue that, contrary to prevailing Western theory, East Asian state building was not a defensive response to aggression but followed on recognition of the value of the Chinese example. Long concerned with the phenomenon of 'revolutionary waves' (Perea Ozerin, Chapter 8, this volume), scholars in comparative politics pondered the role of practical models in the post-Socialist 'color revolutions' of 2000–2006 and the later Arab Spring, including the presumed demonstration effect of one revolution

---

[4] Jackson Free Press, 'Governor Rejects State Lockdown for COVID-19: "Mississippi's Never Going to be China",' March 23, 2020, Online: https://www.jacksonfreepress.com/news/2020/mar/23/governor-rejects-state-lockdown-covid-19-mississip/ (accessed November 17, 2023).

upon the next, the active promulgation of detailed templates by NGOs and the US Department of State in its 'democracy promotion' phase, the availability of these templates to authoritarians as a guide to their own vulnerabilities, and the diminishing efficacy of the templates the farther they were carried from the Eastern European settings from which they had been abstracted (for example, Beissinger 2007; Lawson 2015).

The recent history of violent extremism illustrates the ways in which performances can be tailored to meet the practical needs of potential emulators. Extremist entrepreneurs work hard to make their examples available, not only through the visible propaganda of the deed but through supporting materials online: the manifesto intended to guide reflective judgment, the documentation of planning and process meant to encourage the next attack. In this way, the perpetrators of the massacres at the Norwegian summer camp in 2011, the church in Charleston in 2015, the mosque in Christchurch in 2019, and the Buffalo supermarket in 2022 furnished methods and inspiration one to the next, each citing the prior examples and urging others to follow. Research on neofascist accelerationism suggests that enabling the spread of disruptive assaults through the online transmission of process – and the achievement of exemplarity thereby – are more important to most perpetrators than the immediate 'kinetic' result.[5]

Citation and emulation are thus the last stage of the first round of the – idealized – process through which examples proliferate. They relate the example, now amplified and properly judged, to a pressing political situation, sustaining and amplifying the original example and sometimes assisting its conversion into another mode, for instance by codifying it as rule or banalizing it into practice or procedure. Alternatively, an emulatory performance may be taken up as a new example in its own right, initiating a new loop in the exemplary spiral.

The power of examples

By emphasizing the felicity conditions under which a potential example moves through the path laid out in our stylized model, we have to some extent sidestepped a question that is central to the disciplinary discourse of IR: the question of power. Identified by Hans Morgenthau both as the

---

[5] NBC News, 'Buffalo Suspect Exposes Dangers of Accelerationist, Neo-fascist Lone-actor Violence,' May 21, 2022, Online: https://www.nbcnews.com/think/opinion/buffalo-shooting-suspect-manifesto-livestream-exposes-accelerationist-rcna29881 (accessed November 17, 2023); see also *The Washington Post*, 'Buffalo Suspect Allegedly Inspired by Racist Theory Fueling Global Carnage,' May 15, 2022, Online: https://www.washingtonpost.com/nation/2022/05/15/buffalo-shooter-great-replacement-extremism/ (accessed November 17, 2023).

central concern of states and their leaders in international politics and as pivotal concept for its analysis, the meaning of 'power' has since been parsed and expanded in the discourse of international theory (for example, Guzzini 1993; Barnett and Duvall 2005; Berenskoetter and Williams 2007). If we understand it as 'the production, in and through social relations, of effects that shape the capacities of actors to determine their circumstances and fate' (Barnett and Duvall 2005, 42), that is, as social causation that is not exclusively based on persuasion and consent, it is indisputable that some kind of power is exerted through exemplarity.

The common sense of exemplarity captures only part of it. The commemorative afterlives of such figures as Napoleon, Gandhi, Brandt, or Rosa Parks tempt us to conclude that great men (and occasionally women) make history. This is what people often have in mind when speaking of the 'power of example.' If we turn, however, from the reified exemplar to the exemplary deeds that created their fame and set their trajectories, we move beyond the individual actor. The deed is in fact a cumulative collective achievement involving precedents and repertoires, stages and sponsors, performers, amplifiers, evaluating audiences, and emulators. We know from Derrida (1982) that every iteration alters what it purports to reproduce. The cultural object that is the example thus moves through a process that builds resonance and shifts import at each stage, with the added complexity of multiple branching points and ever-changing participation. Moreover, even networked agency is not independent of structural dynamics. Brandt's *Kniefall* did not directly cause a reorientation in Germany's foreign policy, and Kaepernick's taking a knee was only one episode in the Black Lives Matter movement and the ensuing backlash. Nonetheless, they made a difference.

How they made a difference becomes graspable if we shift our attention from the effective causes of social change to the form of its expression. Despite the importance of protagonists in examples – no Kniefall without Brandt and no taking a knee without Kaepernick – our account of exemplarity highlights precisely the inertias and the dynamisms of form. The political significance of kneeling was both shaped by past performances and reconfigured by the new situation and audience. Actors acted and social forces pushed them in various directions, but what they could and could not do was also shaped by the available forms and the possibilities they afforded. We share this sensibility with both performance accounts (Alexander 2004; Ringmar 2012; Mälksoo 2021) and practice theory (Adler and Pouliot 2011; Bueger and Gadinger 2015; Schindler and Wille 2019). In alignment with these approaches, we contend that the how of social action is as important as the what or why. Our account also has some affinities with post-humanist theories of politics, in that we trace the uneven but expansive distribution of agency across unexpected networks of interaction (Barad 2003; Latour 2005; Bueger 2015). The distinctive feature that separates our account of exemplarity from these approaches and allows for a productive exchange is our focus on the single, situated performance of an identifiable, committed actor as launching and anchoring the transmission of a cultural object. Practice, with its innumerable agents, iterations, and variations, may be thought of as a meshwork within which no single twist is salient. Exemplarity, in contrast, is an irregular, point-to-point network, in which relationship and resemblance are claimed across distance and difference. Human will and effort, along with contingency and particularity, are therefore highlighted at every stage.

What kind of power are we talking about then? Despite the cumulative resonance of examples over time, the framework of symbolic power, inhering in symbolic systems such as art, religion, science, or even language itself, is too narrow for exemplarity (Bourdieu 1979; see Swartz 1997, ch 4). Examples are not *primarily* about meaning to energize consensus, but about form to provoke action: they shape and transmit action in embodied, graspable, memorable ways. Readily amplified and cited, they propose the means of emulation that will carry them forward.

In this sense, although examples cannot coerce, they compel. We use the word in a sense common in English usage: an argument or a theatrical interpretation may be compelling; we might feel compelled to do something or, in a more pathological vein, 'have a compulsion' to do something. A performance of conduct is powerful – it sets an example – to the degree that it commands our attention, stimulates us to revisit and reckon with it, generates feeling and volition that lead us toward action. Although explicit propositions and rational evaluation may be involved in this process, it is fundamentally affective and embodied. At least in its initial stages, exemplarity is transitive, with a sender and receivers. Under the right conditions, if an example is so quickly and broadly diffused that it is effectively 'in the air,' it may launch the communicative power of citizens envisioned by Arendt (1998 [1958]), creating a 1968-style effervescence or perhaps just a phase shift that allows a transformative law to pass. In contrast to Arendt's conception, however, exemplarity is fundamentally strategic, insofar as at least some actors at every stage of the process seek, in some fashion, to exert influence over others.

In other words, exemplarity enacts rhetorical power. Rhetoricians themselves, who drink in exemplarity with their first reading of Aristotle (Gelley 1995; Eriksen, Krefting, and Rønning 2012; Lyons 2014; Lowrie and Lüdemann 2015), might wonder why it took us so long to get here; they have elucidated the mechanics of the judgment and citation phases of our model in vital detail. We took a different starting point, because a core aim of this book is to show the imbrication of these phases in larger scales and more obviously political modalities of action. Inspired by the ambitious framing of Kenneth Burke (1969 [1945]), who understood rhetoric as the primary reduction and staging of reality that enables actors to act in the first place, we think of exemplarity as a foundational cultural mechanism that is grounded in the compelling action of the moment but serves above all to knit those moments together, creating genuinely global and world-historical networks.

Because culture is form and not spirit, rhetorical power is imbricated with material power, but they do not move in lockstep. Examples are transmitted through an uneven global landscape by actors with a variety of purposes and differing access to exemplary repertoires and the machinery of amplification. Forceful examples in turn can be crucial instruments for launching actors toward material and institutional power. They point to a vision of change and offer a form of action that can lead to it: in this way they can mobilize publics with great rapidity. Excitement and solidarity generated around an example can therefore lead to the provision of material and coercive resources, most obviously when the courage of massed protesters convinces an army or police force to change sides.

A significant secondary effect of example is the authority that accrues to its protagonist, individual or collective. An actor accorded the status of exemplar often gains access to social rewards, economic opportunities, and institutional office. The prestige of the example may allow structural resistance to be overcome, to varying degrees: consider the rise of the Italian and Yugoslav Communist Parties as a result of their Partisan successes in the Second World War. But durable elevation almost inevitably leads to the tarnishing of the exemplar, through the failure to follow through or simple corruption: the sad oxymoron of Mexico's Partido Revolucionario Institucional is not unique. Exemplary authority also provides actors with a platform for revised or new purposes, as when eminent scientists become antiwar activists or tech bros become political influencers.

Once actors are in office, the ongoing power of the examples that got them there can help to sustain what Gramsci (1988, part VI) calls cultural hegemony, the saturation of the discursive environment that generates consent – or at least grudging acceptance of what seems inevitable. This very saturation, however, drains the exemplary process of its energy. A naturalized reality does not demand citation and emulation. Well aware of this effect, elites seek to revitalize attention to their legitimating examples in various ways, most obviously through the aesthetic impact of societal rituals and prominent fictions. In more repressive settings, imitation can be forced. Emulation, which engages the reflective and creative energies of the actor, cannot be. This is evident in the foot-dragging, irony, and parody so evident in colonial, authoritarian, and totalitarian societies (Scott 1990).

Although emulation cannot be forced, it can be incentivized. Here the power of exemplarity is mingled with material and institutional resources to significant effect. Most obviously, exemplarity often interacts with practice to energize the diffusion of innovation. Public resistance to the new practice of vaccination in Denmark-Norway was countered by the much-amplified inoculation of Crown Prince Christian in 1760 (Eriksen 2010).[6] Aerial images of long lines of first-time voters proclaimed the installation of electoral democracy to South Africa in 1994, and the arrival of same-sex marriage in the US in 2008 was made real to a wide public with the much-amplified wedding of Star Trek's Mr Sulu, George Takei.[7] Moreover, the celebrity example is translated to grassroots social networks by the emulation of the early adopter: the technological innovations of Alexander Graham Bell or Elon Musk became tangible through the first family in a neighborhood to acquire a telephone or an electric vehicle.

Foucault (1977) famously described the passage from repressive example to productive discipline in the modern era. However incomplete in practice, this passage generated a new kind of exemplar: the role model. Although the saints and Jesus himself remained the cardinal exemplars of Christian pedagogy, the functional specializations, social aspirations, democratization, and expanding choices of the modern world demanded visible exemplars closer to the self. Exemplars generated within or tailored for what Robert Merton (1957) called a 'reference group' provided both intrinsic motivation, being achievable, and extrinsic reward in the form of acceptance, promotion, prizes, and so on. Institutions especially urged such role models upon subaltern actors, with the promise of inclusion if a template was followed (Povedák 2016; Wadia, Chapter 10, this volume), a logic that applied also to states within the institutions of the so-called liberal international order (Zarakol, Chapter 9, this volume; Subotić, Chapter 13, this volume).

An instructive case of examples converging toward a generalized pattern and being mobilized for a disciplinary project is the American Dream. The narrative of an individual exercise of freedom, inaugurated by an act of will, sustained by ongoing effort, and rewarded with economic prosperity, combines a material incentive with a compelling vision of the future and a strategy for getting there. The American Dream still motivates individuals around the globe after two centuries of saturation because it offers them the promise of setting their own example. Identification with a national project is constantly re-energized by the endless generation of particular real and fictional examples at all scales of ambition and in all social locations: Abraham Lincoln, Horatio Alger's heroes, the American uncle, the employee of the

---

[6] Today's anti-vaxxer, offering an example to justify others in rejecting the now established practice, falls under a different logic to be discussed in our conclusion.

[7] https://www.cbsnews.com/pictures/mr-sulu-gets-married/ (accessed November 17, 2023).

month, the woman who breaks the glass ceiling, the visionary innovator who changes our way of doing things.

The failure of this generalized promise is a powerful motive for the reversal or overthrow of established examples. The 'dream deferred' of African Americans[8] generated a civil rights movement that became an example to the world. More recently, the souring of the liberal promise has been recognized as a significant motive for anomie and political reaction in both domestic settings (for example, Hochschild 1996 for the US) and international (Ikenberry 2018; Krastev and Holmes 2019). Exemplarity offers an explanation of the intensity of populist bitterness, for the personal character of the promise in democratic exemplarity creates a personal investment in the national narrative. The failure of individual emulation to achieve inclusion in proclaimed success is an injury to self-respect.

Dissatisfaction inspires a search for alternative examples, but these gain energy from proximity to the exemplary center – the sociopolitical space in which dominant examples are reproduced and promoted. To negate a dominant example or elevate a stigmatized exemplar is more affectively powerful than to introduce something wholly new. Revolutionaries often triumph through their exploitation of the exemplary center, co-opting its stages and means of amplification. The use of performance to compel attention is a classic 'weapon of the weak.' Actors coerced into imitating imposed examples are often the most skilled at pulling back the curtain, revealing the machinery that produces what better-situated actors take for granted. As James Scott (1990) demonstrates, the shock of an act that breaks repressive silence or openly debunks the naturalized surround of power may generate almost instantaneous emulation, snowballing into transformative revolt.

So what to make of exemplarity?

Exemplarity is a thing in the social world. But is it a good thing? Exemplarity itself is inherently normative in that the example claims to unite what is and what should be (Ferrara 2008). More broadly, the collective judgment that turns a performance into an example implicates it in some ethos: a valorized way of life with its associated norms. Add the aesthetic, affective appeal of a well-staged example and it will be very hard for the scholar to keep a neutral and disinterested stand. But as this volume attests, exemplarity serves reaction as well as progress; there is nothing inherently virtuous about it. Like other modes of cultural transmission, *a priori* it seeks

---

[8] https://www.poetryfoundation.org/poems/46548/harlem (accessed November 17, 2023).

its own success. Human agents try to wrest it to a range of purposes, but the impossibility of coordinating these across agents, the contingencies of situations, and the differential force of performances themselves entail highly indeterminate outcomes.

These limitations do nothing to assuage the current hunger for examples and exemplars, whether strongmen or influencers. In a time of multiple crises and mounting uncertainty, when traditional norms and rational institutions are losing their hold on social life, exemplarity may be all that is left to us. Yet as the demand for examples becomes more urgent, their very proliferation vitiates the power of exemplarity to orient action and give focus to social and political process. Amid the current flood of global examples – social movement saviors and tinpot Mussolinis, institutional templates and grassroots improvisations, catastrophically disruptive interventions and quietly suggestive alterations – the performances most likely to triumph in the short term are those that most aggressively compel attention; competition leads to escalation, and the path from unthinkable to normal is often hastened by violence. To recognize this dynamic is hardly sufficient to correct it, but offers a first step. By bringing exemplarity into international theory and beginning to map it as a social process, this volume calls for focused examination of a long-neglected political force that is ever more rapidly transforming the contemporary world.

References

Aalberts, Tanja, Xymena Kurowska, Anna Leander, Maria Mälksoo, Charlotte Heath-Kelly, Luisa Lobato, and Ted Svensson. 2020. 'Rituals of World Politics: On (Visual) Practices Disordering Things.' *Critical Studies on Security* 8 (3): 240–264.

Adler, Emanuel, and Vincent Pouliot. 2011. 'International Practices.' *International Theory* 3 (1): 1–36.

Alexander, Jeffrey C. 2004. 'Cultural Pragmatics: Social Performance Between Ritual and Strategy.' *Sociological Theory* 22 (4): 527–573.

Arendt, Hannah. 1992. *Lectures on Kant's Political Philosophy*, edited by Ronald Beiner. University of Chicago Press.

Arendt, Hannah. 1998 [1958]. *The Human Condition*. 2nd ed. University of Chicago Press.

Austin, John L. 1962. *How to Do Things with Words. The William James Lectures*. Clarendon Press.

Barad, Karen. 2003. 'Posthumanist Performativity: Toward an Understanding of How Matter Comes to Matter.' *Signs: Journal of Women in Culture and Society* 28 (3): 801–831.

Barnett, Michael, and Raymond Duvall. 2005. 'Power in International Politics.' *International Organization* 59 (1): 39–75.

Bataille, Georges. 1985 [1933]. 'The Notion of Expenditure.' In *Visions of Excess: Selected Writings, 1927–1933*, edited by Allan Stoekl. University of Minnesota Press.

Bauman, Richard. 1984. *Verbal Art as Performance*, 3rd ed. Waveland Press Inc.

Beissinger, Mark R. 2007. 'Structure and Example in Modular Political Phenomena: The Diffusion of Bulldozer/Rose/Orange/Tulip Revolutions.' *Perspectives on Politics* 5 (2): 259–276.

Berenskoetter, Felix, and Michael J. Williams, eds. 2007. *Power in World Politics*. Taylor and Francis.

Bourdieu, Pierre. 1979. 'Symbolic Power.' *Critique of Anthropology* 4 (13–14): 77–85.

Bourdieu, Pierre. 1984. *Distinction: A Social Critique of the Judgement of Taste*. Harvard University Press.

Braun, Benjamin, Sebastian Schindler, and Tobias Wille. 2019. 'Rethinking Agency in International Relations: Performativity, Performances, and Actor-Networks.' *Journal of International Relations and Development* 22 (4): 787–807.

Breiner, Peter. 2024. 'The Paradigmatic Example of Weimar and Postwar Political Science: The Case of Otto Kirchheimer.' In *Weimar's Long Shadow*, edited by Richard Ned Lebow and Ludvig Norman. Cambridge University Press.

Bueger, Christian. 2015. 'Making Things Known: Epistemic Practices, the United Nations, and the Translation of Piracy.' *International Political Sociology* 9 (1): 1–18.

Bueger, Christian, and Frank Gadinger. 2015. 'The Play of International Practice.' *International Studies Quarterly* 59 (3): 449–460.

Burke, Kenneth. 1969 [1945]. *A Grammar of Motives*. University of California Press.

Butler, Judith. 1997. *Excitable Speech: A Politics of the Performative*. Routledge.

Buzan, Barry, Ole Wæver, and Jaap de Wilde. 1998. *Security: A New Framework for Analysis*. Lynne Rienner Publishers.

Dayan, Daniel, and Elihu Katz. 1992. *Media Events: The Live Broadcasting of History*. Harvard University Press.

Debord, Guy. 1994 [1967]. *The Society of the Spectacle*, translated by Donald Nicholson-Smith. Zone Books.

Derrida, Jacques. 1982. *Margins of Philosophy*, translated by Alan Bass. University of Chicago Press.

Duxbury, Neil 2008. *The Nature and Authority of Precedent*. Cambridge University Press.

Eco, Umberto. 1984. *Semiotics and the Philosophy of Language*. Indiana University Press.

Ejdus, Filip. 2018. 'Critical Situations, Fundamental Questions and Ontological Insecurity in World Politics.' *Journal of International Relations and Development* 21 (4): 883–908.

Eriksen, Anne. 2010. 'A Case of Exemplarity: C.F. Rottböll's History of Smallpox Inoculation in Denmark-Norway, 1766.' *Scandinavian Journal of History* 35 (4): 351–370.

Eriksen, Anne, Ellen Krefting, and Anne Birgitte Rønning, eds. 2012. *Eksemplets makt: Kjønn, representasjon og autoritet fra antikken til i dag.* Scandinavian Academic Press.

Ferrara, Alessandro. 2008. *The Force of the Example: Explorations in the Paradigm of Judgment.* Columbia University Press.

Flyvbjerg, Bent. 2001. *Making Social Science Matter: Why Social Inquiry Fails and How It Can Succeed Again.* Cambridge University Press.

Foucault, Michel. 1977. *Discipline and Punish: The Birth of the Prison,* translated by Alan Sheridan. Pantheon.

Geertz, Clifford. 1980. *Negara: The Theatre State in Nineteenth-Century Bali.* Princeton University Press.

Gelley, Alexander 1995. *Unruly Examples: On the Rhetoric of Exemplarity.* Stanford University Press.

Gramsci, Antonio. 1988. *The Antonio Gramsci Reader: Selected Writings 1916–1935,* edited by David Forgacs. NYU Press.

Guzzini, Stefano. 1993. 'Structural Power: The Limits of Neorealist Power Analysis.' *International Organization* (47) 3: 443–478.

Hesford, Wendy S. 2013. 'Introduction: Facing Malala Yousafzai, Facing Ourselves.' *JAC* 33 (3–4): 407–423.

Hochschild, Jennifer L. 1996. *Facing Up to the American Dream: Race, Class, and the Soul of the Nation.* Princeton University Press.

Huang, Chin-Hao, and David C. Kang. 2022. *State Formation Through Emulation: The East Asian Model.* Cambridge University Press.

Hymes, Dell. 1981. 'Breakthrough into Performance.' In *'In Vain I Tried to Tell You': Essays in Native American Ethnopoetics.* University of Pennsylvania Press.

Ikenberry, G. John. 2018. 'The End of Liberal International Order?' *International Affairs* 94 (1): 7–23.

Kant, Immanuel. 2000 [1790]. *Critique of the Power of Judgment,* edited and translated by Paul Guyer. Cambridge University Press.

Krastev, Ivan, and Stephen Holmes. 2019. *The Light That Failed: Why the West Is Losing the Fight for Democracy.* Pegasus.

Kuo, Raymond C. 2021. *Following the Leader: International Order, Alliance Strategies, and Emulation.* Stanford University Press.

Latour, Bruno. 2005. *Reassembling the Social: An Introduction to Actor-Network-Theory.* Oxford University Press.

Lawson, George. 2015. 'Revolutions and the International.' *Theory and Society* 44 (4): 299–319.

Lebow, Richard Ned, and Ludvig Norman. 2024. 'Weimar and Modernity.' In *Weimar's Long Shadow,* edited by Richard Ned Lebow and Ludvig Norman. Cambridge University Press.

Lévi-Strauss, Claude. 1963. *Totemism*, translated by Rodney Needham. Beacon Press.
Lowrie, Michèle, and Susanne Lüdemann. 2015. *Exemplarity and Singularity: Thinking Through Particulars in Philosophy, Literature, and Law*. Routledge.
Lyons, John D. 2014. *Exemplum: The Rhetoric of Example in Early Modern France and Italy*. Princeton University Press.
Machiavelli, Niccolò. 1975 [1532]. *Il Principe*. Rizzoli.
Mälksoo, Maria 2021. 'A Ritual Approach to Deterrence: I Am, Therefore I Deter.' *European Journal of International Relations* 27 (1): 53–78.
Mallin, Eric S. 1990. 'Emulous Factions and the Collapse of Chivalry: Troilus and Cressida.' *Representations* 29: 145–179.
Merton, Robert K. 1957. *Social Theory and Social Structure*. Free Press.
Mitzen, Jennifer. 2006. 'Ontological Security in World Politics: State Identity and the Security Dilemma.' *European Journal of International Relations* 12 (3): 341–370.
Mitzen, Jennifer. 2013. *Power in Concert: The Nineteenth-Century Origins of Global Governance*. University of Chicago Press.
Neumann, Iver B. 2002. 'Returning Practice to the Linguistic Turn: The Case of Diplomacy.' *Millennium: Journal of International Studies* 31 (3): 627–651.
Noyes, Dorothy. 2015. 'Inimitable Examples: School Texts and the Classical Register in Contemporary French Politics.' In *Registers of Communication*, edited by Asif Agha and Frog. Finnish Literature Society.
Noyes, Dorothy. 2020. 'The Napoleonic Monopoly and its Challengers: Exemplarity's End?' Paper presented at 'Exemplarity: Performance, Influence, and Friction in Political Innovation.' The Ohio State University Mershon Center for International Security Studies. February 28.
Olcott, Jocelyn. 2017. *International Women's Year: The Greatest Consciousness-Raising Event in History*. Oxford University Press.
Povedák, István. 2016. 'Exemplary Romas and their Identification Patterns.' In *Religion, Culture, Society 3*, edited by Gábor Barna and Orsolya Gyöngyössy. MTA-SZTE Vallási Kultúrakutató Csoport.
Rauer, Valentin. 2006. 'Symbols in Action: Willy Brandt's Kneefall at the Warsaw Memorial.' In *Social Performance: Symbolic Action, Cultural Pragmatics, and Ritual*, edited by Jeffrey C. Alexander, Bernhard Giesen, and Jason L. Mast. Cambridge University Press.
Ringmar, Erik. 2012. 'Performing International Systems: Two East-Asian Alternatives to the Westphalian Order.' *International Organization* 66 (1): 1–25.
Schauer, Frederick 2008. 'Why Precedent in Law (and Elsewhere) is Not Totally (or Even Substantially) About Analogy.' *Perspectives on Psychological Science* 3 (6): 454–460.
Schindler, Sebastian, and Tobias Wille. 2019. 'How Can We Criticize International Practices?' *International Studies Quarterly* 63 (4): 1014–1024.

Scott, James C. 1990. *Domination and the Arts of Resistance.* Yale University Press.

Subotić, Jelena. 2016. 'Narrative, Ontological Security, and Foreign Policy Change.' *Foreign Policy Analysis* 12 (4): 610–627.

Swartz, David. 1997. *Culture and Power: The Sociology of Pierre Bourdieu.* University of Chicago Press.

Turner, Victor. 1974. *Dramas, Fields, and Metaphors.* Cornell University Press.

Vasari, Giorgio 1966–1987 [1550]. *Vite de' più eccellenti architetti, pittori et scultori italiani.* Sansoni.

Veblen, Thorstein. 2009 [1899]. *The Theory of the Leisure Class.* Oxford University Press.

Wagner-Pacifici, Robin. 2017. *What Is an Event?* University of Chicago Press.

Webber, Sabra. 2025. 'Spectacular Dissent.' In *Emerging Perspectives in the Study of Folklore and Performance*, edited by Solimar Otero and Anthony Bak Buccitelli. Indiana University Press.

Zarakol, Ayşe. 2011. *After Defeat: How the East Learned to Live with the West.* Cambridge University Press.

PART II

Individuals and Inspiration

3

Gandhi's Exemplarity

Ramachandra Guha

Editors' note: This chapter is the expansion of a speech presented in 2011 at the United Nations Headquarters for the International Day of Non-Violence, celebrated since 2007 on Gandhi's birthday. In his opening remarks, Secretary-General Ban Ki-Moon praised the efficacy of that year's non-violent protests in Tunisia and Egypt. He also emphasized the interpersonal and historical connections among international exemplars of non-violence across India, South Africa, the US, and UN.

Non-violence

In contemporary times, September 11, or 9/11 for short, is a date remembered and memorialized for the attack on the World Trade Center in New York that took place in the year 2001. But in the long sweep of history, it is another 9/11 that may yet prove to be more significant. On that day in 1906, some 3,000 men and women assembled in the city of Johannesburg in South Africa. Mostly Indians and Chinese, they had come to protest a new, racial law imposed by the Government of the Transvaal, of which province Johannesburg was the capital.

The Transvaal Government had passed an Ordinance seeking to end Asian immigration and to place sharp restrictions on Asians already in the colony. They were to produce fingerprints, carry an identity card at all times, and be confined to locations, so that they would not, so to say, 'contaminate' the ruling whites. The resistance to the Ordinance was led by Mohandas K. Gandhi. Once a lawyer, Gandhi was now a full-time activist, and a figure of considerable authority in the immigrant community.

To protest the Ordinance, the Indians of the Transvaal organized a public meeting on September 11. On the day, shops and stalls run by Indians stopped work at 10 a.m. The meeting began at three in the afternoon; however, the doors were opened at noon, to accommodate the people coming in from the suburbs and the countryside. By 1.30 the theater was packed to overflowing. The scene inside was described by a correspondent of the *Rand Daily Mail*:

> Even in its palmiest days [wrote the journalist], the old variety theatre could never have boasted of a larger audience than that which assembled yesterday. From the back row of the gallery to the front row of the stalls there was not a vacant seat, the boxes were crowded as surely they had never been crowded before, and even the stage was invaded. Wherever the eye lighted was fez and turban, and it needed but little stretch of the imagination to fancy that one was thousands of miles from Johannesburg and in the heart of India's teeming millions.

Five resolutions were presented to and passed by the meeting. One outlined what in the Ordinance was repugnant; a second asked the Transvaal Government to withdraw it. Two others conveyed the sentiments of those present to the Imperial authorities in London. The crucial resolution enjoined the audience to court arrest if their demands were not met. It said that

> In the event of the Legislative Council, the local Government, and the Imperial Authorities rejecting the humble prayer of the British Indian community of the Transvaal in connection with the Draft Asiatic Law Amendment Ordinance, this mass meeting of British Indians here assembled solemnly and regretfully resolves that, rather than submit to the galling, tyrannous, and un-British requirements laid down in the above Draft Ordinance, every British Indian in the Transvaal shall submit himself to imprisonment and shall continue to do so until it shall please His Gracious Majesty the King-Emperor to grant relief.

Speaking to the audience, Gandhi said the responsibility for advising them to go to prison was his. 'The step was grave, but unavoidable,' he remarked: 'In doing so, they did not hold a threat, but showed that the time for action – over and above making speeches and submitting petitions – had arrived.' Gandhi added that he had 'full confidence in his countrymen.' He 'knew he could trust them, and he knew also that, when occasion required an heroic step to be taken, he knew that every man among them would take it.'

Gandhi warned his compatriots of the hardships along the way. 'It is quite possible,' he said, 'that some of those who pledge themselves may weaken at the very first trial.' For 'we may have to remain hungry and suffer from extreme heat and cold. Hard labor is likely to be imposed upon us in prison. We may even be flogged by the warders.' Gandhi nonetheless urged his colleagues to join him 'in pledging ourselves, knowing full well that we shall have to suffer things like these.' The leader was clear that the 'struggle will be prolonged.' But, 'provided the entire community manfully stands the test,' he foresaw that 'there can only be one end to the struggle, and that is victory.'

Thus far, the movement to get the Indians a fair deal in South Africa had followed a strictly legalistic route. Letters, petitions, court cases, delegations – these were the means by which Gandhi and his fellows had attempted to challenge policies which bore down unfairly on them. Now, however, they were threatening to defy this new law and go to jail.

The meeting of September 11, 1906 rejected the cautious incrementalism of petition-writers. But it also rejected the violent methods then very fashionable among revolutionaries. In Europe, anarchists and socialists sought to bring about political change by assassinating kings, generals, and prime ministers. These methods were being emulated in India, where young radicals sought likewise to kill colonial administrators in a bid to frighten the British into leaving the country.

When the Transvaal Government refused to yield, Gandhi and his colleagues courted arrest. They declined to carry passes – or burnt them – defied night-time curfews, and hawked without a license. Between 1907 and 1914, several thousand Indians were put in jail by the South African authorities. Gandhi himself served three long prison sentences.

The methods of protest mandated by that other 9/11, the first 9/11, were given a particular name by Gandhi. He called them *satyagraha*, or truth force. After he returned to India in 1915, he applied them with even greater force, and as much truth, to mobilize public opinion in favor of political freedom. Gandhi led three major, countrywide campaigns of civil disobedience against British colonial rule. These scrupulously eschewed violence. Millions of Indians participated in these protests. They came from all strata of society – in His Majesty's prisons, lawyers rubbed shoulders with peasants, artisans with mill-owners.

Gandhi as national and trans-national

In India, Gandhi is known as the Father of the Nation. This is just – for he did more than anyone else to prepare Indians for freedom, to make them aware of the cleavages of religion, caste, and gender, to nurture the democratic and plural ethos of the Indian Constitution. India's debt to Gandhi is immense. Gandhi's own debts, however, ranged beyond India. While influenced by indigenous traditions of non-violence, his ideas were modified and refined through reading the works of the Russian Leo Tolstoy, the Englishman John Ruskin, and the American Henry David Thoreau. And it was South Africa, not India, that was the first, crucial crucible of his experiments in non-violent resistance.

Gandhi was, and remains, a genuinely trans-national figure. He was trans-national in the range of his influences and in the reach of his thought. Since his death, his techniques of non-violent protest have been successfully emulated and advanced by social movements in several continents. Martin Luther King and his colleagues applied the force of truth to shame the American Government into overturning racial legislation. Across Soviet-controlled Eastern Europe, Lech Walesa, Vaclav Havel, and their comrades used the power of non-violence to replace Communist dictatorships with democratic regimes. The heritage and methods of Gandhi can also be discerned in environmental and civil liberties movements around the world.

That meeting in Johannesburg in September 1906 thus sowed many seeds – seeds of resistance to colonial or authoritarian rule – that helped usher in the end of imperialism and the emergence of democratic regimes. Even when countries are formally free and formally democratic, non-violence can play a crucial role in challenging injustice and discrimination. Such was the case in the United States of the 1950s and 1960s, when the denial of equal rights of citizenship for African-Americans was confronted, and overcome, by the civil rights movement. And such is the case in India today, where multi-party democracy and an independent judiciary exist side-by-side with pervasive social inequalities.

In his own country, Gandhi's methods of satyagraha have been applied in different ways and to different ends. In the 1970s, peasants in the Himalaya launched the Chipko movement, protesting deforestation caused by timber merchants by threatening to hug the trees. In the 1980s, tribals in central India launched a series of satyagrahas in protest against a massive dam that would submerge their homes, lands, and shrines and devastate large areas of forest as well. Most recently, this past year in New Delhi, tens of thousands of Indians have held rallies and fasts to protest against the large-scale corruption of the country's political class. These movements have all drawn inspiration from Gandhi, carrying his portrait, humming the hymns he liked, starting or ending their campaigns on the day he was born, October 2, or the day he died, January 30.

Those two days are important in the life of an individual, *any* individual, who, whether famous or obscure, is known by when he or she entered this world and when he or she left it. However, when considered as a historical figure, as a figure of past importance and contemporary relevance, a third day is perhaps as significant in Gandhi's life. This is September 9, 1906, the day when, speaking to a crowd of merchants, hawkers, and laborers in Johannesburg, Gandhi gave birth to the idea of protesting against unjust laws and against authoritarian rulers, but doing so non-violently.

May the 9/11 that destroyed the World Trade Center never be repeated; but may the 9/11 whose ripples and echoes helped hasten the end of apartheid, bestowed freedom on India, enabled African-Americans to claim equal rights, and ended Communist rule in Eastern Europe live on in public memory, to animate the non-violent struggles for democracy and social justice that have still to be waged in our imperfect and insecure world.

Inter-faith dialogue

The theory and practice of non-violence was undoubtedly Gandhi's greatest contribution to public affairs. But there were other contributions too. One such was to the theory and practice of inter-faith harmony.

Gandhi was born in 1869, a decade after the publication of Charles Darwin's *The Origin of Species*. This was a time of widespread skepticism among the educated classes in Europe, a sentiment captured in the title of Thomas Hardy's poem, 'God's Funeral.' Outside the Continent, this was also a time of heightened missionary activity. In their new colonies in Africa and Asia, European priests sought to claim the heathen for Christianity.

For his part, Gandhi rejected both the atheism of the intellectuals as well as the arrogance of the missionaries. He did not think science had all the answers to the mysteries of the universe. Faith answered to a deep human need. Yet Gandhi did not think that there was one privileged path to God either. He believed that every religious tradition was an unstable mixture of truth and error. From these three beliefs followed a fourth, which was that Gandhi rejected conversion and missionary work. He encouraged inter-religious dialogue, so that individuals could see their faith in the critical reflections of another.

Gandhi once said of his own faith that he had 'broaden[ed] my Hinduism by loving other religions as my own.' He invented the inter-faith prayer meeting, where texts of different religions were read and sung to a mixed audience. At an International Fellowship of Religions, held at his *ashram* in Sabarmati in January 1928, he said that

> We can only pray, if we are Hindus, not that a Christian should become a Hindu, or if we are Mussalmans, not that a Hindu or a Christian should become a Mussalman, nor should we even secretly pray that anyone should be converted [to our faith], but our inmost prayer should be that a Hindu should be a better Hindu, a Muslim a better Muslim and a Christian a better Christian. That is the fundamental truth of fellowship.

What does it mean to be a better Hindu, or Muslim, or Christian? The sacred texts of all religions have contradictory trends and impulses, sanctioning one thing but also its opposite. Gandhi asked that we affirm those trends that oppose violence and discrimination or that promote non-violence and justice. The high priests of Hinduism claimed that the practice of Untouchability was sanctioned by the scriptures; Gandhi answered that in that case the scriptures did not represent the true traditions of the faith. Islamic texts might speak of women in condescending or disparaging terms in one place and in terms of reverence and respect in another; surely a Muslim committed to justice would value the second above the first? Likewise, a Christian must privilege the pacifism of Jesus' life above passages in the Bible calling for retribution against people of other faiths.

There was, in Gandhi's life and work, an inseparable bond between non-violence and religious pluralism. When, in the late 1930s, violent conflicts erupted between Jewish settlers and Palestinian peasants, with both sides claiming to act in the name of their faith, Gandhi remarked that 'a religious act cannot be performed with the aid of the bayonet or the bomb.' A decade later, aged 77, Gandhi walked through the riot-torn districts of eastern Bengal, healing the wounds. When independence came to India the following August, Gandhi refused to celebrate, for political freedom had come on the back of sectarian violence. When the violence would not abate, Gandhi began a fast-unto-death in Calcutta. His act shocked and shamed the people of the city, who came around, slowly. A group of representative Hindus and Muslims met him with a written promise 'that peace and quiet have been restored in Calcutta once again.' The undertaking added: 'We shall never again allow communal strife in the city. And shall strive unto death to prevent it.'

Gandhi now called off his fast, and proceeded to Delhi. The Muslims of this city had been savagely attacked by Hindus and Sikhs, themselves inflamed by pogroms against their co-religionists in Pakistan. Gandhi abhorred this politics of revenge and retribution. He went on another fast in protest. His health rapidly declined. He was persuaded to break his fast after an all-party delegation pledged that 'we shall protect the life, property and faith of Muslims and that the incidents which have taken place in Delhi will not happen again.'

An old, frail, man, had, by the force of moral example, helped bring peace to two very large cities. He now wished to proceed to the Punjab, where the rioting had been especially fierce. Before he could go, he was murdered by a religious fanatic. But his example, and achievements, lie before us. For we live now in a time marked by arrogant atheism on the one side and religious bigotry on the other. Bookshops are awash with titles proclaiming that God does not exist; the streets are muddied and bloodied by wars between competing fundamentalisms. Gandhi's faith may be of vital assistance here, in promoting peace and harmony between people who worship different Gods or no God at all.

Back in 1919, while seeking to forge an *entente cordiale* between India's two major religious groupings, Gandhi asked them to collectively take this vow:

With God as witness we Hindus and Mahomedans declare that we shall behave towards one another as children of the same parents, that we shall have no differences, that the sorrows of each will be the sorrows of the other and that each shall help the other in removing them. We shall respect each other's religion and religious feelings and shall not stand in the way of our respective religious practices. We shall always refrain from violence to each other in the name of religion.

It only remains for me to add: what Gandhi asked of Hindus and Muslims in India in 1919 should be asked again of them today, asked also of Jews and Arabs in Palestine, of Hindus and Buddhists in Sri Lanka, and of Christians and Muslims in Europe, North America, the Middle East, and Africa.

Reconciliation

Gandhi was, so to say, a serial or multiple reconciler. He sought to reconcile Hindus and Muslims, but also men and women, low castes and high castes, and North Indians and South Indians. Through his satyagraha campaigns, Gandhi brought more women into public life than any other modern politician. Apart from the great Dalit leader B. R. Ambedkar, no one did more than Gandhi to delegitimize the practice of Untouchability. And Gandhi vigorously promoted linguistic pluralism.

Gandhi and the Indian National Congress helped inspire struggles for democracy and freedom in other parts of Asia and in Africa too. For a full 50 years after its founding in 1912, the African National Congress (ANC) followed the path of non-violence. It was with some reluctance and much deliberation that it decided that the white racist regime was too deeply entrenched to be shaken by satyagraha. Still, the violence the ANC used was highly focused, designed to minimize the loss of human life. State offices and state infrastructure projects were attacked, but not state officials, and never civilians. In some 30 years of 'armed struggle' perhaps a few hundred people were killed. It was not violence, but the cumulative impact of decades of mass struggle, that finally ended apartheid and brought in a democratic political order.

As a resister, Nelson Mandela did not strictly follow the Gandhian method. But as a ruler he unquestionably did. After the ending of apartheid, he too promoted the path of reconciliation – with the white race, and among the different sections of South African society. That the Constitution of democratic South Africa refused to privilege a particular race, religion, or linguistic group owed something to the Indian, or one might even say, Gandhian, experience.

Freedom and justice, but with reconciliation – that is the message of Gandhi and Mandela, King and Havel, the Dalai Lama It is a message that must resonate with the fighters for freedom in authoritarian countries, so that democratic transitions are not succeeded, as has been the case so often in the past, by sectarian conflict.

Humility

In 1998, the editors of *Time Magazine* chose the scientist Albert Einstein as the 'Person of the Century.' They ranked Gandhi joint second, along with Franklin Delano Roosevelt. One doesn't know about FDR, but Einstein would have been both appalled and embarrassed at being placed above Gandhi. He venerated Gandhi, writing to him in September 1931 that

> you have shown through your works, that it is possible to succeed without violence even with those who have not discarded the method of violence. We may hope that your example will spread beyond the borders of your country, and will help to establish an international authority, respected by all, that will take decisions and replace war conflicts.

Eight years later, Einstein expressed his admiration for Gandhi in even more extravagant terms. This is what he wrote about him:

> A leader of his People, unsupported by any outward authority, a politician whose success rests not upon craft nor the mastery of technical devices, but simply on the convincing power of his personality; a victorious fighter who has always scorned the use of force; a man of wisdom and humility, armed with resolve and inflexible consistency, who has devoted all his strength to the uplifting of his people and the betterment of their lot; a man who has confronted the brutality of Europe with the dignity of the simple human being, and thus at all times rises superior. Generations to come, it may be, will scarce believe that such a one as this ever in flesh and blood walked upon this earth.

Einstein had no doubt that Gandhi was the greatest person of his age; perhaps of any age. In the early 1930s, when he was teaching in Berlin, portraits of three icons hung in his study. These were the physicists Max Planck and Michael Faraday, and Mohandas K. Gandhi. In the early 1950s, when Einstein was based in Princeton, a photograph of Gandhi was still displayed in his office. But Planck and Faraday had disappeared. When asked about this, Einstein replied that the discoveries of physics had recently resulted in the atom bomb. On the other hand, the reputation of Gandhi had been further enhanced in the last decades of his life.

What remains of Gandhi today? What *should* remain of Gandhi today? Some of his teachings are plainly irrelevant. For example, his ideas on food (his diet consisted chiefly of nuts and fruits and boiled vegetables), medicine (he wished to treat cancer with water baths), and sex (he imposed a strict celibacy on his followers) can hardly find favor with the majority of humans. That said, there are at least four areas in which Gandhi's ideas remain of interest and importance.

The first (and perhaps most obvious) area is non-violent resistance. That social change is both less harmful and more sustainable when achieved by non-violent means is now widely recognized. A study of some 60 transitions to democratic rule since World War II, by the think-tank Freedom House, found that 'far more often than is generally understood, the change agent is broad-based, non-violent civic resistance – which employs tactics such as boycotts, mass protests, blockades, strikes, and civil disobedience to de-legitimate authoritarian rulers and erode their sources of support, including the loyalty of their armed defenders.' These, of course, were all methods of protest pioneered by Gandhi.

The second area is faith. Gandhi was at odds both with secularists who confidently looked forward to God's funeral, and with monotheists who insisted that theirs was the one and true God. Gandhi believed that no religion had a monopoly on the truth. He argued that one should accept the faith into which one was born (hence his opposition to conversion), but seek always to practice it in the most broad-minded and non-violent way. And he actively encouraged friendships across religions. His own best friend was a Christian priest, C. F. Andrews. At the time, his position appeared eccentric; in retrospect, it seems to be precocious. In a world riven by religious misunderstanding, it can help cultivate mutual respect and recognition, and thereby diminish conflict and violence.

The third area is the environment. The rise of China and India has brought a long suppressed, and quintessentially Gandhian, question to the fore: How much should a person consume? So long as the West had a monopoly on modern lifestyles, the question simply did not arise. But if most Chinese and most Indians come, like most Americans and most Englishmen, to own and drive a car, this will place unbearable burdens on the earth. Back in 1928, Gandhi had warned about the unsustainability, on the global scale, of Western patterns of production and consumption. 'God forbid that India should ever take to industrialization after the manner of the West,' he said. 'The economic imperialism of a single tiny island kingdom [England] is today keeping the world in chains. If an entire nation of 300 million took to similar economic exploitation, it would strip the world bare like locusts.'

Gandhi's life and legacy have profound implications for the way we live and relate to the environment today.

An aphorism attributed to him runs as follows: 'The world has enough for everybody's need, but not enough for everybody's greed.' Recent scholarship suggests that he never said these precise words in this exact order. However, the sentiments they convey and contain are undoubtedly his own.

Gandhi's respect for other religions, other races, other species, was intimately connected with his philosophy (and practice) of non-violence. He opposed injustice and authoritarian rule, but without arms. He reached out to people of other faiths, with understanding and respect. Where the proselytizer took his book to the heathen – backed sometimes with the bayonet and the bomb – Gandhi chose rather to study Islamic and Christian texts, bringing to them the same open, yet not uncritical, mind that he brought to Hindu scriptures. And in promoting a resource-conserving lifestyle, Gandhi sought to eschew violence to the earth itself.

The fourth area where Gandhi matters is public life. In his *Reflections on Gandhi*, George Orwell wrote that 'regarded simply as a politician, and compared with the other leading political figures of our time, how clean a smell he has managed to leave behind!' In an age of terror, politicians may not be able to live as open a life as Gandhi. There were no security men posted outside his ashram; visitors of any creed and nationality would walk in when they chose.

The politicians of today would do well to emulate Gandhi's lack of dissembling and his utter lack of reliance on 'spin.' His campaigns of civil disobedience were always announced in advance. His social experiments were minutely dissected in the pages of his newspapers, the comments of his critics placed alongside his own.

Gandhi's political practice holds a salutary lesson (or two) for those who seek to change the world today. Gandhi once spoke of making a 'Himalayan Blunder'; but contemporary activists, as much as contemporary politicians, are loath ever to admit to a mistake. Gandhi's heightened self-awareness and openness to self-criticism stands in striking contrast to the arrogance of those in position of power, who, in this decade after the more famous (and more notorious) 9/11, have promoted the politics of revenge and retribution, contributing to an escalating cycle of violence and counter-violence which may at last, and not a day too soon, be finally ebbing. This might then be the time then to recall the other 9/11, the 9/11 in Johannesburg which mandated non-violence as a means of securing justice, the 9/11 whose best exemplars have seen their adversary not as a demon or enemy but as a being as human, and as fallible, as themselves.

Gandhi was a prophet, of sorts, but by no means a joyless one. On a visit to London in 1931 he met a British monarch for the first and last time. When he came out of Buckingham Palace after speaking with George the Sixth, a reporter asked whether he had not felt cold in his loin-cloth. Gandhi answered: 'The King had enough on for both of us.' Another version has

Gandhi saying: 'The King wears plus-fours; I wear minus-fours.' In those self-deprecatory jokes lies a good deal of (still enduring) wisdom.

Some 70-odd years after his death, Gandhi matters for his pioneering of non-violent techniques of protest, or *satyagraha*; for his willingness to stake his life in the cause of religious peace and religious pluralism; for his respect for other living beings and for the earth; for the transparency and honesty of his personal and public life. For these reasons, and more, Gandhi matters, still.

Documentation for the episodes described in this chapter may be found in Ramachandra Guha's two biographies: 'Gandhi Before India' (Penguin Random House, 2013) and 'Gandhi 1914–1948: The Years that Changed the World' (Penguin Random House, 2018). Ban Ki-Moon's opening remarks may be found at https://www.un.org/sg/en/content/sg/speeches/2011-09-30/remarks-special-event-occasion-international-day-non-violence

4

Tyrannicides, Tyrants, and Emperors: Exemplarity in the Graeco-Roman World

Fritz Graf

Introduction

The societies of Greece and Rome understood themselves as ruled and regulated by traditions, πάτριοι νόμοι in Greece, *mos maiorum* in Rome. The terms indicate that these traditions were thought of as initiated by earlier members of their group whose actions and values were perceived as being exemplary. For the Roman world, Karl-Joachim Hölkeskamp (1996) and (in more detail) Matthew Roller (2018) have analyzed this exemplarity and described its structure; no comparable study for Greece exists, despite the wide use of exemplarity in rhetorical practice and Aristotle's theorization. Both Hölkeskamp and Roller insist on the ethical perspective of exemplarity: an exemplary individual shows what a good man or woman is. The following account of the Athenian tyrannicides Harmodios and Aristogeiton not only highlights a well-known couple of Greek exemplary men but insists on the political dimension of their exemplarity. By their radical resistance to the transgressions of a tyrant, they modeled how important even the violent defense of individual freedom was for Athenian democracy.

Tyrannicide, the act of killing an evil autocrat, had become part of democratic ideology once Athenian democracy of the earlier 5th century BC construed the tyrant (*tyrannos* in Greek) as the inversion of democratic ideals, reflecting various forms of Greek and Near Eastern authoritarian rulers. A tyrant in this construction came to power by his own machinations, not by election or another form of consent among the citizens, nor did he answer to the institutions of democracy; he made his own laws and followed his own interests, often relying on violence of all sorts. And since there was no democratic institution to remove him, killing him was a legitimate way of getting rid of him: hence, a tyrannicide was an exemplary savior of the democratic state.

The Athenian tyrannicides

In the summer of 490 BCE, a large Persian army was about to invade the Greek mainland via the East coast of Attika at the advice of Hippias, the son of Athens' former tyrant Peisistratos who was now in exile at the Persian court. The commanders of a small Greek force from several independent city-states debated whether they should run or try to fight them. As was customary, each federal general gave his vote, while their commander-in-chief, the Athenian Miltiades, was not allowed to vote; city politics was more important than the immediate military needs. But Miltiades could at least advise the leader of the Athenian contingent, one Kallimachos, and according to Herodotus (6.109)[1] he urged him to leave 'a memorial (μναμόσυνα) such as not even Harmodios and Aristogeiton have left.' Fighting the Persians was equivalent to freeing the city from the renewed threat of Hippias, the potential tyrant who was coming back with the Persians (Herodotus, *Histories* 6.109.3, translation after the Loeb edition). The passage is the first developed instance of the example of the Peisistratean tyrannicides that we meet in written Athenian sources. It illustrates the key themes of exemplarity: it is based on collective memory, is invoked in a critical moment, and should inspire emulation, to the extent that the emulator would do even better than the original actor.

A few images are earlier than Herodotus' text and demonstrate how fast the historical event became in civic memory an exemplary tale, a template with the normative power of a myth. Three red-figured vases of 475/470 BCE depict the moment when the tyrant is slain by two attackers, the bearded and older Aristogeiton and his beardless, adolescent companion Harmodios (Syriskos Painter, *Stamnos*, 475–470 BCE, Martin von Wagner Museum, Würzburg, L 515; Shear 2012). Athenian vases almost never depict scenes from history but show either scenes from daily life or, much more often, scenes from mythology: already by 475/470 the tyrannicide narrative had entered the realm of tradition. The vases are contemporary with the dedication of the famous statue group of the tyrannicides on the Athenian agora by the two sculptors Kritios and Nesiotes; the bronze original is lost, but we have many smaller reproductions and a life-size Roman copy,

---

[1] This and all subsequent references to antique texts utilize the shorthand citation method (author, book, volume and line number) common in Classical scholarship.

now in the Archeological Museum of Naples, again with a bearded and an adolescent swordsman (Brunnsåker 1971, Thompson 1972, 155–159). Its base must have carried a dedicatory epigram; among the epigraphical and literary fragments that qualify for such an epigram there are many that would fit this bill, and none is more convincing than any other (Day 1985; Lebedev 1996).

The statue group at the center of the agora was the first bronze image to honor humans in a public space in Athens that only slowly and sparingly accepted other honorary statues, and even then only those of 'good generals and the tyrannicides,' not of sundry athletes and benefactors as in other cities (Lykourgos 51; Ma 2013, 104). The next image in honor of a human was set up almost a century later, in the 380s BCE, for the Athenian general Konon who ended the Spartan domination over Athens and its allies. The orator Demosthenes explained the reason for it, referring back to the decree of the assembly: 'In breaking up the empire of the Lacedaemonians, Konon had ended no insignificant tyranny' (Demosthenes, *Against Leptines* 70). Other images followed slowly during the next centuries, but decrees that granted them were careful to exclude the neighborhood of the tyrannicide group: the group should not be eclipsed by other images (*IG* II² 450, 314/313 BCE; *IG* II³ 853 295/2 BCE).

We know of only two exceptions before the epoch of the Roman emperors; both were in debatable taste and rather short-lived. In order to honor the Seleucid kings, Antigonos and his son Demetrios, who in 307 BCE freed Athens from the rule of Kassandros, the rival king of Macedonia, the Athenians 'voted to set up golden statues of Antigonus and Demetrius in a chariot near the statues of Harmodius and Aristogeiton and ... to consecrate an altar to them, calling it the altar of the Saviors' (Diodorus Siculus 20.46.1; Ma 2013, 118). The implication of this honor, spelled out in the religious epithet the Seleucids received at their altar, is again not just the restoration of democracy, but of Athenian identity. It did not bother the Athenian voters that they exchanged one monarch, Kassandros, for another, Antigonos, both Macedonians. A century later, the Athenians would change their minds and abolish most of these honors.

The other case we know of happened much later, after the Ides of March of 44 BCE. When Marcus Brutus and his close friend Cassius came to Athens in the late summer of 44, the Athenians received them enthusiastically and 'voted them bronze images by the side of those of Harmodius and Aristogeiton' (Dio Cassius 47.20.3; Raubitschek 1957). The Roman tyrannicides, two very close friends (although not lovers like Harmodios and Aristogeiton), appeared as having lived up to the much older, classical example. The Athenians had no reason to regard Julius Caesar as a tyrant with regard to their own city. They simply wanted to be on the right side of history – rather prematurely, as it turned out, and we don't know whether the images were ever set up; if so, they must have disappeared rather fast again.

In both cases the bronze images of the Athenian tyrannicides functioned as 'lieux de mémoire' as conceived by Pierra Nora (1989), spots in space to which later actors and events could be tied back to gain their political meaning. It deserves to be stressed, however, that in neither case the exemplarity of the Athenian tyrannicides was used to promote a specific future action (unlike as in Miltiades' advice to Kallimachos before Marathon); it was always interpreted as a past event that justified exceptional honors.

At the same time, the original statue group on the agora did not simply preserve the memory of a specific political act. To be granted the right to erect a highly visible statue was a signal honor that Greek states conveyed to their benefactors until the very end of antiquity, not all of them with the moderation of the Athenians; among possible places, the agora is the most exquisite. In the case of the Athenian tyrannicides, this signal honor went together with other distinctions. They received an annual sacrifice during the Panathenaia, the annual festival in which Athens celebrated itself; it was performed either at the statues on the agora or on their grave outside the city, on the road to the Academy, the suburban grove of the hero Akademos (Shear 2012; Pausanias 1.29.15). Their male descendants received lifelong dining privileges in the *prytaneion*, the city hall, together with the city leaders and other honored personalities, and they were freed from any taxes (Aristotle, *Constitution of Athens* 58.1; Demosthenes, *Adversus Leptinem* 18).

The same preference for evaluation and judgment without calling for active emulation is visible in most of the instances in Athenian and wider Greek literature that refers to the tyrannicides. I only give a few examples. The first is in a comic vein. Aristophanes's *Knights*, a comedy put on stage in 424 BCE, attacks the powerful demagogue Kleon. In an address to the personified People (*Dēmos*), Kleon promises him a soft bed instead of the hard soil on which other politicians have bedded him. The Demos reacts, overjoyed: 'Are you by chance a descendant of Harmodios?' (Aristophanes, *Equites* 786; Aristophanes, *Lysistrata* 630–635). This reaction is double-edged, and it confirms the link of the tyrannicides with Athenian radical democracy. Aristophanes detests Kleon, and to compare the tyrannicides with him makes them demagogues, not positive examples – a rare negative evaluation of their deed that we find again a generation later in another skeptic of Athenian democracy, Plato (*Hipparchus* 229 BE).

Most other earlier references come from the Athenian orators of the 4th century whose speeches most often reflect widely accepted attitudes and values. With them, the tyrannicides usually figure as reference points for 'manly virtue' (ἀρετή). They have 'earned high praise not because of their nobility, but because of their ἀρετή,' said the orator Isaios (Isaeus, *Against Dikaiogenes* 47). They were benefactors of the entire Athenian people, despite their love for each other, according to Aeschines (Aeschines, *Timarchides* 140; Wohl 2002). And in his funeral oration for the dead of the Lamian War of 322 where the general Leosthenes and his officers defended Athens and its allies against the Macedonians and died in battle, Hypereides asserts that the fallen leaders of this war did something as outstanding as what Harmonios and Aristogeiton did, 'nor are there any heroes with whom the tyrannicides would rather talk in the underworld than these' (Hyperides, Epitaphios 39; Demosthenes, *Adversus Leptinem* 29).

If we want to find the Athenian tyrannicides as inspiration for future action, we have to look elsewhere: to a group of Athenian symposiastic songs, the so-called *skolia*, and an Athenian law that intended to incite resistance to tyranny.

The law in question is not preserved in its original inscription, but cited by an orator, verbatim and with an exact date, 410 BCE. It stipulates that each and every Athenian citizen has to take a solemn oath to 'kill with word, act, vote and, if I am able, with my own hand' whoever 'undoes the people's rule (δημοκρατία) over Athens, holds a public office when the people's rule has been undone, installs himself as a *tyrannos*, or works together with a *tyrannos*' (*IG* II³ 1 320). The killer shall not only be free of punishment and religiously pure despite the murder; if he dies in the attempt, the Athenians 'shall treat him and his children as benefactors, in the same way as they have treated Harmodios, Aristogeiton and their descendants' (*On the Mysteries* 96–98; Teegarden 2014, ch 1). As part of this citizen oath, the example of the well-known honors to the two tyrannicides and their descendants serves as a strong appeal for all future tyrannicides to do the same.

The law was voted upon in a reaction to an attempt at overthrowing democracy by a group of oligarchs in summer 411. By not just legitimizing but inciting a tyrannicide, it supplanted an earlier and much tamer law that exiled tyrants and that had not been able to prevent Peisistratos from making himself the sole ruler of Athens in the 550s; the new law, however, in turn would not stop the harsh rule of the next group of oligarchs, the infamous Thirty in 404/403.

At the same time, the new law was the outcome of a development that goes back to much earlier in the 5th century and that intended to familiarize young members of the political elite with the civic duty to kill a tyrant, with a way to do it, and with the honors that would follow. In a rare example of indoctrination through inebriation, this program was expressed in drinking songs. We know of four such *skolia* that all go back to at least the earlier 5th century, although they are attested for the first time as late as the year 411 BCE, in a comedy of Aristophanes (Aristophanes, *Lysistrata* 630–635). It was an Athenian banqueting custom that a banqueter would sing a short song and accompany himself on the lyre, and then challenge another guest to do the same; this would turn into a contest among the usually nine guests, and the winner would earn a drinking cup called 'the Singer,' ὠιδός (Athenaeus 11.110). The custom is well attested in the fifth and fourth centuries; it might well be older, given the roots of the banquet in the aristocratic society of the Archaic Age (Antiphanes frg. 14 Kock = Athenenaeus 15.47; Murray 1990). We know a number of these songs; their topics were mostly erotic, but could be political, as in our case. The four tyrannicide songs echo each other (performance, not originality counted: any well-educated Greek aristocrat could sing and play the lyre). I give you two variations that indicate the width of the genre (Athenaeus 15.50). One song addresses Harmodios:

> Most dear Harmodios, you never died:
> They say you are on the Isles of the Blessed,
> Where they say the swift Achilles is
> and Diomedes, Tydeus' son.

Compared to this praise of the tyrannicides as heroes among the most prominent heroes of Homer and where the praise functions only as an indirect and tame invitation to do the same, the other song that is somewhat more indicative of the genre is more forceful and direct:

> I will carry my sword hidden in a myrtle bough
> like Harmodios and Aristogeiton,
> when in Athens during a sacrifice
> they slaughtered the tyrant Hipparchos.

The text describes the trick of the murderers to kill the tyrant with a concealed weapon during a religious ritual whose participants could not carry weapons and thus, in the tyrant's eye, presented no danger. The example turns into a very useful lesson in the training of future tyrannicides.

So far, so good: we seem to have all the elements of exemplarity we expect from the paradigm – the exemplary action, its memory encoded in a public monument, in institutionalized songs and in public rituals, and the use of the example to evaluate other, later emulations. I could stop here, were things not much more complicated in Athens on two levels.

First there is the statue group of the tyrannicides on the agora that played such a role in some inscriptions and in my argument. This famous statue group by Kritios and Nesiotes is dated to 477/476 BCE (*Marmor Parium, IG* XII: 5.444), and the three contemporary vases I mentioned reflect the impression this statue made on Athenians. The vases do more: as wine containers, they were standard banqueting tools, and I imagine a close relationship between these large and colorful pots and the drinking songs of the same topic: the image on the pots illustrated the songs or even inspired the singers. The songs then would be much older than their first attestation in 411 BCE; nothing prevents the assumption that they are as old as the statue group.

The statue group of Kritios and Nesiotes, however, had a prehistory. It replaced a group made by a different sculptor, one Antenor, that goes back to an uncertain date in the late 6th century BCE. When, a decade after Marathon, the Persian king Xerxes conquered and destroyed Athens, he took Antenor's statue group and abducted it to his capital, Susa. It must already then have been closely tied to the exemplarity of the tyrannicides: this is why the Athenians wanted to replace it fast when they rebuilt their city after Xerxes' defeat in 479 BCE. They did this much faster than they rebuilt the destroyed temples whose ruins recalled the Persian impiety, as an admonition to maintain the civic unity that had vanquished the enemy. The statue group was perceived as vital in the tricky transitional period of the 470s, when Athens returned to democracy and rapidly expanded its power: in this unstable time, it mattered to have a memorial that alluded to the problem of tyranny and recalled the civic obligation of tyrannicide. Like the *skolia*, the vases of 475/470 are also a proof how the democratic elite thought.

As an aside: when after 333 Alexander conquered the Persian empire, he found the Athenian statue group in Susa, and at least some authors credit him with the initiative to ship it back to Athens. Others connected it with later kings; but we know how Alexander favored democracy in Greek cities, so I am willing to credit him with the deed. From then on, there were two statue groups of Tyrant-Slayers in Athens; around the middle of the 2nd century CE, the travel writer Pausanias described them both, standing side by side (Pausanias 1.5.8).

The 6th-century statue group finally forces me to look at the historical event it commemorates, the termination of the Peisistratid tyranny and the invention of Athenian democracy. According to all later sources, from the drinking songs of the early 5th century to the 4th century orators and Hellenistic popular historians, the merit of doing away with tyranny by slaying the tyrant Hipparchos, the son of Peisistratos, went to Harmodios and Aristogeiton who gave their lives during the undertaking. Unfortunately the oldest and most reliable historians, Herodotus, Thukydides and Aristotle, disagree with this story (Jacoby 1949, 152–168).

Herodotus, born around 485 BCE, between the battles of Marathon and Salamis, wrote one generation after the Persian Wars. He insists that nobody was correctly informed about the end of the Peisistratid rule: 'When Hipparchos, son of Peisistratos and brother of the tyrant Hippias, had been slain ... by Aristogeiton and Harmodios ... after this the Athenians were subject for four years to a tyranny not less but even more absolute than before' (Herodotus 5.55.1).

With this, Herodotus corrects the later accounts on two counts. The victim of the tyrannicides Harmodios and Aristogeiton was not the tyrant

Hippias – he survived the attempt and later went to Susa – but his brother Hipparchos. And it did nothing to remove tyranny; if anything, it made it harsher than before, and Hippias stayed in power another couple of years. The historian spells this out in a later passage: Harmodios and Aristogeiton 'only enraged the remaining sons of Pisistratos by killing Hipparchos, and did nothing to end tyranny' (Herodotus 6.123.2).

Thukydides and Aristotle in their much longer narrations agree with this and add two details. The motif of the tyrannicides was not political only but also personal and, at least in part, erotic: Hipparchos was a rival of Aristogeiton in his love for the young and beautiful Harmodios, but was rebuffed by the young man, for which he took revenge on Harmodios' sister. And their attempt at tyrannicide was rather bungled: they and their helpers planned to murder the ruling Hippias during the sacrifice of the Panathenaia, but because some nervous would-be tyrant-slayer assumed wrongly that the plot was known to the tyrant, they acted much too early and in an improvised manner which killed the wrong man and caused the death of both Harmodius and his lover Aristogeiton (Thucydides 1.20.2).

Thus, at the latest in the middle of the 5th century BCE, there were two available narrations on the end of tyranny in Athens. There was the one in which two young men, Harmodios and Aristogeiton, killed the tyrant Hipparchos, thus ending the rule of one powerful family over Athens and opening the way for the rule of the many, democracy, although the tyrannicides themselves did not survive their action. A leading modern historian called this account 'the official conception as sanctioned by the State' (Jacoby 1949, 159). Then there was the story adopted by the major ancient historians in the century after the event, Herodotus, Thukydides, and Aristotle. In this account, the tyrannicides were improvising, and they bungled; they killed not the major tyrant, Hippias, but his less significant younger brother, and they were killed in the attempt; they did not succeed in restoring democracy; and they acted only partially for political reasons. Accordingly, Hippias, the oldest son and heir of Peisistratos, ruled several more years and then was finally deposed by the Spartans, but was allowed to live in exile at the Persian court: from here, he led the Persian armies back to Marathon in 490 BCE (Thucydides 6.55.1).

The exemplarity template helps explain why the Athenians selected the first account: they needed a story of a successful regime change from tyranny to democracy by the action of two exemplary heroes. This account was already present in the minds of the Athenian citizens who voted to erect and pay for the first statue group of Harmodios and Aristogeiton that preceded the occupation by Xerxes in 480 BCE; it could well date to the late 6th century BCE, but we lack the means to determine a clear date. Presumably in the same decree of the popular assembly that granted them the bronze statues, the Athenians also voted to institute an annual sacrifice to the tyrannicides at the Panathenaia; we can assume that the same decree granted dining and tax privileges to their descendants. These three items were justified by the story of the exemplary performance capable of inspiring future defenders of democracy to risk their lives in the defense of the state. If we look for the agents who helped decide the selection of the story, there is an obvious candidate. This construction of history with its various *lieux de mémoire* fits the radically reformed form of Athenian self-government that we associate with the Kleisthenes in about 510 BCE, and that followed upon the expulsion of the tyrant Hippias. Kleisthenes' aim was not just to replace tyranny with democracy, the rule by the one with the rule by the many, but to create radically new democratic institutions. Their complex geographical structure, dissolving earlier local boundaries, made any tyranny impossible, because they prevented one single local aristocratic family from amassing enough power and followers to dominate the state. And should this institutional safeguard not suffice, the new example of Harmodios and Aristogeiton provided an additional safety mechanism to block tyranny. It anchored itself in a highly visible statue group on the center of the agora; in a ritual during the main state festival, the Panathenaia; in the dining privileges of the descendants of the tyrannicides; and perhaps already then also in the banqueting songs. The songs narrated the story, while the statues triggered it, since they represented the two men, the mature bearded and the young beardless one, in full aggressive action which needed an explanation. The sacrifice needed an explanation and might already have come with an explanatory prayer; the dining privileges finally guaranteed the daily interaction of the descendants with the leading city magistrates to keep the story alive.

When Xerxes in 480 BCE abducted the statue to Susa, he knew what he was doing. He was not simply collecting yet another war trophy; in order to prepare Athens to be run by a Persian satrap, he removed a powerful symbol of resistance against the rule of one man. Like his father Dareios the Great, he must have followed the advice of an Athenian insider, if not again Hippias then another descendent of Peisistratos still living at his court (Thucydides 6.55.1). The Athenians in turn were again fully aware of this exemplarity: this is why they replaced the abducted image so quickly, maybe then also inventing the banquet song that become so successful throughout the 5th century. In 411 BCE, however, they realized the hard way that despite all these measures a tyranny was still possible when not done by one man but in committee (technically, then it was not a tyranny, but an oligarchy); to react to this, they introduced the compulsory oath of every citizen to kill anyone who attempted to do away with democracy and served in such a government. As we saw, the law again made reference to the exemplary tyrannicides. Similar decrees against tyranny then became common throughout Greece in the course of the 4th century, as David Teegarden in his 2014 book *Death to the Tyrants!* has shown – and already around 450 BCE, one city, Kyzikos, advertised on its coins the successful removal of a local tyrant (who had ruled with Persian help) with the image of the Athenian tyrannicides (Teegarden 2014, 144–145). Thanks to the fame of the statue group, the example survived several centuries. When in 88 BCE a philosopher, Aristion, made himself tyrant of Athens with the help of king Mithridates of Pontus and against the Romans who at the time were the overlords of Greece, Athenian dissenters fled to the army of Sulla whom the senate had sent to restore Rome's rule; on their propaganda coins issued in Sulla's camp, they represented a naked swordsman that numismatists have read as Aristogeiton, and inscribed δῆμος, 'the people' as the issuer (Jongkees 1947).

As an aside, I cannot refrain from mentioning another image whose story was generated by the exemplary account of the two tyrannicides. A statue of a lioness stood outside the entry of the Athenian acropolis; it was said to have no tongue. Athenians explained this image again with the tyrannicides, as a monument that the grateful citizens had put up to honor the courtesan Leaina (Lioness), a close friend of Harmodios; after the putsch, she like Harmodios died under torture without giving anything away. The invention is obvious – but it is also obvious how exemplarity is eager to attach itself to other monuments by creating new stories.

Postlude in Rome

We saw how the Athenians connect their tyrannicides with the famous Roman ones, Marcus Brutus and Cassius. There is of course also the older Brutus, Lucius, who was said to have ended the rule of the kings and founded the Roman Republic. Like Harmodius and Aristogeiton in Athens, he had a statue on the Capitol in Rome that showed him, sword in hand, somewhat ironically but tellingly among the statues of the Roman kings (Plutarch, *Brutus* 1). We do not know whether this image consciously imitated Athenian statues, but Romans could perceive a relationship between the two events; the Elder Pliny noted that the Athenian and the Roman killing happened at the same time (Pliny *Natural History* 34.16).

During most of Rome's Republican era, we do not see any trace of exemplarity being claimed for Lucius Brutus' deed. Unlike Athens, Rome seemed to be deeply convinced that its democratic institutions would withstand any pressure, and one might remember that Cicero described Rome's constitution not as democratic, aristocratic, or monarchic, but as the blend of these three basic and traditional forms; already in Greek theory, this blend was thought to be most resistant against change (Cicero's *De re publica* 1.69). Cicero's analysis, however, was too optimistic, as we know (and as he himself tragically would realize soon): tyranny was on the horizon in his time. And none other than the second Brutus, Caesar's murderer, would be the first we know of to exploit the exemplarity of the first. When Marcus Brutus was moneyer in 54 BCE, he used his office to mint coins that used a portrait of his older namesake to promote tyrannicide, and he also used the example of another early tyrannicide, C. Servilius Ahala; Brutus' mother claimed descent from him (Plut. *Brutus* 1.5). The would-be tyrant at whom this was aimed was left unspoken. It cannot be the later tyrant Caesar, who at the time was far away conquering Gaul; this leaves Pompey, the most powerful aristocrat of the time. Nine years later, when Caesar had become tyrant, Romans used the statue of the older Brutus to extol his example by scribbling on it 'If only Brutus were alive!' in order to shame the younger Brutus into action (Plut. Brutus 5). Brutus reacted accordingly, as we know; and when he took an oath from his followers, he did it by using the very sword with which Lucretia had killed herself. Our source (Dionysius of Halicarnassus, *Antiquities* 4.71.1) is not wholly reliable – but, in the spirit of exemplarity, 'se non è vero, è ben trovato.'

With the victory of Caesar's heir, Octavian Augustus, the example of Brutus disappeared in Rome: there was no republic left to be restored by tyrannicides. Rather, it is illuminating that the poet Lucan in his poem *On the Civil War*, intended to denounce the inadequacy of Nero's rule, never referred to Brutus as an exemplary figure; Lucan's exemplar is the honest and upright philosopher Cato who killed himself in Africa, as Lucan would kill himself when his implication in an attempt to kill Nero was revealed. Rome now needed a monarch, and the best one could hope for was a philosophically enlightened Stoic. The exemplary tyrannicides were too tightly tied to democracy to remain useful once the political system had changed so radically.

Conclusion

To summarize, the attempt to get rid of Hippias, the tyrant of Athens, was narrated in two ways – as an unprofessional putsch resulting in no immediate regime change, and as the successful event that allowed to restructure Athens as a radical democracy. The Athenians selected the second version because they needed an exemplary account in order to prevent any further tyranny. To fulfill this purpose, it was anchored in a highly visible statue, an annual sacrifice during Athens' main city festival, the customary singing of banquet songs by young elite men, and privileges for the descendants of the tyrannicides; after a new attempt at tyranny, this was bolstered by the institution of a compulsory oath by all citizens to resist and kill any tyrant. This complicated structure survived centuries and became irrelevant only under Roman rule. The Roman parallel, the tyrannicide Brutus, was much less prominent. His exemplarity had a short life in the troubled period at the end of the Roman

Republic, due to radically changed political circumstances. It is obvious that the life of these two examples was tied to the political framework in which they existed; but the *mise-en-scène* of these examples mattered much more.

In a short coda, I cannot refrain from adding another instance of the Brutus narration, in radically new times. After the death of the emperor Justinian, centuries after Caesar, the chronicler John Malalas returned to the story of Brutus. He did not turn the older Brutus into an exemplary hero of a democracy that had long ceased to exist. Rather, Malalas' Brutus was now the inventor of the ritual for freeing slaves that was used by Roman emperors and aristocrats. Although freedom had long lost its importance as a political value, it remained tied to the example of Marcus Junius Brutus; from politics, however, it now pertained to individuals in the context of private law (Malalas' *Chronographia* 7.9). I do not know a more impressive example of how flexible an exemplary template can remain.

References

Brunnsåker, Sture. 1971. *The Tyrant-Slayers of Kritios and Nesiotes*. Svenska Institutet i Athen.

Day, Joseph W. 1985. 'Epigrams and History: The Athenian Tyrannicides.' In *The Greek Historians: Papers Presented to A. E. Raubitschek*. Stanford University, Department of Classics.

Hölkeskamp, Karl-Joachim. 1996. 'Exempla and Mos Maiorum: Überlegungen zum kollevtiven Gedächtnis der römischen Nobilität.' In *Vergangenheit und Lebenswelt: Soziale Kommunikation, Traditionsbildung und historisches Bewusstsein*, edited by Hans-Joachim Gehrke and Astrid Möller. Narr.

Jacoby, Felix. 1949. *Atthis*. Oxford University Press.

Jongkees, Jan Hendrik. 1947. 'Notes on the Coinage of Athens.' *Mnemosyne* 13: 145–164.

Lebedev, Andrei. 1996. 'A New Epigram for Harmodios and Aristogeiton.' *Zeitschrift für Papyrologie und Epigraphik* 112: 263–268.

Ma, John. 2013. *Statues and Cities. Honorific Portraits and Civic Identity in the Hellenistic World*. Oxford University Press.

Murray, Oswyn, ed. 1990. *Sympotica: A Symposium on the Symposion*. Oxford University Press.

Nora, Pierre. 1989. 'Between Memory and History: Les Lieux de Mémoire.' *Representations* 26: 7–24.

Raubitschek, Antony Erich. 1957. 'Brutus in Athens.' *Phoenix* 11: 1–11.

Roller, Matthew B. 2018. *Models from the Past in Roman Culture: A World of Exempla*. Cambridge University Press.

Shear, Julia L. 2012. 'The Tyrannicides, their Cult and the Panathenaia: A Note.' *Journal of Hellenic Studies* 132: 107–119.

Teegarden, David A. 2014. *Death to Tyrants! Ancient Greek Democracy and the Struggle against Tyranny*. Princeton University Press.

Thompson, Homer A. 1972. *The Agora of Athens: The History, Shape and Uses of an Ancient City Center.* The American School of Classical Studies at Athens.

Wohl, Victoria. 2002. *Love among the Ruins: The Erotics of Democracy in Classical Athens.* Princeton University Press.

5

The Child Greta:
The Exemplar as Embodied Future

Kyrre Kverndokk

Greta Thunberg got out of bed earlier than usual on the morning of August 20, 2018. She put her textbooks, some food, and a water bottle in her backpack. This morning she also brought a seat pad and some warm clothes. She got on her bike, but instead of going to school she set off toward the city center of Stockholm. She parked the bike outside the parliament building. Then she carefully placed the seat pad on the ground and sat down. She had brought with her 100 copies of a leaflet, and she placed them in from of her (Ernman et al 2020, 223–225). This leaflet explained:

> We children don't usually do/ what you say./ We do what you do./ And because you grown-ups / don't give a damn about my future, neither do I. / My name is Greta and I am in 9th grade./ And I am going on strike from school for the climate/ until Election Day. (Ernman et al 2020, 223)

She asked a person passing by to take her picture, which she posted on Instagram and Twitter. Thunberg was a shy teenager and at this point she had just a handful of followers on social media. But still, within just a few minutes her picture was re-tweeted and started to spread (Ernman et al 2020, 226). Already on the second day another youngster joined her, and soon a small group of young people were on strike for the climate (Ernman et al 2020, 230). This is how the Thunberg-Ernman family's autobiography *Our House Is on Fire: Scenes of a Family and a Planet in Crisis* (2020) tells the story of how a 15-year-old girl became an exemplar for young activists across the globe.

Greta Thunberg has been compared with other young female pioneers of social movements, such as Malala Yousafzai, Ahed Tamimi, and Emma González.

However, there is one major difference between them and Thunberg. None of these activists would be portrayed as children, at least not in positive terms. Thunberg, on the other hand, presented herself as a child when she sat down in front of the Swedish Parliament, and she continued to do so in her speeches and public appearances that soon followed.

To be a child is not usually something that gives authority in political debates. This seems, however, not to be the case in climate change discourse. The trope of the child plays a significant role in the rhetoric and the performances of Thunberg and also in the public reception of her as an activist. The chapter will discuss what kind of significance the trope might have for her position as an exemplar.

The example as model and sample

Dorothy Noyes has emphasized that an exemplar is a person 'that stands forward to be imitated' (Noyes 2016, 78).[1] In that regard, it is a social status that takes its shape through performative practices. Like other performances, the exemplary act is shaped in the interplay between the performer, the performed message, and the response of the audience. As Noyes and Wille point out, exemplarity is 'a mode of cultural transmission' (Chapter 1, this volume). In order to be transmitted and widely distributed, the act of the exemplar must not only represent something creatively new. It also has to resonate with the interests, norms, and values of the audience (for example, Ortutay 1959). Its success evolves in the tension between innovation and tradition, and between the exceptional and the representative. Hence, the performances of the exemplar must necessarily contain echoes and traces of what is already performed (Noyes 2016, 80; see Bakhtin 1986).

Thus, an exemplar evolves in the tension between the unique and the representative, between what literary scholar Alexander Gelley has termed Platonic and Aristotelian examples. Platonic examples are, according to Gelley, paradigmatic ideals that might be used as models for action. The Aristotelian example, on the other hand, is inductive and serial. Such an example is a sample, it is one of many, and as such it points towards a general statement or abstract principle (Gelley 1995, 1). These two kinds of examples might be regarded as *aspects* of exemplarity, rather than distinct *kinds* of examples, and they are often entangled. Folklorist Anne Eriksen puts it this way: 'The example is both one of a series and one of a kind, and it is in this doubleness that its power resides. Functionally, the example is a point of exchange between the regular and the exceptional, and from

---

[1] In the quoted article Noyes uses the German term *Vorbild*.

this stems its cultural and rhetorical energy' (Eriksen 2019, 358; see Eriksen et al 2012, 12–14). In this chapter, I will explore the entanglement of the Aristotelian and Platonic example, of the model and sample, in Thunberg's case (see Watanabe, Chapter 11, this volume).

This book focuses on exemplarity as a performative act. But examples are also rhetorical figures, and the performance of the exemplar might be entangled with spoken or written rhetorical means. In Thunberg's case, her exemplarity does not just depend on her practices, it also depends on her speeches and her rhetorical skills. I will therefore consider exemplarity both as a certain kind of performative practice that invites emulation and as a discursive practice. The chapter discusses how the modeling and serial aspects of an example are combined in the interplay between Thunberg's discursive and performative practice.

Methodological approach

The analytical approach is narratological and the chapter explores how the performativity of Thunberg as an exemplar is narratively embedded. The amplification of an exemplar might take shape as narratives, as stories about the exemplary performance. At the same time, the exemplar itself might explicitly or implicitly use and refer to specific narratives or cultural macro-narratives when they communicate their message. While I have examined the first kind of narrative embedding of Thunberg elsewhere (Kverndokk 2025), this chapter will focus on the latter kind. I will identify what kind of narratives are implied by her speeches: more specifically, how Thunberg's use of the trope of the child relates to a grand narrative structure of a climate-changed future and how this trope relates to life narratives and family expectations. The narratological approach also implies an identification of the narrative functions of the different actors that are addressed in her speeches: are they given an active subject position as heroes or villains, a passive object position, or functions of a different kind, such as helpers or judges (see Greimas 1983)?

Through this narrative approach the chapter focuses on the embedded futurity of the trope of the child. The temporal orientation embedded in this trope will be examined through a reading of Thunberg's speeches from her first year of protest, from August 2018 to September 2019. The analysis will mainly be based on the transcripts published in the book *No One Is Too Small to Make a Difference* (Thunberg 2019a). I will additionally use recordings and transcripts of her speeches, which are available online. Thunberg's speeches draw partly on a repertoire of narrative motifs and powerful rhetorical tropes that are creatively combined and developed throughout the period I have studied. I focus on the sequences of her speeches in which she explicitly uses the trope of the child and in which the temporality of this trope is most clearly addressed.

The grand narrative of a climate-changed future

'We don't need Whitney Houston to tell us; we already believe the children are our future', writes literary scholar Rebekah Sheldon (2016, 3). She remarks that the relationship between the children and the future is often regarded as self-evident. This temporal aspect of the trope of the child is fundamental for an understanding of the school strike. Climate change is by itself a temporal phenomenon and for the strikers the temporality of the trope intersects with the temporality of a changing climate. As a first analytical step I will therefore look closely at the way Thunberg connects the trope of the child to the temporality of climate change.

Thunberg often uses the child position to talk about expected, possible and no longer possible futures. One example is her address to the British Houses of Parliament on April 23, 2019. She introduced herself in this way: 'My name is Greta Thunberg. I am sixteen years old. I come from Sweden. And I speak on behalf of future generations. I know many of you don't want to listen to us – you say we are just children' (Thunberg 2019a, 57). She continued:

> Many of you appear concerned that we are wasting valuable lesson time, but I assure you we will go back to school the moment you start listening to science and give us a future. Is that really too much to ask? In the year 2030 I will be twenty-six years old. My sister, Beata, will be twenty-three. Just like many of your own children or grandchildren. That is a great age, we have been told. When you have all of your life ahead of you. But I am not so sure it will be that great for us. I was fortunate to be born in a time and place where everyone told us to dream big; I could become whatever I wanted to. I could live wherever I wanted to. People like me had everything we needed and more. Things our grandparents could not even dream of. We had everything we could ever wish for and yet now we may have nothing. Now we probably don't even have a future anymore. (Thunberg 2019a, 57–58)

In this quote, the year 2030 refers to the IPCC special report on the 1.5-degree target of the Paris Agreement. This report points out that the level of emissions of CO_2 must be severely reduced by that year in order to reach the target (Masson-Delmotte et al 2018). In another passage of the same speech where she says: 'Around the year 2030, 10 years 252 days and 10 hours away from now, we will be in a position where we set off an irreversible chain reaction beyond human control that will most likely lead to the end of our civilization as we know it' (Thunberg 2019a, 59). By imagining her life in 2030, she is connecting her personal expectations to a climate change discourse. Her task is, however, not to talk about 2030 as such, but to point out that it is time for immediate action. The present moment decides the future outcome. In narratological terms, it is 'a point of time filled with significance, charged with a meaning derived from its relation to the end' (Kermode 1967, 47).

Her way of arguing leans on a commonly used narrative model for imagining a climate-changed future, often referred to as apocalyptic (for example, Hulme 2008, 10–13; Skrimshire 2014; Cochet 2015; Northcott 2015; Lilly 2016). Yet, it is not apocalyptic in the strict sense of the term. It is rather a dual-plot grand narrative of a climate-changed future, organized around three key concepts: the contemporary 'climate crisis' as a decisive turning point, and 'the climate catastrophe' and 'sustainable development' as two possible outcomes of the crisis (Kverndokk and Eriksen 2021, 8). These two latter terms are complementary and represent alternative, opposite endings. This conceptual triad works as a narrative device, a plot that produces and structures stories of different kinds and at different scales and produces intertextual relationships between them.

Climate change, family time, and the child

The way Thunberg uses the year 2030 to connect her personal prospects to climate science and politics relates her expectations and worries about the future to this grand narrative. Her imagining of 2030 also draws on a notion of being young as a stage of becoming, characterized by hopes, dreams, and possibilities: 'I was fortunate to be born in a time and place where everyone told us to dream big; I could become whatever I wanted to.' This statement is combined with a rather conventional modern idea of history as progress (see Sjögren 2020): 'People like me had everything we needed and more. Things our grandparents could not even dream of.' The changing conditions for her expectations and possibilities and the notion of historical progress are connected through a family term – 'our grandparents.'

Within just a few sentences, Thunberg combines quite different scalar levels of time: historical time (and the time of climate change), individual time, and what might be termed family time. Social historian Tamara Hareven discusses the relationship between these different temporalities, pointing out that the individual lifespan is generally embedded in family rhythms and cycles. Key life events such as childhood, adolescence, weddings, childbirth, and parenting are just as much family events as they are individual experiences, and they add a cyclical aspect to the individual lifetime. As a result, there is a close relationship between individual time and family time. But family time also has the ability to transcend the individual lifespan. As generational time, it includes the lifetimes of parents, grandparents, children, and grandchildren. Through family relations, this timescale connects the past and the future to the present and to individual experiences and expectations. By doing so, it works as a timescale between individual time and historical time (Hareven 1977, 59–61). It is a kind of temporality that brings past and future events closer to everyday life and makes them imaginable.

The family way of organizing time is even more explicitly expressed in a TED Talk from November 2018:

> If I live to be 100, I will be alive in the year 2103. When you think about the future today, you don't think beyond the year 2050. By then, I will in the best case, not even have lived half of my life. What happens next? The year 2078 I will celebrate my 75th birthday. If I have children or grandchildren, maybe they will spend that day with me. Maybe they will ask me about you, the people who were around, back in 2018. Maybe they will ask why you didn't do anything while there still was time to act? What we do or don't do right now will affect my entire life and the lives of my children and grandchildren. What we do or don't do right now, me and my generation can't undo in the future. (Thunberg 2018)

Again, Thunberg combines different levels of time. The years 2050 and 2100 are key dates in climate research and politics. The year 2050 is set by the European Union as the deadline for a transition to a so-called climate neutral society, while 2100 is the year when most climate prognoses end. Both the 1.5-degree target and the 2-degree target of the Paris Agreement refer to the rise in global temperatures (in Celsius) by that year, compared to pre-industrial levels. The measurable, linear time of climate politics is related to her lifespan by associating the turn of the century with her 100th birthday three years later. Finally, she also talks about the future in family-timed terms, by describing an imagined conversation between herself and her grandchildren on the celebration of her 75th birthday.

Thunberg is not the first person to imagine herself in the future, talking to her grandchildren about climate change and 'why you didn't do anything while there still was time to act.' Al Gore does the same thing in his influential book *An Inconvenient Truth* (2006), asking his readers to envision themselves in the future, talking to their children: 'Imagine now that they are asking: "What were you thinking? Didn't you care about the future? Were you really so self-absorbed that you couldn't – or wouldn't – stop the destruction of Earth's environment?"' (Gore 2006; quoted from Sheldon 2016, 37–38). While climate research and policy are dominated by a linear temporality and refers to fixed dates and years such as 2030, 2050, and 2100, the future in popular climate discourse is more often described in family-timed terms such as the future of our children and grandchildren (Kverndokk 2020).

Life-scripted future

Thunberg's use of a family conversation to imagine the future is surprisingly conventional. It draws on a kind of futurism that Sheldon (2016), with reference to queer theory, characterizes as heteronormative and reproductive. It is a futurism that reproduces dominant social norms and family values by projecting them onto the future. It might perfectly well be criticized from a queer perspective. At the same time, it is due to the familiarity of these norms and values that the future becomes imaginable for a broader audience. Sheldon (2016) has convincingly demonstrated how the future is described in such reproductive terms in American environmentalism, and how the child, and also the unborn child, is conceived as embodied future. This notion of the future is, however, not specifically American. To connect the present to the future through family cycles has been common in transnational popular climate discourse from the very beginning, in the late 1980s.

One illustrative Scandinavian example is the Norwegian TV documentary *The Year 2048* from 1988. This was a two-episode documentary on climate change and the ozone hole, that received several international prizes and was broadcast in 183 countries (Flaarønning 2020). Based on interviews with internationally leading researchers, it describes the consequences of climate change by the mid-21st century. These scenarios were dramatized through short sequences from a fictional TV news show dated to 2048. A male news anchor announced the latest news, portraying a chaotic world, apparently due to severe environmental problems. The introduction to the documentary was supposed to set the mood for the audience's imagining this distant future and preparing them for watching the fictional news. It opens with a series of posters saying that the year 2048 may seem far away, but it is not: 'Many of us will be alive, most certainly our grandchildren and the children born today …' (Nome and Morvik 1988). Then follows a short film sequence that sketches a life-story. The first scene is just a glimpse marked by the year 1988 and shows a picture of a newborn child in the arms of his mother. The next one, dated 1995, displays a smiling seven-year-old boy with a cat in his arms. The third scene, dated 2013, is of a flirting heterosexual couple in their mid-20s. While the fourth and final one shows an elderly looking man, presumably at the age of 60, with a smiling little girl on his lap, apparently his granddaughter. They look at a photo album before they turn on the TV news. The story ends and the news begins. This final sequence is dated 2048.

This life story is not told through specific, named character and elaborated action, scenes, or scenography. It is not a developed fabulation about what might happen, but instead provides a sketched narrative framework of what *will* happen – the children will grow up, get children of their own, and eventually grandchildren. It follows a conventional narrative model for telling a life, a so-called life script (see Frykman 1992, 261), portraying a notion of the good life, structured by familial cycles with a happy childhood, finding a spouse in the mid-20s, having children, then grandchildren in the mid-50s. It is a generalized plot, which the viewers might use as a resource to imagine their family futures. In folkloristic terms, it is a narrative type for telling the future.

This life-scripted narrative type is the same one that Thunberg uses when she is imagining herself surrounded by her grandchildren at her 75th birthday party. It is a narrative type that has been reproduced numerous times in climate change discourse since the 1980s.

Moreover, Thunberg's description of her future, both the one of herself as a 26-year-old in 2030 and the other one of herself as a 75-year-old in 2078, have an inherent tension between a ruined world and hopes for a good life. She is supposed 'to dream big' about the future, 'to become whatever [she] want[s] to' and 'live wherever [she] want[s] to,' while climate change, on the other hand, is described as the opposite: as unpredictability, as causing chaos and limitations, leading Thunberg to conclude: 'Now we probably don't have a future anymore' (Thunberg 2019a, 58). The same kind of tension is present in the Norwegian documentary from 1988: while the life story of a boy born in 1988 represents the good, family life, the news show from 2048 presents devastation on a global scale. Both Thunberg's vision of the future and the documentary draw on the tension between 'sustainable development' and 'the climate catastrophe' in the dual-plot grand narrative of a climate-changed future. Thunberg's concerns about her future, and how these concerns challenge her hopes and dreams, form an individualized variant of this narrative. By using a conventional middle-class life-script, she makes both her future and the possible consequences of a changing climate imaginable and tellable.

The child talks back

In climate change discourse, the trope of the child is most often used in plural with the possessive pronoun 'our', as in 'our children and grandchildren.' Both Al Gore and the Norwegian documentary use it in this way. This plural form is family-timed and implies a 'we' of parents/grandparents. This 'we' is widely used as a position of enunciation in popular climate change discourse (see Kverndokk 2020 for further discussions). Emmanuel Macron's speech to the US Congress in April 2018 offers an example of how this position is used. Among the topics he addressed was the importance of international agreements to handle the climate crisis and to bring about a transition to a low-emission society. One of the rhetorical highlights was when he looked out at his audience and declared: 'I believe in building a better future for our children, which requires offering them a planet that is still habitable in 25 years.' And he added: 'Because what is the meaning of our life, really, if we work and live destroying the planet, while sacrificing the future of our children?' (Macron 2018). The way he contrasts 'a better future of our children' to the one that will occur if international agreements fail, implies the same narrative tension as in Thunberg's vision of her future life.

Macron leans on a well-established rhetorical tradition of using family-based analogies for society. When he claims that 'the future of our children' is at stake, he puts himself in a symbolic position of a responsible 'father' caring for his and others' children. To conceptualize society as an extended family is a way of making societal issues concrete. It is a rhetorical strategy for scaling up parental obligations to planetary concerns, in the sense that taking care of children implies taking care of the future in terms of the Earth system (see Sheldon 2016, 37). In this kind of rhetorical framing, the children and their future become the object of climate policy. The children are not ascribed any agency. They simply represent a future to be saved. Macron and his peers, on the other hand, are the responsible and caretaking adults. They fill an active subject position (see Greimas 1983) as the possible heroes of the story of climate change.

Thunberg mirrors this rhetoric. Let me return to the introduction to her address to the British House of Parliament in April 2019:

> My name is Greta Thunberg. I am sixteen years old. I come from Sweden. And I speak on behalf of future generations. I know many of you don't want to listen to us – you say we are just children. But we're only repeating the message of the united climate science. (Thunberg 2019a, 57)

By speaking 'on behalf of future generations,' she explicitly places herself in the symbolic position of 'our children and grandchildren.' But instead of being a passive object waiting for the adults to take care of her future, she steps up on the stage and talks back to the adults, demanding action and a future. While Macron talks about the importance of international agreements, Thunberg demands that they are carried out. 'We want you to follow the Paris Agreement and IPCC reports,' she declares (Thunberg 2019a, 35). When she turns 'the child' into an active position, it is not as the subject of the story in a Greimasian sense. The 'adults' are still the potential heroes or villains. Instead, she steps into a morally judging position. She takes the position of judge in several of her speeches. When introduced at the UN Climate Action Summit in September 2019, she was asked: 'What is the message to the world leaders today?' She replied: 'My message is that we'll be watching you.' And she ended her speech by emphasizing that: 'The eyes of all future generations are upon you. And if you choose to fail us, I say: we will never forgive you' (Thunberg 2019b).

She fills this position by stepping forward as an embodiment of 'our children and grandchildren.' On a discursive level, she exemplifies the much-used rhetorical trope of the child, while her physical appearance makes her also a living sample of the world's children. Her performance is made powerful by this interplay between the discursive practice of using 'our children and grandchildren' as a trope and her physical appearance as an exemplar. Literary scholar John Lyons has argued that using examples as a rhetorical device is 'a way of gesturing outside the pure discourse of the speaker/writer toward support in a commonly accepted textual or referential world' (Lyons 1989, 28). Macron's use of the trope 'our children' works the same way. The trope is gesturing outside of pure discourse of the speaker toward support in the family life of the audience. This gesture would have been made even more concrete if he had exemplified the children by naming them. On a discursive level, Greta Thunberg is that named child. If we understand her example not as a discursive, but as a performative practice, the dynamic between discourse and the referential world works the other way around. When Thunberg steps forward as an embodiment of 'our children and grandchildren', she is not gesturing *out of* but *into* discourse. She is a form of embodied reality that breaks through into discourse.

Thunberg is not the first one to do this. A well-known example of a teenager using the same rhetorical strategy is 17-year-old Brittany Trilford from New Zealand. She was invited to speak at the opening session of the UN Conference on Sustainable Development (Rio+20), in Rio de Janeiro in June 2012. In front of the world leaders present, she said: 'My name is Brittany Trilford. I am seventeen years old. I am a child. Today, in this moment, I am all children. Your children. The world's three billion children. Think of me as half the world' (Trilford 2012). Another example is Canadian Severn Cullis-Suzuki. In 1992, at the age of 12, she spoke on behalf of the Environmental Children's Organization at the UN Conference on Environment and Development (UNCED), also in Rio de Janeiro. She declared that 'I am here to speak for all generations to come' (Cullis-Suzuki 1992). Trilford and Cullis-Suzuki creatively turned the passive notion of 'our children and grandchildren' into an active position of enunciation, years before Thunberg. Thunberg, however, takes this rhetorical strategy a bit further. Based on how the future is embedded in the trope of the child, she steps forward as a time-traveler, traveling back in time from the future to the present.

The prophetic tone

Her often-quoted speech at World Economic Forum in 2019 opens by stating: 'Our house is on fire./ I am here to say, our house is on fire.' And she returns to the same metaphor at the end of the speech:

> Adults keep saying: 'we owe it to the young people to give them hope.'
> But I don't want your hope.
> I don't want you to be hopeful. I want you to panic.
> I want you to feel the fear I feel every day.
> And then I want you to act.
> I want you to act as you would in a crisis.
> I want you to act as if our[2] house is on fire.
> Because it is. (Thunberg 2019a, 24)

The urgency depicted through the fire metaphor draws on scientific knowledge – it is apparently based on the IPCC special report on the 1.5-degree target of the Paris Agreement (Masson-Delmotte et al 2018):

> According to the IPCC, we are less than twelve years away from not being able to undo our mistakes. In that time, unprecedented changes in all aspects of society need to have taken place – including a reduction of our CO^2 emissions by at least 50 per cent. ...
>
> [Those numbers do not] include tipping points or feedback loops like the extremely powerful methane gas released from the thawing Arctic permafrost. (Thunberg 2019a, 19–20)

The usage of deadlines and tipping points in climate discourse has been criticized for having an eschatological bias (for example, Hulme 2008, 11). The same bias is present in Thunberg's way of using the term fire to illustrate the countdown toward 2030. The fire, though, is not just a metaphor for the contemporary crisis. With its apocalyptic connotations, it also implies the devastating outcome of the crisis.

This metaphor is firmly related to the emotional terms Thunberg is using – *fear*, *panic*, and her rejection of *hope*. She pronounces *fear* with a pitch and an intensity that leaves no doubt that it is deeply felt. The word is performed in what literary scholar Isak Winkel Holm has termed a prophetic tone. Holm defines this tonality as 'the perception of the precatastrophic present ... affectively charged by the imagination of a postcatastrophic future'

---

[2] When performing the speech, Thunberg said 'the house,' while the printed version reads 'our house.'

(Holm 2021, 91). This tonality or mode is at the same time aesthetic and rational. He calls it, 'a hybrid of sensibility and rationality, of *aisthesis* and *logos*' (Holm 2021, 91, original italics). This hybridity is elaborated further in Thunberg's speech at the UN Climate Action Summit in September 2019. With a trembling voice, she said:

> This is all wrong. I shouldn't be up here. I should be back in school on the other side of the ocean. Yet you all come to us young people for hope. How dare you!
>
> You have stolen my dreams and my childhood with your empty words. And yet I'm one of the lucky ones. People are suffering. People are dying. Entire ecosystems are collapsing. We are in the beginning of a mass extinction, and all you can talk about is money and fairy tales of eternal economic growth. How dare you! (Thunberg 2019b)

Then she started to list up scientific facts and predictions, and her voice switched to a neutral, reporting mode. Throughout the speech, her voice continually switched between a flat, reporting mode and an intense emotional one, used when addressing her audience in accusatory language like 'How dare you!' and 'You are failing us.'

In this affective mode of performance, scientifically informed knowledge and imaginings of the future intersect. This kind of interplay has, again according to Holm, a looped temporal structure (Holm 2021, 93–94; see Dupuy 2005, 13). This structure is clearly exposed in one of the speeches quoted earlier:

> The year 2078 I will celebrate my 75th birthday. If I have children or grandchildren, maybe they will spend that day with me. Maybe they will ask me about you, the people who were around, back in 2018. Maybe they will ask why you didn't do anything while there still was time to act? (Thunberg 2019a, 11)

She is placing herself in a post-catastrophic future, looking back at the present. It is worth noting that, in one of the other speeches just quoted, she speaks about her expectations and future possibilities in the past tense, as if it is already too late:

> I *was* fortunate to be born in a time and place where everyone told us to dream big; I *could* become whatever I wanted to. I *could* live wherever I wanted to. People like me *had* everything we needed and more. Things our grandparents could not even dream of. We *had* everything we could ever wish for and yet now we may have nothing. (Thunberg 2019a, 58, my italics)

The past tense indicates that the present is no longer pre-catastrophic. It is instead perceived in light of the future catastrophe. The potential for her to become 'whatever I wanted to' and of living 'wherever I wanted to' is described as something that would have taken place if it was not for the coming catastrophe.

The future she envisions becomes an experience that works as the basis for her affective, performative mode. It is this mode, unfolding as an entanglement of the future and the present, of prospection and retrospection, of vision and presence, of sensibility and rationality, that Holm characterizes as prophetic (Holm 2016, 93). He emphasizes that this tonality is not apocalyptic. It is not predicting an ending in a cosmological sense. He argues that the prophetic and apocalyptic tone 'should be approached as two cultural conditions of possibility for the way in which we are sensing time in a world threatened by disaster which is *not now*' (Holm 2021, 104, original italics). The prophetic tone is underscoring the urgency, but it is still possible to act. Unlike the apocalyptic tone, the tonality of *too late* (see Bjærke 2021, 182–183) or of resignation, the prophetic tone encourages action. It is a performative mode that calls for emulation through affective identification.

A prophet is a person to stand out to be listened to and followed, and thus the prophetic tonality carries the potential for being used to start a social movement. In Thunberg's case, she uses this performative mode rhetorically to authorize her trustworthiness and the urgency of following her example.

Conclusion

I have argued that Thunberg authorizes her speech (and performative) position as an exemplar by using well-established climate rhetoric in creative ways. This is rhetoric that draws on dominant family norms and values. Even though her expectations, hopes, dreams, and depictions of the future are colored by her Scandinavian middle-class background, her way of authorizing her message is first and foremost based on her young age and not her social background. It makes it easy to identify with her concerns about the future.

The way she establishes and actively uses 'the child' as her position of enunciation has the potential of transforming what it means to be a child. In Thunberg's school strike, 'the child' is the embodiment of 'our children and grandchildren' and hence an embodiment of a climate-changed future. When she steps forward as a child and speaks 'on behalf of future generations,' she appears as one among many such embodiments. Her message to the world leaders that 'we'll be watching you' could just as well be uttered by any other child. Hence, through her performances, she has invested childhood with political potential. At the same time, climate change is made into a moral issue and to a question about caring for your children.

An exemplary action calls for amplification (Noyes and Wille, Chapter 2, this volume). This is certainly also the case with Thunberg. Her school strike fits well into an interconnected, performative youth culture in which digital and embodied performances are constantly entangled. Her performances have been digitally displayed from the very beginning. She reached almost 10 million followers on Instagram within a year and a half after first sitting down in front of the Swedish Parliament. In a number of her Instagram posts she holds her home-made placard with the words 'School strike for the climate.' Her words and pictures are more than calls for action. They also call for other young activists to follow her example. She has developed a language and a performative form that enable young people to step forward and demonstrate the political and moral power of being children, as moral judges of the politics that will determine their future.

References

Bakhtin, Mikhail. 1986. *Speech Genres and Other Late Essays*. University of Texas Press.

Bjærke, Marit Ruge. 2021. 'Living the Climate Change.' In *Climate Change Temporalities: Explorations in Vernacular, Popular, and Scientific Discourse*, edited by Kyrre Kverndokk, Marit Ruge Bjærke, and Anne Eriksen. Routledge.

Cochet, Yves. 2015. 'Green Eschatology.' In *The Anthropocene and the Global Environmental Crisis: Rethinking Modernity*, edited by Clive Hamilton, François Gemenne, and Christophe Bonneuil. Routledge.

Cullis-Suzuki, Severn. 1992. 'Listen to the Children – Severn Cullis-Suzuki's Famous Speech on the Environment.' Posted October 27, 2017, by United Nations. YouTube, 8:27. https://www.youtube.com/watch?v=JGdS8ts63Ck (accessed June 2, 2025).

Dupuy, Jean-Pierre. 2005. *Petite métaphysique des tsunamis*. Seuil.

Eriksen, Anne. 2019. 'History, Exemplarity and Improvements: 18th Century Ideas about Man-Made Climate Change.' *Culture Unbound: Journal of Current Cultural Research* 11 (3–4): 353–368.

Eriksen, Anne, Ellen Krefting, and Anne Birgitte Rønning. 2012. 'Eksemplets makt.' In *Eksemplets makt: Kjønn, representasjon og autoritet fra antikken til i dag*, edited by Anne Eriksen, Ellen Krefting, and Anne Birgitte Rønning. Scandinavian Academic Press.

Ernman, Beata, Malena Ernman, Greta Thunberg, and Svante Thunberg. 2020. *Our House Is on Fire: Scenes of a Family and a Planet in Crisis*. Penguin Books.

Flaarønning, Guro. 2020. 'Tidligere journalist Petter Nome om klimaendringene: – Jeg skylder på både politikere og journalister.' *Journalisten. no*, March 31. https://journalisten.no/john-olav-egeland-jorgen-randers-klima/tidligere-journalist-petter-nome-om-klimaendringene--jeg-skyl der-pa-bade-politikere-og-journalister/403713 (accessed June 2, 2025).

Frykman, Jonas. 1992. 'Biografi och kulturanalys.' In *Självbiografi, kultur, liv: Levnadshistoriska studier inom human- och samhällsvetenskap*, edited by Christoffer Tigerstedt, J.P. Roos, and Anni Vilkko. Symposion.

Gelley, Alexander. 1995. *Unruly Examples: On the Rhetoric of Exemplarity*. Stanford University Press.

Gore, Al. 2006. *An Inconvenient Truth: The Planetary Emergency of Global Warming and What We Can Do About It*. Rodale.

Greimas, Algirdas Julien. 1983. *Structural Semantics: An Attempt at a Method*. University of Nebraska Press.

Hareven, Tamara K. 1977. 'Family Time and Historical Time.' *Daedalus* 106 (2): 57–70.

Holm, Isak Winkel. 2016. 'Under Water within Thirty Years: The Prophetic Mode in True Detective.' *Behemoth: A Journal on Civilisation* 9 (1): 90–107.

Holm, Isak Winkel. 2021. 'The Prophetic Tone in True Detective: Sensing the Time of the Future Climate Disaster.' In *Climate Change Temporalities: Explorations in Vernacular, Popular, and Scientific Discourse*, edited by Kyrre Kverndokk, Marit Ruge Bjærke, and Anne Eriksen. Routledge.

Hulme, Mike. 2008. 'The Conquering of Climate: Discourses of Fear and their Dissolution.' *The Geographical Journal* 174 (1): 5–16.

Kermode, Frank. 1967. *The Sense of an Ending: Studies in the Theory of Fiction*. Oxford University Press.

Kverndokk, Kyrre. 2020. 'Talking About Your Generation: "Our Children"' as a Trope in Climate Change Discourse.' *Ethnologia Europaea* 50 (1): 145–158.

Kverndokk, Kyrre. 2025. 'The Greta Story and the Narrative Authority of the Exemplar.' *Cultural Analysis* 23 (2): 29–46.

Kverndokk, Kyrre, and Anne Eriksen. 2021. 'Climate Change Temporalities: Narratives, Genres, and Tropes.' In *Climate Change Temporalities: Explorations in Vernacular, Popular, and Scientific Discourse*, edited by Kyrre Kverndokk, Marit Ruge Bjærke, and Anne Eriksen. Routledge.

Lilly, Ingrid E. 2016. 'The Planet's Apocalypse: The Rhetoric of Climate Change.' In *Apocalypses in Context: Apocalyptic Currents through History*, edited by Kelly J. Murphy and Justin Jeffcoat Schedtler. Fortress.

Lyons, John D. 1989. *Exemplum: The Rhetoric of Example in Early Modern France and Italy*. Princeton University Press.

Macron, Emmanuel. 2018. 'French President Emmanuel Macron Addresses Congress.' Posted April 25, 2018, by C-SPAN. YouTube, 48:32. https://www.youtube.com/watch?v=_JwrRXozCXA (accessed June 2, 2025).

Masson-Delmotte, Valérie et al. 2018. *Global Warming of 1.5°C*. Intergovernmental Panel on Climate Change. https://digitallibrary.un.org/record/3893415?ln=en&v=pdf (accessed June 11, 2025).

Nome, Peter, and Torbjørn Morvik. 1988. *Året 2048* [Documentary]. NRK. no. https://tv.nrk.no/serie/aaret-2048/1988/FOLA03007487/avspiller (accessed June 2, 2025).

Northcott, Michael. 2015. 'Eschatology in the Anthropocene: From the Chronos of Deep Time to the Kairos of the Age of Humans.' In *The Anthropocene and the Global Environmental Crisis: Rethinking Modernity*, edited by Clive Hamilton, François Gemenne, and Christophe Bonneuil. Routledge.

Noyes, Dorothy. 2016. 'Gesturing Toward Utopia: Toward a Theory of Exemplarity.' *NU* 53: 75–95.

Ortutay, Gyula. 1959. 'Principles of Oral Transmission in Folk Culture.' *Acta Ethnographica* 8: 175–221.

Sheldon, Rebekah. 2016. *The Child to Come: Life after the Human Catastrophe*. University of Minnesota Press.

Sjögren, Hanna. 2020. 'Longing for the Past: An Analysis of Discursive Formations in the Greta Thunberg Message.' *Culture Unbound: Journal of Current Cultural Research* 12 (3): 615–631.

Skrimshire, Stefan. 2014. 'Climate Change and Apocalyptic Faith.' *WIREs Climate Change* 5: 233–246.

Thunberg, Greta. 2018. 'The Disarming Case to Act Right Now on Climate Change.' *TEDxStockholm*, https://www.ted.com/talks/greta_thunberg_the_disarming_case_to_act_right_now_on_climate_change/transcript?language=en (accessed June 2, 2025).

Thunberg, Greta. 2019a. *No One Is Too Small to Make a Difference*. Penguin Books.

Thunberg, Greta. 2019b. 'Transcript: Greta Thunberg's Speech at the U.N. Climate Action Summit.' *NPR*. https://www.npr.org/2019/09/23/763452863/transcript-greta-thunbergs-speech-at-the-u-n-climate-action-summit (accessed June 2, 2025).

Trilford, Brittany. 2012. 'A Date with History: 17 yr old Brittany Trilford Addresses World Leaders at the UN Earth Summit.' Posted on June 20, 2012, by Global Call for Climate Action. YouTube, 4:54. https://www.youtube.com/watch?v=karQQb-B8Uk (accessed June 2, 2025).

PART III

The Complexities of Uptake

6

The Truths of Suffering and Injustice: Confucian Exemplarity in the History of Exemplar-Prisoners

Ying Zhang

I spent the spring of 2020 reading materials about exemplary figures from two very different worlds: writings by and about imprisoned officials in imperial China, and a cascade of images and texts that captured both heroism and sufferings in Wuhan, the epicenter of what was to become a global pandemic. I could not help but notice some continuity on a deeper level, not only in the paradigm of Chinese exemplarity but in the ways it has been (mis)interpreted. Examples promoted by the authorities, in imperial China and the PRC, are often seen as propagandistic products developed by a strong state to encourage people to emulate normative behaviors and keep their faith in the existing system. Although some historical scholarship has discussed the agency of premodern Confucian moral exemplars and modern revolutionary role models (Lu 2008; Fei 2012; Hershatter 2014), inadequate effort to explore exemplarity as a dynamic process has limited our imagination about how it operated. I would further argue that seeing premodern Confucian exemplarity as indoctrination is as reductive as seeing its contemporary counterpart in oppositional terms.

The stakes are high. Take Fang Fang's globally renowned *Wuhan Diary* as an example. In addition to documenting her personal experience during the first lockdown in the world, the daily jottings posted online by the Chinese writer accused the state media of covering positive news excessively but not enough about the problems on the ground or the officials who should be held accountable for their failures. During those long weeks, competing political, literary, and commercial interests generated bitter divisions over Fang Fang and her diary among both the cultural elite and ordinary netizens in China. When she gained international fame and her lockdown diary translated into English in April, the contention escalated and many Chinese attacked her for 'lending a knife' to the Western critics and damaging the Chinese example in controlling the virus on the global stage. Meanwhile, in the West, her diary continues to be hailed mostly as oppositional literature. Had we developed a better understanding of the paradigm of Chinese exemplarity in the past, we would not have read her work in such a reductive manner but instead could see a more dynamic state-society relationship in her writing.

This chapter draws on cases from the premodern history of imprisoned officials to show Confucian exemplarity to be a process of performance, amplification, judgment, citation, and emulation at the intersections of politics, art, and religion. A temporally expansive survey of this history reveals that affective empathy, that is, identification with the physical suffering of and the injustice experienced by the exemplars, lay at the heart of this lived tradition of exemplarity. These cases are particularly useful for us to observe Chinese exemplarity as a process of critical reflection shaped by Confucian political ethics and its entwinement with other religious systems, through which elite and non-elite people assumed and assigned responsibility and accountability in and beyond their relationship with the state.

First, I look at the establishment of the earliest exemplar-prisoners by the educated elite in imperial China through their identification with the exemplars' physical suffering and injustice. While many imprisoned officials in imperial China were recognized as moral exemplars, only a few fall into the analytical category of what I call 'exemplar-prisoners' because their extraordinary experience of imprisonment was essential to their exemplary status and historical legacy. I then discuss a few cases from the Ming dynasty (1368–1644) to illustrate how shared concerns about physical suffering and injustice led the elite and the common folk to play different roles in the making of exemplar-prisoners. In contrast to the elite's reflexive emulation, common folk venerated these exemplar-prisoners for protection. Last, I connect the history of Chinese exemplarity to the image war during the COVID-19 pandemic, using contemporary material to illustrate the importance of appreciating Chinese exemplarity as a complex of meaningful political and spiritual processes.

Reflexive emulation through historiography

The first Chinese exemplar-prisoner is the Confucian sage ruler King Wen of Zhou (ca 1112–1056 BCE). According to the Grand Historian Sima Qian 司馬遷 (ca 145–86 BCE) in his monumental work, *Historical Records* (Shiji 史記), the King of Shang imprisoned King Wen out of the fear that his virtuous leadership would threaten Shang dominance. While a prisoner at the Youli 羑里 Castle, King Wen (who was called the Earl of the West at the time) worked out the 64 hexagrams that formed the *Book of Changes* (Sima Qian). King Wen would later be revered by the Confucians as a sage ruler, and the *Book of Changes* became a Confucian classic, thanks to Sima Qian's amplification.

In addition to documenting this event, Sima Qian memorialized his own emulation of King Wen in the 'Self-Narration' section of *Historical Records*. Imprisoned by the emperor for defending Li Ling 李陵 (d. 74 BCE), a general who lost a military campaign and surrendered to the enemy, Sima Qian was given two awful options: death or castration. He chose the latter and justified this decision with his duty to complete a historical project, an obligation to his father as well (Sima Qian).

Sima Qian wrote about his emulation of King Wen in his 'Letter in Reply to Ren An':

> The Earl of the West was an earl, yet he was imprisoned at Youli. Li Si was chief councilor, yet he suffered all the five punishments. Huaiyin was a king, but he was put into fetters at Chen. Peng Yue and Zhang Ao each faced south and called himself 'the lonely one,' but both were arrested and put into prison for the charges brought against them. … All these men achieved the positions of kings, lords, generals, or councilors, and their fame reached to neighboring states. But when they committed crimes and sentence was passed upon them, not one was able to 'open a channel' and end his own life. (Klein 2018, 161)

Together, the 'Self-Narration' and the 'Letter in Reply to Ren An' laid the foundation for the future image of Sima Qian as a virtuous man who, like King Wen, overcame extreme hardship in order to complete extraordinary intellectual work. Without *Historical Records*, King Wen might not have been remembered as the first exemplary prisoner.

Claiming to imitate an exemplar served as a means for Sima Qian to explain his decisions and establish his own example. However, in contrast to the immediate acceptance of his writing about the imprisoned sage king, some questioned Sima Qian's claim of emulation. As Esther Klein shows, Sima Qian's presentation of his own political actions, his imprisonment and castration, and his *Historical Records* was strongly rejected, for instance by Ban Gu 班固 (CE 32–92), whose reputation as a historian rivaled Sima Qian's own (Nylan 1998–99; Klein 2018). Competing interpretations of Sima Qian's political actions and self-image were intricately connected to the intense scrutiny of both his ethics and his scholarship.

This phase of judgment continued after Sima Qian's citation of King Wen initiated a process of representation and reflection, with its uptake by the Neo-Confucians in the Song dynasty (960–1279) who fully recognized not only Sima Qian's claim to emulate the sage king but also his status as an exemplar-prisoner. They also established his superiority to Ban Gu as a consequential historian and as an exemplary man (Klein 2018). Those who immortalized him as an exemplar framed his political experience as that of an official 'not meeting the times' (Klein 2018, 201). This framing helped enhance the relatability of Sima Qian's circumstances to the Song literati-officials who were looking for ways to express their frustrations with autocratic emperors or factionalist colleagues. Importantly for our purpose here, what cemented Sima Qian's status as an exemplar-prisoner in the Song dynasty was the sympathetic and even romanticized consensus on the suffering and injustice that he had sustained (Klein 2018, chs 3–4).

The following quotes signaled a consolidated attitude at the time toward Sima Qian's historical legacy as an exemplar-prisoner. They vividly illustrate the affective dimension of judgment:

> I am so fond of how Sima Qian writes about Wei Bao and Peng Yue not being ashamed of imprisonment and going to their punishment. He says, 'They had no ulterior motives, and their wisdom surpassed that of other people. They worried only that they would lose their lives. If they could but get the smallest leverage, clouds could mass and dragons transform [i.e. symbols of great success]. They longed for that which would let them achieve the full scope of their ambitions, and that was why they allowed themselves to be hidden away, imprisoned, and did not take their leave [i.e. commit suicide].' (Klein 2018, 216)

> '[We] see that when Sima Qian was tried for recommending Li Ling and was sent down to the Silkworm Chamber (jail), it was really a punishment that resulted from Emperor Wu's private anger. That is why the punishment and the crime seem not to fit at all.' (Klein 2018, 240)

The Song thinker Zhu Xi 朱熹 (1130–1200), whose interpretation of the Confucian classics was to become orthodoxy in late imperial China, seriously challenged those who advocated Sima Qian's example and scholarly accomplishments. However, Zhu's opinion on Sima Qian was largely sidelined. In the literati's identifying and sympathizing with Sima Qian, emotional resonance and identification outweighed official orthodoxy. After the Song, as Martin W. Huang (2006) shows, Sima Qian firmly stood as the ancestor of a gendered literary tradition, in which literati-officials portrayed themselves as emasculated by imperial politics. Speaking in the voices of abandoned wives, concubines, and prostitutes, their self-representations drew attention to the humiliating circumstances they were subject to at court (Klein 2018, chs 1–2). Empathy and sympathy underlay this literary insistence. The consolidation over the centuries of Sima Qian's image as an exemplar-prisoner shows how exemplarity, even among the

Confucian-educated elite, was a process of critical reflection rather than imposed or indoctrinated.

The impact of the two earliest exemplar-prisoners in Chinese historical records, King Wen and Sima Qian, was tremendous. In Ming China, for instance, many imprisoned officials studied and produced scholarship on history and the *Book of Changes*. Sima Qian's path to exemplarity leaves a pattern of reflexive emulation that navigated complicated connections among the various factors of Confucian exemplarity: ethics, judgment, and writing. It also shows how emotional reactions to injustice and physical suffering played a decisive role in shaping the practice of exemplarity among the Confucian-educated elite, a distinctive fusion of amplification, judgment, citation, and amplification. The Confucian orthodox authority represented by Zhu Xi, or the imperial state behind it, did not cast the final words or stop the literati from engaging in critical reflection or expressing themselves in creative ways through the exemplars.

Mediated emulation through art

Fan Pang's 范滂 (137–169) journey toward the status of exemplar-prisoner also began in historical writing. His biography in the *History of the Latter Han* (Hou Hanshu 後漢書) records two instances of imprisonment due to political factionalism. A famous passage of this biography presents a heartbreaking conversation between Fan Pang and his mother prior to the second arrest, which eventually led to his death. Concerned about his mother's safety, Fan Pang decided not to flee. His mother came to see him off to prison. She told Fan Pang: 'Your reputation now can rival that of [the exemplary officials] Li and Du. You should not feel regret even if you die. You have earned a fine reputation. If you seek longevity, do you think you could really have both?'

Fan Pang's biography in *History of the Latter Han* garnered more attention in the Song dynasty, when waves of political factionalism sent many officials into imprisonment and exile. The consolidation of Fan Pang's status as an exemplar-prisoner resulted not only from a heightened sense of injustice but also from the increasing importance of the Confucian ethics of filial piety among literati-officials (Zhang, C. E. 2020).

During the Song, the artwork of the official Huang Tingjian 黃庭堅 (1045–1105), a prominent victim of political persecution, played a decisive role in rendering Fan's example tangible and even collectible. This famous calligrapher was repeatedly demoted and exiled. Sheltered in a shabby hut in the remote Yizhou (in modern-day Guangxi), at the request of a sympathetic official he produced a magnificent calligraphic copy of the biography of Fan Pang. It was said that he had memorized the whole biography with few errors. Soon this piece of artwork went into print and began to be widely circulated among the literati (Shui 2016, 95). It was inscribed on steles, rubbings of which were then reproduced and disseminated. The calligraphic representation of the biography and its affective value immortalized Huang's own suffering and moral character. It then took on a life of its own, spreading idealized images of both Fan Pang and Huang via print, rubbings, and scrolls in private and imperial collections (Shui 2016, 95). Huang's life not only became inseparable from Fan Pang's biography but also gave the historical exemplar-prisoner materially specific meanings.

Note that these two men's experiences with prison were quite different. Huang produced this artwork outside of prison. He did not replicate Fan Pang's action in confinement, either. What connected them was the extreme adverse circumstances and injustice of the imprisonment. Therefore, as in the case of Sima Qian, the Song literati promoted a moral exemplar by repeatedly reflecting on the precariousness of politics and the sufferings it inflicted on the historical prisoner. Those who cherished the reproductions of Huang's artwork shared an aesthetic of suffering – a dimension of judgment in which agency operated – rather than blind imitation of a particular action.

The construction of the exemplar-prisoner was thus not an ideological work of the state. As the next section shows, beyond official histories, the factors of suffering and injustice seem to be the determining appeal of the exemplars' stories, and, in fact, dependent on art and popular religion to make them powerful. These stories benefited from and also contributed to a pluralistic religious culture rooted deeply in the desire for protection shared by elite and common folk. It was believed that an official who died as a result of their extraordinary performance of the Confucian ethics would become 'a spirit of extraordinary magical prowess, capable of performing a variety of miracles' (Yang 1961, 166).[1] While this belief intentionally and unintentionally encouraged practicing Confucian ethics, it could also radically transform the exemplars and what they represented. Sometimes, a deified hero to which a state-sanctioned 'ethicopolitical cult' was dedicated could even reside in rebellious religious cults as well, effectively connecting the two sites of judgment. As this pattern of exemplarity matured into a tradition, it became a compressed process of amplification, critical reflection, and uptake in a single moment. This process was understood to be an open space of performance and negotiation, participated by the elite and non-elite in their own ways and for different purposes.

From reflexive emulation to veneration

In an imperial compilation of exemplary officials, the Qianlong emperor (1711–1799) of the Qing dynasty called Huang Daozhou 黃道周

---

[1] C. K. Yang calls these cults 'ethicopolitical cults.'

(1585–1646), a Ming loyalist who refused to serve the new dynasty, 'a perfect man of his era' (Zhang 2016, 128). This was a strategic move to promote Confucian ethics among educated men and encourage them to pledge loyalty to the ruling dynasty. While official accounts of Huang's career draw a standard image of an upright, loyal bureaucrat, his popularity then and now derives much from his experience of unjust imprisonment. In particular, the physical suffering caused by crippling torture served as a striking background for his calligraphic reproduction of many copies of the *Classic of Filial Piety*, embodiment of the Confucian masculine virtues of loyalty and filial piety. Huang numbered these copies, the last one numbered 120 and written in blood, and distributed them to prison staff and the public. In the eyes of both the educated and uneducated, Huang's moral example endowed these objects with extraordinary power and was transmitted through them (Zheng 2017).

Elsewhere I have examined the formation of Huang's image as a 'celebrity of loyalty-filial piety' in the literati society during his lifetime (Zhang 2016). A temporally expansive look at how his exemplary status evolved after he died as a loyalist and war captive during the dynastic change sheds light on the paradigm of Confucian exemplarity. Huang almost immediately became deified and worshipped by multiple popular cults in southern China, especially in his home province of Fujian. Unofficial accounts of his life are replete with stories of supernatural phenomena. Some passed on details that depicted him as having a miraculous birth and a diviner's skills. Others suggested that his work on the *Book of Changes*, one of his scholarly obsessions in prison, built on knowledge received from a suprahuman mentor. This narrative did not portray him as emulating King Wen but as similarly blessed with heavenly endowed capabilities. Reproductions of Huang's famous calligraphic works, embodiment of his commitment to Confucian ethics, have been displayed in the temples of Buddhism, regional cults, and even secret societies, radiating protective power in these spaces and through the objects distributed to the common worshippers by these temples. One of the most intriguing examples of the deification of Huang is the temples that worship him as the General of Assuring Success (zhushun jiangjun 助順將軍), such as the Jindegong 晉德宮 Temple in Taiwan (Zheng 2009). There is no scholarly or popular consensus on whether the General was the deified Huang himself or the deified Huang reinscribed onto a previously-deified official-general from the medieval period. Many of the pious participants in the cult of Huang Daozhou were maritime merchants and migrants from the mainland to Taiwan with very little interest in politics. Unlike other cases of martial deification (Wu 2016), Huang had no military experience and was miserably defeated and captured in the only mission he led. Nor had he held any administrative positions in river management or maritime expeditions. He was deified and worshipped by ordinary folk for protection because of his Confucian masculine virtues

(Zheng 2009, 2017).² The connection of his moral excellence, suffering, and magic power was 'obvious' to them, even though dynastic loyalty was largely irrelevant in their lives.

Popular religion played a critical role in endorsing and perpetuating Confucian values, even though it could also inspire and harbor rebellions. As Donald Sutton shows in his research on the cult of Ma Yuan (14 BCE–CE 49) from the medieval to early modern times, 'no regional or national cult could flourish over the long term as an effective instrument of official control without a degree of both popular fervor and literati enthusiasm, for success surely depended on the active participation of widely differing social groups and interests' (Sutton 1989, 113). Because people situated in various social and geographical locations still 'draw on overlapping repertoires of images and associations' (Sutton 1989, 113), the spiritual dimension of Confucian exemplarity must be taken seriously. It has a symbiotic relationship with other traditions in Chinese religion. Confucian values were given significance by the ordinary people, with varied levels of relevance in their everyday life. Meanwhile, as we have seen in the deification of Huang Daozhou, they also radically transformed the exemplar into a protective power rather than emulating him.

Huang's path to deification and cult popularity was not rare in Chinese history and illustrates Confucian exemplarity as Chinese exemplarity. The Confucian-educated literati used writing as art and ritual to position themselves in relation to the ruler, the reading public, the general population, and their imagined future audiences. They were familiar with the process by which the history of Confucian moral exemplars authenticated efficacy in popular religion (Sangren 1987). In other words, they aspired to join the lineage of exemplarity, via literati emulation and ordinary people's veneration of their physical suffering and injustice.

Extraordinary suffering and its audiences

While Huang Daozhou's prison calligraphy implicitly invited the public to imagine its magical power, the official Yang Jisheng 楊繼盛 (1516–1555), imprisoned and tortured for speaking against the powerful Grand Secretary Yan Song 嚴嵩 (1480–1567), explicitly wove supernatural elements into his own account of physical suffering and injustice. Yang expected himself to join the lineage of exemplar-prisoners through reflexive emulation, as evinced by his quoting of Sima Qian in the last letter to his wife and children: 'Death can be as weighty as Mt. Tai, or death can be as trifling as swan's feather'

---

² Also see the inscriptions on the stela established by a few temples dedicated to the General of Ensuring Success in Taiwan in Huang (2019).

(Bossler 2001, 122; Gao Chaoying and Zhao Jindong 2011 Part III, 48). But his rise as an exemplar-prisoner in the public's eyes resulted from an unusual number of details of physical suffering in the autobiography he penned in prison. One of the most famous passages of the autobiography describes how he survived a life-threatening beating:

> Before the beating, I had made up my mind. I decided that, when they beat me, I would keep my mind's eye focused, the tongue pressed against the upper mouth, and the teeth clenched. I would not allow my thought to meander; I would not scream in pain. If I screamed, my *qi* would run uncontrolled, causing the blood to gush into the heart and kill me. After four or five blows, the pain was so overwhelming that my mind started to dash wildly. I reflected on this and worried that my mind might get out of control. So I focused on my mind and treated my body as something external to me. *After fifty or sixty blows, suddenly I began to feel as if someone blanketed me with a piece of clothing and the pain ceded. I must have been protected by some deity?* ... Both legs swelt so much that they became indistinguishable from each other and difficult to make steps. They became so swollen that I could not bend them.

He then describes how he used a piece of a broken teacup to make a sharp tool and cut open one swollen leg, letting out bloody pus. Again, divine power intervened and helped him:

> New flesh is growing on my right leg, while the left leg is as swollen as a little jar, because I did not cut it open. Contaminated *qi* went up and attacked, causing sores in the mouth and on the tongue. *I could not eat anything. I was close to dying. I dreamt of three men in golden robes, followed by a boy in dark clothes who carried a small box. He took a pill from the box and flushed it down my throat with soup. Immediately the pain disappeared.* (Gao Chaoying and Zhang Jindong 2011 Part I, 70–71)[3]

Members of the elite society immediately disseminated these details to the public via print and theater. Wang Shizhen 王世貞 (1526–1590), Yang Jisheng's colleague and friend who invested personally in toppling the powerful Yan Song, played the most important role in shaping Yang's image as a loyal official victimized by Yan Song. Wang excelled in mobilizing his literary network to influence 'public opinion,' which, in turn, helped

---

[3] Emphasis added. For a discussion of Yang Jisheng's self-treatment of his flogging wounds from the perspective of history of medicine, see Yi-li Wu's forthcoming book on traumatology in late imperial China.

enhance his own fame. Yang's detailed descriptions of his physical suffering in the autobiography provided the core material for the most sensational and famous dimensions of his life in the public memory (Hammond 2007; Cao 2018, 145). When I visited Yang's home village in Hebei in 2016, I noticed that he was well known partly due to official and popular interest in the theatrical adaptions of his story. One of the best-educated men in the village told me proudly that he helped design the prison furniture and interrogation tools for its most recent local opera production, affirming the central role of Yang's physical suffering in the establishment of his status as an exemplar-prisoner.

Confucian ethics, Confucian religiosity, and popular religion formed a continuum in which stories of the political elite traveled and morphed. After Yang's execution, two types of shrines dedicated to him appeared. One type was erected by some of the most famous officials and their literati followers, an elite network effort. The court recognized the enshrinement of officials like Yang as a way to right the wrong, while officials, local gentry, and common folk participated in this for a wide range of political, social, and spiritual reasons. The memorial stele of his tomb was deliberately placed on the main road near his hometown in order to make it convenient for travelers to visit. While the officials stated the familiar agenda of moral influence in such commemorating effort, in reality most visitors expressed sorrow over the story of his suffering and prayed for good fortune (Zhang 2019). By the mid-eighteenth century, there were at least five shrines established in that region alone (Gao Chaoying and Zhang Jindong 2011 Part II, 72).

Yang's autobiography, quoted earlier, had already recorded his supra-human powers in prison. Literati supporters spread such elements in their works. The Ming drama *The Crying Phoenix* (Mingfeng ji 鳴鳳記), generally believed to be authored by Wang Shizhen's circle, presented Yang's story not only as that of a Confucian exemplar-prisoner but also as a revelation of heavenly justice. In Scene 23, two newly minted degree-holders go to visit his tomb (Anonymous 1935, 98–99). The play led the audience to think that good people would eventually prevail and evil people be punished. In Scene 36, for instance, an official tells a junior colleague that a member of the 'evil party' encountered Yang's spirit and suffered a sudden death. The junior official agreed that the incident indeed was an 'evil retribution' (e'bao 惡報). In the same scene, upon the arrests of the evil actors and their families, this junior official hears a voice from the sky. He tells the audience: 'Extraordinary! Extraordinary! I heard the exact words said by Yang Jisheng at his execution. I think his spirit of loyalty has not dispersed. Our success today has fulfilled his wishes. We shall bow to the sky and thank him' (Anonymous 1935, 152–153).

The other type of shrine dedicated to Yang borders on treating him as a protective power. In premodern China, religious investment in prison-related issues – physical suffering and injustice – generated an open list of prison deities that included the Prison God (the legendary official Gao Yao 皋陶), deities of popular cults and Buddhism, and deified historical figures (Zhang, Y. 2020). Yang Jisheng eventually joined this list. Orthodox Confucians enshrined historical exemplars to encourage emulation rather than to encourage worshipping for protection, because they considered this to be an impure intention. However, strictly observing this fine line proved to be nearly impossible, even among the Confucian-educated elite themselves. As Chen Xiyuan points out, one of the earliest exemplar-prisoners, the aforementioned Fan Pang, objected to the idea of offering sacrifice and praying to Gao Yao, the Prison God. According to the Confucians, heavenly justice operated on its own terms; anything other than admiring Gao Yao's embodiment of integrity and justice would betray the True Way and only encourage expediency and pragmatism. Fan Pang's stance influenced many colleagues who went to prison at that time (Chen 2018, 184–185). The same attitude can also be found among some late imperial official-prisoners. However, many others shared the popular tendency to invest protective power in historical figures deified for their extraordinary accomplishments, qualities, and sufferings. They worshipped the Prison God and prayed for his protection. They composed poems in which they imagined the Prison God listening to them. Yang Jisheng's shrine in the prison space, in the temple area of the Ministry of Punishments, likely also served multiple purposes. In addition to the notion of heavenly justice, the rich details of his physical suffering in prison readied Yang for worship by ordinary folk. His presence there provoked a range of reactions among the officials, prison staff, and prisoners.[4]

Death and exemplarity

It might be surprising to the students of premodern Chinese history that none of the exemplar-prisoners discussed earlier committed suicide in prison. Official histories and modern scholarship on male loyalty and female chastity have amplified historical subjects who killed themselves to earn state or local recognition as Confucian exemplars. Suicide, however, meant taking the life given by one's parents, which should be avoided unless for the right causes. Imprisonment was not one of them. The first two exemplar-prisoners, King Wen and Sima Qian, refused to take their own lives in confinement. Aversion to suicide in prison among the elite in later periods seemed less a convenient excuse than an effort of emulation. Additionally, imprisonment in the Ming was an investigative procedure. Defying it by suicide theoretically

---

[4] In fact, prison personnel worshipped several 'professional' deities (Li 2013).

meant defying the administrative law, even though it effectively put an end to the investigation.⁵

In the history of the Ming dynasty, for example, I have found only a handful of cases of suicide among more than a thousand imprisoned officials. In most of these cases, the imprisoned officials insisted on their innocence and decried injustice. Had they not chosen to end their own lives, they would have likely been released at some point after the so-called investigation was completed. Among them, Li Zhi 李贄 (1527–1602) might be the most (in)famous case of suicide in prison (Handler-Spitz, Lee, and Saussy 2021). Accused of disseminating inflammatory heterodox writing and disregarding gender norms, Li Zhi entered the prison at the senior age of 75, 20 years after his retirement from the government. The two final poems he composed in confinement read:

> *Floating Tufts of the Flowering Willow*
> The vital spirits are leaving my body
> like horses at a gallop;
> Facing two doors, I cannot choose:
> the one for life, or the one for death?
> The lofting blossoms of the willow enter
> the vision of the prisoner;
> I'm starting to think the underworld
> may have a springtime too.
> *No Hero*
> The man of high ideals never forgets
> he may end in a ditch;
> The man of great valor never forgets
> he may forfeit his head."
> If I do not die today, how much longer must I wait?
> I yearn for the command soon to send me
> back to the world beyond this one.
>
> Li Zhi 2016, 302 and 304

The poems frankly express the anxiety caused by the uncertainty of imprisonment and fate. Rather than dying like a true Confucian hero, the poet wonders about an alternative way to leave this world. Eventually, he died for himself, not for a 'noble' cause.

The official Tu Fei 涂棐 (d. 1468) killed himself in prison to protest the petty accusations by his colleagues that sent him to jail repeatedly, even

---

5   I discuss this question in my forthcoming book on jailing officials in the Ming, and point out that although suicide in jail could cause problems for the family of a jailed official, in reality it rarely had such consequences.

though he had been exonerated each time. The official history records that Tu hanged himself, while the local gazetteer of his home county claims he refused food and starved himself to death. While the former does acknowledge his accusers' abuse of the procedure, the latter conveys more forcefully the image of an outstanding official fallen victim to injustice (*Ming shilu Xianzong shilu*, juan 53, 155; Xu Qingyuan and Li Peixu 1825, 11.29a–30a.). This discrepancy itself suggests the reluctance on the part of the official historiographers to characterize Tu as an exemplar. Complicated political and personal factors seem to have led to these frivolous accusations, making it impossible to identify a typical 'evil force' that could have helped define his Confucian example.[6]

Men like Li Zhi and Tu Fei would not subject themselves to humiliations inflicted by their political enemies or the imperial court, in contrast to many others who believed suicide meant surrender and giving up the righteous battle. Suicide, though extreme as a form of ending suffering or even as martyrdom in some circumstances, falls short as a form of representing suffering in this particular context, in the eyes of both the Confucian-educated elite and ordinary folk. As a result, their prison experience is less impressive than the exemplars'. But one could also argue that the prisoner-exemplars became exemplars precisely because they embodied physical suffering and injustice in such a way that the audience could not turn their eyes away from them while the latter continued to set an example against ongoing indignities. In other words, Confucian exemplarity as a process of critical reflection with empathetic identification was grounded in truths of the precariousness and openness of life.

Reflections during the pandemic

The presence of a powerful central state, political ethics, and diverse religious traditions have continued from the premodern times. Understanding Chinese exemplarity as a meaningful complex of political and spiritual processes in history, especially the complexity of the relationship between the exemplar and the truths of suffering and injustice, informs better appreciation of how it operates today. Let us now return to the debate about exemplars during the COVID-19 pandemic. As Fang Fang's jottings in confinement were being simultaneously praised and attacked on the internet, the Chinese netizens were also wildly circulating a portrait of Dr Zhong Nanshan 鍾南山 (see Figure 6.1), a leading expert on the medical team dispatched to Wuhan by the central government and the de facto official spokesperson on this matter.

---

[6] Tu Fei's interactions with some locally influential figures in his jurisdiction in southern China seemed to have prevented him from receiving unanimous recognition posthumously.

Figure 6.1: 'Defeating One Hundred Viruses, Dispelling All Evils', February 2020

Source: Weibo. Illustration by Liang Shuguang 梁述光. By permission of the artist.

Drawn by an illustrator stuck in the Wuhan lockdown, this portrait features the Thunder God and the Fire God, two deities traditionally sanctioned by the state and worshipped throughout the Chinese empire. Between the two deities, in the middle of this portrait, stands Dr Zhong.

While I am not suggesting that Dr Zhong is being seen as a man with magical power, I do detect the legacy of Confucian exemplarity in this portrait. During the first few months of the pandemic, Dr Zhong became the embodiment of professional excellence, moral integrity, truth, and wisdom. Social media religiously disseminated everything he said about the coronavirus, but also stories about his parents and his everyday life, including his workout regiments and dietary habits. In premodern China, Confucian scholar-officials who demonstrated extraordinary moral integrity and whose job performance benefited the people could earn the honor of a 'living shrine (Shengci 生祠).' Many of the living shrines had a portrait of the exemplary official for the worshippers to pray to. The enshrined image of the exemplary official was often tended by Daoist priests or Buddhist monks (Schneewind 2018). The Fire God and the Thunder God, who assist Dr Zhong in this portrait, indeed belong to the Daoist pantheon and are believed to possess tremendous exorcising power. The two swiftly constructed COVID-19 hospitals in Wuhan were named after these two deities. This portrait immediately went viral in Chinese social media and resonated strongly with the public. Their attachment to the state-endorsed exemplar in this image captured the Chinese perspective at a time of crisis: they looked for protection from both science and divine forces; they connected with both the state and the deities.

We can see a revealing aspect of exemplarity as a complex of social and political processes with empathetic identification in Fang Fang's lockdown diary. She mentions Dr Zhong many times in the diary, as someone she trusts. But Dr Zhong is only one part of the exemplary spectrum. Her contemplation of the national heroes honored by the government reveals ordinary people's attitude and their critical reflection centered around physical suffering and injustice. Commenting on Wang Guangfa 王廣發, the expert who claimed the outbreak in early January 2020 as 'controllable,' 'preventable,' and 'not contagious between people,' Fang Fang wrote these sharp words: 'Dr. Wang may have been recognized by the government for his exemplary contributions, but he still owes a debt to the people of Wuhan. All members of those two teams of specialists owe us a debt. This debt must be repaid' (Fang 2020, 222). She rejected the exemplary status of this specialist and instead demanded justice.

Meanwhile, on another figure honored by the government, Li Wenliang 李文亮, a doctor disciplined by the police for telling friends about a novel virus who later died from infection, received very different remarks in Fang Fang's diary:

> The other person honored at the ceremony today was Dr. Li Wenliang. Li Wenliang was also recognized as an exemplary role model for his actions. I wonder if that is the end of his story? And I wonder if Li Wenliang was watching from the other side; if he could see what was happening, would he laugh or would he cry? (Fang 2020, 222)

Fang Fang was among the many who resisted premature closure in spite of an officially issued exemplary status for Dr Li, the prestigious title of 'Martyr' (Lieshi 烈士). The questions of physical suffering and injustice resonated strongly with them, making his case 'a knot that needs to be untangled' (Fang 2020, 210). What follows is what Fang Fang recorded:

> A few days ago I read an essay about all the people who have been posting messages on Li Wenliang's Weibo page; their messages have transformed Dr. Li's Weibo page into a wailing wall. *These messages are not simply in commemoration of Li Wenliang; their more important function is providing an outlet for people online to release those things that have been pent up inside them.* (Fang 2020, 274)

> Li Wenliang is gone; his Weibo page has become a wailing wall where countless people can go to forever remember him. *Everyone knows that he was not a hero; he lived a normal life like everyone else, and the actions he took are the kind of actions you would expect any ordinary person to take put in his position* ... As for the results of that investigation [of the injustice of the police's discipline], I really don't care anymore. *To be honest, our commemorations are in some sense way for us to commemorate ourselves, to commemorate this experience we went through, and there was one important man who was part of that experience* – his name was Li Wenliang. (Fang 2020, 314)[7]

As Fang Fang notes here, Dr Li was treated posthumously as a listener, and his Weibo page a ritual space. The ordinary people's emotional engagement with this virtual 'wailing wall' after his death, like what we have seen in the case of Sima Qian, ignored pressure from the authority and eventually won him the official status of exemplar. In a quantitative study of about 1.34 million posts on the wailing wall between February 2020 and February 2021, Zhou Baohua and Zhong Yuan point out that social media has made possible an 'extended affective space' in which collective mourning and everyday routines become quickly and fully interpenetrated. They note that this mourning space had been visited by

---

[7] Emphasis added.

'passers-by' (guoke 過客) and regularly maintained by 'tomb guardians' (shoumu ren 守墓人), with the latter capturing a traditional ethico-religious practice of loyalty, filial piety, and friendship. As time moves on, the space has been registering people's everyday emotions most consistently, with 'Good night' (wan'an 晚安) as the dominant message on the wall (Zhou Baohua and Zhong Yuan 2021, 95–102). This data, like the long history of exemplar-prisoners in premodern China, vividly illustrates how exemplarity remains a complex of negotiated political and affective processes, between the state and the people who identify with the exemplar empathetically. Further, as Hinden et al have observed, this space of mourning and memorialization is an inclusive space of creative agency that draws on the power of folklore and religion among Chinese netizens (Hinden, You, and Gao, 2023).

Given the Confucian emphasis on moral cultivation and influence, it seems obvious that exemplars served as the main discursive and governing tool for the imperial system it supported. Indeed, dynastic historiography devotes much space to biographies organized around types that cast moral-political judgments of officials. Opening any local gazetteer, one can also see long lists of exemplary filial sons, loyal officials, and chaste women. However, a closer look at the history of the exemplar-prisoners shared by the elite and non-elite makes one wonder: Perhaps, beneath the conspicuous image of dominance and indoctrination, Confucian exemplarity in China had been quietly but persistently lived as a process of sympathetic identification and critical reflection? Emulation and veneration of the exemplar-prisoners kept the truths of suffering and injustice alive and evocative, which resonated strongly with the premodern people who had to live in political, environmental, and economic precarity. These universal concerns found different articulations and deployments of the exemplar-prisoners by the elite and non-elite, transcending the boundaries between political ethics and religion. Given that popular religion always spoke to the affective dimension of a society, it is not surprising that a dynamic, pluralistic religious culture nurtured this practice of Confucian exemplarity and effectively made it a pattern of Chinese exemplarity. Appreciating Chinese exemplarity as a complex of political and spiritual processes in history and its contemporary legacy sheds light on the importance of going beyond the indoctrination vs. resistance binary. Appreciating examples through the local and historical lens also helps us see the depth of state-society negotiations centered around affect.

References

Anonymous. 1935. *Mingfeng ji* 鳴鳳記, *Liushi zhong qu* 六十種曲 IV. Kaiming shudian.

Bossler, Beverley. 2001. 'Final Instructions by Yang Jisheng (1516–1555).' In *Under the Confucian Eyes: Writings on Gender in Chinese History*, edited by Susan Mann and Yu-yin Cheng. University of California Press.

Cao Yiting 曹依婷. 2018. 'Yang Jisheng yu "Zhongchen Yang Jisheng" zhijian' 楊繼盛與"忠臣楊繼盛"之間：一個明代忠臣之再詮釋. M.A. thesis, Guoli Zhengzhi daxue.

Chen Xiyuan 陳熙遠. 2018. 'Qingdai Zhongyang xiyu zhushen kao' 清代中央繫獄諸神考. *Fazhishi yanjiu* 法制史研究 33: 175–238.

Fan Ye 范燁. *Hou Hanshu* 後漢書. https://ctext.org/hou-han-shu/dang-gu-lie-zhuan/zh (accessed February 6, 2025).

Fang Fang. 2020. *Wuhan Diary: Dispatch from a Quarantined City*, translated by Michael Berry. HarperVia.

Fei, Siyen. 2012. 'Writing for Justice: An Activist Beginning of the Cult of Female Chastity in Late Imperial China.' *The Journal of Asian Studies* 71 (4): 991–1012.

Gao Chaoying 高朝英 and Zhang Jindong 張金棟. 2011. 'Yang Jisheng *Zishu nianpu* juan kaolue' 楊繼盛《自書年譜》卷考略. *Wenwu Chunqiu* 文物春秋 (2–4).

Hammond, Ken J. 2007. *Pepper Mountain: The Life, Death and Posthumous Career of Yang Jisheng*. Kegan Paul.

Handler-Spitz, Rivi, Pauline C. Lee, and Haun Saussy, eds. 2021. *The Objectionable Li Zhi: Fiction, Criticism, and Dissent in Late Ming China*. University of Washington Press.

Hershatter, Gail. 2014. *The Gender of Memory: Rural Women and China's Collective Past*. University of California Press.

Hinden, Adam, Ziying You, and Zhen Guo. 2023. 'Online Activism and Grassroots Memorialization in the Age of COVID-19: Dr. Li Wenliang's Virtual Wailing Wall.' *Cultural Analyais Forum Series* 1: 1–22.

Huang, Martin W. 2006. *Negotiating Masculinities in Late Imperial China*. University of Hawaii Press.

Huang Mengyun 黃孟鋆. 2019. 'Huang Daozhou huihua songshu tuxiang yanjiu' 黃道周繪畫松樹圖像研究. M.A. thesis, Fujian shifan daxue.

Klein, Esther S. 2018. *Reading Sima Qian from Han to Song: The Father of History in Pre-Modern China*. Brill.

Li, Qiao 李喬. 2013. *Hangyeshen chongbai: Zhongguo minzhong zaoshen shi yanjiu* 行業神崇拜—中國民眾造神史研究. Beijing chubanshe.

Li, Zhi. 2016. *A Book to Burn & A Book to Keep (Hidden): Selected Writings*, edited and translated by Rivi Handler-Spitz, Pauline C. Lee, and Haun Saussy. Columbia University Press.

Lu, Weijing. 2008. *True to Her Word: The Faithful Maiden Cult in Late Imperial China*. Harvard Asia Center.

Ming shilu Xianzu shilu 明實錄憲宗實錄. Zhongyang yanjiuyuan lishi yuyan yanjiusuo ziliaoku 中央研究院歷史語言研究所資料庫 http://hanchi.ihp.sinica.edu.tw (accessed February 6, 2025).

Nylan, Michael. 1998–99. 'Sima Qian, A True Historian?' *Early China* 23: 203–246.

Sangren, Steven. 1987. *History and Magical Power in a Chinese Community*. Stanford University Press.

Schneewind, Sarah. 2018. *Shrines to Living Men in the Ming Political Cosmos*. Harvard University Asia Center.

Shui Laiyou 水賚佑. 2016. 'Huang Tingjian "Fan Pang zhuan" tie sanyi ji bawen' 黃庭堅《范滂傳》帖散佚及跋文. *Shufa yanjiu* 書法研究: 95–114.

Sima Qian 司馬遷. *Shiji* 史記. https://ctext.org/shiji/zhou-ben-ji/zh (accessed February 6, 2025).

Sutton, Donald S. 1989. 'A Case of Literati Piety: The Ma Yuan Cult from High-Tang to High-Qing.' *Chinese Literature: Essays, Articles, Reviews* 11: 79–114.

Wu, Delin 伍德林. 2016. 'Zongjiao dui Zhongguo gudai zhanzheng de yingxiang' 宗教對中國古代戰爭的影響. PhD dissertation, Shanghai Shifan daxue.

Xu, Qingxuan 徐清選 and Li Peixu 李培緒. 1825. *Fengcheng xianzhi* 豐城縣誌. National Library of China.

Yang, Ching Kun. 1961. *Religion in Chinese Society: A Study of Contemporary Social Functions of Religion and Some of the Their Historical Factors*. University of California Press.

Zhang, Cong E. 2020. *Performing Filial Piety in Northern Song China*. University of Washington Press.

Zhang, Ying. 2016. *Confucian Image Politics: Masculine Morality in Seventeenth-Century China*. University of Washington Press.

Zhang, Ying. 2019. 'The Confucian Ideal Friend.' In *The Ming World*, edited by Kenneth M. Swope. Routledge.

Zhang, Ying. 2020. *Religion and Prison Art in Ming China (1368–1644): Creative Environment, Creative Subjects*. Brill Research Perspectives in Humanities and Social Sciences.

Zheng Chenyin 鄭晨寅. 2009. 'Chu fang Taibei Jindegong' 初訪台北晉德宮. *Min Tai wenhua yanjiu* 閩台文化研究 2: 118–119.

Zheng Chenyin 鄭晨寅. 2017. 'Huang Daozhou xinyang de wenhua neihan yu fazhan licheng tanxi' 黃道周信仰的文化內涵與發展歷程探析. *Min Tai wenhua yanjiu* 閩台文化研究 4: 89–93.

Zhou Baohua 周葆華 and Zhong Yuan 鍾媛. 2021. '"Chuntian de hua kai qiutian de feng": Shejiao meiti, jiti daonian yu yanzhan xing qinggan kongjian, yi Li Wenliang weibo pinglun (2020–2021) weili de jisuan chuanbo fenxi' 社交媒体、集体悼念与延展性情感空间——以李文亮微博评论（2020-2021）为例的计算传播分析. *Guoji xinwen jie* 國際新聞界 3: 79–106.

7

The Exemplary Normativity of International Precedents

Christopher Daase and Tobias Wille

Introduction

The history of the use of force in international politics is a history of precedents. Moving from case to case, actors and observers have argued about what it means to act in self-defense and under what further circumstances using military force may be permissible. A comprehensive volume edited by Ruys, Corten, and Hofer (2018), for example, assembles 65 case studies mapping the historical and legal narratives from which states, politicians, and lawyers draw their arguments to justify or condemn the use of military force. Each chapter even has a section on the 'precedential value' of the respective case. The question that remains unanswered, however, is why the mere fact of a past action should compel actors to act similarly in the present. What does it mean that a past instance of the use of force has 'precedential value' today? The editors of and contributors to that volume are not the only ones who fail to provide a satisfying answer to the question. To the academic discipline of International Relations (IR), the power of precedent remains mysterious. For given the fact that in international law, precedents 'in the strict sense do not exist' (Kratochwil 1989, 209), since the decisions of international courts have no binding force beyond the parties to a dispute, it is surprising that precedents figure so prominently in international political debates, legal arguments, diplomacy, and international negotiations. Indeed, Thomas Schelling's puzzle (1960, 67) over how precedent can apparently 'exercise an influence that greatly exceeds its logical importance or legal force' remains unsolved 65 years after it was first posed.

In this chapter, we try to solve this puzzle by arguing that precedents have a distinct normativity so far unrecognized by IR scholars. Normativity for us simply denotes the way something provides reasons for action or judgment (Korsgaard 1996, 8–9; Raz 1999, 353). Since we are concerned with international politics, our focus is primarily on such reasons that motivate collective actors to act in relation to other collective actors. As we will show, extant theories of the use of force in international politics know two distinct kinds of normativity; that is, distinct kinds of reasons that motivate states, governments or individual decision-makers to act. The first kind is *instrumental normativity* where actors are motivated by a desire to realize fixed and often material interests and do so by choosing what they deem the best instrumental means to their ends. Practical reasons of this kind take center stage in rationalist theories of international politics and are deeply ingrained in rational choice methodology. The second kind is *deontic normativity* where actors are guided in their behavior by abstract rules that often take the form of moral or legal norms. This kind of practical reason is the main focus of constructivist theories of international politics. When rationalists and constructivists try to conceptualize precedents, they do so in terms of these two kinds of normativity.

In doing so, rationalists and constructivists overlook a third kind of normativity, for which we propose the term *exemplary normativity*. As we will demonstrate, precedents provide reasons for action that are distinct from those reasons that pertain to instrumental or rule-guided conduct. If one acts following a precedent, one acts because of a singular act in the past that is deemed to be exemplary. Instrumental and deontic normativity derive reasons for individual acts from general considerations about the consequences of action or what general prescriptions demand respectively. Exemplary normativity, however, proceeds directly from a particular act in the past to the particular decision to be made or justified in the present. To understand precedents as examples, therefore, one must examine not only the performance that might be seen as 'setting' the precedent, but also how a community of actors judges its relevance for a later act or decision, cites it in political disputes, or even emulates it in action. As we will show, it is precisely in situations of normative uncertainty that political actors turn to precedents, because they provide guidance for action when instrumental and deontic reasons are contradictory, inconclusive, or unavailable. Only if we come to terms with the distinct normativity of precedents can we solve Schelling's puzzle and fully understand the importance of precedents for the use of force in international politics.

Rationalist accounts of precedent

Rationalists in IR have a composite – albeit mostly implicit – model of normativity. Its essence is concisely expressed in James G. March and Johan P. Olsen's description of the 'logic of expected consequences' that according to rationalist theories guides the behavior of social actors. 'History is seen' from this perspective, they write, as the result 'of the interaction of willful actors and is fully understood when it is related to expectations of its consequences and to the interests (preferences) and resources of the actors' (March and Olsen 1998, 950). One source of normativity, that is, one set of reasons actors have for acting, are their preferences. Most often, however, in IR these preferences do not receive much theoretical attention and are assumed to be exogenous and static. They also virtually always are assumed to be self-interested. The second source of normativity, which stands at the very center of rationalist theorizing, results from the linkage between means (that is, the resources), action, and expected outcome. Rationalists assume that social actors have good reasons to act in such a way that they can realize their preferences. In rationalist theory, 'individual actions are "explained" by identifying consequential reasons for them' (March and Olsen 1998, 950). Importantly, these consequential reasons are largely independent of the content of the preferences. We can assess whether the means are rightly chosen to reach a given end regardless of whether we think there are good reasons to pursue that end. Since actions are carried out as a means to a determined end, the kind of normativity presupposed by rationalist IR theories can be termed *instrumental normativity*.

Thinking about precedent in terms of self-interest and instrumental rationality has a long tradition in the literature on judicial decision-making in the US in general and at the US Supreme Court in particular. Segal and Spaeth (1996) have argued that to follow precedents is a key norm of Supreme Court decision-making, but that judges tend to ignore them if they personally disagree with previous decisions. Knight and Epstein (1996, 1021) modified this account, arguing that judges are largely strategic actors trying to 'move the law as close as possible to their personal policy preferences.' Precedents on this account are arguments that are strategically employed by judges in order to advance their individual preferences. Most rationalist accounts of precedent in international law attempt to transfer these theories that explain domestic legal precedent to the international realm (Lupu and Voeten 2012; Pelc 2014; Verdier and Voeten 2014; Larsson et al 2016; De Somer 2019). In essence they argue that actors, be they individual human beings or states, have good reasons to set and follow legal precedents because it allows them to realize their self-interested preferences. As Cohen points out in a chapter that seeks to clear the ground for a theorization of international precedent, 'under this account, interpretations should be invoked or treated as precedent when doing so helps achieve various actors' broader goals' (Cohen 2015, 281). Thus, rationalists try to explain why states cite precedents with reference to their self-interested preferences and their anticipation of what kind of arguments are likely to convince an international court. In turn, court rulings are accounted for by reference to the individual preferences of judges or their attempts so solidify their professional authority.

The idea that all past decisions create a pool of possible precedents from which rational actors can freely choose to strategically advance their interest has an important impact beyond the debates on international law and its application through international courts. Precedent arguments in international politics differ from domestic precedents because there is neither an explicit norm demanding that precedents be followed nor a superior power with the authority to make binding decisions and enforce compliance (see Kier and Mercer 1996, 96–98). According to rationalist scholars, precedents in international politics are therefore first and foremost horizontal coordination mechanisms (for example, Gehring et al 2019, 112–114). The *locus classicus* of this idea is Thomas Schelling's groundbreaking work on strategy and conflict. Schelling was among the first who recognized the importance of precedents in international relations arguing that in coordination games, that is, games with multiple equilibria, precedents help finding 'focal points' around which actors' expectations converge. Schelling's famous example is the distinction of nuclear and conventional weapons, which is not a distinction by nature, but based on 'a powerful tradition that they are different' (Schelling 1960, 260). Although being first and foremost a social construction, the distinction works as a powerful limit to warfare: 'Tradition or conventions are not simply an analogy for limits in war, or a curious aspect of them; tradition or precedent or convention is the essence of the limits' (Schelling 1960, 260). All three derive their authority 'from the sheer perception of mutual acknowledgement, of a "tacit bargain"' (Schelling 1960, 261).

This raises the question of how single events, like precedents, acquire the quality of focal points that form 'each person's expectation of what the other expects him to expect to be expected to do' (Schelling 1960, 57). Evolutionary game theory has tried to solve this puzzle by pointing to the feedback effect of precedents on expectations. According to Payton Young (1998, 6; see also Young 1996), agents, even if not perfectly rational and with incomplete information,

> adjust their behavior based on what they think other agents are going to do, and these expectations are generated endogenously by information about what other agents have done in the past. On the basis of these expectations, the agent takes an action, which in turn becomes a precedent that influences the behavior of future agents.

This feedback loop, Young argues, is the causal mechanism by which path-dependencies evolve and institutions develop.

More recent work in IR and International Law demonstrates that international actors not only take past precedents into account when they deliberate what to do. They also develop strategic attitudes towards precedents. Krzysztof Pelc (2014) demonstrates with statistical methods that states initiate arbitration cases before the World Trade Organization's dispute settlement mechanism in order to create precedents they can later exploit in high-stake trade disputes. Similarly, Pierre-Hugues Verdier and Erik Voeten (2014) use a rationalist model to argue that states tend to follow the prescriptions of customary international law despite the lack of enforcement mechanisms and even if it is against their short-term preferences because they expect precedential effects if their non-compliance will be reciprocated by other states. States comply with customary international law because they fear that non-compliance would set a costly precedent.

In sum, rationalist scholars have tried to make sense of precedents by framing them as focal points that allow international actors to coordinate their behavior. Such a conceptualization is rather thin, however. It reduces precedents to contingent information actors can use strategically to further their interests. Rather than being understood as genuine reasons for acting, precedents are subsumed under the normativity of instrumental action.

Constructivist accounts of precedent

Constructivist scholarship in IR complements the rationalist model with a second kind of normativity. While virtually all constructivists acknowledge that the actors of international politics sometimes act out of self-interest and in an instrumental fashion, they argue that in their practical reasoning actors also consider another kind of reasons. The actors' behavior then is, in March and Olson's (1998, 951) terms, guided by another logic, the 'logic of appropriateness,' within which 'actions are seen as rule-based.' Of course, rule following also has an instrumental dimension – actors think about what behavior will do justice to the rules they consider valid. However, the link is less strict: 'appropriateness need not attend to consequences,' even though 'it involves cognitive and ethical dimensions, targets, and aspirations' (March and Olson 1998, 951). Pertaining to the domain that concerns us in this chapter, constructivists ' "explain" foreign policy as the application of rules associated with particular identities to particular situations' (March and Olson 1998, 951). In the international sphere, behavior is oriented by several kinds of rules, of which in the constructivist literature legal and moral norms have received particular attention. Constructivists believe that the actors of international politics in their practical reasoning consider international law and moral norms as good reasons to do some things and desist from others. Since both morality and law prescribe action through general rules, we refer to this kind of reasons as *deontic normativity*.

Constructivist scholars in IR suspected early on that precedents play an important role in the process of norm creation (Finnemore and Sikkink 1998; Johnstone 2003). However, it turned out to be a formidable challenge to elaborate a convincing theoretical account of how exactly precedents relate to international norms. One obvious possibility is to conceive of precedent-following itself as norm-guided activity. In the common law tradition, the rule that courts should follow precedent is expressed in the principle of *stare decisis*. The legal (and moral) requirement that like cases be treated alike makes similar demands on the state and other authorities (Duxburry 2008, 170–171). In IR, Martha Finnemore and Kathryn Sikkink (1998, 915) have noted, that 'legal arguments are persuasive when they are grounded in precedent, and there are complex rules about the creation of precedent.' Therefore 'an examination of legal mechanisms for norm selection and dissemination will be instructive for IR scholars.' Following this lead, Hawkins (2004, 785) has found that 'the importance of precedent in making decisions and resolving disputes' is an 'implicit, taken-for-granted understandings shared by states.' Thus, following precedents is in itself an international norm, he maintains. Other constructivists have similarly argued that precedents either form part of the 'shared background knowledge' (Gehring and Dörfler 2019, 127) or the standards of 'competent action' (Barnett 2018, 322) that structure international practices. For instance, Vincent Pouliot (2021, 3) argues that 'past interactions, precedents, and tradition' guide informal practices at the UN Security Council and elsewhere. However, reducing precedent-following to an explicit norm or implicit rule of practice is unsatisfactory since it only shifts the explanatory burden to the existence of a meta-norm or the implicit and often embodied rules of social practices.

A more sophisticated theorization of the relationship between norms and precedent can be found in Wayne Sandholtz's writings. He treats precedents as evidence actors can cite in order to justify their positions in normative disputes. Even 'rational maximizer[s],' Sandholtz argues, use normative arguments in support of their aims, 'not because they "believe in" or accept them, but because they offer the best chance of winning' (Sandholtz 2008, 104). Precedents 'shape' such arguments insofar as they 'provide actors with *evidence* of what behavior states have accepted (or condemned) in the past' (Sandholtz 2008, 107, our italics). Consequently, actors in normative disputes will look for as many precedents as possible that support their claim. 'The actor that can offer several pertinent precedents consistent with her interpretation of the current dispute will generally be more persuasive than the actor who cannot cite relevant precedents' (Sandholtz 2008, 107). Sandholtz concedes that the sheer number of precedents does not always win out, but that 'other persuasive reasons' like powerful ethical values sometimes prevail. However, in general precedents seem to draw their justificatory power from their quantity not quality even if sometimes a 'small number of precedents can be crucial in establishing a norm' (Sandholtz 2008, 107). But if this is the case, the question arises as to what makes some precedents more powerful and convincing than others. And what makes acts or decisions precedents in the first place, since, obviously, not all past events become precedents?

In another important theoretical contribution to the problem of precedent, Elizabeth Kier and Jonathan Mercer try to provide answers to these questions by focusing on the process of *setting* precedents. They define precedent 'as an act or statement that serves or is intended to serve as an example, reason, or justification of a later one' (Kier and Mercer 1996, 79). 'To set a precedent,' they argue, 'means to generate a convention,' that is, a common expectation about acceptable behavior (Kier and Mercer 1996, 80). Against a simplistic understanding of precedents, they hold that '[i]n general, efforts to use precedents to create conventions unilaterally will fail' (Kier and Mercer 1996, 79). The reason is that setting precedents is a fundamentally social process: 'Whether an act generates a convention (sets a precedent) depends upon how others interpret the act. The act itself does not create a convention; audiences create conventions' (Kier and Mercer 1996, 80). While this is certainly true, Kier and Mercer do not explain *how* precedents create conventions, understood as arbitrary, self-perpetuating solutions to recurring coordination problems (see Lewis 1969). After all, not every precedent gives rise to a convention.[1] In Kier and Mercer's account of the conventional normativity of precedents, external reasons for action seem to do the trick: 'Indeed, the power of precedents depends, at least to some extent, on the willingness of actors to abide by principles' (Kier and Mercer 1996, 89). This seems to indicate that only if some normative commitment beyond the precedent at hand exists is the precedent able to create 'conventional' normative force.

Sandholtz shares a similar understanding of the normativity of precedent with Kier and Mercer. Both conceptualize precedent in a way that is compatible with rationalist assumptions when they frame them as historical examples of existing norms or conventions that can be strategically chosen by rational actors as evidence in political disputes. Just like their rationalist colleagues and despite their commitment to understanding the social construction of reality, constructivists in IR are unable to account for the way in which evidence translates into normativity, why some precedents are more salient than others, and where their justificatory power stems

---

[1] Precedents *can* lead to conventions, but they are different from them. Precedents create normative regularity insofar behavior is justified with respect to a salient historical event or decision. Conventions function without reference to historical cases but draw on the validity of the regularity itself (see Daase 1999).

from. If in international relations no external norm of *stare decisis* demands that precedents be followed and no superior power enforces compliance, the question remains how precedents can have the power to influence the behavior of states in the first place.

The exemplary normativity of precedents

While rationalists and constructivists in IR are able to grasp some aspects of precedents, modeling them either as result of rational calculation or as rule following, they fail to see that precedents provide a genuine type of reason that states and other actors of international politics can use to justify their own actions and judge the actions of others. Precedents thus have their own normativity. This normativity differs in important ways from instrumental and deontic normativity, which is to say that the reasons a precedent provides differ from the reasons associated with the pursuit of rational self-interest or the following of legal and moral norms. If actors act out of rational self-interest, they do what they do because they expect that it will bring about certain consequences that are in their interest, however these interests may be defined. In instrumental action, practical judgment is limited to a calculation of what the best means are to achieve a given end. In contrast, if actors follow a legal or moral norm, they do what they do because the norm requires it. Their practical judgment applies a rule to the given situation thus subsuming the particular under the general. As we have seen in the previous two sections, extant theories of international politics try to reduce exemplary normativity either to instrumental or deontic normativity. If they talk about precedents at all, they try to account for them in their respective explanatory vocabulary as either instrumental behavior or rule following.

If one wants to explore the genuine normativity of precedent, legal theory provides a helpful starting point (Schauer 1987, 2008; Lamond 2005; Duxbury 2008; Gerhardt 2008). Precedent in general terms is understood there as 'a past event ... which serves as a guide for present action' (Duxbury 2008, 1). In the discussions we find in this literature, the past event is usually the decision of a court and the situation in which action is required is a legal dispute. However, legal scholars recognize that the reach of precedent extends far beyond the sphere of law (Schauer 1987, 2008; Duxbury 2008). For what characterizes a precedent is not primarily the context of action, but the specific way in which the present is related to the past.[2] The crucial point here is that a past act itself becomes a reason for acting in the present. The 'skeleton' structure of a precedent argument is thus: 'The previous treatment

---

[2] Schauer (1987: 573f) illustrate the point with the example of a child who invokes the treatment of their sibling as precedent when negotiating bedtime with their parents.

of occurrence X in manner Y constitutes, *solely because of its historical pedigree*, a reason for treating X in manner Y if and when X again occurs' (Schauer 1987, 571, original italics). Precedents thus are distinct from analogies (Schauer 2008). Analogy is an (often faulty) mode of inference in which a past event or decision and its consequences are used to gain information about structural features of the present situation that can inform action. To invoke 'Munich' is to argue that because appeasement did not work in 1938, it will also fail to work in the present (Khong 1992; see Snyder, Chapter 15, this volume). Precedents, in contrast, create an obligation to act as someone once did simply because of the facticity of the past act. Counterintuitively, they even can 'require judges ... or other decision makers to make decisions contrary to their own best judgment solely because someone else has made what appears to them to be a mistake in the past' (Schauer 2008, 455).

But how can a past act in and of itself be a reason to act in the present? We have seen that neither self-interest nor procedural norms such as *stare decisis* or equal treatment can account for international precedent in a satisfying way. The reason is that precedents neither are rules, nor do they create them (Lamond 2005). Instead, precedents are examples, however examples of a special kind. Social actors cite examples to justify their own actions and evaluate the actions of others. In general, examples are specific instances that stand for a larger whole, however in two very different ways (see Ferrara 2008; Noyes 2016; McNay 2019). Examples of the first kind exemplify a clearly specified rule, regularity, or class. They are, in the terminology laid out in this volume (Noyes and Wille, Chapter 1), samples of a larger whole. Norway may be read as an example of a small state and the UN peacekeeping operation in Cyprus an example of a UN-sanctioned intervention. Reasoning by analogy is one particular use of this first kind of example, albeit a particularly risky one because it infers features of a situation from one single other example without knowing the whole class of relevant phenomena (see Snyder, Chapter 15, this volume). Examples of the second kind, in contrast, stand for something we cannot quite grasp yet. There is no general rule they instantiate, and still they appear to have importance for other, similar cases. Precedents are examples of this second kind; they are not instances of a clearly specified rule, regularity, or class, but rather a singular point of reference that can orient action in similar situations.

The two kinds of examples correspond to two kinds of judgment Immanuel Kant has identified in his *Critique of Judgment* and Hannah Arendt has transferred to the sphere of politics. The first kind are determinate judgments, which 'subsume the particular under a general rule' (Arendt 1992 [1970], 83). Determinate judgment is the central operation of rule following. One takes a general rule and applies it to the particular case. If in war states shall not use means that disproportionately affect the civilian population and cluster ammunition do exactly this, then states shall not use cluster ammunition in any particular war. The second kind of judgments are reflective judgments, which '"derive" the rule from the particular' (Arendt 1992 [1970], 83). This second kind of judgment operates in a very different way: it starts from the particular case and then moves towards similar instances. According to Arendt (1992 [1970], 85), most concepts in history and the social sciences gain their meaning through examples of the second kind, they 'have their origins in some particular historical incident and we then proceed to make it "exemplary,"' by which she means 'to see in the particular what is valid in more than one case.' Precedents thus have 'exemplary validity' (Arendt 1992, 84). To recognize them as precedents means to recognize them as part of something larger the contours of which are not fully defined yet.

Just like norms, precedents are intersubjective. To have effects in the social world, their validity has to be accepted by a community of relevant social actors. Kier and Mercer (1996, 80) are thus right to point out that whether an act sets a precedent 'depends upon how others interpret the act.' Claims to precedent however differ from references to rules in how exactly they appeal to those they address. While empirically, actors only rarely agree which moral and legal rules are valid and how they should be applied, at least in principle these questions can be resolved through rational arguments. How international actors debate the validity and correct application of norms is at the core of the recent literature on norm contestation (Wiener 2018; Zimmermann et al 2023). Claims of precedent, in contrast, are debated differently. The reason is that reflective judgments do not compel agreement the same way determinate judgments do. Social actors can only 'woo' or 'court' the consent of others (Arendt 1992b [1970], 72). If one wanted to claim that the Kosovo intervention of 1999 was legal, one would have to name the legal rules that made it permissible and demonstrate that they apply to the specific case. If, in contrast, one wanted to argue that the Kosovo intervention is a precedent that can offer guidance in a similar situation of mass atrocities, one would have to appeal to the addressee of the claim to accept that the given situations is similar enough to justify the same action. This conclusion does not compel; it needs to be felt.[3]

Even though precedents provide reasons for action that do not take the form of general rules, they usually play out in thick normative contexts of which moral and legal rules form an important part. A precedent can thus be understood as a situational judgment that takes both the normative

---

[3] Drawing on Kant, Arendt argues that this feeling can be communicated because it is rooted in the *sensus communis*, a shared common sense. However, we do not make this assumption. Arguing from a broadly constructivist point of view, for us factual intersubjective agreement of the relevant actors is sufficient to constitute a precedent as a social fact.

context and the specific historical facts into account (see Lamond 2005). If in the past, certain (possibly conflicting) rules were applied in a situation with certain features and led to a certain decision, then this will provide reasons to apply the same rules in a latter situation with the same features in the same way. Furthermore, if a number of possible counter-arguments did not weigh heavy enough to lead to a different decision in the situation that serves as precedent, the same counter-arguments alone also should not lead to a different outcome in a later decision. Precedents thus provide reasons for action that do not take the form of general rules. Rather, they mark decisions made in a context and accepted as justified by a relevant community, which commit all participants to act the same way again in a situation where the same reasons for action are present and no further, new counter-arguments are available. If, in contrast, a later situation is different in that either some of the arguments that supported the initial decision of the precedent are lacking or additional counter-arguments are present, the precedent loses its normative force. This is precisely because they are not general rules but context-dependent judgments.[4] Contra Sandholtz, as well as Kier and Mercer, we thus argue that precedents neither create norms nor prove the validity to existing ones. Instead, precedent merely commits the international community to weigh norms, laws, and other reasons in the same way as it did in similar cases in the past.

The use of force and the Kosovo precedent

In the following, we will apply our understanding of precedent and exemplary normativity in a brief study of the debate about humanitarian intervention. Since the end of the Cold War, Western states, above all the United States, have tried to re-interpret the principles of *ius ad bellum*, the right to wage war. In the normative discourses that have accompanied these attempts, precedents and their exemplary normativity have played an important role. Proponents have invoked precedents to justify the legitimacy of non-legal action, while critics have warned of 'dangerous' precedents that could endanger the integrity of international law. Some events have been instrumentalized with the intention to initiate norm-building processes through the 'setting of precedents,' while others have been mobilized to prevent such processes from developing. Exemplary normativity, it seems, is indeed consequential, but in a somewhat unpredictable, poorly understood way.

---

[4] In the common law tradition, courts thus have the option to either follow a precedent or to distinguish the present case from it, that is, assert that it is sufficiently different so that the precedent does not apply (Lamond 2005).

The legal principle of non-use of force, on the surface, is clearly stated in the UN Charter. It prohibits the use of force by states except for individual or collective self-defense under Article 51 or peace enforcement mandated by the Security Council under Chapter VII (Gray 2000, 24–50). It has been argued by some, however, that in cases of genocide and grave human rights violations, international law is too restrictive and military intervention must be allowed to prevent atrocities and save lives. In the resulting controversies, precedent arguments played an important role. For although Western states made every effort not to let the Kosovo intervention in 1999 become a precedent, it became exactly that: a precedent for humanitarian intervention without a UN Security Council mandate. Moreover, this precedent, or rather the fear of it, was the starting point for a process aimed at codifying humanitarian intervention and qualifying the principle of non-intervention by transferring the responsibility for protecting the population to the international community when a state is unable or unwilling to ensure the well-being of its citizens.

However, this process failed for several reasons. The forced juridification of humanitarian intervention pursued by Western states met with rejection not only from the traditional advocates of state sovereignty, especially China and Russia, but also from many states in the Global South. The overstretching of the UN Security Council's original 2011 R2P mandate in Libya further undermined the willingness to insert references to the responsibility to protect into Security Council resolutions out of fear that it could again be misused as a justification for the unilateral use of force. The academic discussion also remained inconclusive. To this day it is controversial whether the responsibility to protect could also be assumed by individual states or groups of states and whether the use of military force to uphold human rights is permissible without a UN mandate. To the extent that the norm-building process inspired by 'Kosovo' came to a halt, the event of the intervention itself re-emerged and gained normative significance as an exemplary case, that is, as a precedent, ready to be invoked as a normative reason to act when a humanitarian catastrophe occurs and the Security Council is blocked.

How was this possible? Serious human rights violations in the territory of the former Yugoslavia led Western states to consider military measures to stop Serbia's aggression. Because Russia prevented a UN Security Council mandate, NATO states decided on an unauthorized military intervention (even though its members implausibly claimed that the intervention was covered by previous Security Council resolutions). In order to keep the impact of such controversial measure on the international order as small as possible and to calm domestic opposition, Western representatives, among them German Foreign Minister Klaus Kinkel, emphasized that the use of military force was necessary in this particular case but should not become a precedent (Simma 1999). US Secretary of State Madeleine Albright stressed that Kosovo was a *sui generis* case and would have no impact on future events.[5]

The opposite happened. A commission set up by the UN Secretary General and headed by former judge Richard Goldstone concluded that NATO's military action had been illegal but legitimate (Independent International Commission on Kosovo 2000, 4). This verdict fueled the debate about amending international law by creating a norm that would make such action legal. By closing the gap between legality and legitimacy, it was hoped that clear, legal guidelines for legitimate military intervention would emerge and the room for misuse could be minimized. Without such guidelines, UN Secretary General Kofi Annan feared, humanitarian interventions like the one in Kosovo would set 'dangerous precedents for future interventions without clear criteria to decide who might invoke those precedents and in what circumstances.'[6] The Independent International Commission on Kosovo followed this view and took up the task. It proposed a plan for legal reform to make the law of humanitarian intervention more congruent with what was said to be the 'international moral consensus' (Independent International Commission on Kosovo 2000, 4).

This plan added to a growing body of literature advocating either the codification of humanitarian intervention or the development of new standards through a forced change in customary international law. Between 2001 and 2005, a number of UN commissions refined the idea of the 'Responsibility to Protect.' Although the UN stressed the complexity of the concept and emphasized its diplomatic and preventive components, the public debate concentrated on the controversial question of the use of military force to uphold human rights. Although the basic idea behind the responsibility to protect enjoyed general acceptance at that time, it did not solve the dilemma surrounding humanitarian interventions. It is still controversial whether the responsibility to protect is a legal or a moral norm; whether it empowers only the international community or also regional organizations, coalitions of the willing or individual states; whether it constitutes a right or also an obligation; and whether the use of military force requires a UN mandate or not.

International lawyers claim 'that the NATO intervention in Kosovo has next to no precedential value' for assessing humanitarian interventions (Franchini and Tzanakopoulos 2018, 619; see also Simma 1999). We argue the opposite. Given the aborted process of legalizing humanitarian intervention, the Kosovo precedent is one of the few normative facts that

---

[5] US Secretary of State Madeleine Albright Press Conference in Singapore, July 26, 1999.

[6] Report of the Secretary General, 54th Session of the General Assembly, September 20, 1999, A/54/PV.4.

can be referred to in justificatory discourses of future cases. If in the future a humanitarian crisis or catastrophe occurs that bears a resemblance to the situation in Kosovo in 1999, we expect the Kosovo precedent to be invoked as justification for a possible humanitarian intervention.

Conclusion

When it comes to the use of force in international politics, the most important precedents have not been set by courts or tribunals. They did not arise simply because leaders (or scholars) insisted on the relevance of an event or action, nor were they prevented from arising by simple denials of the latter's relevance. Precedents are established when the justification of a state's action by reference to a past act is accepted by the international community as a valid reason for present action. Against this background, we agree with Verdier and Voeten (2014) that states care about the precedential impact of their behavior, but we argue that they do so because the collective judgment of the international community gives examples their normative force. This implies that the precedential effect of an action may be diminished if it is widely criticized or even sanctioned. In turn, individual states that seek to suppress the precedential impact of their actions by declaring them an exception will only succeed if they can convince others of their interpretation.

Scholars and decision-makers tend to overestimate the normative weight of past events when they present them as 'precedents' that, like Pandora's box once opened, will lead to a more permissive use of military force in the future. Precedents are not freestanding social facts, but situated judgments that have consequences in specific contexts of justification. Scholars and decision-makers also tend to give too much weight to governments' insistence that their actions are *sui generis* and therefore should not set a precedent, overlooking the fact that judgment in politics is necessarily a collective process. Such a lack of understanding of how precedents work has led to bad policy, for example when governments expected domestic and foreign support for military intervention that did not materialize. In other cases, they were surprised by the normative consequences of their interventions, which in retrospect appear to outweigh the political and humanitarian benefits. Our conceptualization of precedents can help to more accurately assess the normative significance of past events, and thus improve the congruence between political action and its normative justification in situations of normative uncertainty.

Although precedents do not establish norms that would allow resolving normative conflicts in the sense of determining judgments, neither are they simply arbitrary statements whose relevance is in the eye of the beholder alone. Rather, they are examples to which a special normative significance is collectively attributed. As such they can help to resolve normative conflicts through reflective judgments that allow case-specific weighing of normative claims. This is also the answer to Schelling's question why precedents are so prominent in international politics. They offer a basic normativity with which actors can 'drive by sight' and orient themselves on a case-by-case basis when more general rules are suspended or their meaning has become uncertain. In view of the current disintegration of the liberal international order and the questioning of hitherto central norms of international politics, precedence arguments could indeed become a last bastion of normative argumentation constraining the use of force.

References

Arendt, Hannah. 1992 [1970]. 'Imagination.' In *Hannah Arendt: Lectures on Kant's Political Philosophy*, edited by Ronald Beiner. University of Chicago Press.

Barnett, Michael. 2018. 'Human Rights, Humanitarianism, and the Practices of Humanity.' *International Theory* 10 (3): 314–349.

Cohen, Harlan G. 2015. 'Theorizing Precedent in International Law.' In *Interpretation in International Law*, edited by Andrea Bianchi, Daniel Peat, and Matthew Windsor. Oxford University Press.

Daase, Christopher. 1999 'Spontaneous Institutions: Peacekeeping as an International Convention.' In *Imperfect Unions: Security Institutions over Time and Space*, edited by Helga Haftendorn, Robert O. Keohane, and Celeste A. Wallender. Oxford University Press.

De Somer, Marie. 2019. *Precedents and Judicial Politics in EU Immigration Law*. Springer.

Duxbury, Neil. 2008. *The Nature and Authority of Precedent*. Cambridge University Press.

Ferrara, Alessandro. 2008. *The Force of the Example: Explorations in the Paradigm of Judgment*. Columbia University Press.

Finnemore, Martha, and Kathryn Sikkink. 1998. 'International Norm Dynamics and Political Change.' *International Organization* 52 (4): 887–917.

Franchini, Daniel, and Antonios Tzanakopoulos. 2018. 'The Kosovo Crisis (1999).' In *The Use of Force in International Law: A Case-Based Approach*, edited by Tom Ruys, Olivier Corten, and Alexandra Hofer. Oxford University Press.

Gehring, Thomas, and Thomas Dörfler. 2019. 'Constitutive Mechanisms of UN Security Council Practices: Precedent Pressure, Ratchet Effect, and Council Action Regarding Intrastate Conflicts.' *Review of International Studies* 45 (1): 120–140.

Gehring, Thomas, Christian Dorsch, and Thomas Dörfler. 2019. 'Precedent and Doctrine in Organizational Decision-Making: The Power of Informal Institutional Rules in the United Nations Security Council's Activities on Terrorism.' *Journal of International Relations and Development* 22 (1): 107–135.

Gerhardt, Michael J. 2008. *The Power of Precedent*. Oxford University Press.

Gray, Christine D. 2000. *International Law and the Use of Force*. Oxford University Press.

Hawkins, Darren. 2004. 'Explaining Costly International Institutions: Persuasion and Enforceable Human Rights Norms.' *International Studies Quarterly* 48 (4): 779–804.

Independent International Commission on Kosovo. 2000. *The Kosovo Report: Conflict, International Response, Lessons Learned*. Oxford University Press.

Johnstone, Ian. 2003. 'Security Council Deliberations: The Power of the Better Argument.' *European Journal of International Law* 14 (3): 437–480.

Khong, Yuen Foong. 1992. *Analogies at War: Korea, Munich, Dien Bien Phu, and the Vietnam Decisions of 1965*. Princeton University Press.

Kier, Elizabeth, and Jonathan Mercer. 1996. 'Setting Precedents in Anarchy: Military Intervention and Weapons of Mass Destruction.' *International Security* 20 (4): 77–106.

Knight, Jack, and Lee Epstein. 1996. 'The Norm of Stare Decisis.' *American Journal of Political Science* 40 (4): 1018–1035.

Korsgaard, Christine M. 1996. 'The Normative Question.' In *The Sources of Normativity*, edited by Onora O'Neill. Cambridge University Press.

Kratochwil, Friedrich V. 1989. *Rules, Norms, and Decisions: On the Conditions of Practical and Legal Reasoning in International Relations and Domestic Affairs*. Cambridge University Press.

Lamond, Grant. 2005. 'Do Precedents Create Rules?' *Legal Theory* 11 (1): 1–26.

Larsson, Olof, Daniel Naurin, Mattias Derlén, and Johan Lindholm. 2016. 'Speaking Law to Power: The Strategic Use of Precedent of the Court Of Justice of the European Union.' *Comparative Political Studies* 50 (7): 879–907.

Lewis, David Kellogg. 1969. *Convention: A Philosophical Study*. Harvard University Press.

Lupu, Yonatan, and Erik Voeten. 2012. 'Precedent in International Courts: A Network Analysis of Case Citations by the European Court of Human Rights.' *British Journal of Political Science* 42 (2): 413–439.

March, James G., and Johan P. Olsen. 1998. 'The Institutional Dynamics of International Political Orders.' *International Organization* 52 (4): 943–969.

McNay, Lois. 2019. 'The Politics of Exemplarity: Ferrara on the Disclosure of New Political Worlds.' *Philosophy & Social Criticism* 45 (2): 127–145.

Noyes, Dorothy. 2016. 'Gesturing Toward Utopia: Toward a Theory of Exemplarity.' *NU* 53 (1): 75–95.

Pelc, Krzysztof J. 2014. 'The Politics of Precedent in International Law: A Social Network Application.' *American Political Science Review* 108 (3): 547–564.

Pouliot, Vincent. 2021. 'The Gray Area of Institutional Change: How the Security Council Transforms Its Practices on the Fly.' *Journal of Global Security Studies* 6 (3): 1–18.

Raz, Joseph. 1999. *Engaging Reason: On the Theory of Value and Action.* Oxford University Press.

Ruys, Tom, Olivier Corten, and Alexandra Hofer, eds. 2018. *The Use of Force in International Law: A Case-Based Approach.* Oxford University Press.

Sandholtz, Wayne. 2008. 'Dynamics of International Norm Change: Rules against Wartime Plunder.' *European Journal of International Relations* 14 (1): 101–131.

Schauer, Frederick. 1987. 'Precedent.' *Stanford Law Review* 39 (3): 571–605.

Schauer, Frederick. 2008. 'Why Precedent in Law (and Elsewhere) is Not Totally (or Even Substantially) About Analogy.' *Perspectives on Psychological Science* 3 (6): 454–460.

Schelling, Thomas C. 1960. *The Strategy of Conflict.* Harvard University Press.

Segal, Jeffrey A., and Harold J. Spaeth. 1996. 'The Influence of Stare Decisis on the Votes of United States Supreme Court Justices.' *American Journal of Political Science* 40 (4): 971–1003.

Simma, Bruno. 1999. 'NATO, the UN and the Use of Force: Legal Aspects.' *European Journal of International Law* 10 (1): 1–22.

Verdier, Pierre-Hugues, and Erik Voeten. 2014. 'Precedent, Compliance, and Change in Customary International Law: An Explanatory Theory.' *American Journal of International Law* 108 (3): 389–434.

Wiener, Antje. 2018. *Contestation and Constitution of Norms in Global International Relations.* Cambridge University Press.

Young, H. Peyton. 1996. 'The Economics of Convention.' *Journal of Economic Perspectives* 10 (2): 105–122.

Young, H. Peyton. 1998. *Individual Strategy and Social Structure. An Evolutionary Theory of Institutions.* Princeton University Press.

Zimmermann, Lisbeth, Nicole Deitelhoff, Max Lesch, Antonio Arcudi, and Anton Peez. 2023. *International Norm Disputes: The Link between Contestation and Norm Robustness.* Oxford University Press.

8

Exemplarity in Global Resistance: Beyond Epics and Romanticism

Iratxe Perea Ozerin

Alternative reimaginations of the world, and the way we act upon them, constitute a powerful mobilizing force in world politics.[1] Opposition to the status quo seeks inspiration in previous attempts to transform it, adopting and reinterpreting alternative ideas and practices of resistance from these struggles. The examples set by episodes of collective action, thus, have the capacity to travel across time and space and inspire contestation elsewhere. Revolutionary theorists have particularly underscored the exemplary as a key aspect in the international impact of revolutions (Skocpol 1979, 3; Halliday 1999; Bukovansky 2002, 194; Lawson 2015). While also highlighting their direct and tangible effects, these scholars have mostly connected exemplarity in revolutions with the 'inspiration and ideological example' (Halliday 1999, 180), that is, their more indirect and intangible effects, related with their capacity to inspire other revolutionary processes, as well as to unleash counterrevolutions (Lawson 2015, 314–315; 2019, 35). Drawing on this literature, as well as feminist and postcolonial approaches, I have reconsidered the *exemplary* as an analytical framework to study the legacies of resistance (Perea Ozerin 2021).

In line with this book's aims, such a framework allows us to think of exemplarity as a political process that produces change, beyond more symbolic and ideological understandings of the example that dominate

---

[1] I would like to thank Dorothy Noyes and Tobias Wille for their insightful, encouraging, and helpful engagement with the chapter.

the mobilization of this notion in the study of collective action. It involves critically exploring the conditions of exemplarity in global resistance, in particular, as well as its limitations. These conditions do not only relate with the ideological and intangible. When revolutionary Cuba articulated the Organization of Solidarity with the People of Asia, Africa, and Latin America (OSPAAAL) and the Latin America Solidarity Organization (OLAS) in the 1960s, in order to coordinate with revolutionary movements in these regions, this was also part of an exemplary attempt to export the revolution abroad, to spread the example (Halliday 1999, 116–124, 230–233). Such attempts can also be identified as conditions of exemplarity in revolutions. I distinguish, thus, between direct and indirect exemplarity in global resistance. While direct exemplary legacies lead us more clearly to a material analysis, indirect exemplarity allows us to explore more intangible effects in the long term (Perea Ozerin 2021).

In terms of direct and material exemplarity, then, I propose to look at the material support and the transnational connections and infrastructures built by a movement or site of resistance in order to transcend a local or national scenario. Regarding indirect and immaterial exemplary legacies, I have considered four instances of analysis: first, the alternative ideas and the political cultures of opposition, resistance, and creation (Foran 1997, 2014) spread in the contestation process; second, the type of collective action deployed and its implications in terms of collective memory and shared emotions; third, the scope of the social transformation achieved; and, fourth, the politics of containment. While most of these conditions relate to performance, they will also allow us to analyze the rest of the stages in the process of exemplarity (see Noyes and Wille, Chapter 2, this volume).

Similarly, we must consider how all these factors interact with an international scenario of intersecting structural inequalities that shapes and constrains exemplarity in resistance, determining all the levels in the process. This involves considering not only whether the example of an episode of resistance remains valid to cite or emulate in the current international conditions, but also how those complex inequalities are reproduced within activism, producing exclusions and violences that limit exemplarity. The framework, thus, encourages us to rethink the narratives and knowledge produced on episodes of resistance, reconsidering: why are some examples taken up and others forgotten?

Indeed, the limits of the exemplary expose exclusionary legacies of activism, or even the non-exemplarity of certain challengers and projects, often the most radical ones, that get marginalized in a movement and subsequently silenced. The exemplarity of classic revolutions such as the French and the Russian results, to a great extent, from their challenging character, the alternative they posed not only at a domestic level, but to the international system (Halliday 1999; Lawson 2015). They constituted social revolutions

(Skocpol 1979) that aimed to transform political *and* socioeconomic structures, and they persist as an example of revolutionary transformation. However, the scope of the challenge and the changes introduced by these revolutions, and, not least, our knowledge and perception about them, are shaped and constrained by an uneven distribution of power and resources. The politics of resistance, and the politics of exemplarity *too*, are 'infused with power' (Enloe 2014), so what is exemplary and what is not responds to structural intersecting inequalities. Interrogating exemplarity and its limits, thus, exposes the complex evolution of trajectories of resistance and the sometimes contradictory ways subsequent activists and movements relate to previous sites of contestation.

In other words, such analysis seeks to facilitate the complicated but crucial task, especially for activism, of learning from our past without romanticizing it (Lorde 2007, 256). With that aim, the chapter discusses two forms of resistance through the lens of the exemplary: revolutions and transnational collective action, with special attention to the examples of the Haitian revolution in the Age of Revolutions' context, and the women's rights transnational movement of the 19th century and its connections with the abolitionist movement.

Revolutionary exemplarity: Haiti and the Age of Revolutions

Both International Relations (IR) and revolutionary theorists have often underestimated the international dimension of revolutions. IR has treated revolutions as isolated events that disrupt the normal course of events: once the revolution is overthrown the international order is reinstated (Halliday 1999, 20–21, 293–323). To the contrary, revolutionary theorists engaged with the international have insisted on the centrality and constitutive role of these phenomena in international relations (Halliday 1999, 2001; Lawson 2015). Causes, trajectories, and outcomes of revolutions are inextricably linked with the international. Changes in the international system like wars, economic crisis, or the decline of hegemonic powers can help create revolutionary situations, while revolutionary trajectories are shaped by the interconnections between local and transnational revolutionary actors. Similarly, revolutionary outcomes range from realignment of states' alliances to counterrevolutionary movements and demonstration effects (Lawson 2015). Indeed, revolutions introduce irreversible changes in the international order, to a great extent, through the example they set.

This is so because, beyond the pragmatic component of revolutionary diplomacy, revolutionaries have a more ambitious aspiration to transform the world, which stems from an understanding of the international system as the cause of their oppression (Halliday 1988, 1999; Lawson 2011). As a result, revolutions can challenge basic principles and institutions of the international order and pose alternatives that inspire contestation elsewhere, resulting in far-reaching international effects. In Lawson's (2019, 7) words, revolutions 'stand as a challenge to status quo authority, both at home and abroad, by virtue of the example they set in overcoming seemingly overwhelming forces and in their capacity to generate substantial changes both to the texture of their home societies and to international orders.' In that sense, 'and in the power of example they provide for oppressed people, [revolutions] do change the world' (Lawson 2019, 27).

From this perspective, scholars of revolutions have underlined the significance of the revolutionary period between late 18th and mid-19th centuries in the making of the modern world. Hobsbawm (1996, 112) argued that one of the greatest legacies of the French revolution was the creation of models of political uprising that could be used by revolutionary movements elsewhere. The French example shaped the European revolutions of the 1815–1848 period. The politics and the ideology of the 19th century, Hobsbawm said, were born under its influence. The ideas of the French revolution would inspire national and social movements, as well as intellectuals like Marx and Lenin, and subsequent anticolonial leaders (Skocpol 1979, 3). However, we cannot forget that in the Age of Revolutions, as Shilliam (2017) expresses, 'white Europeans and North Americans spoke of natural rights and freedoms while they remained traffickers and brutal exploiters of African flesh.'

It was only as a result of the Haitian revolution that in 1794 slavery was abolished (albeit temporarily) in the French empire (Dubois 2004a; Sala-Molins 2006).[2] For Dubois (2004a, 3), 'these events represented the most radical political transformation' of the period. Each step in the Haitian revolutionary process, starting with a mass insurrection in 1791 and culminating 'in the emergence of a modern "black state",' as Trouillot (1995, 89) writes, 'challenged further the ontological order of the West and the global order of colonialism.' As a result of this challenge and the successful overthrow of slavery, Haiti remains an example in anticolonial, antiracist and abolitionist trajectories of resistance.

If we look at the *direct and material exemplary legacies* of Haiti, the revolutionaries extended material support in the form of money, arms, and a printing press to Simón Bolívar's campaign for independence in South America (James 1989), for which Alexandre Pétion demanded in return the abolition of slavery in the region (Geggus 2002, 27–29). There had been previous contacts with pro-independence leaders in Venezuela and

---

[2] Napoleon reestablished slavery by the early 1800s and steps towards equality were overturned (Dubois 2004b; Sala-Molins 2006).

Colombia, and Haitian revolutionaries had supported various rebellious attempts. Haiti became the stronghold of revolutionary exiles. Still, it constituted an example of radical and violent Black revolution that also inspired fear and reluctance among conservative forces in the movement for independence. In the case of Bolívar, his exile in Haiti changed his view towards a more positive consideration of the Haitian revolution. After a failed expedition in 1816 supported by Haiti, Bolívar wrote to Pétion praising the example they had given to South America and stated that 'the principles of Haiti' would be found 'in all regions of the New World.'[3]

As well as a pragmatic interest in building alliances, Pétion's decision to back these efforts was also influenced by a revolutionary ambition to spread his anticolonial and antislavery ideals in the region. Indeed, under the Haitian influence, the revolution in South America radicalized and adopted a social component. In 1819 in the Congress of Angostura, Bolívar promoted a constitution that did include slaves' emancipation. Once the war was over, though, their allies in South America distanced themselves from Haiti for fears that it might nurture further rebellions. As a result of these material connections, thus, Haiti spread its example among abolitionist forces, but it persisted as an anti-model for conservative elites in the region (Martínez Peria 2016).

In terms of *indirect and immaterial exemplary legacies*, the ideological and symbolic challenge posed by the Haitian revolution was huge. In a world dominated by European powers, in which the racial supremacist project gained legitimation, Haiti's first constitution prohibited white ownership of land and was later amended to offer citizenship to anyone of African or Indian descent who took up residence in the country (Geggus 2001). Born as the first Latin American and Caribbean independent state in December 1804, Haiti's new Taíno name symbolized a break with its colonial past. The small state stood as an example for the rest of the colonies, as an alternative. Indeed, Trouillot (1995, 89) described the Haitian revolution as 'largely part of the unthinkable until the twentieth century.' 'For many who fought slavery – especially slaves elsewhere in the Americas – the Haitian revolution became an example of what could be accomplished and a source of hope. For those who defended slavery, it became an illustration of the disastrous consequences of freedom' (Dubois 2004a, 2).

The Haitian example nurtured an anticolonial and abolitionist political culture of resistance in the region. It established 'a theme of sorts' as slave revolts and antislavery struggles spread in the Americas (Selbin 2010, 145). Songs, symbols, and stories of the Haitian revolution immediately traveled through Jamaica, Cuba, Trinidad, US, and Brazil (Geggus 2001, x–xi).

---

[3] Letter from Bolívar to Petión, September 4, 1816, cited in Martínez Peria (2016, 10).

Haiti, thus, remained relevant for subsequent struggles for the abolition of slavery in the Americas and influenced movements for independence in Latin America and the Caribbean (Selbin 2010, 152). It also became 'a powerful story for the decolonization of Africa' (James 1989; Selbin 2010, 152). In terms of collective action, Haiti was an example in 'overcoming seemingly overwhelming forces,' as it defeated the world powers at the time: France, Britain, and Spain.

Besides, the alternative understanding of human rights in the Haitian revolution was 'not in the abstract, but in the actual overthrow of slavery' (Fick 2007, 395). This social transformation, however, was not later accompanied by further improvement in living conditions and welfare for the majority of Haitians. According to Carolyn Fick (2007), the political and economic structures of the state, masculine military values and the institution of the family were reinforced. Trouillot highlights the contradiction between the imposition of a system of 'militarized agriculture' and the revolutionary ideals to which Haitian people did hold. This was exacerbated, though, by efforts to reestablish economic dependence and the 'total disdain' for the Haitian independence from European and US leaders (Trouillot 1990, 35–58).

Indeed, as it inspired large insurrections in the region, especially in the decades that followed the 1791 uprising, fears of 'another Haiti' also unleashed an international counterrevolution that has influenced contemporary international relations. Ideologically and symbolically, the Haitian example nurtured emancipationism and abolitionism (Blackburn 1988), and it fueled a backlash in the form of conservatism and racism (Geggus 2001). Haiti functioned as a pretext to tighten slave and race codes in Cuba, US, or Brazil. Its victory against Bonaparte's France in 1804 'put all pro-slavery forces into a state of exceptional mobilization and brought down upon Haiti itself a Cold War that was to last until at least the 1860s, with the effect of fostering militarization and commercial isolation' (Blackburn 2001, 17).

US refusal of diplomatic relations with Haiti would last until 1862. Diplomatic and economic relations with France were restored in 1825, only after Haiti agreed to pay 'a fine for revolution.' Supported by their allies in the Congress of Vienna, which included a secret agreement that allowed France to attempt the reconquest of Haiti (Nesiah 2021, 254), the French demanded an indemnity of 150 million francs for their financial losses as a result of Haitian independence. In order to pay, Haiti had to borrow loans from French banks, entering a long cycle of debt (Dubois 2004a, 303–304) that would last until 1947. Dependence on US banks to pay the French debt opened the door for US intervention in the country that continues today, exposing the limited recognition of Haitian sovereignty in the 1825 deal. This was also clear in the hostility of the French response to former Haitian president Aristide's request in 2003 for the return of 21 billion dollars of indemnity funds. In 2004, France and the US collaborated in the *coup d'état* against Aristide. Today's Haitian national debt is 3.5 billion dollars, about a third of its GDP (Nesiah 2021).

Despite this ideological and material example, accounts of the Age of Revolutions emphasize the international role of the French or North American revolutions and scarcely mention Haiti (Trouillot 1995, 99). Modern ideas of equality are linked to these revolutions, ignoring how in North America enslavement and segregation persisted after the revolution, or how the French maintained other forms of domination and exclusion (Bhambra 2015, 269). Historical and academic silence over the Haitian revolution's role in world politics reflects 'a history of uneven power' (Trouillot 1995) that must be considered in order to explore exemplarity. It was in the context of the US antiracist struggles in the 1960s, and with the influence of C. L. R. James' (1989 [1938]) work, reedited in 1967, that an international counternarrative on Haiti emerged, contesting dominant discourses in Western academia that erased or undermined the international relevance and revolutionary nature of the Haitian process, as well as the agency of Haitian revolutionaries (Trouillot 1995, 70–107).

Despite its historical silencing[4] Haiti has once again resonated in the Black Lives Matter (BLM) movement, as an example for any social movement emerging 'in response to anti-Blackness.' As Grégory Pierrot has put it:

> Think about what it means to be Black in hegemonic white countries, and what it means to see again, year after year, people get executed by police and see absolutely no consequences. And the effort to organize politically in response to this, to me evokes the Haitian Revolution, because I consider it the moment when Blackness became political.[5]

Ibram X. Kendi has also referred to the Haitian revolution as an example of the possibility of sweeping social change, as 'quite possibly the most impossible moment of change in modern history happened in Haiti.'[6]

---

[4] In terms of academic silence, in a revision of the last decade's scholarly work on the Haitian revolution, Popkin (2021) argues that even if the silence exposed by Trouillot was already being addressed a decade ago, this literature still needs to confront the problems and dilemmas he identified at the time, and there are many aspects of the revolution that remain to be explored. This neglect has also been acknowledged in revolutionary studies (see Selbin 2010; Lawson 2015).

[5] Cited in Tayo Bero, 'How the Black Lives Matter movement redefines "common good",' CBC Radio. April 8, 2021, Online: https://www.cbc.ca/radio/ideas/how-the-black-lives-matter-movement-redefines-common-good-1.5976575 (accessed June 9, 2025).

[6] Cited in 'Ibram Kendi talks to Coloradans about racism.' The Colorado Trust. August 4, 2021, Online: https://www.coloradotrust.org/stories/ibram-kendi-talks-to-coloradans-about-racism/ (accessed June 9, 2025).

Exemplarity in transnational social movements: feminist legacies

If we further revisit the example of the French revolution, neither the idea of liberty nor that of equality were extended to women. Despite an important participation of women, Moghadam (1997, 139–142, 2018, 34) has described it as a patriarchal model of revolution. According to Jane Abray (1975, 62), revolutionary feminism in France put forward 'a comprehensive program for social change, perhaps the most far-reaching such program of the Revolution.' It was this radicalism, Abray (1975) suggests, that ensured the minimization of feminist activism at the time and in subsequent accounts of the process. Indeed, erasures of gender and women have been persistent in accounts of revolutions and social movements (Moghadam 1997, 133; 2000, 57–59), generating limiting and misleading understandings of feminist legacies and trajectories of resistance. As a result, women's struggles and feminist examples have been underresearched and depoliticized. In particular, the 19th-century women's rights movement constituted an early example of transnational organizing that has been often downplayed, and sometimes romanticized, in accounts of resistance.

In terms of *direct and material exemplary legacies*, feminist activists had articulated transnational infrastructures by the end of the 19th century, including the still active International Council of Women (ICW) (Keck and Sikkink 1998, 41–58). This campaign followed the transnational organization of the abolitionist movement. The Anglo-American campaign to abolish slavery in the US extended between 1833 and 1865, and the first World Antislavery Convention took place in London in 1840, more than two decades before the 1864 founding of the workers' First International. Women's and antislavery organizing constitute early cases of transnational social movements (TSM), a form of resistance that reached a climax with the intensification of neoliberal globalization in the 1980s and 1990s, consolidating these type of movements as international actors. Both campaigns played an important role in transnationally diffusing repertoires and tactics (such as petitioning or boycott) that have been inherited by contemporary TSMs (Keck and Sikkink 1998).

Crucially, at an *indirect and immaterial* level, activists within these movements with an intersectional understanding of the struggle offered an example, albeit 'failed' at the time, of intersectional movement building. As Angela Davis (1981, 50–134) documented, 19th-century activists such as Maria Stewart, Sojourner Truth, Frederick Douglass, Lucrecia Mott, or Sarah and Angelina Grimke identified the possibilities of establishing connections between antislavery and feminist struggles, rooted in an intersectional understanding of oppression. According to Davis (1981, 109), activists like Angelina Grimke were 'far more advanced than most of her contemporaries' in identifying 'that the democratic struggles of the times – especially the fight for women's equality – could be most effectively waged in association with the struggle for Black Liberation.' These activists were also aware of how exclusionary ideas and practices could be reproduced in resistance.

Indeed, abolitionist women were excluded from the World Antislavery Convention, and Black women were absent at the Seneca Falls Convention in 1848 and erased from the convention's documents. The demands of women working in wage labor were also ignored in the Seneca Falls Declaration, even if US women mill workers, for example, had organized since the late 1820s, long before Seneca Falls, around a discourse on the 'double oppression' they suffered as women and industrial workers. By the 1840s, 'women workers were in the leadership of labor militancy in the United States' (Baxandall, Gordon, and Reverby 1976, 66; cited in Davis 1981, 88). Black feminist activists like Anna Julia Cooper also framed their condition as 'doubly enslaved' (hooks 2015, 19).

These frames on 'double oppression' and 'double enslavement' constitute early examples of intersectional thinking in resistance. As Patricia Hill Collins and Sirma Bilge (2016, 23) remind us, intersectionality's central contribution as a way to understand the world is the idea 'that major axes of social divisions in a given society at a given time, for example, race, class, gender, sexuality, dis/ability, and age operate not as discrete and mutually exclusive entities, but build on each other and work together.' In Audre Lorde's (2007, 255) words, 'there is no such thing as a single-issue struggle because we do not live single-issue lives.' This understanding of social problems is of particular relevance in transnational collective action, as these activists attempt to interconnect issues and transcend frontiers (Hill Collins and Bilge 2016, 255–263).

Despite efforts by these activists, though, the alternative ideas and praxis of intersectionality were not predominantly embraced by the early abolitionist and feminist transnational movements. Indeed, white abolitionists and advocates of women's rights were not in general antiracist, even if this idea has predominated in romanticized accounts of the movement. Still, the discourse on racist and sexist oppression and the call for political solidarity from Black feminists in the 19th-century movement, such as Mary Church Terrell, Josephine St. Pierre Ruffin, Fannie Barrier Williams, or Anna Cooper (hooks 2015, 223–360), did transcend across time and space. Sojourner Truth's 'Ain't I a woman?' speech at a women's convention in Akron, Ohio in 1851 – even if an inaccurate version of the original discourse[7] – is one of the most quoted slogans of the 19th-century women's movement (Davis 1981, 96). Truth's thinking and practice inspired Black feminist activists and research

---

[7] See *The Sojourner Truth Project*, https://www.thesojournertruthproject.com/ (accessed June 9, 2025).

that pioneered the conceptualization and praxis of intersectionality, such as the US movement of the 1970s Combahee River Collective,[8] and landmark works on the matter by bell hooks (2015) or Kimberlé Crenshaw (1989).

Research on intersectionality by Black and Third World feminists since the 1960s–1970s (see Mohanty and Alexander 1997; Carty and Mohanty 2015), constitute arguably one of the most important contributions for contemporary TSMs, both from an ideological and practical perspective. It has informed (re)conceptualizations and debates on *transnational feminism* since the 1990s (Nash 2021), a conception that 'not only marks connections that cross national borders but also places those articulations under critical scrutiny to diagnose how power operates within them in asymmetric and multidirectional ways' (Tambe and Thayer 2021, 4). Crucially, intersectional approaches expose how 'abstract universalisms,' also in struggles for social justice, have failed to include structurally oppressed groups. They have influenced the praxis of movements such as BLM, in which intersectionality becomes a pragmatic tool to avoid 'second marginalization,' that is, reproducing *within* movements the hierarchies that exist in the wider society. These activists incorporate a 'margin-to-center ethic' in its practices that seeks to prioritize the lives of the most marginalized (Woodly 2019), putting forward wider and more inclusive political cultures of resistance. This understanding of activism and movement building constitute an important social transformation in which 19th-century Black feminists have had an influence.

In terms of collective action, the 19th-century abolitionist and women's rights movements were exemplary for contemporary TSMs in their effective use of petition (Davis 1981, 65), tactics of civil disobedience, boycott and symbolic politics, as well as less resonant tasks such as exchanging letters and visits (Keck and Sikkink 1998, 39–78). However, Black feminists' call for political solidarity and broad alliance-building did not materialize. As Audre Lorde (2007, 261) put it,

> militancy no longer means guns at high noon, if it ever did. It means actively working for change, sometimes in the absence of any surety that change is coming. It means doing the unromantic and tedious work necessary to forge meaningful coalitions, and it means recognizing which coalitions are possible and which coalitions are not.

---

[8] See 'A Black Feminist Statement' (Combahee River Collective 2004 [1977]). It is noteworthy in terms of exemplarity that the name of this organization comes from the guerrilla action led by Harriet Tubman on June 2, 1863, in South Carolina, that freed more than 750 enslaved people. Like the group stated, it was 'the only military campaign in American history planned and led by a woman' (Combahee River Collective 2004 [1977], 244).

Given the persistent complexities of 'building solidarity across differences' (Baksh and Harcourt 2015, 22–23), the example of these 'failed' challengers (see Perea Ozerin 2021, 9) in the 19th-century movement remains relevant, particularly in TSMs. It resonates, for example, in the emphasis put by transnational networks born in the context of the Alter-globalization Movement, such as the World March of Women, on alliance-building and cross-sectoral alliances (Conway 2007; World March of Women 2008, 39–40; Conway 2017). Still, it is a case whose exemplarity is not properly recognized in mainstream academic narratives and literature on the 19th-century movement.

In general, the example set by 19th-century abolitionist and women's rights activism for contemporary TSMs has been downplayed in literature on social movements. As an expression of this marginalization, accounts of global resistance in the 1960s and 1970s have referred to feminist collective action in that period as part of the so-called 'new' social movements, which also included antiracist, peace movements, or environmental activism (see Kaldor 2003; Della Porta and Diani 2020). These trajectories of resistance were obscured by the centrality of the male labor movement and national liberation movements in the study of global resistance. André Günder Frank and Marta Fuentes (1990) also pointed at a focus on the evolution of the nation-state in contemporary history. As a result, labor and national liberation movements, which targeted the state and identified 'taking power' with state's control, would have overshadowed these 'other' activists in accounts of trajectories of resistance. At the same time, accounts of the 19th-century women's rights movement in US contemporary history long ignored the role of Black feminists, overemphasizing their commitment to the antiracist struggle and suggesting this precluded involvement in the women's rights movement (hooks 2015, 296–299). Such oversimplified accounts neglect the example of non-dominant radical challengers in broader episodes of collective action, misreading trajectories of resistance and movements' legacies.

Understanding (exemplary) trajectories of resistance

The analytical lens of the exemplary deepens into the long-term legacies of episodes of contestation across time and space, resituating accounts of revolutionary and social movement trajectories. From an activist perspective, it seeks to be a tool to learn from the past, considering past instances of resistance and the process of exemplarity in their complexity, and recognizing how they shape current struggles without romanticizing them.

So, what example did the Haitian revolution set? And, what do we learn from it? Most importantly, Haiti stands as the possibility of change. Haitian revolutionaries challenged the international colonial order and defeated the great colonial powers at the time, which produced an important symbolic legacy for antiracist movements that persists today. As an unthinkable performance at the time, the Haitian example immediately resonated in abolitionist thinking and organizing, and influenced subsequent anticolonial and antiracist struggles. However, status quo powers and elites perceived it as an example that had to be contained, which affected the scope of the social transformation achieved, also limited by domestic factors.

Such containment politics reached Western accounts and narratives on Haiti that have sought to downplay its revolutionary character and scope, as well as the agency of Haitian revolutionaries, in contrast to political and academic narratives that have emphasized the international and social transformations introduced by the North American and French revolutions. As a result, amplification and emulation were contained and the exemplarity process limited. This trend on Haiti, though, started to be internationally countered in the context of the antiracist struggles in US in the 1960s that judged it as an example to be amplified. This shows how exemplarity is a political process shaped and constrained by uneven power relations, which also questions our role as scholars and researchers in critically exploring historical examples and accounts of exemplarity. Outside Haiti, the Haitian example persisted in the discourse and practice of revolutionary and social struggles, which ultimately facilitated a shift in the academic narrative.

In the case of the women's rights movement from the 19th century, there were radical challengers within the movement that were exemplary in their ideas and proposals on double oppression and cross-sectoral alliance-building. These ideas were not embraced by the dominant trends of the movement and the example actually failed in practice and was not emulated. However, this performance has resonated in Black feminist scholars' accounts that have more fully grasped the complexities in 19th-century feminist activism, over more limited and romanticized depictions of the movement's legacies. As a result, this radical project of the 19th century managed to be amplified and inspired subsequent theorizations of intersectionality and transnational feminism by Black and Third World feminist scholars and activists. It persists as a crucial example for contemporary transnational collective action, especially in a world scenario of intensified neoliberal globalization and restructuring – with uneven and variegated patterns but global scope- that affects multiple societal sites (see Bakker and Gill 2003, 2019; Marchand and Runyan 2011; Bruff and Tansel 2019).

This example is also of utmost importance for the study of the international impact of collective action, including the analysis deployed here. While the international effects of the 19th-century abolitionist and women's rights transnational campaigns have been explored in terms of their achievements vis-à-vis their most immediate aims (abolition of slavery and women's suffrage) and the use of tactics that would be later deployed by TSMs (see Keck and Sikkink 1998), reconsidering exemplarity and its limits exposes how activism matters beyond their most immediate achievements (or failures) and not only because of the diffusion of tactics, but as a result of the radical challenge they pose to international orders.

Failures in amplification, emulation, and citation leading to limited or non-exemplarity might result from revolutionaries' or activists' agency and failed social transformation projects, but also from containment politics against radical challengers. As we have seen in this chapter, these include counterrevolutionary policies, often 'making an example of the transgressor' (see Noyes and Wille, Chapter 2, this volume), marginalization or repression within movements, as well as oversimplified, depoliticizing accounts of performances. Limits in exemplarity should also be connected with the gendered nature of the politics of resistance (Marchand 2003), particularly considering that movements targeting the 'public' space of the state through more spectacular actions have been historically considered more exemplary, while antisystemic movements radically questioning the 'private' origins of power politics and often using more 'unromantic and tedious' or everyday tactics have been underestimated and depoliticized.

References

Abray, Jane. 1975. 'Feminism in the French Revolution.' *The American Historical Review* 80 (1): 43–62.

Bakker, Isabella, and Stephen Gill, eds. 2003. *Power, Production and Social Reproduction: Human In/Security in the Global Political Economy*. Palgrave Macmillan.

Bakker, Isabella, and Stephen Gill. 2019. 'Rethinking Power, Production, and Social Reproduction: Toward Variegated Social Reproduction.' *Capital & Class* 43 (4): 503–523.

Baksh, Rawwida, and Wendy Harcourt, eds. 2015. *The Oxford Handbook of Transnational Feminist Movements*. Oxford University Press.

Baxandall, Rosalyn, Linda Gordon, and Susan Reverby. 1976. *America's Working Women: A Documentary History, 1600 to the Present*. Random House.

Bhambra, Gurminder K. 2015. 'On the Haitian Revolution and the Society of Equals.' *Theory, Culture & Society* 32 (7–8): 267–274.

Blackburn, Robin. 1988. *The Overthrow of Colonial Slavery, 1776–1848*. Verso.

Blackburn, Robin. 2001. 'The Force of the Example.' In *The Impact of the Haitian Revolution in the Atlantic World*, edited by David Patrick Geggus. University of South Carolina Press.

Bruff, Ian, and Cemal Burak Tansel. 2019. 'Authoritarian Neoliberalism: Trajectories of Knowledge Production and Praxis.' *Globalizations* 16 (3): 233–244.

Bukovansky, Mlada. 2002. *Legitimacy and Power Politics: The American and French Revolutions in International Political Culture*. Princeton University Press.

Carty, Linda E., and Chandra T. Mohanty. 2015. 'Mapping Transnational Feminist Engagements. Neoliberalism and the Politics of Solidarity.' In *The Oxford Handbook of Transnational Feminist Movements*, edited by Rawwida Baksh and Wendy Harcourt. Oxford University Press.

Combahee River Collective. 2004. 'A Black Feminist Statement.' In *This Bridge Called My Back: Writings by Radical Women of Color*, edited by Cherríe Moraga and Gloria Anzaldúa, 4th ed. State University of New York Press.

Conway, Janet. 2007. 'Transnational Feminisms and the World Social Forum: Encounters and Transformations in Anti-Globalization Spaces.' *Journal of International Women's Studies* 8 (3): 49–70.

Conway, Janet. 2017. 'Troubling Transnational Feminism(s): Theorising Activist Praxis.' *Feminist Theory* 18 (2): 205–227.

Crenshaw, Kimberlé. 1989. 'Demarginalizing the Intersection of Race and Sex: A Black Feminist Critique of Antidiscrimination Doctrine, Feminist Theory and Antiracist Politics.' *University of Chicago Legal Forum* 1: 139–167.

Davis, Angela Y. 1981. *Women, Race & Class*. Random House.

Della Porta, Donatella, and Mario Diani. 2020. *Social Movements: An Introduction*. 3rd ed. Wiley-Blackwell.

Dubois, Laurent. 2004a. *Avengers of the New World: The Story of the Haitian Revolution*. Harvard University Press.

Dubois, Laurent. 2004b. *A Colony of Citizens: Revolution and Slave Emancipation in the French Caribbean, 1787–1804*. University of North Carolina Press.

Enloe, Cynthia. 2014. *Bananas, Beaches and Bases: Making Feminist Sense of International Politics*. University of California Press.

Fick, Carolyn E. 2007. 'The Haitian Revolution and the Limits of Freedom: Defining Citizenship in the Revolutionary Era.' *Social History* 32 (4): 394–414.

Foran, John, ed. 1997. *Theorizing Revolutions*. Routledge.

Foran, John. 2014. 'Beyond Insurgency to Radical Social Change: The New Situation.' *Studies in Social Justice* 8 (1): 5–25.

Fuentes, Marta, and Andre Gunder Frank. 1990. 'Civil Democracy: Social Movements in Recent Word History.' In *Transforming the Revolution. Social Movements and the World System*, edited by Samir Amin, Giovanni Arrighi, Andre Gunder Frank, and Immanuel Wallerstein. Monthly Review Press.

Geggus, David P., ed. 2001. *The Impact of the Haitian Revolution in the Atlantic World*. University of South Carolina.

Geggus, David P. 2002. *Haitian Revolutionary Studies*. Indiana University Press.

Halliday, Fred. 1988. 'Three Concepts of Internationalism.' *International Affairs* 64 (2): 187–198.

Halliday, Fred. 1999. *Revolution and World Politics: The Rise and Fall of the Sixth Great Power*. Palgrave Macmillan.
Halliday, Fred. 2001. 'The Great Anomaly.' *Review of International Studies* 27 (4): 693–699.
Hill Collins, Patricia, and Sirma Bilge. 2016. *Intersectionality*. Polity Press.
Hobsbawm, Eric. 1996. *The Age of Revolution: 1789–1848*. Vintage Books.
hooks, bell. 2015. *Ain't I a Woman: Black Women and Feminism*. 2nd ed. Routledge.
James, C.L.R. 1989. *The Black Jacobins: Toussaint L'Ouverture and the San Domingo Revolution*. 2nd ed. Vintage Books.
Kaldor, Mary. 2003. *Global Civil Society: An Answer to War*. Polity Press.
Keck, Margaret E., and Kathryn Sikkink. 1998. *Activists beyond Borders: Advocacy Networks in International Politics*. Cornell University Press.
Lawson, George. 2011. 'Halliday's Revenge: Revolutions and International Relations.' *International Affairs* 87 (5): 1067–1085.
Lawson, George. 2015. 'Revolutions and the International.' *Theory and Society* 44 (4): 299–319.
Lawson, George. 2019. *Anatomies of Revolution*. Cambridge University Press.
Lorde, Audre. 2007. *Sister Outsider: Essays and Speeches*. Crossing Press.
Marchand, Marianne H. 2003. 'Challenging Globalisation: Toward a Feminist Understanding of Resistance.' *Review of International Studies* 29: 145–160.
Marchand, Marianne H., and Anne Sisson Runyan. 2011. *Gender and Global Restructuring: Sightings, Sites and Resistances*. 2nd ed. Routledge.
Martínez Peria, Juan Francisco. 2016. 'Entre el terror y la solidaridad: La influencia de la revolución haitiana en las independencias de Venezuela y Nueva Granada (1804–1825).' *Anuario del Instituto de Historia Argentina* 16 (1): 1-20. https://www.anuarioiha.fahce.unlp.edu.ar/article/view/IHAv16n1a06 (accessed June 9, 2025).
Moghadam, Valentine M. 1997. 'Gender and Revolutions.' In *Theorizing Revolutions*, edited by John Foran. Routledge.
Moghadam, Valentine M. 2000. 'Transnational Feminist Networks: Collective Action in an Era of Globalization.' *International Sociology* 15 (1): 57–85.
Moghadam, Valentine M. 2018. 'Feminism and the Future of Revolutions.' *Socialism and Democracy* 32 (1): 31–53.
Mohanty, Chandra Talpada, and M. Jacqui Alexander, eds. 1997. *Feminist Genealogies, Colonial Legacies, Democratic Futures*. Routledge.
Nash, Jennifer C. 2021. 'Beyond Antagonism: Rethinking Intersectionality, Transnationalism, and the Women's Studies Academic Job Market.' In *Transnational Feminist Itineraries: Situating Theory and Activist Practice*, edited by Ashwini Tambe and Millie Thayer. Duke University Press.
Nesiah, Vasuki. 2021. 'A Double Take on Debt: Reparations Claims and Shifting Regimes of Visibility.' In *Routledge Handbook of International Law and the Humanities*, edited by Shane Chalmers and Sundhya Pahuja. Routledge.

Perea Ozerin, Iratxe. 2021. 'The Exemplary in Transnational Social Movements: The Legacies of the Alterglobalization Movement.' *International Political Sociology* 15 (2): 232–250.

Popkin, Jeremy D. 2021. 'The Haitian Revolution Comes of Age: Ten Years of New Research.' *Slavery & Abolition* 42 (2): 382–401.

Sala-Molins, Louis. 2006. *Dark Side of the Light: Slavery and the French Enlightenment*. University of Minnesota Press.

Selbin, Eric. 2010. *Revolution, Rebellion, Resistance*. Zed Books.

Shilliam, Robbie. 2017. 'Race and Revolution at Bwa Kayiman.' *Millennium: Journal of International Studies* 45 (3): 269–292.

Skocpol, Theda. 1979. *States and Social Revolutions. A Comparative Analysis of France, Russia and China*. Cambridge University Press.

Tambe, Ashwini, and Millie Thayer, eds. 2021. *Transnational Feminist Itineraries: Situating Theory and Activist Practice*. Duke University Press.

Trouillot, Michel-Rolph. 1990. *Haiti: State Against Nation*. Monthly Review Press.

Trouillot, Michel-Rolph. 1995. *Silencing the Past: Power and the Production of History*. Beacon Press.

Woodly, Deva. 2019. 'Black Feminist Visions and the Politics of Healing in the Movement for Black Lives.' In *Women Mobilizing Memory*, edited by Ayşe Gül Altınay, María José Contreras, Marianne Hirsch, Jean Howard, Banu Karaca, and Alisa Solomon. Columbia University Press.

World March of Women. 2008. *1998–2008. Una Década de Lucha Internacional Feminista (2008)*. http://www.inmujer.gob.es/publicacioneselectronicas/documentacion/Documentos/DE1196.pdf (accessed June 9, 2025).

PART IV

Exemplary Orders

9

Exemplarity and Hierarchy

Ayşe Zarakol

Introduction

The power of example is celebrated in liberal discourse, which prides itself also on its egalitarianism, or the promise of such. But even the most liberal orders produce their own inequalities, and liberalism can sometimes act as a cover for very sharp social hierarchies. In this chapter, therefore, I will explore the ways[1] in which the mechanism of 'exemplarity'[2] can intersect with dynamics of (social) hierarchies, within the specific context of International Relations (IR).

'Hierarchy' can be defined as any system through which actors are organized into vertical relations of super and sub-ordination (Bially-Mattern and Zarakol 2016; Zarakol 2017). The question of exemplarity within hierarchy can be approached from a number of angles. In any given hierarchy, there are actors who occupy the higher ranks and benefit most clearly from the way that particular hierarchy is organized. Then there are those who are at lower rungs and are most disadvantaged. Finally, some actors occupy middle positions, harboring aspirations of moving up. The proportion of actors in each rank varies depending on the hierarchy. Such differences between hierarchies notwithstanding, we can generally ponder about what functions 'exemplarity' can serve in any given hierarchy and how the notion of 'exemplarity' can factor into the mobility strategies of actors in each level of the hierarchy.

---

[1] Parts of this chapter borrow from my previous work (as cited throughout) in order to engage the concept of exemplarity with standing theoretical discussions.

[2] For definitions, see Chapter 1 and Chapter 2 of this volume.

In this chapter, I start from the observation that 'exemplarity' is particularly useful in political orders that have the outward appearance of egalitarianism while continuing to depend on hierarchies to function and that allow (or claim to allow) upward mobility for lower ranked actors. Hierarchies in 'liberal' orders – domestic or international – fit this description very well, including the 'liberal international order' and its precursors in the 20th century (for liberal hierarchies see Zarakol 2018; Adler-Nissen and Zarakol 2021; see also Ikenberry 2012, 2020; Lake, Martin, and Risse 2021 on the liberal international order more generally). This does not mean that exemplarity is inherently hierarchical (see also Noyes and Wille, Chapter 2, this volume). Nor does it imply that exemplarity is only useful for liberal orders or the actors in those orders. What it does mean is that liberal orders have a particular dynamic that imbues the notion of exemplarity with a specific kind of political power.

In liberal orders, higher-ranking middle actors can tap into a narrative of exemplarity to improve their status within the implicit hierarchies of these orders if they are following emulation strategies that bring them closer to the norms of the core (or higher-ranking actors). At the same time, the presence of such exemplary actors serves the interests of the higher-ranking actors within the liberal order as well because it creates the impression (or in some cases, the illusion) that whatever status hierarchy that currently exists is temporary and ephemeral, and that the system is in fact egalitarian and inclusive in its essence. This argument can be used against detractors to insist that equal recognition and treatment for lower-ranking (or even outside) actors is possible if said actors follow the necessary steps. The presence of exemplary actors that are claimed to have achieved a betterment of their status is then used by higher-ranking actors to legitimize the existing order. There is an inherent tension in this process, however: the exemplary actors often become attached to their exemplary status, and their continued exemplary status undercuts promises that the existing hierarchy will in the future transform into an egalitarian order. In a truly egalitarian order, exemplarity as a status would either not exist or be ephemeral.

This chapter proceeds in four sections. The first section briefly reviews recent debates in IR about the relationship between anarchy and hierarchy in order to contextualize the concept of exemplarity within IR theorizing. The second section discusses the ways the modern international order – the Liberal International Order and its precursors – has functioned as a social hierarchy for much of its existence. The third section illustrates how the narrative of exemplarity has been used by certain countries as a strategy within the social hierarchy of the international order. The chapter concludes with considering the limits of the exemplarity strategy in international relations of the past as well as going forward.

Anarchy, hierarchy and exemplarity in IR

Anarchy has been one of the most foundational assumptions for IR. Most IR textbooks teach that what separates international politics from domestic politics is the fact that international relations are characterized by a structure of anarchy whereas domestic politics is characterized by hierarchy (Waltz 1979). States are understood to exist in a context of anarchy because there is no world government that is sovereign over them. When the American Political Science Association was formed in 1903, the study of political science 'was basically synonymous with the state,' which was conceptualized juristically: 'This conception of sovereignty depicted the state as an expression of supreme authority over a territorially defined political community' (Schmidt 1997, 79). From this perspective, 'states occupied a position similar to that of the individuals living in a state of nature' and therefore international law (which 19th-century jurists had recognized) did not embody the 'true characteristics of law' (Schmidt 1997, 79). In other words, in the 20th century, states have been understood in IR – rhetorically and conceptually – to be the equivalents of individuals (Ringmar 1996). The notion of sovereign equality among states mirrors basic assumptions of liberalism about individual autonomy and equality of opportunity (see also Zarakol 2018). We will return to this point later.

The importance of the anarchy assumption in IR theorizing was further cemented in the latter part of the 20th century, after the success of Waltz's *Theory of International Politics* (Waltz 1979). According to Jack Donnelly, the success of the anarchy concept in IR after Waltz can be explained in reference to three factors: its association with structural realism, which offered the promise of an elegant systemic theory of international politics (and thus became the dominant approach in the last quarter of the 20th century), its appeal to rationalist approaches as a starting assumption and its presentation 'as an analytically neutral demarcation criterion' (Donnelly 2015, 401). As a result, until recently, most (mainstream) IR theories – at least in the US – assumed anarchy (and thus sovereign equality) to be a given in world politics and did not bother to theorize very much about stratification or inequality between states.

In recent years, however, the 'hierarchy turn' in IR[3] has challenged the idea that anarchy is the best starting point in thinking about international politics.

---

[3] See, for example, Wendt and Friedheim 1995; Lake 1996, 2007, 2009, 2013, 2017; Keene 2002, 2013; Cooley 2003, 2011; Dunne 2003; Kang 2003, 2004, 2005; Simpson 2004; Hobson and Sharman 2005; Donnelly 2006; Nexon and Wright 2007; Goh 2008; Bowden 2009; Hobson 2012; Butt 2013; Barder 2015; Bially Mattern and Zarakol 2016; Phillips 2017, 2018; Suzuki 2017; Zarakol 2017a, 2017b, 2017c; Mcconaughey, Musgrave, and

This turn advocated for taking hierarchy in international politics more seriously for a number of reasons. First, world politics have been rather hierarchical for much of history: there are many more examples in the past of empires, tributary systems, feudal arrangements, and so on, than of states that legally recognize each other as sovereign equals. Because so much of IR theorizing relies on history, it is important to get the conceptual lens right, and projecting anarchy back in time often distorts the past (Zarakol 2020, 2022). Second, given that historical norm in world politics used to be hierarchy rather anarchy, and that we now seem to be at a moment of international crisis, there is every possibility that we may be headed to a future in international politics that is more formally or explicitly hierarchical (Zarakol 2017c). Third, and most importantly, despite the superficial fact of anarchy, even today's international system is characterized by many hierarchies: social, economic, political. Thus, to understand world politics better we need to think about its hierarchical aspects: in what ways are 'international relations' hierarchical, where do international hierarchies come from, how do international actors operate in hierarchies, how are international hierarchies reproduced and so on. The mechanism of exemplarity, as explored in this volume, is one of the things that can also help us in this quest.

Of course, IR scholars have been studying hierarchies even before the 'hierarchy turn.'[4] A comprehensive survey of the existing IR literature[5] reveals that hierarchies have been understood in a number of fundamental ways in IR. To briefly summarize: first, IR scholars observe that the structures of differentiation at the core of hierarchical systems are deeply implicated with power. Hierarchical systems are thus intrinsically political. Second, in world politics, hierarchies stratify, rank, and organize the relations not only among states but also other kinds of actors as well, and often even a mix of different actors within a single structure of differentiation. Third, there are many different kinds of hierarchical relations in international politics. However, since different hierarchies can and often do intersect each other, these logics can be nested.

Nexon 2018; Musgrave 2019; Musgrave and Nexon 2018; MacKay 2019; Nedal and Nexon 2019; Schulz 2019; Spanu 2020; Subotić and Zarakol 2020; and so on.

[4] There are also various schools of thought such as Marxism and its variants, including World Systems approaches (for example, Wallerstein 1984; Arrighi 1994; Frank 1998) and approaches rooted in Uneven and Combined Development (for example, Rosenberg 2013; Anievas and Nisancioglu 2015), or post-colonial approaches (for example, Grovogui 2016; Barkawi and Laffey 2006), which never conceded the anarchy assumption to begin with.

[5] For extended versions of this discussion, see Bially Mattern and Zarakol 2016; Zarakol 2017b, 2017c.

As I have also explained elsewhere (Zarakol 2017b), IR research on hierarchy thus far could be observed to have gravitated toward two major research questions: (A) 'What is the nature of hierarchy?' (with the accompanying questions of: 'What is hierarchy made of?'; 'How is hierarchy made?'; 'Where does hierarchy come from' and so on), and (B) 'How do actors exist in hierarchies?' (with the accompanying questions of: 'How do actors use/navigate/reproduce/resist/escape existing hierarchies?'; 'How do existing hierarchies function?'; 'How are existing hierarchies sustained or dismantled?'). The mechanism of exemplarity operates under B), but in order to understand how, we first need to briefly review how hierarchies are made.

One dominant strain of IR research, associated closely with neoliberal institutionalism, understands hierarchies – and a given actor's position within a hierarchy – as arising in the first place from bargained solutions to problems of order. In this understanding, hierarchies are founded on exchanges in which actors trade degrees of freedom for a desired social or political arrangement. Accordingly, hierarchies institutionalize interests in that order, and this distinctively affects actors' incentives and disincentives to create compliant and non-compliant outcomes. This line of research generally operates with a *narrow* conception of hierarchy as legitimate authority. To put it another way, this vein of research is primarily interested in how and why hierarchies are deliberately erected by specific actors as solutions to problems of anarchy, that is, in the origins of hierarchies. This is why the bulk of this research has focused on superordinate states, and in particular, the incentives they face to exercise self-restraint in spite of their right to govern through power as they see fit.

In direct contrast to the agentic-contractual accounts outlined, another dominant strain of IR research conceives hierarchies *broadly* as structures of organized inequality. Such accounts of hierarchy suggest that hierarchy does not just shape the behaviors of actors in world politics but rather produces *both* the actors and the space of world politics in which they act. In such accounts, hierarchies shape actors within their structure of differentiation as particular kinds of agents with particular capacities for action that belong, or do not, in some space of world politics. Hierarchies create the actors of world politics and/or their repertoires for action. They also produce the boundaries that define who and what belongs where in world politics. We tend to find this kind of understanding of hierarchy within critical approaches within IR that focus on social or economic inequalities.

One of the most important avenues of research on hierarchies in IR is actor behavior within and in response to existing hierarchical environments. This is where the concept of exemplarity can come in. This growing body of IR research is much less focused on the nature of hierarchy and much more on *how existing hierarchies shape actors*. This line of research generally asserts that the content of what actors want and what is important to them depends in part on where they are *positioned* in a hierarchical order. But clearly more work is still needed in exploring how hierarchies are maintained and reproduced, and how actors navigate hierarchies. As the next sections will demonstrate, the narrative of exemplarity can be strategically deployed by middle-ranking actors in order to improve their standing within an existing hierarchy.

The narrow understanding of hierarchy in IR as a designed institution assumes that hierarchies, once erected, will function more or less as planned. Actors' initial choices are significant in explaining the design of such hierarchies. The broad understanding of hierarchy as structure assumes that understanding the content of inequality and/or the shape of the structure will reveal more or less everything about how actors exist in hierarchies, and one does not need to pay much attention to the actors. The narrow approach, because it was operating with an implicit structure as anarchy assumption, has not considered very well how an institutional hierarchy, once erected, may interact with broad hierarchies, that is, structures of inequality. It has also not considered the impact of broad hierarchies in shaping actors and their choices. The broad approach, however, has not considered the possibility that the solution to the problems created by broad hierarchies may be hierarchies of the narrow type. One solution is for researchers focused on either understanding to consider the other in new empirical settings.

Thinking about exemplarity can also help us get at these questions in a more focused manner because the strategic deployment of the exemplarity discourse is particularly powerful in areas *where narrow and broad hierarchies intersect*. Exemplarity often implies a certain hierarchical relationship between the example ('role model') and those the example is supposed to serve as a model for. The dimension of hierarchy is almost always built into the concept itself. Furthermore, examples do not occur in a vacuum; whether something is considered an example or not depends on how the actors understand, interpret and narrate the situation, which points to more agentic understandings. At the same time, whether something can be cast as an example within a given narrative depends on shared understandings of what is normal and what (and who) is comparable, which depends on structural dimensions of hierarchy.

Is exemplarity a feature of all world political hierarchies or can there be exemplarity in (real) anarchy? It is unlikely that exemplary actors can exist in a genuine anarchy (though it is also debatable whether the latter has ever existed in human relations). This is because exemplarity within a given order implies both the notion that some kind of upward mobility is possible (because the example is rising above others in similar rank) and the notion that more than one actor is occupying each rank (because otherwise there would be no commensurability between the example and those that need to heed the example). There is both a vertical and a horizontal promise in exemplarity. Yet that observation also implies that exemplarity is also not very useful as a mechanism in very rigid hierarchies that did not allow for movement or commensurability among actors. In other words, if a given order consisted of a hierarchy that assigned each actor in the order of a distinct rank wherein neither upward nor downward mobility was not possible, there would be no need for 'exemplarity' in that order.

Neither type of society – pure anarchy or pure hierarchy – exists in practice, but thinking about the mechanism of exemplarity by using these hypotheticals underlines the point made in the introduction of this chapter: the mechanism of exemplarity is particularly useful in an interim kind of order, that is, that produced by liberalism and its discourse of (theoretical or future) equality. Using the hypothetical examples of full anarchy and full hierarchy at either end, we come to realize which type of society is more likely to use exemplarity as a form of maintaining and reproducing existing hierarchies: those hierarchies in which actors are understood to bear some type of similarity no matter the rank, where some kind of upward mobility is at least theoretically possible and acknowledged within the legitimating ideology of the hierarchy. A final observation linked to the notion of upward mobility: the exemplar is rarely the highest-ranking member of the hierarchy. The expression 'lead by example' is confusing precisely because modernity (especially liberal modernity) aims to obscure the existence of hierarchies and obscure the distance between those at the top of the hierarchy and those ranking lower, to create at least the impression that actors are interchangeable. Most pre-modern societies did the opposite because their legitimating ideologies did not depend on a belief in upward mobility but rather the idea that hierarchies were natural (God-given) and unchanging.

Now that this section has established the basic theoretical contours of how exemplarity can figure into IR discussions of anarchy and hierarchy, the next item on the agenda is to review the ways the modern international order has functioned as a social hierarchy despite surface appearance of anarchy and sovereign equality. This is the task of the next section. The following section after the next one will then discuss the ways the 'exemplarity' dynamic has been used by various actors as a stigmatization coping mechanism against such a backdrop of social hierarchy in world politics.

Social hierarchies in the modern (liberal) international order

For reasons explained in the previous section, the argument about exemplarity in the modern international order hinges on seeing the modern international order as a social hierarchy, notwithstanding the ostensible commitment to liberal principles and sovereign equality by core actors. In such an understanding, non-core actors understand and navigate the international order as a hierarchy and develop strategies to mitigate the effects of hierarchy. They may, for instance, join the narrow institutions of the liberal international order to improve their social standing within the broader structural hierarchies of world politics (see Adler-Nissen and Zarakol 2021).

IR scholarship, by contrast, has always attributed the attraction of the liberal international order for non-Western states to more rational incentives: investment and commitment of the US, the primary post-World War II hegemon; economic incentives; the persuasiveness of liberalism's normative model and norm entrepreneurs; the strength of liberal international institutions and rules or their cooperative-security practices.[6] What has been largely overlooked in these explanations are the historical and social broad hierarchies on which the liberal international order has rested. The current liberal international order, like its precursors, has functioned on the back of political, economic but especially social (religious, cultural, racial, and so on) hierarchies that have characterized relations between the West and the non-West since the emergence of the international system in the 19th century. Let's first review the arguments for thinking of the modern international order as a broad social hierarchy before we turn to why stigmatization against such a backdrop makes the utilization of the exemplarity discourse a potential coping strategy for middle-ranking actors.

The 19th century was a pivotal moment in the creation of modern international order not just because economic indicators in 'the West' clearly surpassed that of Asia for the first time (Buzan and Lawson 2015). Equally important was the emergence during the long 19th century of a particular social hierarchy that would characterize international relations for the next century and beyond (Zarakol 2011, 2014). In this dynamic, 'the West' came to be seen as the center of the international system and its political, economic, cultural, social standards came to define what was seen as 'normal.' The 19th-century European worldview was increasingly characterized by the belief that self-interest was not only rational but also moral. E. H. Carr called this worldview 'the harmony of interests' doctrine, and argues that it was first pushed along 'by the unparalleled expansion of production, population and prosperity, which marked the hundred years following the publication of *The Wealth of Nations* and the invention of the steam engine' (Carr 2001, 43–45). As competition got tougher, this worldview got a second push from the

---

[6] See, for example, Keohane 1984; Finnemore and Sikkink 1998; Keck and Sikkink 1998; Lake 1999; Ikenberry 2001, 2012; Pevehouse 2002; Adler 2008; Eichengreen and Leblang 2008; Simmons 2009; Lake 2010; Marinov and Goemans 2013; Nye 2017; Ikenberry 2018.

doctrine of evolution, which was applied to international politics to justify the ruthless land grab of the latter part of 19th century:

> The path of progress is strewn with the wreck of nations; traces are everywhere to be seen of the hecatombs of inferior races, and of victims who found not the narrow way to greater perfection. Yet these dead peoples are, in very truth, the stepping stones on which mankind has arisen to the higher intellectual and deeper emotional life of to-day. (Carr 2001, 47)

Not only was this seen as an apt description of how things were, but also of things should be. For example, Cecil Rhodes wrote: 'I contend that we are the first race in the world, and the more of the world we inhabit the better it is for the human race' (Carr 2001, 48). Note that this period is often taught in mainstream IR textbooks as the beginnings of a 'liberal' international order.

Imperialism was not a phenomenon unique to the 19th century (Zarakol 2022), but the particular tenor and justifications of it (as rooted in liberalism and Enlightenment) were (see also Bell 2007, 2016). As pointed out by Hobson and Sharman (2005), prior to the 19th century, a superior Europe-as-West identity had gradually emerged as Europeans, originally held together by a loose tie of Christendom, increasingly came to define themselves negatively against the natives in Africa and Americas, and also the infidels of the Ottoman Empire. This would crystallize into a fully-fledged racist ideology in the 18th and especially the 19th centuries, affecting even the understandings of what constitutes a 'Great Power.' Echoing Carr, Hobson and Sharman note that 'the British (and others) engaged in imperialism not simply because "they could" (as materialists assume). Rather they engaged in it because they believed they should' (Hobson and Sharman 2005, 85). Governing over large areas in the 'inferior non-European' world was taken as a mark of great power status.

All of these ideas were clearly manifested in 19th-century international law, which was centered around a premise that states had to meet a 'Standard of Civilization' in order to be treated as equal participants in the international system. Edward Keene observes that Grotius, who as a 17th-century legal thinker is usually credited with the idea of a European society of states, was quite comfortable with the hypothetical idea of equality between European and non-European states. By the 19th century, however, the international system was very much divided: 'there was an order promoting toleration in Europe, and an order promoting civilization beyond' (Keene 2002, 109). Focusing only on the former obscures the degree to which international dynamics beyond most of Europe were constituted along hierarchical principles (see also Zarakol 2011, 2014, 2018).

Those who fell short of these expectations were stigmatized, initially formally via the 'Standard of Civilization' which deprived states that were not considered 'civilised' of equal legal recognition, but increasingly in the 20th century more informally: 'modern vs backward,' 'developed vs developing,' and so on. The principle of sovereign equality replaced the 'Standard of Civilization' but the social hierarchy established in the 19th century between the West and the rest of the world never fully dissipated in the 20th century. Building on Norbert Elias, I have characterized this hierarchy (Zarakol 2011) as an 'established-outsider' relationship: those who are 'established' in a social setting (or early-comers) have the power to set norms and stigmatize those who are 'outsiders' (or late-comers) even if material differences between them are insignificant. This social power allows the difference to grow and/or to be reproduced over time (Zarakol 2011).

Stigmatization differs from simple discrimination or exclusion and a crucial component of stigma is its internalization by the stigmatized actor (Goffman 1963). Once stigma is established, the options open to stigmatized actors are limited: they can try to correct their stigma or to embrace it, but both choices are essentially reactions to stigmatization and usually leave the social hierarchy intact (Zarakol 2011, 2014; Adler-Nissen 2017). Stigmatized actors cannot but help react to their stigma for two reasons: first, stigmatization presents an existential recognition problem: stigmatized actors are by definition recognized as 'less than.' Second, lack of recognition (or lack of equal recognition) has material consequences: for example, in the 19th century stigmatized actors in the international system had less legal recognition and thus fewer economic protections than 'normal' actors. Thus, stigmatization is nearly impossible to ignore (for more on this dynamic see Zarakol 2011, 2014).

Exemplarity as a stigma coping strategy

The 20th century was characterized by two types of stigma-management strategies by the 'outsiders' of the international system. A few countries attempted to embrace their stigma and their lack of recognition from the core. The Soviet Union was the most high-profile experiment of this kind, wherein an 'outsider' actor attempted to create its own normative universe by embracing its stigma and get recognition from similarly situated actors. However, the USSR never really challenged the primary narrative underwriting the social hierarchy of the modern international order: that is, the notion that the non-West had to 'catch up' with the West. More common was the strategy wherein many non-Western states attempted to move their states up in the social hierarchy of the international system by correcting their stigmatizing attributes, that is, by assimilating into the 'Western order.' The late 19th and early 20th centuries are full of examples of 'non-Western' states adopting 'Western' norms from seemingly trivial matters such as dress codes to more serious ones such as legal codes. It is the former strategy which is particularly suitable for the deployment of the exemplarity mechanism. Let me demonstrate what I mean by zooming in on two cases discussed in more detail in my previous work. In *After Defeat* (2011), I analyzed Turkey and Japan as countries that pursued an emulation strategy in the 20th century in order to gain recognition from the Western core of the international order (see also Zarakol 2010, 2014). We can see the strategy of exemplarity clearly at play in their attempts to move up the social hierarchy of the 20th century international order(s).

In the early part of the 20th century, both the Ottoman Empire (the predecessor of the Republic of Turkey) and Japan experimented with revisionist grand strategies with the intent of capturing what they thought was their rightful place in the new international system. The Ottoman Empire's bout with revisionism was short and bitter, lasting less than eight years; Japan sustained it for about twice as long. However, instead of earning them a seat among the 'established' members of the international society, these revisionist policies ended in failure. Thus, not only did the defeat of the Ottoman Empire in World War I and Japan in World War II cost the titular nations their empire, but also reinforced the very 19th-century social hierarchy these states were trying to escape (as discussed in the previous section). At some point in the 20th century, therefore, both countries found themselves stigmatized, defeated, and restigmatized because of having fought to overcome the position of stigma, at an inferior social status to the West. They emerged from their respective wars even further away from the 'established' core of the modern international order.

Both in Turkey and Japan, revisionist governments were then replaced by regimes very receptive to Western norms, ideas, and institutions. In the 1920s, Turkey chose a domestic system which was designed to overcome the stigmatized position of being an outsider in the international system. The choice was made in the context of a normative ideal which placed a premium on modernity as a sign of civilization and tied the right to be independent to the level of modernity. The domestic choices, in turn, brought Turkey closer to the West in the 1930s. Turkey accepted that it had to prove to the West that it deserved to belong to the family of civilized nations through actual, visible steps, but simultaneously asserted that this was a choice Turkey was making and was capable of making. Turkish leaders insisted on the moral and intrinsic equality of the Turkish nation to the West, and presented Turkey's situation of defeat and lowered status as the result of a combination of factors such as historical happenstance, fault of the West, and the exaggerated influence of religion in Ottoman affairs. Because the logic was acceptable, the content of the normative ideal was not questioned.

The obsession with cosmetic changes, such as the hat law, makes sense when seen in this light. It was as if Turkey was a man who intrinsically belonged in the family of civilized nations, or great powers, and he just happened to be placed out of it because he was wearing the wrong dress, used the wrong calendar, and so on. Such stigmatizing attributes could be replaced. All of the Westernizing reforms were justified to the domestic public with the logic that all the powerful, civilized countries were doing things in this particular way, and Turkey naturally belonged in that group, therefore Turkey should also adopt the same ways.

Pre-WWII Japan was motivated by the same desire to overcome the civilization hierarchies that shaped Turkey's post-defeat choices. Japan's quest for inclusion in the civilization of Western powers reached a feverish nationalist pitch in the interwar period. This was a Japan that was manifesting the worst aspects of Western civilization – that is, imperialism and condescension – through a military regime duly propped up and legitimized at home by reference to how the West had been acting until then, on the one hand, and also with the emperor divinity cult, on the other. While the devastating defeat Japan suffered in World War II was traumatic, it did not put an end to Japan's quest for status; it merely transformed its dominant manifestation. By the time World War II broke out, the original 'Standard of Civilization' – even in its quasi-legalized form (through the League of Nations) – was becoming obsolete, making way for a more teleological view of human development, modernity, and progress. Japan continued to care deeply about its ranking among nations within this emerging manifestation of the broader hierarchy. Japan did not get over the trauma of World War II until Japan's GNP carried the country to a top rank. The 1964 Tokyo Olympics marked a definite shift in the mood of the country, and international organization memberships sealed the deal for Japan (Jansen 2000; Klien 2002; Buruma 2003).

The economy-first doctrine of Yoshida was chosen deliberately. Besides the obvious benefits of economic development, emphasizing economic growth and trade was the only way a country could advance, status wise, within an international system dominated by two powers. Furthermore, this choice was very much in line with dominating normative discourse in the international system, which had shifted from civilization to development. It also allowed Japan to further its stature by presenting itself as a model of successful Asian development. This course was sustainable and had legitimacy because it delivered the kind of power-prestige that the domestic audience demanded.

But especially important for our purposes in this volume is how both countries strategically used the narrative of 'exemplarity.' Despite the loss of empire, both Turkey and Japan after defeat maintained an interest regaining a leadership role in their respective regions. However, in both cases, the ability to pursue such a strategy to its full extent was constrained by the desire to gain equal recognition from the West as 'normal' states. Both countries attempted to maintain a delicate balance between emphasizing their success in emulating Western models while underlining their ties to their regions. If a choice had to be made between the two, the latter was compromised for the former. The notion that both countries were examples for their regions helped maintain this difficult balance for much of the 20th century.

In other words, instead of trying to regain a more powerful status by committing fully to regional causes (and becoming advocates for regional complaints), both Turkey and Japan attempted to frame their Western orientation as the reason why they should matter in their regions. Implicit in this attitude was an endorsement and legitimation of the modern/Western ontology of ranking states. Modernization was the right thing to do – Turkey and Japan had something to teach states in their respective regions because they had traveled down that path first, just as they had themselves learned from the West.

Here is how the exemplarity mechanism functioned in reproducing the social hierarchy between the West and the non-West: by their own constant attempts to prove that Turkey deserved to join the community of civilized, modern nations, the leaders of Turkey legitimized the norm of interwar mandate regime that sovereignty was indeed something that needed be earned and that a nation needed to prove itself to the world community before it could become fully independent. For all of the anti-imperialist rhetoric of the war years, Turkey turned out to be the best emissary for imperialist norms – if it was possible for Turkey to successfully transform itself, the implication was that there was no inherent structural problem with civilization standards. Of course, Turkey took it even further than that. Under the guise of an 'anti-imperialist' rhetoric Turkey actively encouraged other 'outsider' countries to commit to the same advancement strategy as Turkey. The Japanese case is slightly different, but we see the same dynamic at work as the Japanese actively pushed the Japanese model of development in Asia, and remained aloof to regional and Third World efforts to question the international economic order. In both cases, problems in the 'Third World' were severed from their international context and reduced to being responsibilities of various local governments – if Turkey and Japan could solve their modernity problem, so could other disadvantaged states, and if they couldn't, the implication is that because they were not as deserving. This is a good example of how the discourse of exemplarity can be used to reproduce and even strengthen social hierarchies within the international order.

Conclusion

The examples discussed in the previous section belong more to the earlier part of the 20th century, but our current liberal international order was formed against this same historical background and is shaped by similar dynamics. Acutely aware of the social hierarchies of the international order and having suffered from the material consequences of these hierarchies, many states outside the core of the international system joined the liberal order (either during the Cold War or in its immediate aftermath) because they saw it as the inner circle of the international system with special rewards and privileges for its members. The choice was thus not about (or just about) the substantive quality of this order but between a desired label ('Western' or 'First world') vs. its undesirable corollaries.

What makes our time different from the earlier part of the 20th century discussed in the previous section is that emulation strategies seem to have reached the end of their appeal. There are a number of reasons for this: emulation, that is, the attempt to move up in the social hierarchy by mimicking the features of the high-ranked actors, never quite works in garnering equal recognition for the assimilating actor because the act reminds the community of both the original stigmatizing difference and the arbitrariness of the normative order. The 'established' cannot afford to have all of the emulating outsiders join their ranks because doing so would result in a loss of status and this is where exemplarity comes in as discussed in previous sections. The international hierarchy between the West and the non-West was also maintained by shifting the normative goal post as soon as it was close to being approximated (see Bourdieu 1984; Bauman 1991; Zarakol 2014). However, these are only temporary solutions: resentments over unattained social equality (despite the presence of formal, sovereign equality) continued to grow. All of this suggests that the utility of exemplarity as a status improving mechanism (at least as it pertains to the Liberal International Order) will also be fading in the 21st century. Of course, that does not at all preclude the possibility that the mechanism will find life in the next international order.

References

Adler, Emanuel. 2008. 'The Spread of Security Communities: Communities of Practice, Self-Restraint, and NATO's Post-Cold War Transformation.' *European Journal of International Relations* 14 (2): 195–230.

Adler-Nissen, Rebecca. 2017. 'Are We "Lazy Greeks" or "Nazi Germans"?' In *Hierarchies in World Politics*, edited by Ayşe Zarakol. Cambridge University Press.

Adler-Nissen, Rebecca, and Ayşe Zarakol. 2021. 'Struggles for Recognition: The Liberal International Order and the Merger of Its Discontents.' *International Organization* 75 (2): 611–634.

Anievas, Alex, and Kerem Nisancioglu. 2015. *How the West Came to Rule: The Geopolitical Origins of Capitalism*. University of Chicago Press.

Arrighi, Giovanni. 1994. *The Long Twentieth Century: Money, Power, and the Origins of Our Times*. Verso.

Barder, Alexander. 2015. 'International Hierarchy.' In *Oxford Research Encyclopedia of International Studies*, edited by Nukhet Sandal. Oxford University Press.

Barkawi, Tarak, and Mark Laffey. 2006. 'The Postcolonial Moment in Security Studies.' *Review of International Studies* 32 (2): 329–352.

Bauman, Zygmunt. 1991. *Modernity and Ambivalence*. Cornell University Press.

Bell, Duncan. 2007. *Idea of Greater Britain: Empire and the Future of World Order, 1860–1900*. Princeton University Press.

Bell, Duncan. 2016. *Reordering the World: Essays on Liberalism and Empire*. Princeton University Press.

Bially-Mattern, Janice, and Ayşe Zarakol. 2016. 'Hierarchies in World Politics.' *International Organization* 70 (3): 623–654.

Bourdieu, Pierre. 1984. *Distinction: A Social Critique of the Judgement of Taste*. Harvard University Press.

Bowden, Brett. 2009. *The Empire of Civilization*. University of Chicago Press.

Buruma, Ian. 2003. *Inventing Japan, 1853–1964*. The Modern Library.

Butt, Ahsan. 2013. 'Anarchy and Hierarchy in International Relations: Examining South America's War-Prone Decade, 1932–41.' *International Organization* 67 (3): 575–607.

Buzan, Barry, and George Lawson. 2015. *The Global Transformation: History, Modernity and the Making of International Relations*. Cambridge University Press.

Carr, E. H. 2001. *The Twenty Years' Crisis, 1919–1939*. Palgrave.

Cooley, Alexander. 2003. 'Thinking Rationally about Hierarchy and Global Governance.' *Review of International Political Economy* 10 (4): 672–684.

Cooley, Alexander. 2011. *Logics of Hierarchy*. Cornell University Press.

Donnelly, Jack. 2006. 'Sovereign Inequalities and Hierarchy in Anarchy: American Power and International Society.' *European Journal of International Relations* 12 (2): 139–170.

Donnelly, Jack. 2015. 'The Discourse of Anarchy in IR.' *International Theory* 7 (3): 393–425.

Dunne, Tim. 2003. 'Society and Hierarchy in International Relations.' *International Relations* 17 (3): 303–320.

Eichengreen, Barry, and David Leblang. 2008. 'Democracy and Globalization.' *Economics & Politics* 20 (3): 289–334.

Finnemore, Martha, and Kathryn Sikkink. 1998. 'International Norm Dynamics and Political Change.' *International Organization* 52 (4): 887–917.

Frank, Andre Gunder. 1998. *ReORIENT: Global Economy in the Asian Age*. University of California Press.

Goffman, Erving. 1963. *Stigma: Notes on the Management of Spoiled Identity*. Simon & Schuster.

Goh, Evelyn. 2008. 'Hierarchy and the Role of the United States in the East Asian Security Order.' *International Relations of the Asia-Pacific* 8 (3): 353–377.

Grovogui, Siba. 2016. *Beyond Eurocentrism and Anarchy: Memories of International Order and Institutions*. Springer.

Hobson, John M. 2012. *The Eurocentric Conception of World Politics: Western International Theory, 1760–2010*. Cambridge University Press.

Hobson, John M., and J. C. Sharman. 2005. 'The Enduring Place of Hierarchy in World Politics: Tracing the Social Logics of Hierarchy and Political Change.' *European Journal of International Relations* 11 (1): 63–98.

Ikenberry, John G. 2001. 'American Power and the Empire of Capitalist Democracy.' *Review of International Studies* 27 (5): 191–212.

Ikenberry, John G. 2012. *Liberal Leviathan: The Origins, Crisis, and Transformation of the American World Order*. Princeton University Press.

Ikenberry, John G. 2018. 'The End of Liberal International Order?' *International Affairs* 94 (1): 17–23.

Ikenberry, John G. 2020. *A World Safe for Democracy: Liberal Internationalism and the Crises of Global Order*. Yale University Press.

Jansen, Marius B. 2000. *The Making of Modern Japan*. Belknap Press.

Kang, David C. 2003. 'Hierarchy and Stability in Asian International Relations.' In *International Relations Theory and the Asia-Pacific*, edited by Michael Mastanduno and John Ikenberry. Columbia University Press.

Kang, David C. 2004. 'The Theoretical Roots of Hierarchy in International Relations.' *Australian Journal of International Affairs* 58 (3): 337–352.

Kang, David C. 2005. 'Hierarchy in Asian International Relations: 1300–1900.' *Asian Security* 1 (1): 53–79.

Keck, Margaret E., and Kathryn Sikkink. 1998. *Activists Beyond Borders: Advocacy Networks in International Politics*. Cornell University Press.

Keene, Edward. 2002. *Beyond the Anarchical Society: Grotius, Colonialism and Order in World Politics*. Cambridge University Press.

Keene, Edward. 2013. 'International Hierarchy and the Origins of the Modern Practice of Intervention.' *Review of International Studies* 39 (5): 1077–1090.

Keohane, Robert O. 1984. *After Hegemony: Cooperation and Discord in the World Political Economy*. Princeton University Press.

Klien, Susanne. 2002. *Rethinking Japan's Identity and International Role: An Intercultural Perspective*. Routledge.

Lake, David A. 1996. 'Anarchy, Hierarchy, and the Variety of International Relations.' *International Organization* 50 (1): 1–33.

Lake, David A. 1999. *Entangling Relations: American Foreign Policy in its Century*. Princeton University Press.

Lake, David A. 2007. 'Escape from the State of Nature: Authority and Hierarchy in World Politics.' *International Security* 32 (1): 47–79.

Lake, David A. 2009. *Hierarchy in International Relations*. Cornell University Press.

Lake, David A. 2010. 'Making America Safe for the World: Multilateralism and the Rehabilitation of US Authority.' *Global Governance* 16 (4): 471–484.

Lake, David A. 2013. 'Great Power Hierarchies and Strategies in Twenty-First Century World Politics.' In *Handbook of International Relations*, edited by Walter Carlsnaes, Thomas Risse, and Beth Simmons. Sage.

Lake, David A. 2017. 'Laws and Norms in the Making of International Hierarchies.' In *Hierarchies in World Politics*, edited by Ayşe Zarakol. Cambridge University Press.

Lake, David A., Lisa Martin, and Thomas Risse. 2021. 'Challenges to the Liberal Order: Reflections on International Organization.' *International Organization* 75 (2): 225–257.

MacKay, Joseph. 2019. 'Legitimation Strategies in International Hierarchies.' *International Studies Quarterly* 63 (3): 717–725.

Marinov, Nikolay, and Hein Goemans. 2013. 'Coups and Democracy.' *British Journal of Political Science* 44 (4): 799–825.

Mcconaughey, Meghan, Paul Musgrave, and Daniel H. Nexon. 2018. 'Beyond Anarchy: Logics of Political Organization, Hierarchy, and International Structure.' *International Theory* 10 (2): 181–218.

Musgrave, Paul. 2019. 'Asymmetry, Hierarchy, and the Ecclesiastes Trap.' *International Studies Review* 21 (2): 284–300.

Musgrave, Paul, and Daniel H. Nexon. 2018. 'Defending Hierarchy from the Moon to the Indian Ocean: Symbolic Capital and Political Dominance in Early Modern China and the Cold War.' *International Organization* 72 (3): 591–626.

Nedal, Dani K., and Daniel H. Nexon. 2019. 'Anarchy and Authority: International Structure, the Balance of Power, and Hierarchy.' *Journal of Global Security Studies* 4 (2): 169–189.

Nexon, Daniel H., and Thomas Wright. 2007. 'What's at Stake in the American Empire Debate.' *American Political Science Review* 101 (2): 253–271.

Nye, Joseph S. 2017. 'Will The Liberal Order Survive: The History of an Idea.' *Foreign Affairs* 96 (10): 10–16.

Pevehouse, Jon. 2002. 'Democracy from the Outside-In? International Organizations and Democratization.' *International Organization* 56 (3): 515–549.

Phillips, Andrew, 2017. 'Making Empires.' In *Hierarchies in World Politics*, edited by Ayşe Zarakol. Cambridge University Press.

Phillips, Andrew. 2018. 'Contesting the Confucian Peace: Civilization, Barbarism and International Hierarchy in East Asia.' *European Journal of International Relations*, 24 (4): 740–764.

Ringmar, Erik. 1996. 'On the Ontological Status of the State.' *European Journal of International Relations* 2 (4): 439–466.

Rosenberg, Justin. 2013. 'The "Philosophical Premises" of Uneven and Combined Development.' *Review of International Studies* 39 (5): 569–597.

Schmidt, Brian C. 1997. *The Political Discourse of Anarchy: A Disciplinary History of International Relations*. SUNY Press.

Schulz, Carsten-Andreas. 2019. 'Hierarchy Salience and Social Action: Disentangling Class, Status, and Authority in World Politics.' *International Relations* 33 (1): 88–108.

Simmons, Beth A. 2009. *Mobilizing for Human Rights: International Law in Domestic Politics*. Cambridge University Press.

Simpson, Gerry. 2004. *Great Powers and Outlaw States: Unequal Sovereigns in the International Legal Order*. Cambridge University Press.

Spanu, Maja. 2020. 'The Hierarchical Society: The Politics of Self-Determination and the Constitution of New States after 1919.' *European Journal of International Relations* 26 (2): 372–396.

Subotić, Jelena, and Ayşe Zarakol. 2020. 'Hierarchies, Emotions, and Memory in International Relations.' In *The Power of Emotions in World Politics*, edited by Simon Koschut. Routledge.

Suzuki, Shogo. 2017. '"Delinquent Gangs" in the International System Hierarchy.' In *Hierarchies in World Politics*, edited by Ayşe Zarakol. Cambridge University Press.

Wallerstein, Immanuel. 1984. *The Politics of the World-Economy: The States, the Movements and the Civilizations*. Cambridge University Press.

Waltz, Kenneth. 1979. *A Theory of International Politics*. Addison-Wesley Publishing.

Wendt, Alexander, and Daniel Friedheim. 1995. 'Hierarchy under Anarchy: Informal Empire and the East German State.' *International Organization* 49 (4): 689–721.

Zarakol, Ayşe. 2010. 'Ontological Insecurity and State Denial of Historical Crimes: Turkey and Japan.' *International Relations* 24 (1): 3–23.

Zarakol, Ayşe. 2011. *After Defeat: How the East Learned to Live with the West*. Cambridge University Press.

Zarakol, Ayşe. 2014. 'What Made the Modern World Hang Together: Socialisation or Stigmatization?' *International Theory* 6 (2): 311–332.

Zarakol, Ayşe, ed. 2017a. *Hierarchies in World Politics*. Cambridge University Press.

Zarakol, Ayşe. 2017b. 'Introduction: Theorising Hierarchies.' In *Hierarchies in World Politics*, edited by Ayşe Zarakol. Cambridge University Press.

Zarakol, Ayşe. 2017c. 'Why Hierarchy?' In *Hierarchies in World Politics*, edited by Ayşe Zarakol. Cambridge University Press.

Zarakol, Ayşe. 2018. 'Sovereign Equality as Misrecognition.' *Review of International Studies* 44 (5): 848–862.

Zarakol, Ayşe. 2020. 'Use of Historical Analogies in IR Theory.' H-Diplo/ISSF Roundtable on *Thucydides's Trap? Historical Interpretation, Logic of Inquiry, and the Future of Sino-American Relations* by Steve Chan. November 9, 2020.

Zarakol, Ayşe. 2022. *Before the West: Rise and Fall of Eastern World Orders*. Cambridge University Press.

10

The Violence of the Exemplar: The French Civilizing Mission in French and Algerian Memories, 1918–Present

Guillaume Wadia

Colonization is a past that cannot pass between France and Algeria; or at least not yet. In January 2021, Benjamin Stora, arguably France's foremost historian on Algerian history, issued a long-awaited report commissioned by French President Emmanuel Macron on how to address the contentious history of French colonization in Algeria and the Algerian War. Stora's report recommends that French officials create a 'memories and truth commission' and give historians the tools they need to work out the history of colonization and the Algerian War. Macron's reasons for requesting a report and Stora's conclusions are not merely suggestions aimed at correcting the historical record, but a way of officially recognizing that the complicated history between France and Algeria is a festering wound in both French and Algerian society (Stora 2021).

Why is France's colonization of Algeria still a source of tension between both countries as well as within each country? In part, the answer lies in *la mission civilisatrice*, the civilizing mission. *La mission civilisatrice* was more than a rhetorical device to justify empire: it was the framework that guided French actions as they set about making modern citizens out of what they considered uncivilized people. They endeavored, or so they claimed, to export exemplars of French civilization via people and institutions that embodied the values of the Enlightenment, the Revolution, rational government, and science. In the name of the civilizing mission, they also claimed to train Algerians using those techniques of administration which in France had transformed peasants into Frenchmen and which would inevitably transform Algerians into modern citizens (Weber 1976). Entreating colonial subjects to fight for the Republic, encouraging fluency and rhetorical mastery in French, and learning the history of France and accepting it as their own were examples of how colonial subjects might show they were civilized.

But the civilizing mission and the colonial project were also, as Achille Mbembe puts it, 'a historical way of dominating, violence exercised on spaces, bodies, objects, imaginaries, and souls, a relationship of exchange and negotiation, fraudulent in the way it humiliated its victims, rewarded its valets, punished dissidents, created relationships as lovers and persecutors, executor and protector' (Mbembe 1993, 85). French exemplarity expressed through the *mission civilisatrice* in Algeria consisted of 132 years of violent occupation during which the French gaslit Algerians, first denigrating their identity and then convincing them they could be civilized if they worked hard at it. In the end, however, no matter how well Algerians emulated the examples the French provided, the French argued that they were never quite civilized enough, consigning French colonial subjects to what Dipesh Chakrabarty called 'the waiting room of history,' where the colonized were entreated to wait while the colonizer gauged their readiness to participate in the civilized world (Chakrabarty 2007, 8).

In fact, the civilizing mission, as a repository of exemplars and a framework for action, continues to consign both French and Algerians to the waiting room of history. France, as 'daughter of the Enlightenment,' historian Pascal Ory notes, 'believed itself for a very long time to be exemplary, but has found shouldering this responsibility difficult, especially after Vichy and decolonization' (Rérolle 2016). French politicians have consequently sought to rehabilitate the civilizing mission as a humanitarian endeavor and attempted to create around it internal social and political cohesion by emphasizing the idea of a Republic that has always been benevolent and that has always supported democratic values.[1] In many ways, this has led successive French governments since the Algerian War (1962) not only to deny the trauma of the civilizing mission but to reproduce its logics, especially when dealing with Algerians.

Meanwhile, across the Mediterranean, everyday Algerians continue to work through the legacy of the civilizing mission in their lives, in part because the trauma is multi-generational, but also because they have claimed

---

[1] The impulse of political actors from former colonial empires wishing to rehabilitate or redeem their history is not quintessentially French. How this impulse expresses itself, however, varies dramatically. Whereas France still seeks to put a positive spin on its colonial empire and the civilizing mission, the Netherlands found value in acting as a 'guide-country' and 'unique decolonizer' by recognizing its complicated relationship with its former colonies. See de Bruin, Chapter 12, this volume.

for themselves the values and tools of the civilizing mission and continue to transform them into something uniquely Algerian.

Negotiating and denying early examples of the civilizing mission

On July 28, 1885, Jules Ferry, then the Prime Minister of France, rose to give one of the most important speeches in French politics. France having occupied Algeria in 1830, Tonkin and Annam in 1881 and 1883, and Tunisia in 1881, Ferry clamored on the floor of parliament that 'superior races [had] a right in regards to inferior races ... to civilize them,' and that France, as the country of the Rights of Man, had the obligation to exercise that right (Ferry 1885). French public opinion was split on the matter of France's overseas conquests. At stake were concerns about France's place in the world. Indeed, French capitulation during the Franco-Prussian War (1871) and the loss of Alsace and Lorraine to the Germans durably scarred the nation (Girardet 1972, 51). But although the French of the Third Republic (1870–1940) remembered daily their humiliation at the hands of the Prussians, they were remarkably confident in the superiority of French culture and the universal application of the French Revolution.

Ferry and other proponents of the French colonial empire capitalized on the public's fear of decline but also its sense that the values of the Enlightenment and the Revolution were unique in the world. Colonialists drummed up support for adventures abroad that would inevitably bring law, order, proper administration, and commerce to 'primitive' people and prove to the world and themselves that France was a great power. They believed that compared to the violent British and German empires, French civilization would appeal to what they called 'savages' who in turn would gladly jettison ignorance, superstition, and despotism for science, reason, and law. Indeed, French colonizers believed in the perfectibility of mankind and intended to accompany the 'evolution of inferior peoples toward civilization' with 'patience, by providing good examples, and through education' (Leroy-Beaulieu 1882, 332). By the late 1880s, school textbooks and the popular press gave myriad examples to children and their parents of the civilizing mission abroad as 'savage' Africans and Asians welcomed the French as liberators and embraced the gift of civilization that the French had brought with them (Le Petit Journal 1911).

French propaganda dazzled some Algerians too. Algerians saw the French invasion in 1830 as a cataclysmic event that demanded they reconsider their place in the world. They looked at the French contrast of the order their own military had brought to Algeria with the chaos created by native brigands. They looked at the scientists and capitalists who set up their experimental farms, laboratories, and factories in Algeria and contrasted that with Algerian elites, whom they blamed for scientific decline and economic mismanagement. They read the laws the French brought with them and contrasted that with the arbitrary decisions of the Dey of Algiers, representative of the Ottoman Empire. French exemplarity awed them, and espousing the civilizing mission became a way not only to seek new opportunities in the French empire, but also to understand the world (Dzanic 2015). Yet Algerians also carried in their memory the savagery that accompanied the civilizing mission. French directives in the early days of the occupation encouraged soldiers to 'kill all men from the age of 15, take all the women and children, destroy buildings, send them to the Marquise islands or elsewhere, in a word, annihilate everything that doesn't crawl at our feet like dogs' (Julien 1992, 232).

Algerian nationalists embodied this tension as they navigated pathways to acquire a greater say in how empire was run while softening colonial administration. They called their strategy of renegotiating the terms of empire 'resistance through dialogue' (Djeghloul 1988, 4). Algerians could not resist the French military, but French military operations were costly, so Algerians banked on French officials looking for moderate intermediaries between them and the colonial masses to smooth French rule. Indeed, the French considered armed resistance an indicator of the Algerian's savage nature, and consequently Algerian reformists set about securing greater rights and more responsibilities in local administration by actively performing the examples put forth by the French (McDougall 2006).

The Young Algerians traveled to France extensively. They trained in French schools as teachers, lawyers, journalists, doctors, and engineers. They utilized the French language masterfully, interacted with French political and commercial elites, and created innumerable civic associations in France. Some married French women. The work of becoming fluent in French, studying and working and living in France, engaging in French civic life, and integrating through marriage enabled Young Algerians to better understand French civilization, gave them practical training in the kind of civic life necessary to a functioning democracy, and taught them to translate the demands of Algerians into language that might be better understood by French authorities (Ageron 1983, 26).

To that end, Algerian reformists published pamphlets and newspapers in French to present their case for reform to a public consisting mostly of Algerian *évolués*, that is to say, Algerians who were evolving to become civilized by learning French, as well as French and European settlers. In much the same way that the Enlightenment *philosophes* discoursed on rights, representation, and rational government, Algerian reformers put forth programs to ensure France remained an empire by advocating for greater equality in law and in taxation. Additionally, because the goal of the civilizing mission held up the French citizen as an exemplar of modernity, Algerian nationalists also entreated French officials to make French citizenship more widely available to Algerians who had emulated the examples of civilization and worked toward the grandeur of French civilization (Ageron 2005).

The Great War was one opportunity to emulate the civilized French and help shoulder the burden of securing French civilization. Indeed, about 380,000 Algerians took part in the war effort between 1914 and 1918, of whom 48,000 were killed in action, the highest rate of casualties among soldiers from the French empire (Jansen and Jomier 2014, 38). Beginning in 1915, French politicians seeking to enlist more Algerians for the European fight began to consider the possibility of awarding French citizenship to Algerian soldiers (Gastaut, Yahi, and Blanchard 2014, 135). That idea was quickly put to rest for fear that Algerians with political representation proportional to their numbers might upset the sovereignty of France over Algeria and the power of European settlers over Algerians (Stora 2004, 76). But the Young Algerians, encouraged by promises of one day being recognized as civilized and acceding to citizenship, continued to believe and work in a future in which Algerians were increasingly welcomed by the French.

Indeed, for Young Algerians like Ferhat Abbas, an Algerian nationalist who sought greater cooperation with France before the Second World War, the civilizing mission was so great a prize that it demanded that Algerians reconcile with the French if they made good on all their claims to bring civilization to Algeria. 'The griefs of conquest are being erased from our memories,' he wrote in 1930, 'and this country which fell into terrible anarchy will see its race reborn through French thought. In the villages … The houses multiply. The school, the court, the hospital, the post office, the police station. There is hygiene, medicine, security' (Abbas 1981, 165). Abbas' writing, scrutinized as it was by French authorities, prodded the French to let go of violence and accelerate the political, intellectual, and material outcomes of the civilizing mission. He reminded his readers that the core of France's mission, that of civilizing Algerians and imbuing them with 'French thought,' was still ongoing, and required the French to better exemplify the behaviors of the 'liberal and republican France' that built schools and hospitals, not those of the violent 'colonialist and tyrannical France' that killed, maimed, and humiliated Algerians (Abbas 1962, 111).

As Algerians grew disillusioned with French rule, Algerian nationalists continued to couch their message within the civilizing mission, now in order to better develop a framework of action against the French. In 1946, Abbas, no longer interested in Algeria's integration into France, wrote in a report titled 'The colonial regime is the negation of justice and civilization' that 'French democracy' was in fact the natural ally of Algerians seeking independence (Abbas 1946, 15). Abbas continued to look to the Enlightenment and the French Revolution to craft political messages that entreated the Algerians and the French to resist tyrannical settlers and colonial officials, 'feudal lords' like the ones French revolutionaries had removed from power. He used the civilizing mission to build a nation, while encouraging the French to rediscover their revolutionary heritage so that France might also live up to its civilizational ideals (Abbas 1946, 16). Justice, democracy, civilization, and reason, those values which Jules Ferry and others claimed to want to gift Algerians, figure extensively in the texts of the Young Algerians as proof that they understood the values of French civilization, accepted them as their own, and transformed them into actionable policy that in turn served as models to others.

But, as successful as the Young Algerians were in coopting the civilizing mission to create the foundations for political action at first, and revolutionary action later, French colonial authorities rarely engaged Algerians who used said mission to make claims. At times the French argued that it was the racial composition of colonial subjects that prevented them from being civilized, at others that charges of colonial abuses were instigated by outsiders seeking to destabilize the French empire. They claimed to want to make Algerians civilized, but the goalposts were always moved. Once it became clear that the French would never make good on their promises to colonized people, independence became the only way for Algerians to achieve the civilizing mission and put into practice the universal values that the French claimed to admire (Cooper 2014, 4).

The lingering trauma of exemplarity in the postcolonial Algerian

Independence, however, did not bring an end to the tensions created by the civilizing mission. It gave Algerians a nation, but did not give them the feeling of parity with the French (who, as we will see, refused to critique the civilizing mission), nor were the applications of the civilizing mission fully resolved at the time of independence. Indeed, Algerians continue to ask themselves more intimate questions about their identity and their sense of belonging in the world. As Karima Lazali, a psychoanalyst with practices in Algiers and in Paris, puts it, there is 'an unnamed, but fully active inability to forget' how the French applied the civilizing mission, even among generations that neither experienced colonization nor lived in Algeria (Alcaraz 2017, 1).

A recent case in point occurred during Algeria's transition to biometric passports in 2009 and 2010, which was accompanied by the transliteration of patronyms from French to Arabic. This was another reckoning with the civilizing mission's present-day legacy, as Algerians reenacted the destruction of their names a century earlier. As part of French modernization efforts, officials had traveled the colony registering the names of its native inhabitants in French. This interaction between colonizer and colonized, suffused as it was with violence, accounted for more significant transformations than mere transliteration. Tuaregs, for example, whose names incorporated paternal as well as maternal lineages were known only by their patronyms after French colonizers registered them in their ledgers (Benramdane 2000, 81). Algerians, the French claimed, could rejoice: by changing their names to better integrate them into the modern *cité*, the French had excised 'deficiencies proper to the native, son of the savage.' Yet, for all their talk of civilizing the native and introducing rational administration, the French officials who went about naming their charges had no official guidelines, resulting in multiple French versions of the same Algerian name. In other cases, French officials mandated under penalty of death that the inhabitants of a particular village choose patronyms starting with the letter A, the next village with the letter B, and so on. Some French officials simply refused to assign a name to Algerians, giving them the denomination SNP, *Sans Nom Patronymique*, Without a Patronym. In the most abhorrent cases, French officials assigned as last names French insults and French names of animals (Ouldennebia 2008, 8). As Algerians renewed their passports and presented their birth records in 2009, Algerian officials were overwhelmed by demands to change names, restore spellings, and correct errors made in the service of a French system that was more arbitrary than rational. Changing and erasing names cut Algerians off from the socio-cultural and political markers that linked them to a particular group of people. In some cases it also severed people from places, facilitating expropriation (Algeria-Watch 2014). The change in identification technologies was an occasion for Algerians to recover personal histories by correcting the colonial record and claiming belonging to the Algerian nation (Algeria-Watch 2010).

Civilizing by assigning new last names and erasing lineage was one way to break intimate links between individuals and their families as well as between individuals and their identities. But the French, in their effort to civilize, went further and endeavored to replace Algerian history with French history. The consequences, as Algerian writer Samir Toumi recounts for the French newspaper *Liberation*, remain explosive. Toumi remembered how a single sentence in 2007 from French presidential candidate Nicolas Sarkozy – that the Gauls were the ancestors of the French, including those French of different origins – awoke a painful memory of his father and grandfather. Toumi asked his father one day what 'colonization' meant, and his father replied with a memory of his own dating to the early days of the war of independence. A French teacher in Algeria taught him that his ancestors were the Gauls. This fact had so troubled him that he asked his own father if it was true. The old man screamed in response: 'They're lying! They're liars! Look! That's colonization … to force people to be what they are not by lying about what they are' (Toumi 2017). For Toumi,

Sarkozy's comment on TV had been a moment of reckoning: he imagined his father as a child trying to make sense of the schoolteacher's civilizing instruction and his grandfather coming to grips with the lies of a nation that had couched the civilizing mission in lofty universalist republican rhetoric, but had instead erased Algerian history. A single sentence in 2017 had the power to activate trauma that crossed three generations. Teaching Algerians that their 'ancestors were Gauls' was intended to civilize Algerians by assimilating them into France and imparting those universal gifts that led to an educated citizenry and a well-run Republic (Paligot 2019, 153–163). In reality it uprooted Algerian children emotionally and culturally, as the French colonial schoolteacher contested his pupils' identity in his capacity as agent of the civilizing mission. Children internalized this tension, rejecting a heritage they were incapable of escaping (Amrouche 1994, 329).

Perhaps the most poignant example of this tension between rejection and recovery is the use of the French language by Algerians. As noted earlier, the French language was also a tool of the civilizing mission; Algerians fluent in French believed that their fluency could liberate their genius and facilitate their integration into a more inclusive empire. Yet, as Algerian intellectual and poet Jean Amrouche noted, fluency in French could also be used against Algerians to make them feel inferior from a young age:

> People will say of a paper written in French or a fable recited without too much of a local accent: that's pretty good for a Kabyle or an Algerian. But the European schoolmate will get his revenge: you're only a dirty goat (*bicot*). Get out of here! Still he will try to convert himself slowly, with difficult patience, to France: to grow from what denies him into what has denied him. (Amrouche 1994, 291)

Algerians could be ambivalent about using French, especially if they were educated by French teachers. French was another vehicle for separating them from their history, wedging them away from their regrettably uncivilized ancestors and parents, and alienating Algerians from power. But when Algerians adopted the language, added a native inflection to it, and claimed for themselves France's unique Enlightenment and Revolution, French became a weapon of war. Writing in 'Le Monde,' Amrouche exhorted the French in their native tongue, which 'represent[ed] at the highest degree a universal conception of Man,' to listen to Algerian pleas for political sovereignty (Amrouche 1994, 297). Amrouche's appeal sought to strike at the values and political imaginary of the French to show that support for the Rights of Man also had to include support for Algerian independence.

In another example of Algerians claiming the tools of French civilization for themselves, the famous feminist historian and novelist Assia Djebar entitled her inaugural lecture to the Académie Française '*Cicatriser mes blessures mémorielles'* – 'Healing the Wounds in My Memories.' There is perhaps no greater achievement for francophone scholars than to be invited by peers to hold a chair at the Académie Française. The Académie is the guardian of the French language and has, among its many missions, the vocation to make French a 'modern Latin,' universal and accessible to all. Acceptance into the Académie is the consecration of years of prolific and brilliant work with the French language. It was there, in one of the temples of French civilization, that Djebar felt it important to remind the other Immortals, as the *Academiciens* are called, that 'during my childhood in colonial Algeria (I was called then "French Muslim") we were taught "our ancestors the Gauls," but precisely at the time of the Gauls, North Africa (which was also known as Numidia), my ancestral home, already had a literary culture that was written and of high quality, and in Latin' (Djebar 2006). The French language had been a way for Djebar to explore, communicate, and begin understanding the trauma she endured as a colonial subject not only by producing great works in French, but also by recovering in French the Algerian parts of herself that she felt had been amputated by the civilizing mission.

An unquestionable exemplarity

Whereas Algerians suffer 'memorial bulimia,' the French are amnesiac about their Algerian history. In France, the aftermath of Algerian independence did not allow for an airing out of grievances between the French and Algerians on the topic of the civilizing mission. On the contrary, there was a concerted effort to prevent any possibility of revisiting and understanding the civilizing process in Algeria through the creation of what historian Benjamin Stora calls 'mechanisms to produce forgetting' (Stora 2005, 1). After the Second World War and decolonization, it was imperative to build a consumer society and to participate in the European Common Market (Ross 1995). In both cases, French officials and the media prevented any possibility of dissension over the civilizing mission in an effort to get past those 'times when the French did not like each other very much and even killed one another' and to imprint French civilization on global markets and Europe (Le Monde 1989). There could be no discussion of whether French civilization had failed in Algeria, no second-guessing the intent of the French Republic, and no questioning of whether the French had practiced a virtuous form of government. The French continue to see the civilizing mission as a benevolent force, and mistakenly rely upon their own unexamined exemplarity to formulate responses to seemingly intractable dissension between the state and people with origins in the former colonies.

By preventing discussion, French elites, in some cases deliberately and in others unknowingly, encouraged state agencies to repurpose the civilizing mission for use in policies. Integration, not civilization, was the new operative word, but the demands on Algerian immigrants were the same as the tenets of the civilizing mission. To help Algerians integrate into France, French social workers were tasked with exemplifying French civilization and ensuring that Algerians practiced its lessons. French social workers sought to extinguish those bits in Algerians that did not line up with what they thought befitted life in a modern society. They made sure Algerian Muslims living in France sent their children to public school, tutored them in French, and even took French cooking classes (Lyons 2013, 3). Unsurprisingly, however, social workers argued that no matter their efforts, Algerians simply could not become French. The veils of Algerian women were particularly suspicious; it seemed to these workers that Algerians could not 'fully [grasp] equality,' a central tenet of being French (Lyons 2013, 3). Much like their colonial colleagues, postcolonial authorities in France laid out specious claims to prevent Algerians from fully taking part in modern France.

Politically, support for integration policies for Algerians was always contingent on the economic utility of Algerian immigrants and their abandoning of what made them Algerian. But as the French economy slowed in the late 1970s, politicians seized on the presence of Algerian immigrants to highlight waste in social spending and unemployment among immigrants. Right-wingers also accused Algerians of threatening French civilization by highlighting supposed incompatibilities in customs and religion.

Lurking on the fringes and influencing the harsher aspects of France's new mission to integrate were those forgotten by the Algerian War. Most agents of the war – the soldiers, conscripts, Harkis (Algerian soldiers who fought for France), and settlers – had long been removed from what sociologist Jürgen Habermas calls the public sphere (Habermas 1991). They had hushed their experiences out of shame at the atrocities they committed and the way they were treated in France after leaving their homes and possessions in Algeria (Stora 2005, 10). A few however shared their stories. In the confines of the family at first, and later more vocally and publicly, those who had fought in the war or had been its victims made claims against the state to rehabilitate their overseas contributions to France's civilization. Time changes memories, and efforts to protect the legacy of the civilizing mission by preventing any discussion of it in the aftermath of Algerian independence created echo chambers in which false histories of empire circulated and led to a phenomenon historians call *nostalgérie*/nostalgeria, in which the actors of the colonial drama and their descendants remain stuck in memory loops that prevent them from digesting the colonial past and moving on (Ruscio 2015, 1). *Nostalgérie* accounts for the radicalization of a vocal segment of the French population that believes that Algeria should have stayed French and that France was in fact a civilizing force (Ruscio 2015). These diehards initially found natural allies among supporters of the far-right, who have cited and distorted examples of the civilizing mission in Algeria in order to influence politics in contemporary France.

Indeed, today, the bugaboos of old Algerian hands and their descendants are now mainstream, and if a growing number of French recall the civilizing mission it is because political opportunists on the far-right have managed to convince a majority of French that they themselves risk becoming 'decivilized' (Le Point 2021). The trend towards 'decivilization' began, in fact, in 1962 with France's 'abandonment' of Algeria, according to Eric Zemmour, a far-right polemicist who at one point polled second for the 2022 French presidential elections (Le Point 2021). Thanks to years of denial, obfuscation, and misremembering of France's colonial history, reactionaries have framed discourse on immigration, economic crises, and unemployment as 'fractures' that sully French civilization. They lament the loss of a clear native French identity, the kind they exported when France was still an empire and see immigration as a form of 'reverse colonization.' These reactionaries organize talks, publish in the press and lobby politicians to cast their history as a series of examples in which they worked for the 'collective good.' They are on a 'mission' to reify the civilizing mission and seek to find sympathetic politicians who also believe that France's past can prevent what they believe is the country's decline (IPSOS 2020). To defend against a foreign other that corrupts French identity and the national community, they seek to institutionalized examples of a benevolent France abroad and a history of 'when things were better in France' (Dalisson 2018; see also Savarese 2006). This refusal to contextualize the civilizing mission within French history has led to legislation that promotes historical fiction and retains the framework of the mission's proponents in the late 19th century.

On February 23, 2005, for example, members of parliament introduced bill 2005–158, requiring high schools to teach the 'positive aspects of French colonialism as Jules Ferry intended' (Assemblée Nationale 2004). By specifically including the term 'positive,' French legislators intended to create an official history of French colonialism that highlighted the exemplary nature of the civilizing mission by documenting:

> France's multiple contributions in Algeria, Morocco, Tunisia, as well as in the other territories previously placed under its sovereignty in terms of sciences, techniques, administration, culture, and linguistics. Generations of women and men, of all walks of life and all religions, from here and all of Europe, built in those places communities for the future and built a life for themselves. Thanks to their courage, their entrepreneurship and their sacrifices, those countries were able to develop socially and economically; they contributed to France's grandeur throughout the world. (Assemblée Nationale 2004)

In other words, legislators intended to rehabilitate the civilizing mission by updating it to accommodate 21st-century sensibilities (Boilley 2005). On the floor of parliament, employing nearly word for word the sentences of colonial Governors and Residents General extolling the virtues of the civilizing mission, *députés* grandstanded:

> the facts are these: they built roads, bridges and cities, cultivated the land, built hospitals and schools, they healed and organized the country and added value to the land ... perhaps it was even teachers ... who gave the little children of Algeria the taste of liberty, perhaps even the taste for independence and revolt. (Assemblée Nationale 2005)

Incredibly, French legislators also managed to coopt the Algerian Revolution, and made it into a resounding example of the civilizing mission.

The 2005 law took on its full significance later in the year when riots in French *banlieues*, inhabited by and large by poor and underemployed immigrants, the formerly colonized, and their children, placed front and center the tensions that had always been present in the civilizing mission. The riots began after youths had been chased by police in one of the housing projects of Clichy-sous-Bois. Three young men hid from police in an electrical substation. Two of them were electrocuted and the third suffered severe electrical burns. In the days that followed, violence spread to other parts of Paris and eventually to other *banlieues* across France.

To devise a response to the riots, officials fell back on colonial logics: the suspension of law and the imposition of emergency measures. Public intellectuals, politicians, and the media helped drum up support for the state of emergency by linking violence in the *banlieues* to the Palestinian intifada, the Iraqi insurgency, and nefarious outside agitators. But the most potent argument for proponents of emergency measures was the assertion that the riots were proof that France was another front in a wider 'clash of civilizations,' once again pitting the values of the Enlightenment and the Revolution against the backward superstitions and habits of people originating from the other side of the Mediterranean.

Few bothered to point to the *banlieues*' social, economic, and political marginalization and systemic poverty, underemployment and youth unemployment, the paucity of good quality public services and dismal educational outcomes, the casual racism and everyday police violence that characterized life there as the underlying causes of the riots. Instead, intellectuals launched screeds against supposedly violent youths filled with rage and a French education system that encouraged them to revolt: '[They're] changing the teaching of colonial history and the history of slavery in the schools. Now they teach colonial history as an exclusively negative history. We don't teach anymore that the colonial project also sought to educate, to bring civilization to the savages' (Mishani and Smotriez 2005). French officials today, like their past colonial avatars, remain locked in a way of thinking that interprets the dissent of Algerians (and more generally people from the former colonial empire, people of color, immigrants, and Muslims) against the state not as claims to participate in democratic deliberations, but as 'anti-republicanism' and as an attack on French civilization.

In a way, Benjamin Stora's report, mentioned at the beginning of this chapter, is itself a performance in exemplarity. By bringing forth experts to publicly resolve this lingering tension of empire, France has committed to showing that the French state will attempt to govern itself more harmoniously by accommodating the demands for recognition of minority populations. It has also committed itself to becoming a better partner in broader Mediterranean governance. More importantly however, the report signals to Algeria and Algerians that the French state will attempt to be a fair moderator, giving a platform to Algerian voices in France and in Algeria who will express their trauma and call the French state to account for the atrocities committed in the name of civilization. For Algerians, though, having lived firsthand the effects of the French state's inconsistencies, the Stora report is worth no more than the paper it is printed on so long as France fails to live up to the examples it sets by matching intention with appropriate action.

References

Abbas, Ferhat. 1946. *Le régime colonial est la négation de la justice et de la civilisation*. Editions Libération.

Abbas, Ferhat. 1962. *Guerre et Révolution d'Algérie I, La nuit coloniale*. Juillard.

Abbas, Ferhat. 1981. *Le jeune Algérien. De la colonie vers la provinc.* Garnier.

Ageron, Charles-Robert. 1983. 'L'Association des étudiants musulmans nord-africains en France durant l'entre-deux-guerres. Contribution à l'étude des nationalismes maghrébins.' *Revue française d'histoire d'outre-mer* 70 (258): 25–56.

Ageron, Charles-Robert. 2005. 'Le mouvement "Jeune-Algérien" de 1900 à 1923.' In *Genèse de l'Algérie Algérienne*, edited by Charles-Robert Ageron. Editions Bouchène.

Alcaraz, Emmanuel. 2017. *Lieux de la mémoire de la guerre d'indépendance algérienne*. Editions Karthala.

Algeria-Watch. 2010. 'Les Demandes de Rectification Inondent Les Tribunaux: La Tache Noire de l'état Civil,' https://algeria-watch.org/?p=25046 (accessed October 14, 2021).

Algeria-Watch. 2014. 'Algérien, Quel Est Ton 'vrai' Nom?' https://algeria-watch.org/?p=6341 (accessed October 14, 2021).

Amrouche, Jean. 1994. *Un Algérien s'adresse aux Français ou L'histoire d'Algérie par les textes (1943–1961)*. L'Harmattan Awal.

Assemblée Nationale. 2004. 'N° 1499 – Projet de Loi Portant Reconnaissance de La Nation et Contribution Nationale En Faveur Des Français Rapatriés.' https://www.assemblee-nationale.fr/12/projets/pl1499.asp (accessed October 12, 2021).

Assemblée Nationale. 2005. 'Abrogation de l'article 4 de la loi du 23 février 2005 relative aux français rapatriés.' https://www.assemblee-nationale.fr/12/cri/2005-2006/20060081.asp#P70_2237 (accessed October 12, 2021).

Benramdane, Farid. 2000. 'Qui es-tu? J'ai été dit. De la destruction de la filiation dans l'Etat civil d'Algérie ou éléments d'un onomacide sémantique.' *Insaniyat: Revue algérienne d'anthropologie et de sciences sociales* 10 (2000): 79–87.

Boilley, Pierre. 2005. 'Loi du 23 février 2005, colonisation, indigènes, victimisations.' *Politique africaine* 98 (2): 131–140.

Chakrabarty, Dipesh. 2007. *Provincializing Europe: Postcolonial Thought and Historical Difference*. Princeton University Press.

Cooper, Frederick. 2014. *Citizenship between Empire and Nation: Remaking France and French Africa*. Princeton University Press.

Dalisson, Rémi. 2018. *Guerre d'Algérie: l'impossible commémoration*. Armand Colin.

Djebar, Assia. 2006. 'Discours de Réception, et Réponse de Pierre-Jean Rémy,' Académie Française. https://www.academie-francaise.fr/discours-de-reception-et-reponse-de-pierre-jean-remy (accessed August 17, 2021).

Djeghloul, Abdelkader. 1988. 'La formation des intellectuels modernes, 1880-1930,' in Omar Carlier and Fanny Colonna Lett (eds), *Intellectuels et militants en Algérie, 1880–1950*. Office des publications universitaires, Alger.

Dzanic, Dzavid. 2015. 'Between Fanaticism and Loyalty: Algerian Prisoners within the French Mediterranean Empire.' *The Journal of North African Studies* 20 (2): 204–224.

Ferry, Jules. 1885. 'Les fondements de la politique colonial.' July 28. Assemblée Nationale. https://www2.assemblee-nationale.fr/decouvrir-l-assemblee/histoire/grands-discours-parlementaires/jules-ferry-28-juillet-1885 (accessed October 21, 2021).

Gastaut, Yvan, Naïma Yahi, and Pascal Blanchard. 2014. 'La Grande Guerre des soldats et travailleurs coloniaux maghrébins.' *Migrations Société* 156 (6): 119–136.

Girardet, Raoul. 1972. *L'idée coloniale en France de 1871 à 1962*. La Table Ronde.

Habermas, Jürgen. 1991. *The Structural Transformation of the Public Sphere: An Inquiry into a Category of Bourgeois Society*. MIT Press.

IPSOS. 2020. 'Fractures Françaises: Face Aux Crises Qui Frappent Le Pays, Un Besoin de Protection plus Fort Que Jamais.' https://www.ipsos.com/fr-fr/fractures-francaises-face-aux-crises-qui-frappent-le-pays-un-besoin-de-protection-plus-fort-que (accessed October 24, 2021).

Jansen, Jan C. and Augustin Jomier. 2014. 'Une Autre "Union Sacrée"? Commémorer La Grande Guerre Dans l'Algérie Colonisée (1918–1939).' *Revue d'histoire Moderne et Contemporaine* 61 (2): 32–60.

Julien, Charles-André. 1992. 'Lettre du général Montagnac du 15 mars 1843.' In *Histoire de l'Algérie contemporaine*, edited by Charles-André Julien. Presses universitaires de France.

Le Monde. 1989. 'Comment Georges Pompidou avait justifié la grâce.' *Le Monde*, May 26. https://www.lemonde.fr/archives/article/1989/05/26/comment-georges-pompidou-avait-justifie-la-grace_4147249_1819218.html (accessed October 24, 2021).

Le Petit Journal. 1911. 'France will be free to bring to Morocco Civilization, Prosperity, and Peace.' *Le Petit Journal. Supplément Du Dimanche*. https://gallica.bnf.fr/ark:/12148/bpt6k7169830 (accessed June 9, 2025).

Le Point. 2021. 'Présidentielle 2022: Un Sondage Qualifie Zemmour Au Second Tour.' *Le Point*, October 6. https://www.lepoint.fr/politique/presidentielle-2022-un-sondage-qualifie-zemmour-au-second-tour-06-10-2021-2446523_20.php (accessed October 24, 2021).

Leroy-Beaulieu, Paul. 1882. *De La Colonisation Chez Les Peuples Modernes*. Guillaumin et Cie. https://gallica.bnf.fr/ark:/12148/bpt6k245012 (accessed October 24, 2021).

Lyons, Amelia H. 2013. *The Civilizing Mission in the Metropole: Algerian Families and the French Welfare State during Decolonization*. Stanford University Press.

Mbembe, Achille. 1993. 'Écrire l'Afrique à partir d'une faille.' *Politique africaine* 51: 69–97.

McDougall, James. 2006. *History and the Culture of Nationalism in Algeria*. Cambridge University Press.

Mishani, Dror, and Aurelia Smotriez. 2005. 'What Sort of Frenchmen Are They?' *Haaretz*, November 17. https://www.haaretz.com/1.4882406 (accessed October 24, 2021).

Ouldennebia, Karim. 2009. 'Histoire de L'état Civil Des Algériens – Patronymie et Acculturation.' *Revue Maghrébine Des Études Historiques et Sociales* 1: 5–24.

Paligot, Carole Reynaud. 2019. 'Usages Coloniaux Des Représentations Raciales: L'exemple de La Politique Scolaire.' In *Les Administrations Coloniales, XIXe-XXe Siècles: Esquisse d'une Histoire Comparée*, edited by Samia El Mechat. Presses universitaires de Rennes.

Rérolle, Raphaëlle. 2016. 'Pascal Ory "Ce pays n'est pas tout à fait comme les autres".' *Le Monde*, January 9. https://www.lemonde.fr/societe/article/2016/01/07/pascal-ory-ce-pays-n-est-pas-tout-a-fait-comme-les-autres_4843415_3224.html (accessed October 24, 2021).

Ross, Kristin. 1995. *Fast Cars, Clean Bodies: Decolonization and the Reordering of French Culture*. MIT Press.

Ruscio, Alain. 2015. *Nostalgérie: L' interminable histoire de l'OAS*. La Découverte.

Savarese, Éric. 2006. 'Après la guerre d'Algérie.' *Revue internationale des sciences sociales* 189 (3): 491–500.

Stora, Benjamin. 2004. *Histoire de l'Algérie coloniale (1830–1954)*. La Découverte.

Stora, Benjamin. 2005. *La gangrène et l'oubli*. La Découverte.

Stora, Benjamin. 2021. *Rapport sur les questions mémorielles portant sur la colonisation et la Guerre d'Algérie, Rapport remis au président de la République*. Palais de l'Elysée. https://www.elysee.fr/admin/upload/default/0001/09/0586b6b0ef1c2fc2540589c6d56a1ae63a65d97c.pdf (accessed November 7, 2024).

Toumi, Samir, 2017. 'A Alger, à 8 ans, j'apprenais le mot 'colonisation.' *Libération*. January 2. https://www.liberation.fr/debats/2017/01/02/a-alger-a-8-ans-j-apprenais-le-mot-colonisation_1538688/ (accessed October 21, 2021).

Weber, Eugen. 1976. *Peasants into Frenchmen: The Modernization of Rural France, 1870–1914*. Stanford University Press.

11

Prototyping Events: Creating Child-Oriented Methods of Disaster Preparedness

Chika Watanabe

Design thinking in international cooperation

Across the Pacific Ocean, Japanese and Chilean actors have been cooperating on disaster preparedness since the 1960s. For many years, Chilean seismologists have been traveling to Japan to join training courses, and Japanese scholars on earthquake resistant building codes have visited Chile to learn about architectural practices there. According to a Japanese government official working in Santiago, a major turning point came in 2010 with the Chile earthquake and tsunami, and in 2011 with the Great East Japan earthquake and tsunami (interview, April 16, 2018). Disaster risk reduction (DRR) became a particularly important focus in the cooperation agreements between the two countries. Accordingly, the Japanese Ministry of Foreign Affairs' (MOFA) 2012 Country Assistance Policy for Chile explicitly lists DRR as the primary policy objective (MOFA 2012).[1]

Since 2017, I have been conducting ethnographic research on the international cooperation between Japan and Chile around disaster preparedness, particularly pertaining to activities for children. I have been undertaking this research in collaboration with Dr. Jenny Moreno from the University of Concepción (Chile) and Dr. Shuhei Kimura from the University of Tsukuba (Japan).[2] The children's activities that

---

[1] For a historical analysis of Japan's 'science diplomacy' through seismology, see Jakoby (2021).
[2] In 2024, Jenny Moreno moved to the University of Bournemouth.

we have been studying center around a one-day event called *Iza! Kaeru Caravan* that a Japanese nonprofit organization has designed, where children learn skills to survive the first 72 hours or week after a mass disaster. These skills vary from learning to use a fire extinguisher to how to use everyday objects in emergency situations. Various community and governmental groups across Japan and in other countries, including Chile, have organized their own events based on this model. At first glance, this travelling of *Iza! Kaeru Caravan* from Japan to Chile appears to be a transposition of an example across contexts – in my case study, a Japanese example being applied to a Chilean context. The Japanese example, then, serves as a blueprint for Chilean actors to replicate. However, as this chapter will show, the process of translating *Iza! Kaeru Caravan* to the situation in Chile is not a simple act of copying an example. Chilean participants of the event do the work of what I call prototyping, which leaves the example open-ended and not-yet-formed. The power of the example in international cooperation is determined by its location on the continuum between, on one end, the force of the model (to be replicated) and, on the other end, the possibilities of the prototype (to be tinkered with). The former shows the example-as-authority, whereas the latter shows the example-as-possibility. This tension can explain the diversity of contexts that shape the uptake of examples (see Noyes and Wille, Chapter 2, this volume). Ultimately, I suggest that the location of the example on this continuum is unstable, as prototypes can easily slip into becoming static models, and static models can quickly become open and unauthoritative in the hands of different local actors. In this chapter, I trace the great effort of disaster preparedness actors to ensure that the children's community event would not become static but remain open-ended and participatory.

Japanese aid actors use the term 'international cooperation' (*kokusai kyōryoku*) to refer to a wide range of activities, from projects tackling poverty to the support of people with disabilities in the Global South. The word 'cooperation' first emerged in Japan in reference to war reparations to Burma (now known as Myanmar) in 1954 (Kitano 2011). Subsequently, 'international cooperation' was officially used for the first time in 1974 with the establishment of the Japan International Cooperation Agency (JICA), the government's flagship aid agency.[3] A glance at JICA's activities today evidence the broad scope of 'international cooperation' (JICA n.d.). A comparative look at other countries shows that Japan is not an exception

---

[3] In my work, I have shown how Japanese international cooperation activities were happening since the early 1960s via NGOs, earlier than the establishment of government agencies and state structures of aid (Watanabe 2019).

in this regard. The UK's 2015 Aid Strategy covers not only poverty but also other issues such as security, resilience, and 'global prosperity' (Government Digital Service 2015). This includes disaster preparedness.

The term 'international cooperation' might connote a harmonious and egalitarian relationship across nation-states but it is evident that this is not always the case. In Japan, international cooperation is inseparable from a condescending view of 'developing countries' (Kitano 2011, 45). Other development aid regimes have been accused of reproducing imperialist and colonial hierarchies (Escobar 1995). Yet, international cooperation practitioners and scholars have been aware of these critiques and initiated moves to change the unequal system of aid, promoting participatory, empowerment, and beneficiary-driven approaches (Stiglitz 2002; but see also critiques of participation, for example Cooke and Kothari 2001). Participation is now an orthodoxy in development programs.

Relevant to this chapter is the growing attempt in policy and governance circles to move toward more 'user'-driven programing through design thinking as a new form of participatory method (Bason 2014). There is no singular definition of 'design thinking,' but one of the leading global design firms, IDEO, states:

> Design thinking uses creative activities to foster collaboration and solve problems in human-centered ways. We adopt a 'beginner's mind,' with the intent to remain open and curious, to assume nothing, and to see ambiguity as an opportunity ... To think like a designer requires dreaming up wild ideas, taking time to tinker and test, and being willing to fail early and often. (IDEO n.d.(b))

Thus, designers prioritize collaboration, openness, and tinkering in order to try out different approaches without a fear of failure. Public servants see this approach as a promising way to engage citizens, experts, business actors, and other stakeholders in delivering policy solutions in innovative ways (Kimbell and Bailey 2017). Similarly, international cooperation actors such as from the UK's Overseas Development Institute (ODI) to the Department for International Development (DFID) have grasped onto design thinking. They see it as a way to reenergize and place creativity, co-designed programming, and appreciation for aid recipients' resourcefulness at the heart of the development and humanitarian sectors (HPG 2018; IDEO n.d.(a)). The activities I trace in this chapter are also derived from design thinking in the sphere of disaster preparedness.

The attention to participatory methods and design thinking is premised on the idea that there are binary choices which map onto each other: top-down versus bottom-up approaches, imposition versus participation, predetermined actions versus contingent pathways, and so on. However, in practice, both are always present. There is always both imposition and participation. As I show next, the tension between the two constitutes a continuum of exemplarity in disaster preparedness cooperation. Following the editors' introduction, I see exemplarity as a mode of cultural transmission (see Noyes and Wille, Chapter 1, this volume). In this transmission, an example has the capacity to both replicate itself as an imposition onto others and be open to contingent, participatory adaptations. As Andreas Bandak and Lars Højer (2015) have argued:

> The good example/exemplar is always less than everything and more than itself and ... examples and exemplars point to a constant movement — in both anthropological theory and the ethnographic worlds we attend to — between the general and the specific by suggesting, proposing, and revealing new generalized 'wholes,' standing for a broader class of phenomena, while at the same time always being in danger of being shallow 'exemplars of everything' or reduced to 'mere examples,' standing for nothing other than themselves. (Bandak and Højer 2015, 8)

To be more than itself, the example would need to impose its model onto others, but to be less than everything it would need to allow for local adaptations and potential endpoints to its replication. Examples, then, cannot be fully controlled and are always already subject to the agency of the actors in the uptake (see Noyes and Wille, Chapter 2, this volume). In short, an example is always calibrated along a continuum of seriality (repetition) and becoming (emergence), or example-as-authority and example-as-possibility. Therefore, on one end is the example as pure seriality, where more or less static models are replicated. On the other end is the example as prototype — that is, as an always-emerging and not-yet-whole example. I suggest that all examples have the possibility to fall somewhere on these extremes because even a not-yet-whole example still needs to have some kind of replicability in order to be an example.

Prototypes in design thinking are mock-ups to test and refine solutions to a problem through user engagement. Prototypes resemble examples in that they also aspire to be replicable, or in the editors' words, inspire uptake (Kimbell and Bailey 2017, 218; see Noyes and Wille, Chapter 2, this volume). But they differ in that prototypes are not fully formed examples — the 'model' itself is open to tinkering by various actors. As such, I follow the anthropologist Alberto Corsín-Jiménez (2014, 383) who describes a prototype as 'more than many and less than one.' In other words, it exists in a space prior to unified formation — 'less than one' — and with a promise to bring about an infinite number of reiterations. It is not quite a model yet and does not impose its own repetition.

What the theories of the prototype to date do not emphasize is the labor required to keep something a prototype. Despite the open orientation of design thinking, at least in the area of international cooperation, there is the danger for prototypes to close off into models to be copied, primarily from the Global North to the Global South. Therefore, depending on the social and political interests at play, people put in effort to keep an example as pure seriality – to be copied – or as a prototype – to be tinkered with. This is ultimately about contentions of power. In this sense, even a prototype based on design thinking is not automatically 'open and curious,' as the quote from IDEO seems to indicate. It requires constant work to ensure this openness and indeterminacy. Next, I trace the work of creating open-ended prototypes that happened on two dimensions. On one level, I foreground the continuous work that disaster preparedness actors in Chile put in to keep the event as a prototype so that the international cooperation and preparedness efforts were not simply top-down affairs.[4] I illustrate the importance of acknowledging the labor of people who make something a participatory and open-ended example – the openness of design-thinking is not just based on the intentions of the planners; it is actualized by the people involved in the implementation process. On another level, this chapter shows that the hard work involved in resisting coagulation – in trying to keep the prototype from becoming a unified or static model – is central to both international cooperation and the making of prepared subjects in the face of catastrophic disasters. In short, it is important to understand how disaster preparedness actors labor to ensure the open-endedness of a prototype because it is their everyday labor that exemplifies the kind of relational openness necessary to be prepared for disasters.

Two events across the Pacific Ocean

When I arrived in the coastal city of Talcahuano in south-central Chile in April 2018, everyone in the municipal office was busy preparing for an upcoming event in May. In particular, I found the official in charge of DRR, Boris, running from meeting to meeting across the municipal departments, schools, and other groups to finalize plans.[5] The event he was preparing is called '*la caravana escolar de seguridad*,' or more commonly called '*la caravana*.' It is an event modelled after *Iza! Kaeru Caravan*, conceived by a Japanese

---

[4] In another publication, I illustrate how this openness, or incompleteness of translation, is also central from the Japanese perspective (Watanabe 2021).

[5] I call Boris by his real first name at his request. I will also use the real name for the founder of *Iza! Kaeru Caravan* because I speak of him in his professional capacity. When I refer to Japanese interlocutors I will use their surname with the suffix '-san' to reflect how I talked to them in the field.

nonprofit social design organization called Plus Arts. *Iza! Kaeru Caravan* in Japan combines a toy exchange, where children can bring their old toys to exchange for those of other children, with hands-on activities, boardgames, and card games relating to disaster preparedness skills: for example, how to help people trapped under rubble after an earthquake *Iza! Kaeru Caravan* is an event that various actors across Japan as well as DRR officials and experts in other countries have replicated, including in Chile.[6]

Boris learned about Plus Arts' event in 2012 when he participated in a JICA training program on disaster preparedness in Japan. Talcahuano, along with other regions in Chile, had been struck by a major earthquake and tsunami in 2010, when over 33 people died, over 50,000 more were affected, and more than 13,000 houses were damaged (Torres et al 2018, 22–23). In 2011, the United Nations Development Program (UNDP) officials from the Chile office visited Talcahuano and selected it as one of the pilot cities for creating a municipal-level DRR department. With additional funds from the European Union (EU), the country's first municipal-level department for *gestión del riesgo de desastres* (DRR) was established. Four staff members have been involved with the office over the years, all of whom trained in Japan.

Out of all the trainings that Boris undertook in Japan, he was most taken by Plus Arts' events with children. Since 2014, he has organized various *caravanas* in Talcahuano. Although the toy exchange element of the Japanese version does not exist – because children in Chile do not have that many toys to give away, I was told – the rest of the events' designs are similar, using games to teach children how to survive a disaster. The event in 2018 was one of the largest *caravanas* that Boris had organized. Over 500 students between the ages of 9 and 11 from dozens of schools in the region gathered at a sporting arena. They were there to learn various skills in disaster preparedness through playful, fun activities: first aid, what to do in the case of a tsunami, and other skills for surviving the first 72 hours to a week after a disaster. There were 20 booths at the event, each with a hands-on activity, staffed by adults such as from the different municipal departments and some led by primary school students who had participated in past *caravanas*.

The booths offered interactive activities, and students visited them with their teachers. For example, as I describe later on, one booth showcased local herbs that people could use for physical and psychological treatments during emergencies. Primary school students led the 15-minute sessions for groups of a dozen children each. They had created a large die out of cardboard, which included different senses (taste, touch, and so on). An audience member would be asked to roll the die, and depending on the

---

[6] For an overview of *Iza! Kaeru Caravan*, watch the video here: https://vimeo.com/135238366.

option selected, they would touch or smell the herbs, or taste herb-infused teas. They could then discuss together the benefits of the herbs.

Here we have two events, across the Pacific Ocean, where one is modelled after the other. From one perspective, *Iza! Kaeru Caravan* and the *caravanas* might seem like festivals or carnivals. But the carnival or festival as an analytic does not quite capture *Iza! Kaeru Caravan* in Japan or the *caravanas* in Talcahuano because they do not upend normal hierarchies in the Bakhtinian sense.

The term 'event,' in contrast, allows me to consider the exemplarity of these activities. Anthropologists have always relied on events to make their analyses, as can be seen in our use of ethnographic vignettes. That is, we describe in detail a critical event from fieldwork and proceed to unpack it. Different generations and schools of anthropologists have approached these ethnographic events differently, and many have tended to see them as a 'micro example of macro dynamics' (Kapferer 2015, 18). In this view, everyday events are microcosms of larger structural forces, and ethnographic examples are illustrations of universal laws. In contrast, Bruce Kapferer (2015, 16) proposed that we take an event as an example but not as an illustration of macro dynamics, and instead, as 'a critical site of emergence.' There are processes and phenomena that emerge from everyday events that do not map onto wider structural explanations. This is a view that resonates with Bandak and Højer's (2015) theorization, which foregrounds the example's dynamism between being 'more than itself' and 'less than everything.' Thinking of the event-ness of the example illuminates in particular the moment when it becomes 'more than itself' as a site of conceptual and subject formation. The event is not only an example *of* a societal system but something new that could become an example *for* others.

Prototyping events

One anthropological framework for thinking about events appears in the works of Alain Badiou. For Badiou (2003, 49), the Event, expressed in Christ's Resurrection as 'pure beginning,' disrupts the reproduction of the status quo and reveals an absolute and universal Truth. As a philosopher, much of Badiou's proposition is difficult for anthropologists to accept, such as the insistence on a universal Truth. However, Stef Jansen (2019) suggests ways that anthropologists and other empirical scholars could adapt this conception of the Event. He focuses on Badiou's formulation that an event becomes an event only when subjects are recruited to act faithfully to it (Jansen 2019, 241). Three anthropological questions can be asked along these lines: (1) To whom are certain occurrences an event?; (2) how much is something an event?; (3) how long is an event an event? (Jansen 2019, 244–245). By pursuing these inquiries, Jansen (2019, 253) argues that Badiou can help us examine 'the constitutive relationships between the (after)lives of happenings and subject formation.' These might include actors who are mobilized by the event but not 'faithfully,' and rather, moved by fear. Events and people shape each other in specific historical moments of mutual emergence (see also Humphrey 2008; Demetriou 2007).

As events, then, the *caravanas* are moments of subject-formation, happenings that call forth a response from people who are then constituted as particular kinds of subjects in that call. But the Event, according to Badiou and his anthropological interlocutors, is supposed to be recognized as such. It might mean different things to different participants, but the event, when it is recognized, is a unitary object. That is not the case with the *caravanas*. As described next, the *caravanas* are and should be processual and relational, ultimately always unfinished. It is for this reason that I call them 'prototyping events.'

The founder of Plus Arts, Nagata Hirokazu, conceived of *Iza! Kaeru Caravan* in 2005, and at this point more than 15 years later, it might appear to be a fully formed project. Nevertheless, Nagata-san always emphasized the importance of incompleteness (*fukanzen*). During trainings for community organizers, he stressed the need to leave gaps in the planning so that multiple participants from children to their parents and their neighbors can contribute to the event's realization (Watanabe 2021). For Nagata-san, the making of relationships and connections among members of a community is as important as if not more than teaching children disaster preparedness skills and knowledge. It is this emphasis on incompleteness that makes *Iza! Kaeru Caravan* and the *caravana* akin to the prototype.

Alberto Corsín-Jiménez's formulation of the prototype takes inspiration from the feminist anthropologist, Marilyn Strathern, who in turn built on Donna Haraway's (1991) cyborg manifesto. Strathern (2004 [1991]) argued that the cyborg 'is neither singular nor plural, neither one nor many, a circuit of connections that joins parts that cannot be compared insofar as they are not isomorphic with one another' (54). Thus, parts do not stand for wholes, and parts do not ultimately cohere to become a united whole. Accordingly, events like *Iza! Kaeru Caravan* do not represent a totality such as 'Japaneseness' or a unified DRR method. Or, at least, it is not only that. The series of the *caravanas* in Chile and other similar activities around the world were inspired by *Iza! Kaeru Caravan* in Japan, but it would be a mistake to see these as exact replicas, and it would also be a mistake to see them as completely different from each other. They are 'neither one nor many.' Moreover, if we follow Corsín Jiménez's reformulation of Strathern's theory, the *caravanas* as prototypes are also 'neither singular nor plural.' He argues that 'the prototype indexes a cultural form in turn that is "more than many and less than one": always on the move and proliferating into affinal objects, yet never quite accomplishing its own closure' (Corsín Jiménez 2014, 385).

Iza! Kaeru Caravan, with the emphasis on incompleteness, precisely follows this ethos of non-closure.

The *caravanas* as prototyping events are, therefore, both open-ended and moments of assemblage from which particular subjects emerge. As a performative process, subjects are not pre-established, but rather, are enacted in contingent relationship with each other through the event (Suchman, Trigg, and Blomberg 2002; Wilkie 2014). The incompleteness of the event mobilizes actors to fill those gaps, becoming specific types of subjects in the process. Adhering to design thinking, prototyping events means that all participants, including the prototype itself, have to give up control. Everything and everyone should be ready to change at the event.

Enrollment to the event

One important way that *Iza! Kaeru Caravan* and the *caravana* differ from the prototype in a conventional design project is that they need to be constantly produced as prototypes. Regardless of how many years it has been since its conception, the event needs to be continually co-designed. This is because *Iza! Kaeru Caravan* can only be realized with the cooperation of different actors who plan and run the booths with activities, as well as the children, their families, and teachers who participate in the event. Prototyping the event involves the enrollment of diverse actors, resulting in its fragmentation and condition as 'less than one' (see Star and Griesemer 1989). The event also cannot exist fully-made because it needs to adapt to local concerns and experiences surrounding disasters. To inspire uptake, the example needs to be less-than-fully-formed and welcome input from others.

The enrollment of actors into an event requires work and Boris knew this. On April 20, 2018, a little over a month before the big *caravana*, he had a meeting with two female staff members from the municipal office that supports citizens with disabilities to encourage and explain their participation in the *caravana*. We sat around a long table in one of the top floor offices of the municipality. Using slides on a projected screen as he went along, Boris introduced the *caravana* as having two aims: first, disaster risk reduction, and second, to inculcate values of respect, tolerance, and solidarity among school children. This was not how he explained the event to everyone. DRR was always there, but he changed the second aim depending on the audience. The emphasis on 'respect, tolerance, and solidarity' in this occasion was meant to resonate with the disability support office's aims.

At one point, one of the staff members asked if any of the children being invited to the *caravana* would be disabled. She said: 'If that is possible, it could be very good.' Boris replied that he would ask the schools he had recruited, but that if they had any specific schools, programs, or children in mind, they could also recruit these participants themselves. He went on to explain other aspects of the *caravana*, and concluded by saying: 'The ball is now in your court, and you need to come up with some ideas for your booth.' These two staff members now had to design their own activity.

The enrollment of different actors for the *caravana* is not easy because it constitutes additional work for an already busy group of city employees. But Boris managed to involve a good number of people, many from departments he had never worked with, making the *caravana* in May 2018 a great success. The event was not exactly the same as *Iza! Kaeru Caravan* in Japan, and this variability is part of the design, as the event always depends on who is involved. These variations are what make this event a 'good example' in the form of a prototype, exemplary and replicable but also open-ended, indeterminate, and surprising. It also contains risk in its indeterminacy, as it became evident in the few days before the event when an organization pulled out at the last minute and the *caravana* was left with one booth less than planned. Despite the risks involved, the dynamic tension between example-as-authority and example-as-possibility is critical for international cooperation to work, as certain forms of knowledge are passed on but an openness to local adaptation also needs to exist.

The relational child

It is significant that *Iza! Kaeru Caravan* and the *caravanas* are aimed at children. In many contexts, including in Japan and Chile, the figure of the child often signals a kind of pure, innocent humanity (see Sheldon 2016). By the 17th century in Europe and North America, children were seen to be inherently good keepers of universal truths in the face of horror, and blank slates on which reason and morality could be written (Malkki 2010). They have also been represented as ideal victims who embody a generic, depoliticized humanity that needs protection. Children have been ideal figures of innocence at the heart of liberal personhood, upheld as paragons of human purity but thereby never quite achieving full personhood (Ticktin 2018).

On one level, this view of the child is present in *Iza! Kaeru Caravan*. However, I foreground here the conception of the child as a relational and intergenerational subject (Alanen 2001; Spyrou et al 2018). The child is also multiscalar, as seen in Greta Thunberg's speeches connecting historical, individual, and family time in her speeches (see Kverndokk, Chapter 5, this volume). In many ways, Boris' opening of new and old relationships to construct the event modeled the ways that people should cultivate relations in preparation for disasters – ultimately, it will be family members and neighbors who will help each other in times of disaster. Conceptualizing the child as relational was part of this thinking. As much as the games were aimed at children, Nagata-san and Boris both told me that the presence of adults was also important. In Japan, children came to *Iza! Kaeru Caravan* with their parents and grandparents, and organizers took note of the fact that the latter should also be listening to and participating in the activities. For example, during one *Iza! Kaeru Caravan* in Japan, I saw a girl about eight years old play a game with a miniature model of a bedroom, the aim of which was to secure furniture during an earthquake so that it would not fall onto a toy frog sleeping in a bed. The girl had to use wooden blocks to insert in spaces such as between a wardrobe and the ceiling. The volunteer running the booth then shook the bedroom using a sliding mechanism to show her and the other children there how the block stopped the wardrobe from falling onto the frog. The girl's mother was watching beside her. At the end, she commented to her daughter that when they return home, they should really check if their furniture was secured properly (fieldnotes, January 11, 2020).

In Chile, children came to the *caravanas* with their school teachers. Boris also stressed the importance of having the adults, both the teachers and the volunteers, watch and participate in the games when appropriate. In both countries, the hope is also that children will share what they learn with their parents, friends, and even neighbors after the event. As disaster scholars have noted, targeting children in disaster preparedness efforts is thought to be more effective in community-based DRR because the assumption is that parents will listen to their children more than to experts (Matsuura and Shaw 2014, 78). This does not necessarily happen in reality, as I found that children who participate in the *caravanas* do not always talk about the disaster skills they learned with their families, or about the event at all. But the assumption is that the child is a relational and multiscalar subject, a node of relations and temporalities through which disaster preparedness knowledge can travel. The *caravana* is meant to be so exciting and novel that it will trigger a chain of communication about disaster risks and preparedness techniques from children to their carers and friends.

New connections were also enabled through and with the child before the event. Ahead of the large *caravana* in May 2018, a group of five to six students from one primary school worked with a community organization of women gardeners to create a game showcasing local herbs that people could use for physical and psychological treatments during emergencies. In the course of weekly workshops with the women, the students had chosen different herbs and designed together a game around these plants. The women had also shown the students how to create seedlings out of seeds harvested from their plants. I met this group of children and women at a school during one of their last rehearsals before the *caravana*.

The first pair of students started their run-through of the activity by asking the women, two of us from the municipal office, and the other students – the audience – why we thought they chose the title 'herbs to the rescue' (*yerbas al rescate*) for this game. We shrugged and one of the women asked them to tell us. The two students took turns explaining the uses and benefits of each herb: rue, lemon balm, and the leaf of a fig tree. They seemed slightly nervous, with low voices and not quite meeting our eyes. They then showed us two drawings, which showed a man with a stomach ache and another who looked stressed. 'What is happening to this person,' asked one student as he pointed to one of the drawings, 'and which herb do you think we need based on the explanations we gave earlier?' One of the women suggested an answer, correctly, and we spent a few minutes discussing the drawings in relation to the herbs.

The second part of the activity involved using a large dice that the students had made out of cardboard. Each side had a different sensory type written on it such as vision, taste, and smell. The students explained that they would ask the participants to roll the dice, and they would then 'interact' with the herbs based on the sensory type that had come up. For example, if 'taste' was rolled on the dice, the students would prepare some herb-infused tea at that point so that participants could taste it. 'What did you learn from this?' asked one of the students at the end. One of the students in the audience raised his hand: 'Lemon balm is good for stress.'

In the weeks leading up to the *caravana*, children, teachers, municipal officials, and other people from Talcahuano like the women gardeners discussed worked together to design each activity. Boris gave them some ground rules such as the fact that the games needed to be participatory and not a demonstration of impressive skills by the adults. Beyond that rough framework, everyone had to come up with their own ideas for the booths, without which the event would not be possible. It might have been easier for Boris to use the same games as in Japan or designed all of them himself. But he purposefully *underdesigned* the *caravana*, spending considerable time and energy visiting different actors across the municipal offices, schools, and community organizations to convince them to co-design the event. He built relationships across different municipal departments, institutions, and individuals, and others did the same. As a result, everyone felt ownership for part if not all of the *caravana* and worked hard to make it a success.

Opening relations as preparedness

Prototyping events requires work from multiple actors to ensure openness, a task made especially challenging when the prototype has been around for many years and can easily be taken as a static model. It is also a challenge when people are busy with other daily tasks and would rather be told what to do than have to create something new. But this openness of the example is essential not only for international cooperation programs to work but also for the production of prepared persons. In the process of constituting the event, the relationships between people and among institutions became essential. Boris exemplified prototypes of relationships fostered toward one event, just as, at some point in the future, individuals would need to create and rely on relationships within the family, neighborhood, or relevant organization to survive and recover from a mass disaster.

I suggest that what emerged here were relations-as-resilience. Scholars and policy makers of disaster preparedness often state that community-based relations – whether that is argued in terms of 'social capital' (Aldrich and Meyer 2015), participatory methods (Cadag and Gaillard 2012), or ''community resilience' (Moreno and Shaw 2019) – will provide the kinds of support systems necessary for survival and recovery. Considering the making of the *caravana* as a 'performative artefact' (Suchman et al 2002), the idea of preparedness emerged through the event's preparations and implementation, which foregrounded the importance of various kinds of relationships. Thus, it was not a pre-determined idea of preparedness that informed the event, but rather, it was through the assembling of the event that the idea of preparedness emerged, specifically in terms of relations-as-resilience.

Preparedness can be defined in many ways, from a technocratic plan of continuation for systems considered to be vital (Collier and Lakoff 2015) to the simulation of emergencies in which roles such as 'victims' and 'rescuers' are established (Revet 2013). In the *caravanas*, the idea of preparedness as the making and strengthening of relations emerged. Relations were seen as resources to be mobilized for a community's resilience against disasters. For example, when a devastating disaster strikes, children and their families, who had learned survival skills at the *caravana*, could come together to harvest herbs helpful for calming people's nerves and distribute them to affected neighbors. The focus on children, therefore, was valuable because the child was a node in a wider network of relations that could be mobilized for disaster resilience.

The problem with this approach, however, is that relations are erroneously taken to be 'natural' and harmonious, and amenable to bureaucratic instrumentalization (see Li 2011). This is the shortcoming of resilience thinking overall, as many critics have shed light on the concept's depoliticizing effects and neoliberal capitalist underpinnings (MacKinnon and Derickson 2013). Relations in the world, whether within a family, among neighbors, or between institutional actors, are often rife with conflict, or even indifference. They cannot be simply mobilized like a pliable tool. Most significantly overlooked in the notion of resilience are the factors of the wider political economy and systems of governance, which need to be addressed to tackle disaster vulnerabilities; the resilience of individuals, families, and neighborhoods will only go so far. The political system often needs to change to ensure the equitable distribution of resources, for example. The *caravanas* produce the understanding of preparedness-as-relations, and relations-as-resilience, which fit DRR orthodoxies, but this is perhaps limited.

Yet, is there a way to find an openness to the relation-making efforts in Talcahuano, a possibility for something different in the prototyping events? Boris nurtured relationships but never in a coercive or purely instrumentalized way. He invited participants but left it up to them if they wanted to contribute, and how. Relations were not an explicit tool, but rather, a by-product of preparing the event. This was why there was some risk, as participants could suddenly drop out at the last minute, as we saw earlier. If, as the volume's editors state, the power of exemplarity lies in seeing examples as deeds and not as reified exemplars, perhaps it is only as a by-product that relations can be prototypes and not static models. As soon as relations are highlighted as important factors for disaster preparedness, they can quickly become static models, subject to the problems of resilience thinking. Ultimately, then, what Boris shows us is that the openness of an example-as-prototype is accomplished not simply through everyday labor but also through an indirect approach to the prototype in order to keep it open-ended. Some of the best examples might better serve us if we do not call them as such.

References

Alanen, Leena. 2001. 'Explorations in Generational Analysis.' In *Conceptualizing Child-Adult Relations*, edited by Leena Alanen and Berry Mayall. Routledge.

Aldrich, Daniel, and Michelle A. Meyer. 2015. 'Social Capital and Community Resilience.' *American Behavioral Scientist* 59 (2): 254–269.

Badiou, Alain. 2003. *Saint Paul: The Foundation of Universalism*. Stanford University Press.

Bandak, Andreas, and Lars Højer. 2015. 'Introduction.' In *The Power of Example: Anthropological Explorations in Persuasion, Evocation, and Imitation*, edited by Lars Højer and Andreas Bandak [A Supplement issue of the *Journal of the Royal Anthropological Institute*]. Wiley.

Bason, Christian, eds. 2014. *Design for Policy*. Routledge.

Cadag, Jake Rom D., and J.C. Gaillard. 2012. 'Integrating Knowledge and Actions in Disaster Risk Reduction: The Contribution of Participatory Mapping.' *Area* 44 (1): 100–109.

Collier, Stephen, and Andrew Lakoff. 2015. 'Vital Systems Security: Reflexive Biopolitics and the Government of Emergency.' *Theory, Culture and Society* 32 (2): 19–51.

Cooke, Bill, and Uma Kothari, eds. 2001. *Participation: The New Tyranny?* Zed Books.

Corsín Jiménez, Alberto. 2014. 'Introduction.' *Journal of Cultural Economy* 7 (4): 381–398.

Demetriou, Olga. 2007. 'To Cross or Not to Cross? Subjectivization and the Absent State in Cyprus.' *Journal of the Royal Anthropological Institute* 13 (4): 987–1006.

Escobar, Arturo. 1995. *Encountering Development: The Making and Unmaking of the Third World*. Princeton University Press.

Government Digital Service. 2015. 'Official Development Assistance (ODA).' *Government of the United Kingdom*. https://www.gov.uk/government/collections/official-development-assistance-oda--2 (accessed January 31, 2021).

Haraway, Donna J. 1991. 'A Cyborg Manifesto: Science, Technology, and Socialist-Feminism in the Late Twentieth Century.' In *Simians, Cyborgs, and Women: The Reinvention of Nature*. Routledge.

Humanitarian Policy Group (HPG). 2018. 'A Design Experiment: Imagining Alternative Humanitarian Action.' *Overseas Development Institute*. https://www.odi.org/sites/odi.org.uk/files/resource-documents/12009.pdf (accessed January 29, 2021).

Humphrey, Caroline. 2008. 'Reassembling Individual Subjects: Events and Decisions in Troubled Times.' *Anthropological Theory* 8 (4): 357–380.

IDEO. n.d. (a) 'Amplify; Accelerating Innovation in International Development.' https://www.ideo.org/programs/amplify (accessed January 29, 2021).

IDEO. n.d. (b) 'Design thinking defined.' https://designthinking.ideo.com/ (accessed January 29, 2021).

Jakoby, Julia M. 2021. 'Learning from the Earthquake Nation: Japanese Science Diplomacy in the 20th Century.' *Journal of Contemporary History* 56 (3): 485–501.

Jansen, Stef. 2019. 'Anthropological (In)Fidelities to Alain Badiou.' *Anthropological Theory* 19 (2): 238–258.

JICA (Japan International Cooperation Agency). n.d. 'Thematic issues.' https://www.jica.go.jp/english/our_work/thematic_issues/index.html (accessed January 27, 2021).

Kapferer, Bruce. 2015. 'Introduction.' In *In the Event: Toward an Anthropology of Generic Moments*, edited by Lotte Meinert and Bruce Kapferer. Berghahn Books.

Kimbell, Lucy, and Jocelyn Bailey. 2017. 'Prototyping and the New Spirit of Policy-making.' *CoDesign* 13 (3): 214–226.

Kitano, Shu. 2011. *Kokusai kyōryoku no tanjō: kaihatsu no datsu seijika wo koete [The Birth of International Cooperation: Beyond the Depoliticization of Development]*. Sōseisha.

Li, Tania M. 2011. 'Rendering Society Technical: Government through Community and the Ethnographic Turn at the World Bank in Indonesia.' In *Adventures in Aidland: The Anthropology of Professionals in International Development*, edited by David Mosse. Berghahn Books.

MacKinnon, Danny, and Kate Driscoll Derickson. 2013. 'From Resilience to Resourcefulness: A Critique of Resilience Policy and Activism.' *Progress in Human Geography* 37 (2): 253–270.

Malkki, Liisa. 2010. 'Children, Humanity, and the Infantilization of Peace.' In *In the Name of Humanity: The Government of Threat and Care*, edited by Ilana Feldman and Miriam Ticktin. Duke University Press.

Matsuura, Shohei, and Rajib Shaw. 2014. 'Concepts and Approaches of School Centered Disaster Resilient Communities.' In *Community Practices for Disaster Risk Reduction in Japan*, edited by Rajib Shaw. Springer.

Ministry of Foreign Affairs (MOFA). 2012. 'Country Assistance Policy for the Republic of Chile.' *Government of Japan*. http://www.cl.emb-japan.go.jp/doc/Country-Assitance-Policy-for-Chile_ENG.pdf (accessed January 29, 2021).

Moreno, Jenny, and Duncan Shaw. 2019. 'Community Resilience to Power Outages After Disaster: A Case Study of the 2010 Chile Earthquake and Tsunami.' *International Journal of Disaster Risk Reduction* 34: 448–458.

Revet, Sandrine. 2013. 'A Small World: Ethnography of a Natural Disaster Simulation in Lima, Peru.' *Social Anthropology* 21 (1): 38–53.

Sheldon, Rebekah. 2016. *The Child to Come: Life after the Human Catastrophe*. University of Minnesota Press.

Spyrou, Spyros, Rachel Rosen, and Daniel T. Cook. 2018. *Reimagining Childhood Studies*. Bloomsbury Academic.

Star, Susan L., and James. R. Griesemer. 1989. 'Institutional Ecology, "Translations" and Boundary Objects: Amateurs and Professionals in Berkeley's Museum of Vertebrate Zoology, 1907–39.' *Social Studies of Science* 19 (3): 387–420.

Stiglitz, Joseph E. 2002. 'Participation and Development: Perspectives from the Comprehensive Development Paradigm.' *Review of Development Economics* 6 (2): 163–182.

Strathern, Marilyn. 2004 [1991]. *Partial Connections*. Updated edition. Altamira Press.

Suchman, Lucy, Randall Trigg, and Jeanette Blomberg. 2002. 'Working Artefacts: Ethnomethods of the Prototype.' *British Journal of Sociology* 53 (2): 163–179.

Ticktin, Miriam. 2018. 'A World Without Innocence.' *American Ethnologist* 44 (4): 577–590.

Torres Méndez, Mauricio, Beatriz Cid Aguayo, María Teresa Bull, Jenny Moreno, Alejandro Lara, Carlos Gonzalez Aburto, and Bárbara Henríquez Arriagada. 2018. 'Resilencia Comunitaria y Sentido de Comunidad Durante la Respuesta y Recuperación al Terremoto-Tsunami del Año 2010, Talcahuano-Chile [Community Resilience and the Sense of Community During the Response and Recuperation from the Earthquake-Tsunami in 2020, Talcahuano-Chile].' *Revista de Estudios Latinoamericanos sobre Reducción del Riesgo de Desastres (REDER)* 2 (1): 21–37.

Watanabe, Chika. 2019. *Becoming One: Religion, Development, and Environmentalism in a Japanese NGO in Myanmar.* University of Hawai'i Press.

Watanabe, Chika. 2021. 'Translating Disaster Knowledge from Japan to Chile: A Proposal for Incompleteness.' In *Critical Disaster Studies*, edited by Andy Horowitz and Jacob Reemes. University of Pennsylvania Press.

Wilkie, Alex. 2014. 'Prototyping as Event: Designing the Future of Obesity.' *Journal of Cultural Economy* 7 (4): 476–492.

PART V

Trajectories

12

The Soft Power of a Small Country: Self-Perceptions of the Netherlands as a Model for Europe and the World

Robin de Bruin

Exemplarity in EUrope

The European Union (EU) and its predecessors have been aware of the cultural mechanism of exemplarity and have made, and continue to make, conscious use of it. The European Communities (EC) and the EU developed a discourse of themselves as an exemplar, or 'soft power' in Brussels' terminology, to support the transfer of European values, norms and rules to neighboring countries and trade partners (Zielonka 2008). However, exemplarity is not only important in the EU's external relations. Internally, it serves as a crucial mechanism within today's EU, manifested through informal competition between member states and the 'open method of coordination' – an EU instrument in which policy-making is based on a combination of cooperation, reciprocal learning, and the voluntary participation of member states (Heidenreich and Bishoff 2008).

The EU's official and unofficial internal competition of best practices is to be handled with care, as thoughtless comments can arouse resentment. For example, at the end of March 2020, during a meeting on the issue of the partial collectivization of the debts of Eurozone countries through 'coronabonds,' Wopke Hoekstra, the Dutch Christian Democratic finance minister, made some rather blunt remarks about 'certain' [Southern European – RdB] Eurozone countries being less prepared for the COVID-19 pandemic crisis than other countries, such as the Netherlands. He called for the EU to probe why those ill-prepared states hadn't built up the financial buffers to cope better with the economic shocks of the pandemic. This infuriated leading politicians in southern European countries like Portugal and Italy, reopening wounds from the Eurozone debt crisis (Alonso, van de Wiel, and Sadée 2021). In northern Europe, this euro crisis was partly blamed on the fiscal fecklessness of southern European governments – for example, by Hoekstra's predecessor Jeroen Dijsselbloem, who, in 2017, as president of the Euro Group, stated that solidarity with the countries affected by the euro crisis was extremely important, but that these countries could not 'spend all the money on drinks and women and then ask for help' (Mussler 2017).

Dijsselbloem's remarks aroused major political outcry, and he was accused by Portuguese Prime Minister António Costa of racist, xenophobic and sexist remarks. Costa wanted Dijsselbloem to step down as president of the Euro Group (Bugge and Khalip 2017). A few years later, Hoekstra's comments were branded 'repugnant' by this same Portuguese prime minister (von der Burchard, Oliveira, and Schaart 2020), who would become president of the European Council in 2024. In the longer run, Dutch self-image was hit by these controversies, and the Netherlands eventually had to back down in the debate over 'coronabonds.'

The historian Nicholas J. Cull (2021) has argued that the greatest degree of reputational security for a nation may be found in an international 'brand' which emphasizes cooperation with others and collaboration for a collective good. This chapter will show that the same applies to domestic, internal nation branding. Many Dutch politicians and intellectuals like to think of the Dutch as the world's pathfinders and pioneers. That message is usually well received by a large part of the Dutch population. In the early 1970s, many Dutch progressive left-wing politicians thought of their country as a *guide country*, leading like-minded Western countries in the fields of environmental policies, East-West relations in the Cold War and North-South relations, thereby creating leverage for global reforms (Kuitenbrouwer 1999, 183; Snel 2014, 62).

Expressions of the Netherlands as a progressive guide country for Europe and the world partly found their inspiration in views from outside the Netherlands about the Netherlands. The Dutch idea of being a guide country was subsequently picked up and either praised or criticized outside the Netherlands, but not emulated. Ultimately, the cycle of performance, amplification, judgment, citation, and emulation (see Noyes and Wille, Chapter 2, this volume) was primarily an inward-looking process.

This chapter[1] will first explain the meanings of the term *guide country* and its connection with left-wing progressive politics. I will demonstrate how the

---

[1] The author thanks Marjet Brolsma and Remieg Aerts for their contributions to this chapter and Mercedes Arndt for her comments on an earlier version of this chapter.

mechanism of exemplarity provides a strategy for less powerful actors – such as small countries – to construct a position for themselves within a given geopolitical field. Additionally, I will examine how the exemplarity process influences the self-conception of actors, particularly by linking practical successes to claims of ethical superiority.

Second, this chapter will explore how the Western tradition of liberal exemplarity plays out in the EU context. I will highlight the importance of 'Europe' as a lever for global change in the Netherlands' self-image as both a European and global guide country. This lever function of 'Europe' has, until now, been absent in historical explanatory models of the Dutch conceptualization of 'guide country.'

Netherlands as guide country

According to Ben Coates, a journalist from the UK and long-time resident of the Netherlands,

> It's fair to say many people here pride themselves on their industriousness and efficiency. There's a common notion in the country that other nations fail simply because they're not Dutch enough: The cover of an issue of Dutch magazine EW last summer [of 2020 – RdB] depicted Northern Europeans wearing suits and working hard, while Southerners in tight red clothes drink wine and lounge in the sunshine. (Coates 2021)

However, cracks were starting to show in the usually bulletproof Dutch self-esteem, according to Coates, as the country seemed to be outperformed by neighbors and other countries when it came to managing the COVID-19 pandemic crisis: this 'botched handling' of the pandemic appeared to have 'damaged Dutch self-esteem.' He argued that the popular self-image of the Netherlands as a guide country, setting an example for the rest of the world with its boldly progressive policies had started to feel quaint, and cited the Dutch academic Rob de Wijk. The latter had claimed during the COVID-19 pandemic that the Netherlands was 'over' as a guide country: 'Our vaccination strategy is a disaster, we are at the top of the number of infections and have social unrest … Other countries are looking at us with increasing amazement' (de Wijk 2021, as cited in Coates 2021).

A few years after the end of the COVID-19 pandemic, little of this despair remains. The Dutch policy was no less effective than that of neighboring countries. The example does show, however, that many Dutch political and intellectual elites, of whom Rob de Wijk can be regarded as an exponent, want their country to live up to the self-image of a guide country and also want their country to be seen abroad as an exemplar.

Connection with progressive politics

Many Dutch politicians and intellectuals have traditionally thought of the Netherlands as the vanguard of the EU's environmental transition, often with reference to the historically grown Dutch can-do mentality in the field of waterworks engineering (Bregman 2020). While the Dutch government indeed advocated to raise EU ambitions for 2030 from a 40 percent to 55 percent emission reduction since 1990 – presented in the European Commission's 'Fit for 55' program in July 2021 (Netherlands' Government 2021) – the Netherlands itself does not score well compared to other EU member states in the transition to renewable energy or the reduction of nitrogen emissions.

In December 2019, this didn't stop the First Vice President of the European Commission at that time, Dutchman Frans Timmermans, from introducing the new Commission's Green New Deal for Europe at the Dutch Labor Party's annual Joop den Uyl Lecture (named after the former prime minister of the most leftist cabinet in Dutch history between 1973 and 1977). The title of Timmermans' lecture, 'Groeien aan de grens' (Timmermans 2019), was a clear reference to *Grenzen aan de groei*, the title of the Dutch translation of *The Limits to Growth* (Meadows et al 1972), the seminal Club of Rome report about overpopulation and environmental pollution.[2] Thus, the title of Timmermans' lecture in fact referred to the self-image of the Netherlands as a guide country.

This self-image was inspired by a statement from one of the authors of *The Limits to Growth* and was soon adopted by Dutch politicians, especially from the left. The Club of Rome report was officially published in March 1972. Earlier that same month, a committee of Dutch progressive politicians, under the leadership of the Dutch Vice President of the European Commission Sicco Mansholt, and with Labor Party leader Joop den Uyl among its members, had published their own report. Some of these politicians had earlier been sent a draft version of *The Limits to Growth* (Van Merriënboer 2006, 364). In their own report, the Dutch politicians committed themselves to efforts with regard to the nuclear, biological, and chemical arms race, overpopulation/global poverty, and environmental protection, not because they cherished the illusion that the Netherlands really had the (soft) power to save 'space-ship earth,' but as a first step in the right direction (Snel 2014, 62). While awaiting a truly effective global policy of the 'Europe of the Ten' – the then six countries of the EC: Belgium, France, Italy, Luxembourg, the Netherlands and West Germany; together with its assumed new member

---

[2] This title still is regularly being referred to in Dutch media (see, for example, Telegraaf 2020).

states: Denmark, Ireland, Norway[3] and the United Kingdom – Commissioner Mansholt and his fellow progressives argued the Netherlands should be the first country to implement the policies that were needed (Van Merriënboer 2006, 366; Snel 2014, 62). The concept of a guide country was first introduced in a subsection of this Dutch report, titled 'The Netherlands, Guide Country,' in which Dennis Meadows, one of the main initiators of the Club of Rome, was quoted saying that 'if it does not start in Holland, it will not start at all.'[4] Meadows should probably be credited as the real inventor of the concept of a *guide country*, because, at the time the Dutch report was being prepared, he was known to have referred to the Netherlands as a *pilot country* (Snel 2014, 62–63). So, the Dutch self-image was in fact inspired by the view of an outsider.

Meadows has certainly also been important for the spread of the concept of a guide country. In April 1972, while at a conference in the Dutch town of Delft, Meadows reiterated that the Netherlands could act as a guide country for the study of problems related to the limits of economic growth (Snel 2014, 63). The fact that twice as many copies of *The Limits to Growth* had been sold in the Netherlands as elsewhere in the world could, according to Meadows, indicate that the Dutch population was more receptive to warnings about mounting ecological dangers (Volkskrant 1972). He obviously considered this a powerful performance in itself – a signal from the Netherlands that there was nothing ridiculous about advocating idealistic visions in politics.

That the latter view was not widely accepted became evident from the reactions to the notion of a guide country in the conservative press. Despite the rather modest ambition of the Mansholt Committee to take the lead in initiating the first steps toward reforms, it was heavily criticized by an editorial comment in the Netherlands' largest right-wing newspaper *De Telegraaf*, with the title 'The Netherlands – guide country.' According to *De Telegraaf*, the committee had presented a far too ambitious reform plan for Dutch society, Europe and the world. The newspaper commented ironically that, although the Dutch were not yet in charge of the world, 'with the Netherlands as a guide country and Europe as its lever one should be able to accomplish these aims' (Telegraaf 1972).

The Mansholt report served as a source of inspiration for a second report, 'Bombs for Bread.' This second report was written by a group of pacifists who thought that the Mansholt report focused too strongly on the environment.

---

[3] Norway would reject the EC membership in a referendum in September 1972.
[4] The radical-progressive politician Bas de Gaay Fortman, who was not a member of the committee, also claimed to have introduced the 'presumptuous word guide country' (De Gaay Fortman 2001, 375) in an article published on February 22, 1973 (De Gaay Fortman 1973, 112), so almost a year after the publication of the Mansholt committee's report.

The authors of this second report, the renowned polemologist Hylke Tromp, the Protestant ethicist Johannes Verkuyl, and the radical-progressive politician Bas de Gaay Fortman argued that the Netherlands as a small country could fulfil a 'forerunner function in the world.' As a first step towards the removal of nuclear weapons from Europe, the Netherlands could remove all nuclear weapons storage sites from its territory: 'Here lies an opportunity for a small country like ours to exert a major influence: a statement by the Netherlands could also make it clear to the American people that there is a risk that the US can lose the sympathy of its allies with an aggressive nuclear policy' (Post 1972).

Initially, right-wing politicians also made use of the guide country concept. For them, the concept had more to do with a boy-scout-style exploration of best practices than with being a moral compass for the world. The conservative-liberal cabinet minister for Economic Affairs Harry Langman, for example, stated in a parliamentary debate in March 1972 that the Netherlands in fact acted as a guide country within the EC in the field of environmental issues (Snel 2014, 63–64). Although Heinrich Heine (was supposed to have) said that everything in the Netherlands happens 20 years later than elsewhere, Langman argued that the impression he himself had gotten from 'Brussels' was rather the opposite, namely that everything in the Netherlands actually happens 30 years earlier than anywhere else (Netherlands' Second Chamber 1972, 7). Notwithstanding the apparent slowness of the Brussels decision-making process, the Dutch government became an advocate of transferring power to EC institutions in order to 'integrate' the member states' environmental policies. In the words of the historian Marc Dorpema, the Dutch 'became increasingly ardent supporters of binding Community legislation and of granting its institutions the powers to enforce these legislations' (Dorpema 2020, 243–246).

In May 1972, the Dutch foreign minister for the Catholic Party, Norbert Schmelzer, a staunch supporter of European integration, interpreted the idea of a guide country in the same way, when he answered a question in the Dutch senate on whether or not NATO should also be involved in environmental issues: Should NATO stick to its core business of military defense, or not? Schmelzer advocated the 'guide country method' or '*pilot-nation* working method,' which meant that countries would voluntarily participate in new projects when they realized that this would be beneficial for their self-interest (Netherlands' First Chamber 1972, 881). This concept of a guide country recalls the EU's open method of coordination, in which the EU countries' policies are evaluated by one another.

So initially, for some, the term guide country had a fairly neutral connotation, as a group of pathfinding boy scouts, but for others the term also had an explicitly moral connotation, as a group of prophets. In 1974, the Catholic newspaper *De Tijd* dismissed the second idea of the Netherlands as a 'beautiful dream,' but at the same time advocated the first idea, namely the use of the recently reclaimed new land in the Flevo polder, as the ideal breeding ground for the development of a new ecological type of agriculture in Europe (Langenhoff 1974).

Over time, the concept of a guide country became regarded as a progressive left-wing concept of a country which reminded humanity of its role as the steward of the earth. 'The Netherlands must be a guide country for radicals, it must point out a path in its policy that can also lead the other EC and NATO member states to a globally responsible security and development policy,' the radical-progressive politician de Gaay Fortman stated in a 1973 article on peace policy (De Gaay Fortman 1973, 112).

Jan Pronk, the cabinet minister for development aid in the left-wing cabinet led by Prime Minister den Uyl (1973–1977), had been a member of the former Mansholt Committee. In the early years of his tenure as minister, he was guided by the idea that the Netherlands, in cooperation with like-minded countries, should be the driving force behind reforms in the North-South relations (Brandsma and Klein 1996, 50). After its formation in 1973, the enthusiasm of the den Uyl cabinet for development aid went hand in hand with a desire to decolonize the remaining Dutch colony Surinam as soon as possible (Bleich 2008, 320), partly in response to the sense of guilt within the Labor Party for its role in the violent decolonization war of Indonesia between 1945 and 1949. The Labor Party tried to get right in Surinam what they got wrong in Indonesia. A revolt against the Dutch-British oil company Shell on the Antillean island of Curaçao, another remaining Dutch colony, in 1969 acted as a catalyst: Surinam had to become independent, even though not the entire Surinamese population supported independence. The Labor Party wanted the Netherlands, in the words of Jan Pronk, to be a 'unique' decolonizer by providing financial guarantees for the economic development of Surinam (Jansen van Galen 2001, 52–53, 72, 83, 95). One of his other ambitions was to make the Netherlands a guide country for the European Economic Community in its relationship with other 'developing countries' (Trouw 1974), because, according to Pronk, Europe mainly provided aid to its former colonies, and this was only intended 'to restore those colonial relations in economic terms' (Vrije Volk 1975).

Showing a superior progressive moral stance

In the following years, the notion of a guide country also became strongly connected to the act of showing a superior progressive moral stance, or 'getuigenispolitiek' (testimonial policy) in Dutch. In his memoirs, former American Secretary of State Henry Kissinger provides an excellent story about this attitude that he titles 'the den Uyl fiasco' (Kissinger 1999, 570). In May 1975, he and President Gerald Ford had an official dinner at the White House with the Dutch Labor prime minister den Uyl, that, according to Kissinger, was 'one of the most bizarre and tense evenings of my experience in government' (Kissinger 1999, 566). On the evening of the dinner, President Ford had simultaneously started military operations against the Khmer Rouge in Cambodia on three different fronts, in order to liberate the crew of the American merchant ship Mayaguez that had been kidnapped by the Khmer. Not wishing to embarrass his guest, Ford had decided to go ahead with the dinner. Kissinger said of it:

> Den Uyl was not the ideal guest with whom American policymakers involved with monitoring a military operation might have wished to share that evening. Since he was from the pacifist wing of the Dutch Labor Party [in fact he was not a pacifist – RdB], den Uyl's enthusiasm for any Indochina-related military activity was muted, to say the least. He had obviously been briefed to avoid being provocative, a feat he never quite managed. At intervals, den Uyl could not restrain himself from stressing in a professorial manner that he was not passing judgment on any particular military operation but, in principle, he did not consider military force the appropriate way to solve political problems. It was an odd comment from the representative of a NATO ally whose country we had pledged to defend. Nor was it consistent with Dutch history. Den Uyl never vouchsafed to us by what other means we might induce the Khmer Rouge to release the hostages. (Kissinger 1999, 566)

The progressive identity of the Netherlands in the 'long Sixties' that was demonstrated by den Uyl in the White House is often regarded as a surrogate religion for ex-Catholics and ex-Protestants, who had left the Church in previous years (den Uyl himself was a former Calvinist) (Kennedy 2010, 147). 'Getuigenispolitiek' is generally regarded as a remnant of their Christian faith. Anecdotes like Kissinger's about den Uyl are often extrapolated into claims about the 'long Sixties' as a bygone age in which the Netherlands was still its 'true self,' slogans such as 'spreading of knowledge, income and power' and 'power to imagination' (which referred to the Parisian slogan of May 1968: 'l'imagination au pouvoir'), reflecting either a self-confident, forward-looking post-Christian nation, or a country of narcissistic self-aggrandizers (Kennedy 2010, 162).

Den Uyl himself claimed not to like the term 'guide country.' In a 1987 interview he referred to the fact that this term was often used in the 1970s, but that he himself had 'always found it a horrible word. I'd rather throw that term in the corner. You shouldn't want something like that, it's way too pretentious.' However, he also emphasized that back then, the Netherlands 'gained respect through the leading position that we occupied with development policy. ... The Netherlands was a model for advanced thinking. We were listened to. We were taken seriously' (Breedveld and Koelé 1987).

The notion of a guide country had little to do with traditional foreign policy. The main actors weren't just states or diplomats, but also non-state actors, such as the environmental movement, or the Dutch anti-nuclear and anti-cruise missile movement in the late 1970s and early 1980s that cited this notion and incorporated it into their action repertoire. Protests against the deployment of 'American' cruise missiles on 'European' soil under the slogan 'Help get all nuclear arms out of the world, starting in the Netherlands' rejuvenated Dutch missionary self-righteousness. A 1981 rally in Amsterdam against the deployment of nuclear cruise missiles in the Netherlands attracted more than 400,000 people; a 1983 rally in The Hague attracted 550,000 people (Figure 12.1).

The organizers saw the Netherlands as the most fit country to set a good example for Europe on both sides of the Iron Curtain, since the Netherlands, as a small country with the reputation of a loyal NATO country but not a hardliner in the relations with Eastern European countries, in their view was particularly capable of evoking sympathy in the US or the Eastern Bloc. Many Dutch conscripts also protested in military uniform. This performance

Figure 12.1: Former Prime Minister Joop den Uyl at the rally in The Hague against the deployment of nuclear cruise missiles in the Netherlands, 29 October 1983

Source: By permission of the Dutch National Archives CC0, photographer: Marcel Antonisse/ Anefo, permanent url: http://hdl.handle.net/10648/ad8b5f78-d0b4-102d-bcf8-003048976d84

of 'NATO soldiers against nuclear arms' offered a unique twist to the myth of the Netherlands as a loyal NATO: the Netherlands was willing to defend itself but was not prepared to contribute to an arms race that carried the risk of a nuclear Armageddon. Conservative opponents described the philosophy of the peace movement as simplistic and naïve:

> For, they say: We must trigger a chain reaction. When peace movements in Western Europe, which inherently have 'more degrees of freedom' than those in Eastern Europe, take the lead in influencing their governments, Eastern European reform groups will be able to follow. Gradually, rapprochement will grow between Western and Eastern European countries, who together can pressure the respective superpowers, America and Russia, to withdraw ... Optimism in this regard knows no bounds. (Nederlands Dagblad 1982)

At the time, the German-born American historian Walter Laqueur dismissed this attitude as 'Hollanditis,' as if it was an illness. 'Holland has long been known as an exemplary country,' he argued, but this was now a danger precisely because the major European countries were at risk of being infected by the bad Dutch example (Laqueur 1981). He shared with the activists the idea that Europe functioned as a lever for Dutch political demands.

His term, Hollanditis, was quickly adopted by the peace movement as evidence that the guide country role of the Netherlands was also recognized by opponents. The Belgian social democratic member of the European Parliament, and later European Commissioner, Karel van Miert argued, for example, in a speech at the 1981 rally in Amsterdam, 'Let this Hollanditis spread across the world, to the United States, and sew it into the Warsaw Pact' (NRC Handelsblad 1981).

Product of post-war politics, or the progressive incarnation of a long-term practice?

There is an ongoing historical debate in the Netherlands about whether or not the self-image of a guide country was a typical product of post-war politics, or rather the progressive incarnation of a long-term practice in foreign policy. The latter was argued by historians who interpreted the notion of a guide country as the clergyman's face in an age-old ambiguous foreign policy of the commercial impulses of the 'merchant' and the religious impulses of the 'clergyman.'[5] The Dutch political scientist Alfred Pijpers

---

[5] More recent literature characterizes this contrast between egoistic, economic motives and altruistic, idealistic impulses as misleading (van Dam and van Dis 2014, 1636–1637).

argued the first. He explained this idea as part of the compensatory search after the war of independence in, and loss of, Indonesia between 1945 and 1949 (Pijpers 1991). This view was confirmed by the Dutch high official of the EC Edmund Wellenstein who stated at the end of his long life that as a child he 'knew the life of a large colonial empire that didn't want to get in trouble with its neighbors. ... After we had broken free from Indonesia, ... we were suddenly a small country on a devastated continent' (Kuijk 2012).

According to Wellenstein, the country realized that it could only take fate into its own hands if it shared insights and developed policies together with its European neighbors (Kuijk 2012). As a small country, unencumbered by the issues of major powers, it was fit to serve as an example for Europe and the world.

Most of the research on the Netherlands as a guide country has been carried out by the American-Dutch historian James Kennedy, who is rather well-known in the Netherlands for his original analysis of changing Dutch culture in the Sixties in the Dutch translation of his PhD thesis on cultural change in the Netherlands during the 1960s (Kennedy 1995). Instead of focusing on either a 'protest generation' or a 'battery of socio-economic forces,' he argues that the centrist politicians, intellectuals, clerics, newspaper editors and other leaders of the Netherlands were the most important agents of the cultural change of the Sixties: 'In order to "keep up with the times" and thus control and direct a rapidly changing society, these elites either initiated significant changes or (more often) proved to be rather receptive to the "modern" forces with which they were confronted' (Kennedy 1997, 362).

Kennedy interprets the idea of a 'guide land' (Kennedy 1999–2000) as a coherent collective ideology of exemplarity for a better world in this life, not the Christian after-life. According to Kennedy, it ended with the great disillusionment of the second half of the 1980s, which spawned cynicism and materialism (Kennedy 2010, 142–145).

A condition for the development of Dutch missionary internationalism, according to Kennedy, was the lack of a state ideology in the Netherlands like that of the US, as a result of pillarization – the Netherlands was a religiously segmented ('pillarized') society until the 1960s. The country lacked well-defined civic virtues. Dutch 'missionary nationalism' could be regarded as an attempt to fill this gap (Kennedy 2005, 10–12; Kennedy 2010, 130). Subsequently, Kennedy defines the guide country attitude as a 'public religion' or 'public theology' of modern Protestant countries, which should be distinguished from the French secular *mission civilisatrice*. In his analysis, Kennedy emphasizes the massive exodus from 'pillarized,' static church institutions in the Netherlands of the Sixties in combination with the maintenance of individual piety and the rise of anti-traditional global engagement. He sees similarities with the tradition of 'public theology,' the moral campaigns of the evangelicals and Quakers in the predominantly

Protestant Anglo-Saxon world of the 19th century (Kennedy 2010, 106–111, 131). In short, Kennedy sees the idea of a guide country not just as a form of surrogate nationalism, but also as a surrogate religion. The small size of the country does not play a major role in his explanatory model.

Kennedy is absolutely right when he claims that, since the 1960s, many Dutch have the paradigms of inevitable progress and different speeds on the path to modernity in the back of their minds (see Oñorbe Genovesi 2020). However, two arguments can be made against Kennedy's conclusions. In the first place, the basic tradition of seeing the Netherlands as a soft power for Europe and the world is certainly not inseparable from post-Christian progressivism. Examples from a more-or-less conservative angle can also be added to the list, such as criticism on advocates of indisputable multiculturalism from the social democrat Paul Scheffer or the pleas against the alleged 'Islamization' of Dutch culture around 2000 from Pim Fortuyn (until his murder in 2002), Ayaan Hirsi Ali, Theo van Gogh (until his murder in 2004), and Geert Wilders. Here, too, a role was seen for the Netherlands as the initiator of a European, and maybe even a global political debate.

In the second place, ideas about the internationalist mission of the Netherlands did not just play a role in the period between the 1960s and the mid-1980s. In addition to 'development aid' and disarmament, the idea of being a guiding country also played a strong role in medical-ethical issues, such as the policy of harm reduction with regard to 'soft drugs' (1976) and the legalization of abortion under specific conditions (1984). These policies were followed by similar policies after 1985, such as the act on euthanasia in 2001. Euthanasia was made possible in the Netherlands for patients experiencing 'unbearable suffering with no prospect of improvement.' Since then, euthanasia under specific conditions and 'assisted dying' have been legally accepted by some other countries as well. Furthermore, a special source of national pride in the Netherlands after 1985 was the act on same-sex marriage in 2000; the Netherlands was the first of now almost 40 countries to make possible same-sex marriage. A third case of the guide country attitude after 1985 concerned the LibLab consensus in Dutch politics from 1994 to 2002 that was generally seen in the Netherlands as an example for Tony Blair's New Labour and for the American Democratic Party under Bill Clinton. Clinton and Blair actually praised the Dutch Labor prime minister Wim Kok for being their forerunner in using the market mechanism to serve social ends. In 1999, at an international meeting in Washington on the Third Way synthesis between economically liberal and center-left social policies, Clinton introduced him by saying 'Wim Kok, from the Netherlands, actually was doing all this before we were' (Oudenampsen 2021, 45).

A largely similar list could be given of various fields in which the Netherlands regarded itself as a small lighthouse for the world before the 1960s. A fundamental difference between the period before the 1960s and after the 1960s is that the notion of a guide country always explicitly played a role after the 1960s – either as an honorary title to be lived up to, as a model to emulate, or as a cautionary symbol of moral hubris and delusion.

Europe as a lever

Since the 19th century, self-perceptions of European nations had always been inseparably intertwined with images of Europe. Europe was essentially thought 'through' the nation (De Roode 2012) and vice versa. In the 1830s, Johan Rudolf Thorbecke, probably the most important Dutch statesman of the 19th century, had already developed an 'organic' notion of a European order (Aerts 2018, 214–215). Central to the idea of Europeanness of people like Thorbecke was the notion of reciprocity: every nation had a specific task, role, and significance in Europe, but in turn was also shaped by the European 'larger whole.' Following Thorbecke, many Dutch politicians advanced the Netherlands' role as a non-competitor in the European power struggle, or as the perfect mediator between the great powers in post-war Western Europe (de Bruin 2014, 125–132, 142).

Before the occupation of the Netherlands by Nazi Germany from May 1940 to May 1945, the Netherlands was often seen as an exceptional successful colonizer. Publicists from different European colonial powers idealized the Dutch 'professional' and 'rational' systems of colonial exploitation (Wagner 2022, 113–116). The Dutch self-image was comprised of a combination of the notions of the Netherlands as the originator of international law, the patron of neutrality and the advocate of free trade, which was seen by many Dutch politicians as the prelude to world peace. In 1913, the Dutch professor of legal science Cornelis van Vollenhoven advocated a pioneering role for the Netherlands in the establishment of an 'ethical' international order in a book that advocated national concord. 'Honor befalls the nation,' he wrote, 'which leads as a scout' (van Vollenhoven 1913, 63).

Long before the establishment of the EC in the 1950s, Dutch politicians saw Europe as a as a lever for global change. In order to fight the economic crisis of the 1930s, Norway, Sweden, Denmark, the Netherlands, Belgium, and Luxembourg signed the so-called Oslo Convention. The Oslo states wanted to set a good example in trade policy for the major European powers. Nobody suspected these smaller countries of pursuing dominance in Europe. However, these attempts proved to be fruitless because the great powers in Europe could not or did not want to align with the Oslo states. In the British case, for example, the imperial interests stood in the way (van Meurs et al 2018, 25).

So, underneath the skin of historical changes, there were continuities between the pre-war Dutch pursuit of international order and free trade and the strong identification with the project of European integration after the end of the Second World War. The traditional Dutch notion of free trade as a case of morality inspired the fruitful efforts of Dutch politicians like Foreign Minister Johan Willem Beyen to establish a European common market as part of the European peace project (Weenink 2005, 475).

This positive attitude changed temporarily in the 1970s, when the progressive parties only conditionally supported the process of European integration, arguing that the kind of society they wanted to create in the EC was more important than the pace at which the process of European unification took place (Reiding 2013). But overall, from the 1950s to the 2000s, the Netherlands would have the reputation of being a loyal member state of the EU until 1 June 2005, when the Dutch unexpectedly rejected the EU Constitutional Treaty in an advisory popular referendum. (De Bruin 2014, 65).

The organic relation between the Netherlands and Europe also worked the other way around. The tenacity of self-esteem and resilience against the dark side of one's own history, from the Netherlands' role in slave trade to the relative aloofness of the Dutch authorities towards the persecution of Dutch Jewry under Nazi rule or the incapability of the Dutch battalion to intervene during the massacre of Bosnian Muslims in Srebrenica in July 1995, can partly be explained by the awareness that the Dutch behavior did not deviate from a general European pattern.

Conclusion

The idea of effectively influencing other countries by acting as a *pilot country* is attractive for a small state without hard power. However, this does not explain the, from time to time extremely strong, self-identification of the Netherlands as a guide country.

The explanatory historical framework of the Dutch international missionary drive is usually dominated by the small size of the country and by cultural factors, such as the Calvinist root note of Dutch culture, post-Christian progressivism or the tools developed by a divided ('pillarized') nation to find common ground.

This chapter has added the idea of Europe as a lever to this framework, by discussing cases which seem to suggest that the notion of being organically connected with the European larger whole played a major role in Dutch missionary internationalism. National self-images are inseparably intertwined with perceptions of Europe and EU member states essentially see Europe through the lenses of their respective nations. Setting the example for Europe was a task the Dutch imposed on themselves in order to set the example for the world, with Europe as a lever.

As part of this missionary internationalism, the Dutch tend to see the EU and the Eurozone as organizations under construction to become a 'Greater Holland.' This notion went a little off track with Dijsselbloem and Hoekstra's attempts to set their own country as an example to southern European

EU partners. What the examples of their *faux pas* show, is that there are clear limits to branding one's own nation abroad (Gienow-Hecht 2019).

What the case also demonstrates is the usefulness of nation branding for domestic purposes. Although the concept of the Netherlands as a progressive guide country for Europe and the world was, in part, influenced by external perceptions of the Netherlands as a *pilot country*, and although the idea of *Hollanditis* was either celebrated or critiqued internationally, the process of performance, amplification, judgment, citation, and emulation remained largely inward-focused. It is no coincidence that Timmermans referred in his speech on the European Commission's Green New Deal to the enthusiasm with which the Club of Rome report was received in the Netherlands.

Conversely, the notion of the Netherlands as a progressive guide country became an important representation of everything that had gone wrong since the 1960s for the Dutch far-right Partij voor de Vrijheid (PVV), that won a landslide victory in the 2023 elections and formed a coalition government with three other parties in 2024. As a ruling party, the PVV strongly focuses on reducing economic aid to countries in the 'Global South,' an area where the ideal of the Netherlands as a guide country was most prominently expressed in the 1970s (Kuitenbrouwer 1999, 198).

According to Martin Bosma, a prominent PVV politician and chair of the Dutch Second Chamber, Dutch scepticism towards the EU, which first emerged in the 2005 referendum, was rooted in a long-standing Dutch tradition. He portrayed the EU as a proponent of post-1968 values such as 'diversity racism, climate socialism, and the war against the nation-state' and saw the alleged Dutch aspiration to be the 'best student in the European class' as another legacy from the 1960s (De Bruin 2024, 126). This narrative about a tradition of Dutch Euroscepticism, though implausible, gained popularity as part of their new and increasingly influential discourse on the Netherlands and the EU. But it remains to be seen whether this marks the end of the Dutch self-image as a small example for Europe and the world. The PVV's anti-Europeanism has significantly decreased now that their like-minded far-right allies have become an important factor in the European Parliament. It would certainly fit within the Dutch tradition if the PVV were to emphasize the leverage function of those European allies in its propaganda.

References

Aerts, Remieg. 2018. *Thorbecke wil het: Biografie van een Staatsman*. Prometheus.
Alonso, Stéphane, Clara van de Wiel, and Tijn Sadée. 2021. ' "Walgelijk" en "wreed": hoe Nederland in de coronacrisis vijanden maakt in de EU.' *NRC Handelsblad*, March 27. https://www.nrc.nl/nieuws/2020/03/27/walgelijk-en-wreed-hoe-nederland-in-de-coronacrisis-vijanden-maakt-in-de-eu-a3995149 (accessed January 5, 2025).

Bleich, Anet. 2008. *Joop den Uyl: Dromer en doordouwer*. Balans.
Brandsma, Margriet, and Pieter Klein. 1996. *Jan Pronk: Rebel met een Missie*. Scheffers.
Breedveld, Willem, and Theo Koelé. 1987. 'Nederland praat niet meer mee, het praat gewoon na.' *Trouw*, February 14. https://www.delpher.nl/ (accessed January 5, 2025).
Bregman, Rutger. 2020. *Het Water Komt: Een brief aan alle Nederlanders*. De Correspondent.
Bugge, Axel, and Andrei Khalip. 2017. 'Eurogroup chairman Dijsselbloem refuses to quit over "xenophobic" remarks.' *Reuters*, March 22. https://www.reuters.com/article/us-eu-eurogroup-portugal-idUSKBN16T1AU (accessed January 5, 2025).
Coates, Ben. 2021. 'How the Dutch lost their shine.' *Politico.eu*, March 12. https://www.politico.eu/article/netherlands-coronavirus-response-how-the-dutch-lost-their-shine/ (accessed January 5, 2025).
Cull, Nicholas J. 2021. 'H-Diplo Article Review 1041 Nation Branding.' *H-Diplo*, June 8. https://issforum.org/reviews/PDF/AR1041.pdf (accessed January 5, 2025).
de Bruin, Robin. 2014. *Elastisch Europa: De Integratie van Europa en de Nederlandse Politiek*. Wereldbibliotheek.
de Bruin, Robin. 2024. 'The Construction of a Dutch Eurosceptic Tradition by Contemporary Populist Political Parties.' In *Anti-Europeanism, Populism and European Integration in a Historical Perspective*, edited by Andrea Guiso and Daniele Pasquinucci. Routledge.
de Gaay Fortman, Bas. 1973. 'De vredespolitiek van de radicalen.' *Internationale Spectator* 27 (2): 109–113.
de Gaay Fortman, Bas. 2001. 'Nederland gidsland in Noord-Zuidbetrekkingen? Het "gidsland" van de jaren '70.' *Internationale Spectator* 55 (7/8): 375–379.
de Roode, Sven Leif Ragnar. 2012. *Seeing Europe through the Nation: The Role of National Self-Images in the Perception of European Integration in the English, German, and Dutch Press in the 1950s and 1990s*. Steiner.
de Wijk, Rob. 2021. 'Polderen werkt alleen met mooi weer, in crisistijd loopt het van de rails.' *Trouw*, January 29. https://www.trouw.nl/opinie/polderen-werkt-alleen-met-mooi-weer-in-crisistijd-loopt-het-van-de-rails~b7fbbe75/ (accessed January 5, 2025).
Dorpema, Marc. 2020. 'The Netherlands, the Environment, and European Integration in the Early 1970s.' *Journal of European Integration History* 26 (2): 229–246.
Gienow-Hecht, Jessica. 2019. 'Nation Branding: A Useful Category for International History.' *Diplomacy & Statecraft* 30 (4): 755–779.
Heidenreich, Martin, and Gabriele Bishoff. 2008. 'The Open Method of Co-ordination: A Way to the Europeanization of Social and Employment Policies?' *Journal of Common Market Studies* 46 (3): 497–532.

Jansen van Galen, John. 2001. *Het Suriname-syndroom: De PvdA tussen Den Haag en Paramaribo*. Bert Bakker.

Kennedy, James C. 1995. *Nieuw Babylon in aanbouw: Nederland in de Jaren Zestig*, translated by Simone Kennedy-Doornbos. Boom.

Kennedy, James C. 1997. 'New Babylon and the Politics of Modernity.' *Sociologische Gids* 44 (5–6): 361–374. https://ugp.rug.nl/sogi/article/view/19511/16989 (accessed January 5, 2025).

Kennedy, James C. 1999–2000. 'The Myth of Dutch Progressiveness: The Netherlands as "Guide Land."' *The Low Countries* 7: 220–224. https://www.the-low-countries.com/wp-content/uploads/2024/08/TLC7-DutchProgressiveness.pdf (accessed January 5, 2025).

Kennedy, James C. 2005. *De Deugden van een Gidsland: Burgerschap en Democratie in Nederland*. Bert Bakker.

Kennedy, James C. 2010. *Bezielende Verbanden: Gedachten over Religie, Politiek en Maatschappij in het moderne Nederland*. Bert Bakker.

Kissinger, Henry. 1999. *Years of Renewal*. Simon & Schuster.

Kuijk, Leonoor. 2012. 'Beetje elan best belangrijk.' *Trouw*, January 10. https://www.trouw.nl/nieuws/beetje-elan-best-belangrijk~b5db9267 (accessed January 5, 2025).

Kuitenbrouwer, Maarten. 1999. 'Nederland gidsland? De ontwikkelingssamenwerking van Nederland en gelijkgezinde landen, 1973–1985.' In *De geschiedenis van vijftig jaar Nederlandse ontwikkelingssamenwerking 1949–1999*, edited by Jan Nekkers and Peter Malcontent. SDU.

Langenhoff, Vic. 1974. 'Proeftuin voor vluchtelingen.' *De Tijd*, March 1. https://www.delpher.nl (accessed January 5, 2025).

Laqueur, Walter Z. 1981. 'Hollanditis: A New Stage in European Neutralism.' *Commentary*, August. https://www.commentary.org/articles/walter-laqueur/hollanditis-a-new-stage-in-european-neutralism/ (accessed January 5, 2025).

Meadows, Donella H., Dennis L. Meadows, Jørgen Randers, and William W. Behrens III. 1972. *The Limits to Growth: A Report for the Club of Rome's Project on the Predicament of Mankind*. Universe. [Translated to Dutch as: Meadows, Donella H., et al 1972. *De grenzen aan de groei: rapport van de Club van Rome*. Het Spectrum.]

Mussler, Werner. 2017. 'Dijsselbloem: "Ich bedauere, dass es als 'Nord gegen Süd' aufgefasst wurde."' *Frankfurter Allgemeine Zeitung*, March 22. https://www.faz.net/aktuell/wirtschaft/wirtschaftspolitik/nach-interview-in-der-f-a-z-dijsselbloem-ich-bedauere-dass-es-als-nord-gegen-sued-aufgefasst-wurde-14937857.html (accessed January 5, 2025).

Nederlands Dagblad. 1982. 'Lenin en onze naïviteit.' *Nederlands Dagblad: Gereformeerd gezinsblad*, July 21. https://www.delpher.nl/ (accessed January 5, 2025).

Netherlands' First Chamber. 1972. 'Debate on "Topics Related to NATO and European Cooperation Organizations.' *Handelingen Eerste Kamer 1971–1972* (May 16, 1972), https://repository.overheid.nl/frbr/sgd/19711972/0000216130/1/pdf/SGD_19711972_0000027.pdf (accessed January 5, 2025).

Netherlands' Government. 2021. Overview 'Dutch goals within the EU' regarding climate change, https://www.government.nl/topics/climate-change/eu-policy (accessed January 5, 2025).

Netherlands' Second Chamber. 1972. Debate on 'international cooperation in the field of environmental management.' *Handelingen Tweede Kamer 1971–1972* (March 23, 1972), https://repository.overheid.nl/frbr/sgd/19711972/0000216933/1/pdf/SGD_19711972_0000652.pdf (accessed January 5, 2025).

NRC Handelsblad. 1981. 'Grootste demonstratie ooit in Nederland gehouden. Uniek protest tegen raketten.' *NRC Handelsblad*, November 23. https://www.delpher.nl/ (accessed January 5, 2025).

Oñorbe Genovesi, Iñaki. 2020. 'Van Gidsland tot hekkensluiter: Hoe progressief is Nederland nog? Boris Dittrich over abortus, drugs en euthanasie: "Het debat is hier wat ingezakt."' *de Volkskrant*, February 6. https://www.volkskrant.nl/columns-opinie/boris-dittrich-over-abortus-drugs-en-euthanasie-het-debat-is-hier-wat-ingezakt~b89b8f61/ (accessed January 5, 2025).

Oudenampsen, Merijn. 2021. 'The Riddle of the Missing Feathers: Rise and Decline of the Dutch Third Way.' *European Politics and Society* 22 (1): 38–52.

Pijpers, Alfred E. 1991. 'Dekolonisatie, compensatiedrang en de normalisering van de Nederlandse buitenlandse politiek.' In *De kracht van Nederland: Internationale positie en buitenlands beleid*, edited by Niek van Sas. Becht.

Post, Hans. 1972. '"Bommen voor brood": op weg naar nieuw veiligheidsbeleid.' *De Tijd*, October 17. https://www.delpher.nl (accessed January 5, 2025).

Reiding, Hilde. 2013. '1973–1986: De teleurstellende Europese werkelijkheid.' In *Verloren consensus: Europa in het Nederlandse parlementair-politieke debat 1945–2013*, edited by Anjo G. Harryvan and Jan van der Harst. Boom.

Snel, Jan Dirk. 2014. 'Nederland Gidsland: Ontstaan en zin van een betwistbaar begrip.' *Christen-Democratische Verkenningen* 34 (4): 61–72. https://www.tijdschriftcdv.nl/scripts/shared/artikel_pdf.php?id=CD-2014-4-61 (accessed January 5, 2025).

Telegraaf. 1972. 'Nederland – gidsland.' *De Telegraaf*, March 8. https://www.delpher.nl (accessed January 5, 2025).

Telegraaf. 2020. 'Grenzen aan groei: Enquête 65% van Nederlanders wil inperking immigratie.' *De Telegraaf*, February 8. https://www.telegraaf.nl/nieuws/2107687974/enquete-65-van-nederlanders-wil-inperking-immigratie (accessed January 5, 2025).

Timmermans, Frans. 2019. 'Groeien aan de Grens.' *Socialisme & Democratie* 76 (6): 8–16. https://www.wbs.nl/publicaties/groeien-aan-de-grens-den-uyl-lezing (accessed January 5, 2025).

Trouw. 1974. 'Minister Pronk op bijeenkomst: Geld voor werklozen uit de ontwikkelingspot.' *Trouw*, February 4. https://www.delpher.nl/ (accessed January 5, 2025).

van Dam, Peter, and Wouter van Dis. 2014. 'Beyond the Merchant and the Clergyman: Assessing Moral Claims about Development Cooperation.' *Third World Quarterly* 35 (9): 1636–1655.

van Merriënboer, Johan. 2006. *Mansholt: Een Biografie*. Boom. [Translated to English as: van Merriënboer, Johan. 2011. *Mansholt: A Biography*, translated by Ronald Bathgate. P.I.E. Peter Lang.]

van Meurs, Wim, Robin de Bruin, Liesbeth van de Grift, Carla Hoetink, Karin van Leeuwen, and Carlos Reijnen. 2018. *The Unfinished History of European Integration*, translated by John Eyck. Amsterdam University Press.

van Vollenhoven, Cornelis. 1913. *De eendracht van het land*. Nijhoff.

Volkskrant. 1972. 'Prof. Meadows over Nederland: Bevolkingsaanwas nadert limiet, Record oplage rapport Club Rome.' *de Volkskrant*, April 17. https://www.delpher.nl/ (accessed January 5, 2025).

von der Burchard, Hans, Ivo Oliveira, and Eline Schaart. 2020. 'Dutch try to calm north-south economic storm over coronavirus.' *Politico.eu*, March 27. https://www.politico.eu/article/netherlands-try-to-calm-storm-over-repugnant-finance-ministers-comments/ (accessed January 5, 2025).

Vrije Volk. 1975. 'Pronk pakt uit tegen EEG.' *Het Vrije Volk: Democratisch-socialistisch dagblad*, October 6. https://www.delpher.nl/ (accessed January 5, 2025).

Wagner, Florian. 2022. *Colonial Internationalism and the Governmentality of Empire, 1893–1982*. Cambridge University Press.

Weenink, Wim. 2005. *Bankier van de Wereld, Bouwer van Europa: Johan Willem Beyen 1897–1976*. Prometheus/NRC Handelsblad.

Zielonka, Jan. 2008. 'Europe as a Global Actor: Empire by Example?' *International Affairs* 84 (3): 471–84.

13

Exemplary Appropriation: Holocaust Remembrance Practices in Post-Communist Europe

Jelena Subotić

In the aftermath of the communist collapse in 1989 and the breakup of the Soviet Union in 1991, newly independent post-communist states were confronted with the need to carry out a thorough rewriting of their state identities, ideologies, and national myths. This rewriting was necessary to establish different forms of political legitimacy in the newly-emerged confusing, unstable, and unsettled post-communist order.

A large part of the new post-communist international agenda was the project of 'rejoining Europe' after five decades of cultural, political, and social isolation. To 'come back to Europe,' East Central European states needed to systematically erase the legacy of the 50 years of communism that removed them from Europe's center. Instead, they were to replace it with an embrace of perceived core European values, identities, and political cultures. They needed, in other words, to follow Europe's normative examples. Some of this 'return to Europe' was ideational and rhetorical, but much of it was very practical and quite institutionalized. Most directly, it involved applications for membership in various European bodies, and most importantly, membership in the European Union (EU).

Getting rid of the undesirable legacy of communism also meant rearranging state biographies, which were built on historical memories of recent and distant national pasts. Being part of a united European project, after 50 years of ideological fracture, would also mean pursuing a shared history, a common understanding of Europe's past, and following standard examples of remembering (Müller 2002; Judt 2005; Littoz-Monnet 2012). European unity necessitated a patched-up history. One of the central features of this history was the history of the Holocaust but, even more important, the ways of remembering the Holocaust.

As the rest of the chapter demonstrates, the attempt to introduce a cosmopolitan, pan-national memory of the Holocaust as an example post-communist states in Europe were supposed to adopt has been quite politically destabilizing, not only for these states themselves, but also for the larger EU. In fact, much Holocaust revisionism that has followed post-communist transitions and consolidations of nationalist populist regimes in the region has also begun to serve as examples for Western actors, who have increasingly adopted ways of appropriating the Holocaust to buttress narratives of local ethnic victimization instead (Subotić 2023). This is important because if the European process of *Vergangenheitsbewältigung* (working through the past) was the exemplary performance of European postwar narrative consolidation and a foundational block of the EU's moral identity, then the contemporary appropriation of the Holocaust for elevation of national victimhoods is truly a stunning reversal, and one with very high political stakes.

The Holocaust in European contested historical memory

Few events in Europe's 20th century are as broadly meaningful and consequential as the Holocaust. Its various – if often conflicting – narratives of genocide, survival, heroism, rescue, and the promise of 'never again' served as a foundational story of the European Union, one that gave the political project of the EU meaning and broad appeal (Assmann 2014). Not only did the Holocaust become an example of the end point of the politics of racism, exclusion, and violence, but practices of Holocaust remembrance (museums, memorials, monuments, days of remembrance) became widely dispersed and diffused as examples of how the past – other pasts, other histories, and other historical crimes – should be remembered and memorialized (Young 1993).

Over time, as Levy and Sznaider detailed in their influential 2002 essay, the Holocaust became detached from the historical moment of the Nazi Holocaust of Europe's Jews in the 1940s and developed into a broader narrative of crimes against humanity and human rights protection everywhere, at different moments in time. This is what the 'cosmopolitan memory' of the Holocaust came to represent – no longer a memory of the Holocaust alone, but instead a broadly shared – exemplary – narrative of human rights atrocities and their remembrance, a narrative accepted across borders and across national imaginations (Levy and Sznaider 2002; Dubiel 2003; Baer and Sznaider 2017).

This exemplary feature of cosmopolitan Holocaust memory was also evident in the massive proliferation of Holocaust museums and monuments around the world, especially since the 1990s, including in many countries that had very little, if any actual historical relationship to the Holocaust (Duffy 2001). The Holocaust (the historical event of the Holocaust), but also Holocaust memory (remembrance of the historical event of the Holocaust) therefore developed as exemplary models of historical remembrance practices worldwide, but especially in Europe, which was their central geographic, cultural, and political locale.

The implication of this diffusion of cosmopolitan Holocaust memory and memorialization practices was that these models of Holocaust remembrance over time became another way of performing European identity for those states (such as those in post-communist East and Central Europe) for which this identity remained liminal. Holocaust remembrance, in the words of Tony Judt, became a 'European entry ticket' (Judt 2005, 803) for many post-communist states that otherwise had little interest in revisiting the difficult and often implicatory history of the Holocaust. In fact, Holocaust remembrance soon became institutionalized as an important element in the process of 'Europeanization' of the post-communist East. Most specifically, as the EU made its Eastern European enlargement conditional on many domestic reforms, education and memorialization of the Holocaust became one of the explicit expectations that candidate states had to meet.

This expectation – that East European states will follow EU examples and practices – comes directly from the European Union's own self-understanding as an exemplary institution. In fact, the exemplary self-conception of the EU is built into its very foundation and is in many ways its continuing *raison d'être*, regardless of the spotty record of both its own commitment to reckoning with the European past as well as its ability to influence its members. The EU has built its identity and perpetuated its strength as 'normative power Europe' (Manners 2002), and it is this self-identity that has shaped the EU's expectations that others will follow established European examples (Borg 2014).

In the first decade after the collapse of communism, the European Union passed a series of resolutions that dealt specifically with the memory and legacies of the Holocaust such as, for example, the 1995 Resolution on the Return of Plundered Property to Jewish Communities, which contained explicit demands from East European states to return property looted in the Holocaust (European Parliament 1995). In 2000, Sweden convened the 2000 Stockholm Forum on the Holocaust, which served as a major European institutional push to regulate Holocaust remembrance across the continent and define a common framework for European Holocaust remembrance, research, and education (Allwork 2015). The Stockholm Forum also established the International Task Force on Holocaust Education, Remembrance and Research, which was to implement Stockholm recommendations into practice.

In 2005, the European Parliament adopted its most complete resolution on the Holocaust, the Resolution on Remembrance of the Holocaust, Antisemitism and Racism. This resolution established January 27, the day of liberation of Auschwitz in 1945 by the Soviet Red Army, as European Holocaust Memorial Day across the whole of the European Union (European Parliament 2005). In 2012, the Stockholm Task Force was renamed International Holocaust Remembrance Alliance (IHRA). This international organization has since become the main source of international regulation and modeling of Holocaust remembrance practices around the world. It is through IHRA that exemplary models of Holocaust remembrance, including even issues much broader than the Holocaust, such as the definition of antisemitism, become globally diffused (Plessow 2015; Kucia 2016).

While many governments in East Central European states accepted these new resolutions, signed documents, and adopted major models of the memory framework, careful not to jeopardize the delicate process of European Union accession, they also rejected much of the established canon of European memory politics (Mälksoo 2009; Littoz-Monnet 2013). This was especially the case with conservative and populist governments in countries where the initial, more liberal embrace of Western European memory practices (such as, for example, in Poland), was quickly marginalized. European Union accession then further created a moment of memory divergence as joining the European family provided a space for a much more direct and critical assault on Western European mnemonic canon, without concern for international political consequences. This moment, then, allowed for a new cycle of exemplary politics where post-communist states began to model Holocaust remembrance less on the Western cosmopolitan memory model and increasingly, instead, *after each other*.

This new field of mnemonic exemplarity in the post-communist East – a 'field of anticommunism' (Dujisin 2021) – was built on the realization that the cosmopolitan Holocaust memory as developed in the West did not align very well with their own, often quite different set of historical memories. This lack of fit was evident in the lack of centrality of the Shoah as the defining memory of the 20th century experience across the post-communist space. Instead, Eastern European states after communism constructed their national identities on the memory of Stalinism and Soviet occupation, as well as on the search for continuity with pre-communist nation-states. The Western cosmopolitan centrality of the Holocaust, then, was set to replace the centrality of anti-communist and ethnic nationalist frames as the dominant organizing narrative of post-communist states.

This was threatening and destabilizing to these states because it drowned out nationalist appeals to their own victimization and diluted them with appeals to memorialize past Jewish suffering (Vermeersch 2019). To resolve these different memory pulls, many states in post-communist Europe chose instead to embark on radical projects of criminalizing communism (Mälksoo 2014), using much of the language of memory developed to commemorate the Holocaust to, instead, commemorate communist crimes.[1]

In a series of exemplary moves through direct imitation, mimicry, and diffusion, a number of post-communist states (with the Czech Republic, Slovenia, and Lithuania among the most active) pushed for a series of resolutions and legislation about anti-communist memory through the European Parliament (Neumayer 2018, 2015). These efforts were also decidedly transnational – in addition to working with other right and far-right political parties in the European Parliament (many of them members of the European People's Party bloc), these groups also organized networks of transnational memory entrepreneurship as in, for example, the international Platform on European Memory and Conscience (Hogea 2012; Büttner and Delius 2015).

The centrality of the Holocaust as a foundational European narrative, however, was also soundly rejected across much of post-communist Europe (some of the early leaders of this counter-memory were Poland and the Baltic states) because of its perceived elevation of Jewish victimhood above victimhood of other regional majority ethnic groups, a move that was openly resented (Baer and Sznaider 2017). Further, the European Holocaust memory's focus on Jewish suffering was also rejected in much of post-communist Europe because it brought about discussion about extensive and deep local complicity in the Holocaust and material and political benefits of the complete Jewish absence across East and Central Europe (Himka 2008).

It is against this background that the destabilizing effects of Holocaust memory in post-communist Europe can be best understood. Holocaust memory, as institutionalized in the Western mnemonical canon, created significant stress and anxiety as well as deep domestic conflict and contestation in much of the region. It brought up undesirable memories that ran contrary to these states' identities of victimization at the hands of German and Soviet occupiers. To resolve this dilemma – how to nominally accept the Holocaust memory template while rejecting its focus on Jewish suffering and local East European complicity – post-communist states embarked on a new kind of exemplary historical remembrance where the memory, symbols, and imagery of the Holocaust were appropriated to represent other historical crimes. Holocaust remembrance practices, iconography, and visual templates that were constructed on the established Western cosmopolitan memory model were used as examples, but not of how to memorialize the Holocaust (which remained largely underemphasized). Instead, these models and tropes originally developed for Holocaust crimes, as prime exemplars of crimes

---

[1] For a full elaboration of this argument, see Subotić (2019).

against humanity, were now used to memorialize very different types of crimes, such as crimes of communism.

This type of exemplary Holocaust remembrance, I suggest, is best viewed as a form of *memory appropriation*, where the memory of the Holocaust is used to memorialize a different kind of suffering, such as suffering under communism, or suffering from ethnic violence perpetrated by other groups. But this practice of Holocaust remembrance was truly exemplary and not unique or particular to individual countries. As I document in the remainder of this chapter, these models of Holocaust remembrance traveled across the post-communist space, and even found their way into the core of the European Union, the new House of European History in Brussels.

In the next three sections, I illustrate some of these dynamics by grouping exemplary Holocaust appropriation into three main forms: first, remembrance practices that normatively elevate the suffering of non-Jewish national majorities and equate it with the Holocaust; second, remembrance practices that reposition the crimes of communism as the dominant criminal legacy of the 20th century, on par with and sometimes overcoming the legacy of the Holocaust; and, third, remembrance practices that use the appropriated Holocaust remembrance to strengthen myths of European unity.

Exemplary Holocaust appropriation as competitive victimization

In 2017 in Warsaw, a commemorative plaque was unveiled 'In Memory of the 200,000 Poles Murdered in Warsaw in the German Death Camp KL Warschau.'[2] This was a somber ceremony, with the local priest performing Catholic rites and a representative of the army honoring the dead.

The only problem – almost none of this was true. There indeed did exist a camp in Warsaw, where a few thousand Polish citizens died during the German occupation. But after the burning of the Warsaw Ghetto in 1943, this camp was turned into a concentration and extermination camp for Jews brought in from other parts of Europe, who were used as slave labor to clear the charred remains of the ghetto. A total of some 20,000 people died in this camp, most of them Jews.

The Polish group behind this project was not just commemorating victims of their own ethnic group at the expense of other victims – this is an unremarkable and largely ubiquitous feature of commemorative politics everywhere. What is remarkable, however, is that the very clear purpose of this commemoration was to put it in direct competition with the memory

---

[2] For a detailed investigation of the KL Warschau claims in contemporary Poland on which this summary is based, see Davies (2019).

of the Holocaust, especially in Poland, the geographic heart of the genocide. One likely reason for the invented number of 200,000 killed ethnic Poles in KL Warschau is that – when added to the roughly 200,000 Poles killed in the Warsaw Uprising – the total number of Poles killed reaches the number of 400,000, which is often cited as the estimated number of Jews imprisoned (and most consequently killed), in the Warsaw Ghetto.[3] Further, the myth of the KL Warschau includes a story about a tunnel under the rail lines where, the conspiracy alleges, Germans created a massive gas chamber to murder ethnic Poles. This myth, therefore, places ethnic Polish victimization by the Nazis on the very same plane as the victimization of the Jews by equating not only the number of the dead but repurposing the known symbolic and visual imagery of the Holocaust (gassing) to elevate the suffering of non-Jewish others and chip away at the dominance of Holocaust memory where it is not welcome.

In a similar vein, in Hungary, the Memorial to the Victims of the German Occupation erected in 2014 in Budapest memorializes Hungary – the country – as the main victim of the German occupation, by an unsubtle depiction of Germany's imperial eagle crushing of Hungary, which is symbolized by Archangel Gabriel.[4] The memorial was unveiled overnight and with no accompanying official opening ceremony, in order to avoid any public debate and expected protests (Pető 2019).

The memorial, however, immediately produced deep domestic contestation. Outside of the memorial, Holocaust survivors or their family members have placed hundreds of handwritten notes, pictures, and objects that tell the story of 430,000 Jews who were deported from Hungary, mostly to Auschwitz. Their deportation occurred at the fastest rate of any in the history of the Holocaust, taking less than two months and done with the active participation of Hungarian civil servants (Braham 2016).

What this memorial does is use architecture as a tool to express myths of nationhood, as part of a state strategy of visual remembrance that the Hungarian government under the rule of the Fidesz party has been promoting for more than a decade (Palonen 2013). Specifically, it narratively replaces the memory of the Holocaust and the catastrophe of Hungarian Jewish annihilation with that of widescale Hungarian victimhood and innocence as the central memory of World War II in Hungary. It also purposefully removes responsibility for the murder of Hungarian Jews from Hungary's

---

[3] The language used in the plaque ('murdered Poles' and not 'murdered Polish citizens') indicates that the group behind this memory intervention referred to ethnic Poles, not Polish Jews. In fact, this type of nationalist memorialization is always specifically directed at separating and, often, elevating the suffering of ethnic Poles in comparison to the suffering of Polish Jews.
[4] Some of the material in the next section builds on Subotić (2019).

Axis-allied government and places it firmly with Germany, presenting fascism and its exterminationist policies as alien, foreign intrusions into the Hungarian body politic.

This intervention is important because it provides the current Hungarian far-right government a brick-and-mortar visual device to claim a mythical continuity with the pre-Axis sovereign Hungary and its (illiberal, fascist, and antisemitic) regime (Rév 2018, 610). In doing so, it presents the history of World War II as being exclusively the history of Hungary's victimization – through the loss of state sovereignty – and not as the history of genocide of Hungarian Jews.

Here, the largest victims of the German occupation – Hungarian Jews killed in the Holocaust – are erased to make room for the memory of the Hungarian state, which not only was not the largest victim of the German occupation, but in fact directly participated in the genocide. The very purpose of this type of Holocaust appropriation, this 'pathological mourning' (Murer 2018), was ethnic narrative replacement and competitive victimization, which itself served as an attack on liberal cosmopolitan politics of remembrance.

Exemplary Holocaust appropriation as criminalization of communism

In 2014, the Historical Museum of Serbia put up a highly publicized exhibition *In the Name of the People – Political Repression in Serbia 1944–1953*, which promised to display new historical documents and evidence of communist crimes, ranging from assassinations, kidnappings, detentions in camps, to collectivization, political trials, and repression carried out by communist Yugoslavia in the first postwar years. The most stunning visual artifact was a well-known photograph of prisoners from the Buchenwald concentration camp, including Elie Wiesel, taken by US soldier Harry Miller at camp liberation in April 1945. In the Belgrade exhibition, this famous image was displayed in the section devoted to the communist era camp for political prisoners on the Adriatic island of Goli otok in today's Croatia. The exhibition describes the display as 'the example of living conditions of Goli otok prisoners.'[5] In response to an outcry from Holocaust historians (Radanović 2014), a few weeks after the opening a small note was taped underneath the display caption that read, 'A photograph of prisoner boxed beds in Dachau camp.' That nobody bothered to check that the photograph was, in fact, from Buchenwald and not Dachau, is symptomatic of the broad irrelevance with which the Holocaust is met in Serbia. And yet, even when

---

[5] Author observation at the exhibition, May 2014.

its details are considered irrelevant, the Holocaust as an image and a visual model is powerful enough that it serves as an exemplar of other mass crimes, such as crimes of communism. In other words, the Holocaust itself is not what matters here; it is the *idea* of the Holocaust and what it represents that can be emulated for different political and memorialization purposes.

The direct and crude replacement of victims of the Holocaust with victims of communism also affected the memorialization of Judenlager Semlin (Sajmište), the largest concentration and extermination camp in occupied Serbia during World War II, where 6,300 Jewish women, children, and the elderly were gassed in a mobile gas van over the course of a few months in 1941–1942 (Bajford 2011). At the same 2014 exhibition at the Serbian Historical Museum, next to the recaptioned Buchenwald photograph of Elie Wiesel, there was another photograph. This was a pre-war image of the main tower of Belgrade's Fairgrounds, the building that housed the administration of the Judenlager Semlin during the occupation. The photograph caption read: 'The parachute tower becomes a machine gun nest, period 1952–1953 … enemies of all colours were held at Sajmište.' This completely fabricated statement then gives the visitor the impression that Semlin camp was a communist prison for enemies of the state, discipline maintained through machine gunfire. The visitor would not know that Semlin was the place where half of all Jews in occupied Serbia were killed in a few spring months of 1942.

But what *was* extremely relevant for the exhibition organizers was to use the well-known visual imagery of the Holocaust, and especially photographs and material objects that invoke immediate recognition and emotional response (pictures of bunk beds, emaciated skeletal inmates, and so on), to connect semiotically in an exemplary fashion the horrors of the Holocaust with the horrors of communism and make the two appear the same.

This appropriated remembrance practice, however, has not developed in isolation and independently, on its own. Rather, it was a direct result of the first regional and then broader international appeal of the Hungarian House of Terror museum that opened in 2002 in Budapest. The principal narrative message of the House of Terror is to present the story of Hungary's 20th-century experience as a nation victimized by a foreign communist, and to a much lesser extent, a foreign fascist regime. The House of Terror truncates Hungary's 20th-century history to the period 1944–1989, so that the fascist era begins with the German occupation in 1944, and not in 1940 when Hungary first joined the Axis alliance. This shift therefore completely removes the history of the Holocaust in Hungary before 1944, the period that left 60,000 Hungarian Jews killed as early as 1942, the extermination carried out not by Germans, but by Hungarian forces under the rule of regent Miklós Horthy (Braham 2016). This chronology also presents communism as a much longer and far more damaging terror in Hungary than fascism ever was, while the Museum's exhibition narrative remains completely silent regarding the broad and sustained antifascist and communist resistance throughout the war.

The House of Terror goes out of its way to bring home the message that fascism and communism were flip sides of the same coin – there are multiple visual representations of black totalitarianism and red totalitarianism – of the black arrow cross juxtaposed with the red star, of the fascist uniform juxtaposed with the communist uniform. Equating the crimes of the two regimes is not new nor is it particularly surprising. What is more interesting is that the blunt message of this state institution is presented through the exemplary appropriation of not just Holocaust imagery, but also the Holocaust museum's visual display. Most directly, the House of Terror uses the model of the 'Tower of Faces' – portraits of Holocaust victims projected on to the entire length of walls in the United States Holocaust Memorial Museum in Washington, DC – to project portraits of Hungarian 'victims of communism,' while the 'Hall of Tears' in the basement of the Budapest museum is a visual repurposing of the Children's Memorial at Yad Vashem Holocaust Remembrance Center in Jerusalem (Radonić 2017, 283; also Radonić 2020).

The Hungarian House of Terror, however, was only one in a series of very similar museums that opened in very short succession in post-communist Europe. The Museum of Occupations in Tallinn, Estonia, opened in 2003 and it carries an almost identical message to its Budapest sibling.[6] The 'occupations' from the museum's name are the 'twin' occupations by Nazi Germany and the Soviet Union that in this museum are equated as the two totalitarianisms of the 20th century – exactly mirroring the Budapest House of Terror model.

These museums also had previous exemplary models to adopt – the Museum of Victims of Genocide,[7] the top tourist destination in Vilnius, Lithuania, or the Museum of the Occupation of Latvia,[8] both opened within a year of each other in 1992 and 1993 respectively, just a year or so after the independence of the Baltic states from the Soviet Union. The Vilnius Museum sits in a former NKVD/KGB building (which also served as Gestapo headquarters during the Nazi occupation), and it continues to be the most visible institution of memory in Lithuania. The Museum describes its object of representation as 'genocide performed by the Soviet

---

[6] Vebamu Museum of Occupations and Freedom, https://www.vabamu.ee (accessed June 6, 2025).

[7] After intense pressure, much of it international, the Museum changed its official name to Museum of Occupations and Freedom Fights in 2018.

[8] Museum of the Occupation of Latvia, http://okupacijasmuzejs.lv/en (accessed June 6, 2025).

occupiers against the Lithuanian inhabitants, demonstrates the methods and extent of resistance to the occupying regime, and commemorates genocide victims and freedom fighters.'[9] The mission of the Museum, therefore, is to generalize Soviet violence to Lithuanian 'inhabitants' – not specific political or economic classes but all Lithuanians – making the narrative link with what the visitor may understand as 'genocide' more direct. This link is made visually clear by the use of extremely graphic images of executions, death, and torture, images that many visitors would associate with the Holocaust.

The exemplary model of this appropriated remembrance of the Holocaust was to use the existing visual repertoire of the Holocaust to instead portray the suffering of non-Jewish others, to elevate the memory of ethnic majoritarian victimization, but also centrally to criminalize communism as a system of violence indistinct from the Holocaust – to make communism as a historical project reinterpreted as a project of genocide (Mark 2008). By doing so, these exemplary practices created an easy template that can be replicated and reused for different political purposes but using the same practice of appropriation, inversion, and nationalization (Radonić 2018).

Exemplary Holocaust appropriation as myth of European unity

This reordering of European memory received perhaps its clearest physical manifestation in the new House of European History (HEH), which after decades of delays – some political, some administrative – finally opened in Brussels in May 2017. This museum was one of the key European Union projects aimed at shoring up the cultural foundation for EU integration, strengthening European identity and building EU legitimacy across the continent (Kaiser 2017, 518). It is also one of the most direct manifestations of the shifting patterns and directions of exemplarity – the new ways and priorities of remembering developed in East Central Europe reached a critical mass and began to exert exemplary influence on normative representation on behalf of the entire European Union.

The House of European History narrates the history of European unity by weaving together the stories of the Holocaust with those of communist totalitarianism, again subsuming the huge diversity of communist experience under the Stalinist narrative, while marginalizing the centrality of the Holocaust. The House of European History specifically avoids singling out the experience of European Jews and has no separate remembrance of their annihilation – a curating decision agreed upon early in the development of

---

[9] Museum of Occupations and Freedom Fights, http://genocid.lt/muziejus/en/708/c (accessed June 6, 2025).

the Museum (Kaiser 2017). Instead, the Holocaust is woven through other narratives of World War II and post-World War II remembrance, in a way that demonstrates the extent to which the memorial models from East Central Europe have been imported into the European Union memory core (Kaiser 2017). Using the exemplary models of appropriated Holocaust remembrance practices already developed and institutionalized in post-communist Europe, the House of European History makes both the Holocaust and communist terror integral to the history of Europe and leading, teleologically, toward European integration (Hilmar 2016).

Other examples of contemporary populist (often, also, far-right) appropriation of memories of World War II for current national victimization grievance agendas across Western Europe abound.[10] When she spoke at the Fosse Ardeatine massacre commemorations in 2023 (and, again, in 2024), Italian Prime Minister Giorgia Meloni repeatedly claimed that in March 1944 Nazis killed '335 innocent Italians ... simply because they were Italian' (Italian Government 2023). But this was a highly nationalized version of the past – the victims at Fosse Ardeatine were primarily Italian antifascists and civilians, and the massacre was direct retaliation for the Italian antifascist partisan attack on the Nazi occupation forces in Rome the day before. By eliding any context of the Ardeatine massacre, Meloni nationalized Italian victimhood, ignored the existence and legacy of Italian antifascism, and, even more conveniently for her current political needs, ignored Italian fascists' deep alliance with the Nazis and the inconvenient fact that her own party Fratelli d'Italia is rooted in Italian fascism (Angeletti, Posocco, and Meghnagi 2024).

Also in Italy, days after the Hamas terrorist attack on Israel on October 7, 2023, the Italian Parliament approved, after years of delay and negotiations, the establishment of the Holocaust Museum in Rome. This institution, however, was to be housed in Mussolini's former villa, a location that would seem to be the least appropriate place to memorialize crimes of Mussolini's fascists (Barry 2023). Further, the same complex at Villa Torlonia already houses a permanent exhibition of Mussolini's hideout but also the exhibition about Allied air raids against Rome, which are presented as raids against Italian civilians, not raids against the Italian fascist regime (Kuta 2024). These kinds of commemorative decisions, then, are possible examples of the institutional and normative diffusion of museum practices already well established in East and Central Europe that narrate World War II through the lens of local, national victimhood, and fully absolve local regimes of any complicity in wartime mass atrocity. As Daase and Wille elaborate in

---

[10] On the relationship between grievance, resentment, and emotions in world politics more generally, see Subotić (2024).

Chapter 7 of this volume, 'pushing the envelope' of precedent is part of the dynamics of emulation.

These illustrations show how exemplary centers may in fact shift when ambitious social actors revise examples to serve their own political needs – same example, different message. That East and Central European social actors managed to set new examples for a general presentation of memory in the heart of the EU is evidence of their great discursive and performative success.

Conclusion

This short chapter aimed to put practices of Holocaust memory appropriation in a contemporary political context by demonstrating that they are not isolated instances of competing memory, but instead critical elements of exemplary national strategies of political legitimacy. They serve to reposition national narratives in opposition to those of communism but also to those historically embraced by Western Europe, and instead reclaim a national identity that rejects cosmopolitanism and is rebuilt along ethnic majoritarian lines.

More broadly, the examples demonstrate that we cannot understand practices of historical remembrance – of the Holocaust, but also of any other significant historical event – in national isolation. These practices diffuse, spread, and reconstitute in different ways across transnational spaces. Political actors – state actors but also many social actors such as cultural entrepreneurs, historians, or various other memory gatekeepers – look for and are influenced by examples from across their borders. Once these models of remembrance have developed and become salient, they are easily transported and applied to different political and cultural contexts, where they begin to serve different local political needs. They imitate one another, but they also grow and spread through a form of grafting or hybridization – where some elements are adopted and merged with the local model, and some are rejected. It is the ease with which these practices can be malleable and adaptable that makes them so readily transportable. Paying attention to exemplarity helps us understand how practices travel, but also how they are localized, nationalized, and particularized for contemporary political purposes.

Using the case of Holocaust remembrance, my chapter demonstrates that Western powers elaborate a liberal discourse of exemplarity and instrumentalize the ordinary social process of searching for examples of conduct on which to model one's own. They recruit new members via a promise of inclusion if their example is followed. As Zarakol shows in Chapter 9 of this volume, however, that promise is often unfulfilled. My chapter also points to a subversive potential inherent in the exemplary mechanism: an example is not an example until it is cited and emulated, and this makes even powerful incumbent actors dependent in practice on those who take up their example. Temporally, the chapter lines up with those of Wadia and Watanabe (Chapter 10 and Chapter 11) in addressing later stages of the liberal exemplarity process outlined by Zarakol. It also provides a counterpoint to de Bruin's (Chapter 12) argument about how 'old Europe' seeks to update its claim to be the exemplary center.

The practices of memorialization described in this chapter also point to the way in which the imposition of exemplars is a deeply contested political process. The fact that this political contestation played out so dramatically and so visibly within the European Union further speaks to the complex process of resistance to exemplars. This is a denser, more self-aware process of imposing, assuming, but also resisting exemplars, which speaks to a differently constructed power relationship between the exemplar (EU) and the self (East Central European states) and is critical to the self-presentation and positioning of East Central Europe vis-à-vis the EU. Emulation is a negotiation of identity, but its act of revision can set a new example that destabilizes the cited precedent and/or the source milieu. Such skillful emulation can contribute to a shift in the exemplary center, which is arguably happening in the current relationship between Eastern and Western Europe. Exemplarity, then, served to both destabilize state identities and, through the process of resistance, assert those identities in new and different ways. This is why we should understand exemplarity – setting examples, compelling their adoption, and then strategic resistance to them – as also a process of identity contestation and negotiation.

References

Allwork, Larissa. 2015. *Holocaust Remembrance between the National and the Transnational: The Stockholm International Forum and the First Decade of the International Task Force*. Bloomsbury.

Angeletti, Valerio, Lorenzo Posocco, and Micol Meghnagi. 2024. 'Fossil Memory: Unaltered Narratives of Resistance and Deportation in the Oldest Italian Holocaust and Resistance Museums.' *Eastern European Holocaust Studies* 2 (2): 403–429.

Assmann, Aleida. 2014. 'Transnational Memories.' *European Review* 22 (4): 546–556.

Baer, Alejandro, and Natan Sznaider. 2017. *Memory and Forgetting in the Post-Holocaust Era: The Ethics of Never Again*. Routledge.

Bajford, Jovan. 2011. *Staro sajmište: Mesto sećanja, zaborava i sporenja*. Beogradski centar za ljudska prava.

Barry, Colleen. 2023. 'Italian Lawmakers Approve 10 Million Euros for Long-delayed Holocaust Museum in Rome.' *AP News*.

Borg, Stefan. 2014. 'European Integration and the Problem of the State: Universality, Particularity, and Exemplarity in the Crafting of the European Union." *Journal of International Relations and Development* 17 (3): 339–366.

Braham, Randolph L. 2016. 'Hungary: The Assault on the Historical Memory of the Holocaust.' In *The Holocaust in Hungary: Seventy Years Later*, edited by Randolph L. Braham and András Kovács. Central European University Press.

Büttner, Sebastian M., and Anna Delius. 2015. 'World Culture in European Memory Politics? New European Memory Agents between Epistemic Framing and Political Agenda Setting.' *Journal of Contemporary European Studies* 23 (3): 391–404.

Davies, Christian. 2019. 'Under the Railway Line.' *London Review of Books*, May 9, 29–30.

Dubiel, Helmut. 2003. 'The Remembrance of the Holocaust as a Catalyst for a Transnational Ethic?' *New German Critique* 90: 59–70.

Duffy, Terence M. 2001. 'Museums of "Human Suffering"' and the Struggle for Human Rights.' *Museum International* 53 (1): 10–16.

Dujisin, Zoltan. 2021. 'A History of Post-communist Remembrance: From Memory Politics to the Emergence of a Field of Anticommunism.' *Theory and Society* 50 (1): 65–96.

European Parliament. 1995. *Resolution on the Return of Plundered Property to Jewish Communities*. Brussels.

European Parliament. 2005. *Resolution on Remembrance of the Holocaust, Anti-Semitism and Racism*. Brussels.

Hilmar, Till. 2016. 'Narrating Unity at the European Union's New History Museum: A Cultural-Process Approach to the Study of Collective Memory.' *European Journal of Sociology* 57 (2): 297–329.

Himka, John-Paul. 2008. 'Obstacles to the Integration of the Holocaust into Post-communist East European Historical Narratives.' *Canadian Slavonic Papers* 50 (3–4): 359–372.

Hogea, Alina. 2012. 'European Conscience and Totalitarianism: Contested Memory in the European Union.' *Revista Româna de Jurnalism și Comunicare* 7 (3/4): 59–71.

Italian Government. 2023. 'President Meloni's statement on anniversary of the Fosse Ardeatine massacre.' Last Modified March 24. https://www.governo.it/en/articolo/president-meloni-s-statement-anniversary-fosse-ardeatine-massacre/22190 (accessed June 6, 2025).

Judt, Tony. 2005. *Postwar: A History of Europe since 1945*. Penguin Press.

Kaiser, Wolfram. 2017. 'Limits of Cultural Engineering: Actors and Narratives in the European Parliament's House of European History Project.' *JCMS: Journal of Common Market Studies* 55 (3): 518–534.

Kucia, Marek. 2016. 'The Europeanization of Holocaust Memory and Eastern Europe.' *East European Politics and Societies* 30 (1): 97–119.

Kuta, Sarah. 2024. You Can Now Visit Mussolini's Underground Bunker in Rome. *Smithsonian Magazine*.

Levy, Daniel, and Natan Sznaider. 2002. 'Memory Unbound: The Holocaust and the Formation of Cosmopolitan Memory.' *European Journal of Social Theory* 5 (1): 87–106.

Littoz-Monnet, Annabelle. 2012. 'The EU Politics of Remembrance: Can Europeans Remember Together?' *West European Politics* 35 (5): 1182–1202.

Littoz-Monnet, Annabelle. 2013. 'Explaining Policy Conflict across Institutional Venues: European Union-Level Struggles over the Memory of the Holocaust.' *JCMS: Journal of Common Market Studies* 51 (3): 489–504.

Mälksoo, Maria. 2009. 'The Memory Politics of Becoming European: The East European Subalterns and the Collective Memory of Europe.' *European Journal of International Relations* 15 (4): 653–680.

Mälksoo, Maria. 2014. 'Criminalizing Communism: Transnational Mnemopolitics in Europe.' *International Political Sociology* 8 (1): 82–99.

Manners, Ian. 2002. 'Normative Power Europe: A Contradiction in Terms?' *JCMS: Journal of Common Market Studies* 40 (2): 235–258.

Mark, James. 2008. 'Containing Fascism: History in Post-Communist Baltic Occupation and Genocide Museums.' In *Past for the Eyes: East European Representations of Communism in Cinema and Museums after 1989*, edited by Oksana Sarkisova and Péter Apor. Central European University Press.

Müller, Jan-Werner. 2002. *Memory and Power in Post-War Europe: Studies in the Presence of the Past*. Cambridge University Press.

Murer, Jeffrey Stevenson. 2018. 'Four Monuments and a Funeral: Pathological Mourning and Collective Memory in Contemporary Hungary.' In *Fomenting Political Violence: Fantasy, Language, Media, Action*, edited by Steffen Krüger, Karl Figlio, and Barry Richards. Springer.

Neumayer, Laure. 2015. 'Integrating the Central European Past into a Common Narrative: The Mobilizations Around the "Crimes of Communism" in the European Parliament.' *Journal of Contemporary European Studies* 23 (3): 344–363.

Neumayer, Laure. 2018. *The Criminalisation of Communism in the European Political Space After the Cold War*. Routledge.

Palonen, Emilia. 2013. 'Millennial Politics of Architecture: Myths and Nationhood in Budapest.' *Nationalities Papers* 41 (4): 536–551.

Pető, Andrea. 2019. '"Non-Remembering" the Holocaust in Hungary and Poland.' *Polin: Studies in Polish Jewry* 31: 471–480.

Plessow, Oliver. 2015. 'The Interplay of the European Commission, Researcher and Educator Networks and Transnational Agencies in the Promotion of a Pan-European Holocaust Memory.' *Journal of Contemporary European Studies* 23 (3): 378–390.

Radanović, Milan. 2014. 'Kuća terora u Muzeju revolucije.' *Peščanik*, last modified June 2, http://pescanik.net/kuca-terora-u-muzeju-revolucije (accessed June 6, 2025).

Radonić, Ljiljana. 2017. 'Post-communist Invocation of Europe: Memorial Museums' Narratives and the Europeanization of Memory.' *National Identities* 19 (2): 269–288.

Radonić, Ljiljana. 2018. 'From "Double Genocide" to "the New Jews": Holocaust, Genocide and Mass Violence in Post-Communist Memorial Museums.' *Journal of Genocide Research* 20 (4): 510–529.

Radonić, Ljiljana. 2020. '"Our" vs. "Inherited" Museums: PiS and Fidesz as Mnemonic Warriors.' *Südosteuropa* 68 (1): 44–78.

Rév, István. 2018. 'Liberty Square, Budapest: How Hungary Won the Second World War.' *Journal of Genocide Research* 20 (4): 607–623.

Subotić, Jelena. 2019. *Yellow Star, Red Star: Holocaust Remembrance after Communism.* Cornell University Press.

Subotić, Jelena. 2023. 'Holocaust Memory and Political Legitimacy in Contemporary Europe.' *Holocaust Studies* 29 (4): 502–519.

Subotić, Jelena. 2024. 'Resentment and Grievance.' In *The Oxford Handbook of Emotions in International Relations*, edited by Simon Koschut and Andrew A. G. Ross. Oxford University Press.

Vermeersch, Peter. 2019. 'Victimhood as Victory: The Role of Memory Politics in the Process of De-Europeanisation in East-Central Europe.' *Global Discourse* 9 (1): 113–130.

Young, James Edward. 1993. *The Texture of Memory: Holocaust Memorials and Meaning.* Yale University Press.

14

From Exemplarity to Farce? The Career of Cold War Threshold Crossings

Dorothy Noyes

I was proud to step over the line.

Donald J. Trump

'From tragedy to farce' has become a political cliché for a reason. It captures a characteristic intuition of modern state politics: we have been here before; old actions are being replayed but debased in the process. Marx's representative anecdote, the 1851 coup that gave birth to France's Second Empire, posits Louis Napoleon as a grotesque 'second edition' of the problematic but indisputably remarkable original (Marx 1852, I).

All too easily have commentators made satire out of Donald J. Trump's thirst for grandeur. Watching him cross the stone threshold from South to North Korea in June 2019, murmuring to Kim Jong Un, 'Should I come in? Would you like me to come in?,' the diplomacy-watcher of a certain age could hardly resist the temptation of snark. Older images leap to mind, freighted with import: Richard Nixon stepping off of Air Force One in 1972 to shake hands with Zhou Enlai, this icon enhanced by its recreation in John Adams' 1987 opera, *Nixon in China*; and – sufficiently operatic without enhancement – Anwar el-Sadat in 1977, stepping down from his own plane into the Jerusalem night, as the world held its breath and an Israeli military band performed the hastily rehearsed Egyptian national anthem.

Well, Trump exhales opera – of a sort. The strenuous tenor aria 'Nessun dorma,' promising a consummation of the deal when dawn shall come, is, after all, a favored musical number at his rallies. Why, Trump has often asked, have his grand gestures not compelled the critics?

Exemplarity is the answer: the practical and citational connections across performances that situate the immediate gesture. A compelling performance of the body is the foundation of exemplarity, to be sure, and political actions meant to carry exemplary force are carefully staged. The cameras are consequential. But an example is more than a spectacular moment: it lives in transmission. A gesture gains mass for its momentum when it resonates with prior examples; when it plays out upon a broadly significant ground of action; when it is a move in the ongoing interaction of mutually observant, mutually answerable actors; when it is mediated to reach a public across time and space; and when it proposes instrumental follow-though from institutions. These conditions came together during the Cold War, the era of great divides and giant leaps across them. Difficult to sustain as an ensemble, they are complicated above all by the simultaneously powerful and destabilizing synergy between gesture and media.

Even lightweight redeployments of a gesture once deemed significant take part in a process of distributed invention that sustains both particular examples and exemplarity as a whole. The Cold War threshold crossing has a career, shaped within a complex, ever-shifting social network of mutual observation, reflective judgment, citation, and emulation. It emerges into compelling form through the recombination of examples; its cardinal examples are observed, assessed, cited, emulated, and again recombined at multiple scales by actors with a variety of purposes and constraints. Dynamism and omnipresence change the gesture's nature: its performance becomes banal, dismissible as 'empty gesture,' but by the same token enters political habitus. From this residual position, and in assorted archives and sites of memory, it remains available as a resource for future performance.

Exemplarity's inherent dynamism is reinforced by the ethos of modernity. In contrast to the early modern exemplarity of *historia magister vitae* (Koselleck 1985), the spiral of transmission in modern politics privileges the setting rather than the following of examples. It celebrates the *unexampled* action that surpasses the past. This incentive to escalation generates risk, both of absurdity and of disaster. Thus the Second Empire cannot be blamed on the inadequacy of 'Napoléon le petit' alone: the problem was, arguably, with the ambition of Napoleon the original. Trump's determination to astonish has a lineage. Is modern exemplarity destined to play out as farce? Perhaps, if we focus on the actors in the spotlight, but tracing the broader network reveals more complex outcomes.

In this chapter, I briefly present the emergence of the détente-era threshold crossing. I offer a partial visualization of the network within which Nixon's 1972 trip to China and Sadat's 1977 trip to Jerusalem took shape, pointing out the multiple modes of exemplary transmission.[1] I show the growing

---

[1] Surprisingly, a relationship between these two iconic 1970s events has hardly been posited by scholars. Handel's *Diplomacy of Surprise* (1981) expounds commonalities between them

reliance on media spectacle that imperiled Sadat's threshold diplomacy and doomed Trump's 2018–2019 summits with North Korean leader Kim Jong Un . Despite this trajectory, consideration of South Korean president Moon Jae-in's role in that process and a comparison to the 2020 Abraham Accords suggest a more nuanced account of exemplary decay.

Examples of détente

The felicity conditions of exemplarity were singularly united in the Cold War. The possible nuclear consequences of the East-West rivalry created a global common ground of anxiety and fostered an international community of obsessive mutual attention. Unequal and constraining, this community was nonetheless unprecedentedly inclusive, conferring importance on even the smallest nations as indicators of potential shifts in the global balance. With their ideological loyalties at stake, publics were ever more fully incorporated through mass media – print, radio, and increasingly, television, with satellites enabling live intercontinental transmission from the late 1960s. Finally, and regardless of regime, state institutions and mainstream media were robustly funded, deeply invested in the struggle, and tightly networked to the political actors; they had little scope for going rogue or even for incoherence and neglect. With every action so potentially consequential, political representatives could draw on support from teams of advisors, diplomatic services, and press corps and national broadcasters in the planning, execution, and aftermath of significant steps. These conditions produced the golden age of the 'media event' as the 'live broadcasting of history' (Dayan and Katz 1992).

With global cameras on individual bodies, far-reaching consequences were extrapolated from single gestures. In this sense, the 'small step' that became a 'giant leap for mankind' is the period's cardinal example.[2] The US establishment still speaks of 'moonshot' ventures, but the sublime aspiration evoked by the images of the 1969 moon landing obscures the earthly competition driving such attainments. The US-Soviet rivalry, with its uneasy balance between tit for tat and escalatory reciprocity, gave the tone to exemplarity, prompting a paradoxical obsession with the unexampled: boldly

---

in a rational-choice framework, but is not concerned to historicize the cases. Dayan and Katz's influential recognition of the media event as a television macro-genre (1992) is only implicitly historical. Follow-on research recognizes changing technological and historical conditions as undoing the media event's viability, but only for particular 'serials' such as the sequence of Middle East peace performances from 1977 to 1995 does this research program concern itself with historical relations or citation and dialogue across media events (for example, Katz and Liebes 2007).

[2] Thanks to Ned Lebow for this point.

going where no one had gone before. Kennedy's thrilling 1961 exhortation to put a man on the moon by the end of the decade was of course prompted by Sputnik, which panicked the West and spurred massive emulatory investment in science and technology. Sputnik itself was recognized as a kind of euphemism, for it indexed the possession of technologies that could lead to nuclear annihilation. In this sense, all the giant leaps of the Cold War may be said to have taken example by the bombing of Hiroshima and Nagasaki, the atomic gesture that ushered in the new world order (see Handel 1981, 25 n.1). In the domain of politics proper, it was not only the revolutionary regimes that sought transformative global outcomes: Western realists like Henry Kissinger, who famously took example by Metternich and Bismarck, were equally animated by the idea of world-historical innovation (Suri 2015).

Individual leaders put a face to change. Both liberal heroes and defenders of the people were produced through performances and propaganda techniques learned in mutual observation with Fascist regimes and derived from that first exemplar of the unexampled, Napoleon. While Eastern leaders enjoyed the media monopoly that could shape a personality cult, Western leaders benefited from popular narrative forms that naturalized the lone hero as savior. 'Third World' leaders drew on their own epic idioms. Supporting the association of heroic narratives with political representatives was the growing importance and autonomy of the executive power in all political regimes: as guarantor of an expanding state apparatus, arbiter of political disputes, and fount of authoritative communications to the masses.

The sheer density of performance, media amplification, and competitive emulation in this period gave shape to political genres: structures of expectations facilitating the production and interpretation of performances. Daniel Dayan and Elihu Katz developed their influential account of media events after observing the similarities in coverage of the moon landing and Sadat's Jerusalem visit (1992, 125, 255–256). Both, they argued, could be described as 'conquests,' in which a hero challenges norms or nature to cross, against all odds, a material or symbolic threshold. In response, an awestricken audience 'invest[s] … the hero with charisma' (1992, 34–35).

What I am calling the threshold crossing is a specific crystallization of this pattern: a state visit with a difference, exemplified by Sadat in Jerusalem and, before that, Nixon in China. It consists of a leader assuming personal risk to become the first representative of his (sic) nation or bloc publicly to cross the border of an enemy country, stepping off a plane or over a line into its territory. There he is greeted formally by his counterpart; they shake hands in front of international cameras amid dignitaries and soldiers at attention; he is brought into the country, where he will visit sites of national significance, toast understanding at a banquet, and engage in informal leader-to-leader conversation. The double gesture of crossing the threshold and shaking hands with the enemy inaugurates summit diplomacy and is meant to lead to the normalization of relations (Dayan, Katz, and Motyl 1984, 132; Mitchell 2000). It confers recognition upon a pariah nation, admitting it to the larger international or regional community. It is the embodied performance of détente, and as such it proposed an example for the eventual resolution of the Cold War. Often undertaken in opposition to domestic advisors, public opinion, and the leader's established reputation, it constitutes a political and personal as well as diplomatic risk, and counts on the performative force of surprise to leverage reversed expectations into extraordinary success (Handel 1981).

With so many contingencies, the outcome of the performance is unpredictable. Nixon's startling visit to China was quickly taken up by other Western actors and led to gradual opening of relations, justifying Nixon's repeated citations of the moon landing[3] and description of the trip as a 'great watershed in history, clearly the greatest since World War II' (Caldwell 2009, 637–638). Along with its transformative instrumental consequences, the example could be extrapolated to ambitious ventures in new domains. Even the liberal Star Trek franchise appropriated 'Only Nixon could go to China' as 'an old Vulcan proverb' (Hatzivassiliou 2021, 73).

By contrast, Sadat's visit to Jerusalem was stunning in its moment but at best ambiguous in outcome. One in a series of what Sadat called 'electric shocks' to make Egypt an independent power in the region (Handel 1981, 241–297), the Jerusalem visit was imagined as a peaceful revision of his 1973 October War offensive, itself a charismatic reversal of exemplary defeat in the Six-Day War. The 'Hero of the Crossing' of the Suez Canal now sought to cross the 'psychological barrier' with a charged gesture intended to force reciprocity on a similar scale. Sadat invited the Israelis to 'introduce to the entire world the image of the new man in this area so that he might set an example to the man of our age, the man of peace everywhere' (Sadat 1978, 336, 342). Calqued on the shared religious imagery of Abrahamic sacrifice, redoubled in the joking family-reunion atmosphere of Sadat's conversations with his old enemies, the visit moved liberal Israelis to welcome 'my brother Ishmael' (Kahanoff 2011) and was recognized in the Western press as surpassing even Nixon's China visit in world-historical significance and personal daring.[4]

---

[3] For example, *The New York Times*. 'Text of Statements by Nixon and Ceausescu in Bucharest.' August 3, 1969, Online: https://www.nytimes.com/1969/08/03/archives/text-of-statements-by-nixon-and-ceausescu-in-bucharest.html (accessed January 18, 2025); Nixon, Richard. 'Remarks on Departure from the White House for a State Visit to the People's Republic of China.' February 17, 1972, Online: https://www.presidency.ucsb.edu/documents/remarks-departure-from-the-white-house-for-state-visit-the-peoples-republic-china (accessed January 18, 2025).

[4] See, for example, Hoagland, Jim. 'Sadat's Initiative a Bold Break with Old Mindset Taboos.' *The Washington Post*, November 15, 1977, Online:

In the end, so freighted an example had difficulty moving forward. Arab-world suspicion and Egyptian domestic resentments left Sadat largely isolated. On the Israeli side, historical mistrust, domestic political rivalries, and reliance on US support meant that no reciprocating gesture came to validate Sadat's assumption of risk. And the risk was real: Yitzhak Rabin, the one Israeli who arguably did emulate Sadat's example of personal commitment to the peace process, shared Sadat's fate of assassination by extremists on his own side (Liebes and Katz 1997). Only with Jimmy Carter did Sadat find a partner in exemplary innovation, but the outcome of the 1979 Camp David Accords was, in Arab opinion, marred by Sadat's readiness to make pre-emptive concessions: his faith in sacrifice became a reflex that overcame prudence.

Envisioning the exemplary network

Startling as these acts were in context, they did not come from nowhere. Like a performance of song, a performed political action is recombined, at every level, from other performances; its originality lies in the redeployment of cultural resources in a new situation. Heightened, reflexive action shaped to call attention to itself (Bauman and Briggs 1990), a performance is unique in its moment but also constitutes a node in a network of transmission: performers draw, covertly and overtly, on previous performances as both practical models and symbolic referents. Reception is also dialogic, conditioned by the public's familiarity with prior and neighboring performances, especially those impressive, memorable performances that are taken up as examples. These make the new act interpretable, create expectations regarding its meaning and impact, and, depending on their own rarity, wake up attention or justify indifference and cynicism. Judicious adaptation and citation are thus key to success, even for the leader seeking to astonish with novelty. In a complex, competitive environment, the cooperation among actors needed both to carry off the performance and to follow its gesture toward instrumental political consequences is also not easy. Successful examples are exceptions.

All the same, Sadat's heroic performance and Nixon's more robust achievement were thickly networked with other examples, both threshold crossings and 'conquest' events more generally. Figure 14.1 represents a partial mapping of these relationships, derived from tracing contacts among actors as well as allusions and cross-references made in the moment, some by actors themselves, some by key observers. In a few instances, for the purpose of demonstration, I have proposed a link where mutual knowledge

---

https://www.washingtonpost.com/archive/politics/1977/11/16/sadats-initiative-a-bold-break-with-old-mideast-taboos/ef3bc438-eea6-475b-b027-ca018edd64f6/ (accessed January 18, 2025).

Figure 14.1: The threshold crossing network

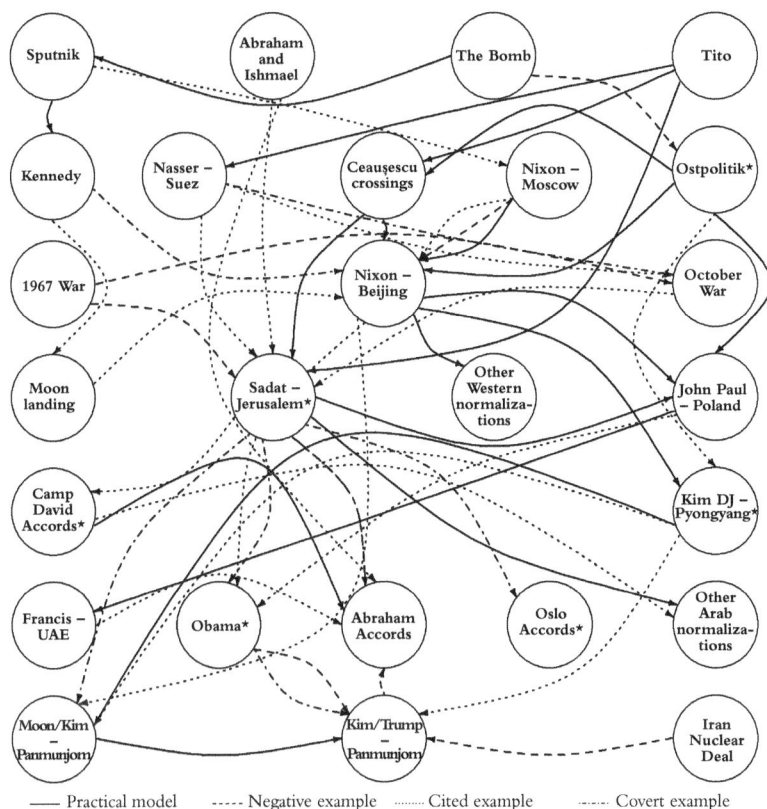

Note: The asterisk denotes a Nobel Peace Prize.

certainly existed and comparison could hardly have been avoided. This network excludes key gestural dialogues between international and domestic politics, where still more astonishing threshold crossings were carried out by unauthorized actors in civil rights and liberation struggles. It excludes an overlapping network of international performances related to walls, most famously in Ronald Reagan's visit to Berlin. It simplifies agency, treating the leader in the photograph as an individual decision-maker rather than the figurehead of a complex foreign policy assemblage. It simplifies transmission pathways, not considering the forms and vehicles through which examples circulate or certain smaller-scale performances that interceded between two network points. It does, however, make visible the centrality of seemingly inconsequential actors such as Romanian president Nicolae Ceaușescu, himself an assiduous crosser of thresholds, without whose entrepreneurial diplomacy and example neither Nixon's nor Sadat's visits would arguably have taken place (Pechlivanis 2019).

As Figure 14.1 suggests, a political action achieves exemplary salience not just directly, against a background of everyday life muddling forward, but within a tissue of connected and comparable actions that encourages its coming to pass and makes it both interpretable and recognizable as extraordinary. The threshold crossing of a singular charismatic hero is the outcome of distributed invention among a differentiated, open network of interactants.

Examples are made from other examples in a less linear process than pure citation would indicate. At the same time, exemplarity is more than the diffusion of innovation: actions clearly differ in weight. (Formal recognitions such as the Nobel Peace Prize, highlighted earlier, confirm the general judgment of such weightiness.) Moreover, new actions draw upon old ones in various ways. Reducing these modes of uptake to ideal types (Table 14.1), we can recognize complementarities among them. A single political action may conceivably cite a sacred national precedent while also overturning a recent negative example, taking practical example from a neighboring success, and being haunted by the shadow of a covert example that might discredit the whole venture.

Alignment with a powerful positive example is thus only the tip of the iceberg of exemplary transmission. In framing his trip to China, Nixon did not simply borrow charisma from the moon landing; he wrested possession of the moon landing toward himself and away from Kennedy, whose idea it had been. Kennedy's ambitions provided, to some degree, the covert example for Nixon's own. Building on his 1962 memoir *Six Crises* – itself composed in emulation of Kennedy's 1956 *Profiles in Courage* at Kennedy's own surely ironic suggestion – Nixon constructed an exemplary lineage of his own actions, leading towards Beijing. His famous 1959 vice-presidential trip to Moscow took pride of place as both a positive example of bold threshold crossing and a negative example of a hostile and suspicious encounter, which he could now claim to have reversed in the dawning of friendly relations with the Chinese. On the contrary, neither Nixon nor the commentariat went out of their way to cite the tightly connected precedent of his 1969 trip to Romania, which received deferential international coverage in its day as a bold threshold crossing resulting in warm relations. This trip, with Ceaușescu's ongoing encouragement of Nixon's China rapprochement, offered a vital practical model for making a success of the China visit; but Bucharest was not Moscow or the moon, to be talked of before the world's cameras.

Table 14.1: Modes of Exemplary Uptake

	Cited	Not cited
Aligned with	Example	Practical model
Distanced	Negative example	Covert example

Where Nixon had the moon landing and his trip to Moscow, Sadat had the Feast of Sacrifice and the 1973 October War to throw glory over his trip to Jerusalem. Sadat sought, unsuccessfully, to shelter his entire subsequent career under the aegis of October, with continual citations, a commemorative holiday, and the 1974 'October Paper' outlining national strategy. More dynamic was his relationship to Nasser's presidency. Sadat was obliged to echo citations of Nasser as exemplary national hero, but rejected Nasser as a practical model by actively distancing Egypt from the Soviet Union. If Nasser's triumph in the Suez Crisis energized Sadat's self-production as the Hero of the Crossing, the most urgent stimulus towards Sadat's 'electric shocks,' both military or peaceful, was the negative example of the 1967 Six-Day War, with its conspicuous and seemingly definitive humiliation of Arab forces. Sadat described his October invasion across the Suez as 'going out in a dark, pitch-black period carrying the torches of light, pointing out the road so that their Nation could cross the bridge between despair and hope.'[5]

Spectacle and suspicion

Richard Nixon was famously conscious of live television's role in his triumphs and debacles, from the 1959 Kitchen Table debate to the 1960 presidential debate to the gleeful taunt of Chicago's 1968 protesters: 'The whole world is watching!' To the extent that the technology, the Chinese government, and the uncertainty of the situation allowed, Nixon sought to make a media event of the China visit.

By 1977, the conventions of televisual 'conquest' were still better established and the technologies more widely diffused. A more intuitive performer than Nixon, Sadat understood early the art of cultivating American journalists. In stepping off the plane from Cairo, he was preceded by Barbara Walters, Walter Cronkite, and John Chancellor, signaling to the Israelis the star power Sadat already commanded (Dayan, Katz, and Motyl 1984, 128–129). Forced to rise to the occasion, Israeli leaders complained that Sadat should win an Oscar instead of a Nobel, but the riveting televisual spectacle brought Israeli life to a halt, and one sympathetic liberal argued that Gandhi too had been a showman (Kahanoff 2011, 233).[6]

---

[5] See Sadat, Anwar. 'Excerpts of a Speech Calling for an Arab-Israeli Peace Conference,' October 16, 1973, Anwar Sadat Archives, Anwar Sadat Chair for Peace and Development, University of Maryland. https://sadat.umd.edu/sites/sadat.umd.edu/files/Excerpts%20of%20a%20Speech%20Calling%20for%20an%20Arab-Israeli%20Peace%20Conference.pdf (accessed January 18, 2025).

[6] See Koven, Ronald. 'Sadat Jokes, Laughs with Golda.' *The Washington Post*, November 21, 1977, Online: https://www.washingtonpost.com/archive/politics/1977/11/22/sadat-jokes-laughs-with-golda/0676c8d2-aa97-4aef-aaa8-79ad880fc043/ (accessed January 18, 2025).

In a comprehensive account of Sadat's gestural trajectory, Egyptian journalist Mohamed Heikal took a darker view. Citations were suspect. Although Kissinger had (remarkably, given his own identification) called Sadat 'the greatest since Bismarck,' Bismarck had used his position of strength to unify the German states; Sadat had divided the Arabs (Heikal 1983, xi). Styles of heroism shifted as one generation responded to another. Hitler was the negative exemplar for the statesmen who made peace in 1945 'since without his malevolent genius the others would not have had their capacities brought on to greatness' (Heikal 1983, 3; see Handel 1981). After them came the generation of revolutionaries – Mao, Ho, Nehru, Tito, Nasser; these were both positive and negative exemplars for Sadat. Finally, 'the world of television, of satellites and computers' created the 'superstar[s],' among whom Heikal numbered John Paul II, Jackie Onassis, Lech Wałęsa, Sadat, and, presciently, international terrorists. The cameras now provoked the escalation and proliferation of political gesture, especially for leaders of small powers, who could hold attention only through compelling, constant, and ever-changing performance. How could Sadat surpass himself as the Hero of the Crossing? 'For audiences who had watched men walking on the moon something more was required ... and this was what Sadat achieved when he made his historic journey to Jerusalem ... Sadat crossed the sound barrier between the normal and the abnormal, between the thinkable and the unthinkable' (Heikal 1983, 5). But Heikal – once Sadat's Minister of Information, later imprisoned by him – saw the ground-level consequences of this escalation. 'A superstar leaps over the frontiers of time and space,' while his people and their demands remain below 'in the shadows,' forgotten by the leader himself until they irrupt into the light of the cameras to demand attention of their own. This happened in the 1981 October anniversary parade, reviving a different exemplary lineage. Said one of Sadat's assassins, 'We wanted to kill him alone, to make him an example for those who came after him' (Heikal 1983, 3, 265).

Heikal's assessment that Sadat became addicted to the cameras, increasingly basing his decisions on fantastic scenarios, need not be fully accepted for his larger argument to be useful. Liebes and Katz demonstrate the diminishing returns of 'media events' as they trace successive performances of reconciliation in the Middle East peace process, such as the signing of the Oslo Accords (1997). Inadequate diplomatic underpinnings, inattention to domestic public opinion, and the incomplete conviction of the leaders themselves were all factors. Equally important, the evolving conditions of mediation no longer permitted performers to claim the crossing of a global threshold (Liebes and Katz 1997, 255). The illocutionary force of 'conquests' depends on their scarcity. They must be rare marvels, unexampled. Instead, a formula had emerged. They must bear some plausible relation to facts on the ground. Instead, recurrent assertions of peace in the Middle East began to sound like the boy crying wolf. Media events must, in Dayan and Katz's model, interrupt regularly scheduled programming and command both global attention and the 'reverence,' or at least acquiescence, of the broadcasters. In the age of CNN, broadcasters emancipated from state control had little to gain from suspending their disbelief or allowing one narrative to monopolize the channels when a world of potential protagonists called for attention, intersecting with a constantly fracturing and recombining global audience. The felicity conditions of Cold War threshold crossings no longer obtained.

A straight line to Donald Trump's first term is easily drawn. Socialized during the Cold War by a competitive father, Trump cared for no league but 'big-league,' and in the US presidency he found a sphere of action commensurate with his self-conception. The challenges facing him certainly existed on a global and indeed planetary scale. But Trump's actor-centered understanding made him still less interested than Sadat in the shadows beyond the spotlight. Instead, for him the performativity of gesture and the necessity of media coverage were axiomatic, determinants of his reality (Poniewozik 2019). Trump's version of the Cold War 'diplomacy of surprise' (Handel 1981) also operated at a different rhythm from that of his predecessors. Nixon had built on the large gestures of mid-20th-century war and diplomacy to create a world-historical moment. Sadat's series of 'electric shocks' whenever stasis threatened, or superpower attention was elsewhere, offered gradually diminishing returns. Adapting to the new formats of reality TV, 24–7 cable news, and the short, sharp shocks of Twitter, Trump monopolized the cameras through continual surprise and disruption, the constant twist of the unexpected. As president, he commanded military and diplomatic force to uphold the power of spectacle, and now he saw the opportunity for unexampled historical accomplishments that would win durable recognitions.

Trump clearly understood the North Korean initiative as his moonshot. To receive Bob Woodward for the opening interview of the book *Rage*, Trump had letters from Kim Jong Un and photographs of their meetings distributed around the Oval Office as 'props.' Trump pointed to the brick ledge delineating the border in the photo of his June 2019 crossing to shake hands with Kim on the northern side of the Joint Security Area. 'That line is a big deal. Nobody has ever stepped across that line. Ever … you know, when you talk about iconic pictures, how about that?' (Woodward 2020, 168–169, 173). The magnitude of the opportunity had become apparent in the first meeting with Kim in Singapore: Trump described the wall of cameras as 'even more than he had seen in Hollywood at the Academy Awards' (Woodward 2020, 106).

'Did you think it's kind of Nixon to China?' suggested Woodward. Fox News commentators had already made this comparison, and the precedent was certainly in the minds of the North Koreans, but Trump brusquely refused any citation, especially in association with China's rise (Woodward 2020, 170). Still, Trump's refrain 'like you've never seen' indicated an obsessively comparative frame of reference in his approach to the presidency. While Nixon in China was surely one of the icons informing Trump's conception of the office, the focus on North Korea had much to do with Barack Obama, a negative exemplar to be reversed and overthrown. Like Nixon and Sadat, Trump struggled in the shadow of a charismatic predecessor, who had achieved both popular acclaim and the elite recognition he sought for himself; Obama's Nobel Peace Prize was a particular irritant. At their January 2016 Oval Office meeting, after which Trump showed himself momentarily swayed by Obama's example, Obama had impressed upon Trump that North Korea was the most dangerous security threat the US faced. Having heard a National Security Council advisor decry Obama's 'strategic patience' as disastrous, Trump immediately inverted the approach to 'maximal confrontation' (Woodward 2020, 26). After the Singapore meetings, Trump famously tweeted: 'There is no longer a Nuclear Threat from North Korea,' and followed up with a second tweet pointing out that Obama had cited North Korea as 'our biggest and most dangerous problem' (Woodward 2020, 107–108). As his interchanges with Kim continued, Trump frequently cast Obama as a failed rival suitor, 'begging for a meeting' that Kim would not give.[7]

If Obama provided a negative exemplar, Kim Jong Un excited a mimetic fascination in Trump that made him a barely covert exemplar. The neoliberal 'bromances' of Blair and Clinton or Obama and Modi had warmed up and personalized the détente-era idiom of friendship. Kim, like Emmanuel Macron and seemingly Vladimir Putin before him, cultivated a still more intense intimacy that exploited Trump's obsession with significant others. Offering mirrors in which Trump could see himself clarified and amplified, they prompted identification expressed in admiration or, if the mirror failed to cooperate with the self-image, ferocious competitive emulation. Kim's celebrity-inflected personal style posed a lower bar for identification than that of Macron or Putin, and more nakedly than either, he embodied an

---

[7] See Edevane, Gillian. ' "What a Clown Show": Trump's DMZ Meeting with North Korea's Kim Jong-Un Prompts Divided Reactions.' *Newsweek*, January 30, 2019, Online: https://www.newsweek.com/what-clown-show-trumps-dmz-meeting-north-koreas-kim-jong-un-prompts-divided-reactions-1446705 (accessed January 18, 2025).

enviable fusion of untrammeled state, mediatic, and personal power. In relaxed moments, Trump joked with his people that they should snap to attention like Kim's; he mused on Kim's personal ruthlessness (Woodward 2020, 27, 169). As the public communications evolved from personal rivalry to falling in love, Trump and Kim began to fuse into a dyad. Kim encouraged the public theatricality of the relationship, drawing on the historic power of threshold crossings, the idiom of celebrity, and, as Kim said, the atmosphere of 'fantasy film' (Woodward 2020, 161). The 'Hollywood-style trailer' that accompanied the demilitarized zone (DMZ) visit joined Kim and Trump in heroic postures with the slogan, 'Two men, two leaders, one destiny' (Kim 2018, 34).

The North Koreans cannily manipulated Trump's Napoleonic yearning to monopolize the global gaze and push the envelope of greatness forward. The theme is constantly urged in the famous 2018–2019 series of 'love letters': 'I'm prepared to cooperate with you in sincerity and dedication to accomplish a great feat that no one in the past has been able to achieve and that is unexpected by the whole world' (Woodward 2020, 100–101). Grasping Trump's purely illocutionary conception of action (Wagner-Pacifici 2017, 93–94), Kim stresses the transformational character of their meetings per se in inaugurating a 'new footing' (Woodward 2020, 161). Institutional follow-through was deferred into a hazy but glorious future.[8]

That future never came. Kim kept deferring the prescribed first step of accounting for his holdings in weapons of mass destruction. Trump changed national security advisors and his team lost focus. The North-South negotiations broke down. By December 2019 the North had resumed nuclear testing and was threatening the US with a 'Christmas present.' The threshold crossing itself failed to come off as a global 'conquest,' for most US and Western media declined to do their part in supporting it. Trump's lack of establishment legitimacy, his record of disruptive gestures unmoored to institutional action, and a longer American history of declaring 'mission accomplished' meant that, although international observers from the Pope to Al-Jazeera offered cautious endorsements, the US commentariat largely dismissed Trump's DMZ crossing as a dangerous 'photo op' and a reality TV production.

---

[8] The emphasis on cooperation for achievement points to the farcical reduction of another set of postwar examples. Berenskoetter's account of friendship in international relations (2007) cites the postwar Anglo-American construction of the 'Western World' and the Franco-German reconciliation at the basis of the European Union as examples of commitment to common projects that both anchor particular relationships and energize the shaping of international order. The Trump-Kim episode jumped from friendship to fusion, and it equally proclaimed rather than did anything to build a new world order. Less gestural authoritarian friendships are doing more work on the ground towards this end.

It would be a mistake, however, to attribute failure purely to Trump's idiosyncrasies, or to understand Nixon and Sadat – figures sufficiently problematic in their own right – as heroic exemplars for Trump's mimetic caricature. The 'tragedy to farce' trajectory cannot be understood as a binary reversal. Instead, the transformation of felicity conditions is a more iterative process. (As has often been observed, Trump is symptom rather than cause of certain transformations in our politics.) Nixon, Sadat, and many others prefigured Trump's grandiloquence, his desire to do something big, his obsession with the cameras, his insistence on leader autonomy, his faith in interpersonal diplomacy, and his taste for diplomatic surprise. The 'imperial presidency' born of the Cold War provided structural reinforcement and institutional power. The developing media environment, as Heikal realized, enhanced the scope of the 'expressive presidency' in which the leader's affective link to the public overrides instrumental concerns (Hennessey and Wittes 2020). Under these conditions, instead of instituting a new example, the violation of expectations is prone to escalate into a 'gleeful' torpedoing of norms or just an artfully produced televisual climax.[9] A leader looking to dominate the headlines will find value in authoritarian exemplars, and spectacle will tend to disentangle itself from substance. Sadat had more faith than Nixon in the gesture itself as decisive; Trump went further than either.

A true believer

In grand lines, then, we might indeed speak of exemplarity returning as farce. But, as the network map indicates, grand lines oversimplify. For a fuller understanding of the threshold crossing's career as an exemplary performance, we must look beyond the protagonists of those most globally visible cases. I will consider the place of Trump's DMZ crossing within a South Korean exemplary trajectory, and then examine the 2020 Abraham Accords from the point of view of the United Arab Emirates negotiators.

If Trump was a stranger to the long, intersecting arcs of Cold War exemplarity, South Korean president Moon Jae-in was profoundly and personally imbricated. His mentor, Kim Dae-jung, had won his own Nobel for a notable threshold crossing, visiting Pyongyang in 2000. From his deathbed, Kim enjoined Moon to continue the 'Sunshine Policy,' and Moon had coordinated the ensuing 'Peace and Prosperity' initiative of President Roh Moo-hyun; attentive to every detail, he had a yellow line

---

[9] See Lozada, Carlos. '150 Books Show How the Trump Era Has Warped Our Brains.' *The Atlantic*, October 6, 2020, Online: https://www.theatlantic.com/ideas/archive/2020/10/chaos-trump-white-house/616616/ (accessed January 15, 2025).

painted along the border to catch the exact moment when Roh would cross it northward during a 2007 summit.[10] After scandals, missteps, and inattention, however, the effort had fallen off; on attaining the presidency, Moon had to relaunch. Unsurprisingly, he took up his mentor's trajectory. A practicing Catholic and a traditional liberal, Moon was doubly socialized into the discourse of leading by example. In addition, as S. Nathan Park observed, he was an expert Go player, accustomed to improve his skills by replaying and re-analyzing old games.[11]

The Korean peace process did not proceed in international isolation. On the North Korean side, Kim Jong-il had visited Beijing in May 2000 for advice on Kim Dae-jung's reception; China's economic opening in the wake of a threshold crossing offered a potent example of opportunity, later countered by the negative example of Moammar Qaddafi, who gave up his nuclear ambitions and was ousted from power. But the South Korean leadership looked away from US-dominated relationships and found a new example for both citation and practical emulation. Before the trip to Pyongyang, Kim Dae-jung visited Berlin and issued the pointedly titled declaration, 'Lessons of German Reunification and the Korean Peninsula.' Citing the parallels between the two countries in war, division, and economic 'miracle' on the democratic, market-driven side of the border, Kim pointed to the good outcomes of Ostpolitik, reassuring the world and no doubt himself that his imminent visit to what was still formally enemy territory would bring progress instead of disaster.

In July 2017, the newly sworn-in Moon Jae-in took his own trip to Berlin and made his own speech. Like Kim Dae-jung, he used the occasion to lay out general principles for advancing peace in the Korean peninsula and moving incrementally towards reunification. To make the risky German example more palatable to the North Koreans, Moon redoubled Kim's insistence that unification must proceed by slow increments of mutual accommodation, pointing to the long-term, locally-negotiated character of Ostpolitik. Moreover, he shifted the venue of his remarks. Kim Dae-jung had spoken in the former West Berlin; Moon spoke from the eastern side of the former wall, in a site chosen to display not just

---

[10] See Fifield, Anna. 'South Korea is Sparing no Effort to Make Summit with Kim a made-for-TV success.' *The Washington Post*, April 25, 2018, Online: https://www.washingtonpost.com/world/asia_pacific/south-korea-is-sparing-no-effort-to-make-summit-a-made-for-tv-success/2018/04/25/3d167350-487a-11e8-ad53-d5751c8f243f_story.html (accessed January 18, 2025).

[11] See Global Asia. 'The Road Remains Open: Moon Jae-in's Berlin Speech as a Pathway to Peace.' June 2019, Online: https://www.globalasia.org/v14no2/cover/the-road-remains-open-moon-jae-ins-berlin-speech-as-a-pathway-to-peace_s-nathan-park (accessed January 18, 2025).

restored prosperity but restored equality and dignity.[12] Moon was explicit in claiming the lineage:

> The Berlin in which we are here today is the very place where 17 years ago President Kim Dae-jung of the Republic of Korea introduced the 'Berlin Doctrine' which laid out the foundation for reconciliation and cooperation between South and North Korea. Moreover, this Altes Stadthaus is a historic site where the German Unification Treaty was negotiated. (Moon 2017, 221)

Moon worked on both Kim Jong Un and domestic public opinion through the occasion of the February 2018 Pyongchang Olympic Games. Despite the overlayer of traditional mutual hostility performed by the proxies of Kim Jo-yong and Mike Pence, which prepared the stage for the charismatic reversal of Singapore, Moon reconstructed the Games as an 'Olympics of Peace,' exemplified in emotional cooperations that won approval on both sides of the DMZ.

The cooperative, friendly tone established at the Games between the two Koreas culminated in a threshold crossing of its own: a stunning media event in South Korea and, to the extent that the world's attention could be wrested from Trump, a global news story. On April 27, 2018, Kim Jong Un became the first North Korean leader to enter the South, stepping over the border at the Joint Security Area to hold a summit with Moon. There was a substantive outcome: the joint Panmunjom Declaration seeking a formal end to the war and 'complete denuclearization' of the peninsula. There were also the affecting visuals of the crossing of the line, the two leaders chatting without minders on a footbridge, and the delegates drinking soju together.[13] Moon made sure the point was not lost on Kim, telling him 'When you crossed the military border for the first time, Panmunjom became a symbol of peace, not a symbol of division.' Nudging Kim to reciprocate, he added, 'I wonder when I can cross to the North' (Shorrock 2018). Kim responded with an immediate invitation, taking Moon's hand as both stepped over the line to the north side; Kim's 'penchant for bold and surprising moves' received due credit in the coverage (see Shorrock 2018).[14] Ordinary Koreans

---

[12] See Ruediger, Frank. 'Navigating Difficult Waters: President Moon Jae-in's Berlin Speech.' *38 North*, July 10, 2017, Online: https://www.38north.org/2017/07/rfrank071017/ (accessed January 18, 2025).

[13] For an extensive summary, see Campbell, Charlie. 'Person of the Year: Moon Jae-In.' *Time Magazine*, Online: https://time.com/person-of-the-year-2018-moon-jae-in-runner-up/ (accessed January 18, 2025).

[14] See Fifield, Anna. 'In a Feel-Good Korea Summit, Kima Lays the Groundwork for Meeting with Trump.' *The Washington Post*, April 27, 2018, Online:

and Korean-Americans were deeply moved by the embodied commitments, even describing the meeting as 'far more important than Singapore,' and Kim's South Korean approval ratings shot up from 20 percent to 80 percent (Kim 2018; Shorrock 2018).

It is a mark of Moon's discipline that he did not seek to equal Kim Dae-jung in taking a Nobel for North-South détente, but told his own cabinet: 'It's President Trump who should receive the Nobel Prize. We only need to take peace' (Kim 2018). Literally pushed out of the photo at the DMZ, Moon made it his business to create exemplary opportunities for Trump and provide him with practical models, but also, when necessary, to provoke him by example. While the official purpose of the April Panmunjom meeting was to prepare for the Kim-Trump Singapore summit, it was clearly also intended to keep Trump up to the mark. Soon after the Olympics, South Korean National Security Advisor Chung Eui-young met with Kim Jong Un in Pyongyang; the April summit was then announced, with the promise that Kim would cross the border to the South. Immediately afterwards, on March 8, Chung flew to Washington unannounced, declaring that he carried a letter from Kim. Trump canceled other appointments, received Chung in the Oval Office, agreed to a future meeting with Kim, and had Chung, a foreign official, announce this major diplomatic step in a sudden evening press conference from the porch of the White House. Observers compared this unprecedented scene to Trump's reality show, 'The Apprentice' (Cha and Fraser 2018). Careful commentators recognized, however, that the South Koreans had been the primary disruptors; Trump was judged to have gone along with this diplomatic surprise 'not to be outdone' by the upcoming inter-Korean summit (Cha and Fraser 2018). The White House announcement allowed the April meeting to be meaningful for Koreans while encouraging the US press to dismiss it as a 'feel-good summit' laying the ground for the real work in Singapore.[15] At Trump's first 2017 visit to Seoul, Moon had praised his dealmaking skills and confirmed that he was making America great again; he assured Trump that the Singapore meeting could earn him the Nobel, and allowed this to be confirmed in public (see Kim 2018, 43).[16] His skill in first driving Trump to participate in the peace

---

https://www.washingtonpost.com/world/asia_pacific/north-and-south-korea-agree-to-work-toward-common-goal-of-denuclearization/2018/04/27/7dcb03d6-4981-11e8-8082-105a446d19b8_story.html (accessed January 18, 2025).

[15] See Fifield, Anna. 'In a Feel-Good Korea Summit, Kima Lays the Groundwork for Meeting with Trump.' *The Washington Post*, April 27, 2018, Online: https://www.washingtonpost.com/world/asia_pacific/north-and-south-korea-agree-to-work-toward-common-goal-of-denuclearization/2018/04/27/7dcb03d6-4981-11e8-8082-105a446d19b8_story.html (accessed January 18, 2025).

[16] Denyer, Simon. 'Japan's Abe won't Confirm Trump Nobel Prize Nomination, but Media Reports Say He Made It.' *The Washington Post*, February 18, 2019, Online:

process, then inducing Trump to commit himself to an outcome by offering him exemplary protagonism, caused Korean-American journalist Suki Kim to christen Moon himself 'the Dealmaker' (Kim 2018).

When out from under the American shadow, Moon did not hesitate to point to his own national example. In the 2017 speech, he represented the Koreas as capable of taking up the world-historical baton and inaugurating a phase shift: 'We will complete in Seoul and Pyongyang the dismantlement of the Cold War which started in Berlin. Furthermore, we will spread a new vision of peace to Northeast Asia and the rest of the world' (Moon 2017, 225). Speaking to the UN General Assembly in September 2019, Moon initially spread the exemplarity around, citing European postwar cooperation, with its 'peace economy,' as 'a fine model for us to emulate' and also praising Trump's 'action in taking Chairman Kim's hand and stepping over the Military Demarcation Line … a declaration of the true beginning of a new era of peace'; he urged both leaders to follow their own example and take further 'huge steps.' But, as in his Berlin speech, Korea again would seize historical protagonism from these precedents. The DMZ itself, Moon proposed, could become an 'international peace zone' and UNESCO World Heritage Site for peace and environmental research towards the UN's Sustainable Development Goals. One hundred years after its anticolonial revolt, he concluded, Korea was now leading global efforts for peaceful coexistence (Moon 2019). By May 2020, when the Republic of Korea was staving off the COVID-19 pandemic as it spread in the West, Moon encouraged his people with Trumpian echoes of national 'greatness' and asserted that 'countries that we wanted to follow have started learning from us. We have set a standard and become a world-class nation' (Moon 2020). In Moon's practice, as with other non-Western leaders, the liberal idiom of exemplarity did not imply perpetual deference to Western models, but facilitated escaping them. The peace process, however, depended on the uptake of more powerful actors, who failed to cooperate. Forced to delegate protagonism to two volatile agents, Moon was unable to complete the exemplary transmission.

With the peace effort blocked, Korean greatness found another avenue, as *The Economist* remarked. The triumph of Moon's late presidency was the signing of series of large deals to sell arms to Australia, Egypt, and the United Arab Emirates; built with American support and practical example, the South Korean weapons industry was now on track to compete with

---

https://www.washingtonpost.com/world/japans-abe-wont-confirm-trump-nobel-prize-nomination-but-media-reports-say-he-did/2019/02/18/26f62310-3337-11e9-946a-115a5932c45b_story.html (accessed January 18, 2025).

its former model.¹⁷ Here is further confirmation that exemplarity does not lodge in the extraordinary moral integrity of individual actors or in any universal standard, but inheres in networks of transmission across particular actions, judged in relation to one another.

After liberal exemplarity

How to pull back from exemplary inflation and exemplary decay? A forlorn liberal might turn back to Barack Obama's 2009 Nobel Prize lecture, a characteristically subtle rereading of Cold War exemplarity tinged by his awareness of not having earned the prize awarded. Obama named the humanitarians and sacrificial heroes who had preceded him in accepting the honor – King, Schweitzer, Mandela, though not the uncitable Sadat – but stipulated that as US Commander-in-Chief, he could not 'be guided by their examples alone'; he also had to follow the US leaders who had faced the negative exemplars of Hitler and Al Qaeda with military force. He invoked Kennedy's example to argue for the American transition from war to global institution-building, achieved over the long term through the ethically ambiguous but forward-looking threshold crossings undertaken by Nixon in China, John Paul II in Poland, and Reagan in perestroika. Implicitly acknowledging the compromised status of all American leaders and leadership in general, he went on to cite the peacekeeping soldier, the protester braving repression, the determined mother educating her child – 'Let us follow *their* example' – and concluded with this grounded rather than transcendent vision of struggle as 'the story of human progress.'¹⁸

Such 'everyday heroes' (Evans 2023) have remained the staple of American public rhetoric, though unmoored to any increasingly implausible narrative of progress, and largely within domestic discourse. The Biden administration did not follow Obama's example in trying to internationalize these individual exemplars. Instead, in a disconcerting blend of habit and hopefulness, its foreign policy establishment once more invoked the nation-state's 'power of example.'

Neither liberal talk nor populist spectacle have exhausted the usefulness of the threshold crossing. On August 13, 2020, in the heat of re-election campaign and with progress in North Korea long off

---

17 See The Economist. 'South Korea Wants to Become One of the World's Biggest Arms Exporters.' February 12, 2022, Online: https://www.economist.com/asia/2022/02/12/south-korea-wants-to-become-one-of-the-worlds-biggest-arms-exporters (accessed January 18, 2025).
18 See Obama, Barack H. 'Nobel Lecture.' *The Nobel Prize*, December 10, 2009, Online: https://www.nobelprize.org/prizes/peace/2009/obama/lecture/ (accessed January 18, 2025).

the table, Donald Trump tweeted the completion of a US-mediated agreement normalizing relations between Israel and the United Arab Emirates. Without explicit mention of the diplomatic achievements of the 1970s, the cover term of the 'Abraham Accords' clearly evoked both Sadat's visit to Jerusalem and the ensuing Camp David Accords, the objective precedent for any Arab-Israeli agreement. Secretary of State Mike Pompeo attempted to uphold a tone, tweeting 'Blessed are the peacemakers,' but even Fox News gave the initial announcement only two minutes before returning to Trump's views on Kamala Harris.[19] Trump himself made little show of taking the rhetoric seriously. In the formal Oval Office announcement, he evoked 'the father of three great faiths,' but quickly joked that he had wanted to call it the 'Donald J. Trump Accord.' Thou shalt have no other exemplars but me was, by then, too familiar a principle for any other presentation to be credible. The White House signing on September 15 passed almost unnoticed, with more media discussion of social distancing than of the ceremony itself.[20] No threshold crossing was embodied in gesture. The agreement produced no lasting icons or visible world emotion.

Even the framing of the event as a 'peace agreement' was dismissed by world observers; it was widely remarked that Israel and the UAE had no border or history of conflict, while the unconsulted Palestinians were made more rather than less vulnerable to Israeli aggression. In keeping with Trump's modus operandi, the agreement was a 'business transaction.'[21] Pushed out by Washington at the eleventh hour to save the re-election and justify the elevation of Jared Kushner, it also helped a beleaguered Benjamin Netanyahu; it gave Crown Prince Mohammed Bin Zayed a claim on US gratitude and a way to change the subject from UAE human rights violations.[22] In addition, the agreement moved existing security cooperation

---

[19] See Singman, Brooke. 'Trump Announces "Historic Peace Agreement" Between Israel, UAE.' *Fox News*, August 13, 2020, Online: https://www.foxnews.com/politics/trump-israel-uae-peace-agreement (accessed January 18, 2025).

[20] See Wulfsohn, Joseph. 'CNN Shames Trumps "Large Crowd," "Little Social Distancing" at WH Event Marking Historic Mideast Peace Deal.' *Fox News*, September 15, 2020, Online: https://www.foxnews.com/media/cnn-shames-trumps-large-crowd-little-social-distancing-at-wh-event-marking-middle-east-peace-deal (accessed January 18, 2025).

[21] See Harb, Imad K. 'The Utter Failure of the Abraham Accords.' *Aljazeera*, May 18, 2021, Online: https://www.aljazeera.com/opinions/2021/5/18/the-utter-failure-of-the-abraham-accords (accessed January 18, 2025).

[22] See, for example, Salloum, Raniah. 'Was der Friedensplan zwischen Israel und der VAE bedeutet.' *Der Spiegel*, August 14, 2020, Online: https://www.spiegel.de/ausland/israel-und-vereinigte-arabische-emirate-was-der-friedensplan-bedeutet-a-130d929d-9039-4e9f-bba2-43dea9e354bb (accessed January 18, 2025).

into the open, creating a 'latter-day Holy Alliance' of conservative autocrats against Iran as well as Islamist and democratic forces in the region and pressing the Saudis to join it.[23]

The outcomes, therefore, were real, if not exactly as advertised. There was emulatory follow-on: similar agreements with Bahrain and Morocco were quickly announced and incorporated into a plural 'Abraham Accords.' The Palestinians were further isolated diplomatically, reducing inconvenience to regional governments. The Emirates were given the hope of access to US-made F-35 jets. Channels were opened for reciprocal communications, including business investment as well as tourism and access to holy sites, and economic investment; Kushner and Treasury Secretary Steven Mnuchin immediately found ways to profit by the new relationships.[24] Preferring reform to populist rupture, the next US administration also made the best of arrangements that were in many ways advantageous. At a virtual anniversary celebration in 2021, Secretary of State Anthony Blinken did his best to draw the agreement into the fold of liberal foreign policy by citing the Camp David Accords and urging the example toward the future: 'May it be a model for others to follow.'[25]

Banal exemplarity was not lacking in the rhetoric on the UAE side, but it had undertones. Consider the language of former Minister of State for Foreign Affairs Anwar Gargash at the first anniversary: 'I would say that the main achievement of the Abraham Accords in the beginning was breaking the psychological barrier.'[26] We need not, of course, posit any psychoanalytic

---

[23] See H-Diplo ISSF Policy Series. 'Policy Series 2021–52: The Trump "Legacy" for American Foreign Policy.' September 22, 2021, Online: https://issforum.org/roundtables/policy/ps2021-52 (accessed January 18, 2025); Aljazeera. 'The Abraham Accords: The PR of the "Peace Deals".' September 19, 2020, Online: https://www.aljazeera.com/program/the-listening-post/2020/9/19/the-abraham-accords-the-pr-of-the-peace-deals (accessed January 18, 2025).

[24] See Kelly, Kate, et al. 'Seeking Backers for New Fund, Jared Kushner Turns to the Middle East.' *The New York Times*, November 26, 2021, Online: https://www.nytimes.com/2021/11/26/us/politics/kushner-investment-middle-east.html (accessed January 18, 2025); Kelly, Kate, and David D. Kirkpatrick. 'Kushner's and Mnuchin's Pivots to Business with the Gulf.' *The New York Times*, May 22, 2022, Online: https://www.nytimes.com/2022/05/22/business/jared-kushner-steven-mnuchin-gulf-investments.html (accessed January 18, 2025).

[25] See Blinken, Anthony. 'At the One Year Anniversary of the Abraham Accords: Normalization Agreements in Action.' *U.S. Department of State*, September 17, 2021, Online: https://www.state.gov/at-the-one-year-anniversary-of-the-abraham-accords-normalization-agreements-in-action/ (accessed January 18, 2025).

[26] See Blinken, Anthony. 'At the One Year Anniversary of the Abraham Accords: Normalization Agreements in Action.' *U.S. Department of State*, September 17, 2021, Online: https://www.state.gov/at-the-one-year-anniversary-of-the-abraham-accords-normalization-agreements-in-action/ (accessed January 18, 2025).

return of the repressed in this echo of Sadat; there are more straightforward empirical mechanisms through which even polluted examples are kept alive. It is surely possible to trace the diffusion of the 'psychological barrier' into diplomatic cliché during the long years of the Middle East peace process. And it is impossible to believe that Anwar Gargash or any statesman of any Arab nation contemplating normalization with Israel would *not* have the example of the other Anwar before him, albeit covertly. Yet however memorable that threshold crossing, the remark supports an interpretation of examples as gestures without substance, for Sadat himself had claimed to break that barrier, and here it was again.

There is a final turn of the screw, however. Soon after the first accord was announced, the Atlantic Council hosted a conversation with Gargash on its implications. No time was wasted on three-great-faiths window-dressing, and the discussion moved quickly from a perfunctory evocation of Palestinian claims to an extended consideration of F-35 sales. Here too, though, was more than sheer transaction. Asked how the UAE's decision would influence other Gulf States and affect the long-term Arab League stance on the Palestinian issue, Gargash evoked a long history of conferences – 'night after night coming from Cairo,' the people demanding 'are we going to see anything more than statements?' With the Israeli commitment to halt annexation, Gargash claimed, 'the UAE clearly is delivering more than a statement.' Here is implied improvement on Egypt's historical example, a claim to regional leadership. Asked again what the UAE position would mean in a Gulf context, Gargash answered with an extended meditation on barriers and thresholds, raising one more example:

> We like to think of ourselves as a dynamic and, you know, Arab country that actually wants to break a lot of barriers, because we feel that an exclusivist view of the world through a purely Arab prism will not allow you to play, you know, up to your potential ... Nobody ever thought that a Catholic pope will visit the Arabian Peninsula. And at the time, that decision of inviting the pope was seen as something that was very risky, that will be injurious to conservative Muslim views, et cetera. And, you know, we pulled one of the most spectacular visits of a Catholic pope.
>
> And we feel we did the right thing ... We want to really come and see where can we actually have our stretch targets? Where can we actually open up the region and make the region more global? Now, this is a different decision, but inviting also the pope to visit the Arabian Peninsula, perhaps from a Western perspective will not be the same. But from a regional perspective, this was considered a taboo. This is something you don't do. So from that perspective

I think the UAE is managing a successful development model here in the region.[27]

Here is yet another threshold crossing. Pope Francis' February 2019 visit to Abu Dhabi did not capture global headlines, but it was a first in the Gulf region and it was clearly significant in the minds of its hosts, opening the way to the agreement with Israel. Pope Francis had revived the pattern of papal visiting inaugurated by John Paul II, who first visited large Catholic nations, then in 1979 famously returned as Pope to the nominally atheistic Poland, in the final iconic threshold crossing of the era of détente. From John Paul's time to Francis', the idioms of human rights and civilizational encounter had taken hold, and the Vatican sought not merely to solace the Catholic guestworkers of the Gulf but to engage in a 'dialogue with Islam.'[28] Delicate as both agendas were, the Emiratis saw an opportunity and themselves issued the invitation.[29]

In the Atlantic Council conversation, Gargash goes on to distance the Emirati stance from the 'high rhetoric' that had accompanied stagnation in the peace process. That, of course, was Sadat's tone; Gargash sounds more like a CEO defending a tricky acquisition. But the deeper logic of entering the international community and becoming a player by means of risky threshold crossings has taken root. Such gestures may have dwindled to banality or degraded into farce for countries weary of the burdens of engagement. For countries seeking to expand their presence, the examples of détente have not lost their import.

This is despite or perhaps because of their thinned resonance. The Hamas attacks of October 7 2023 and the ferocity of Israel's response embarrassed the UAE leadership and confirmed the limitations of a treaty framed around 'stability, peace, and prosperity.' The treaty remains in effect, however. More importantly, like China before it, the UAE has emphasized agency rather than alignment, global economic opening rather than security cooperation. If James Mattis celebrated the UAE as 'Little Sparta,' the

---

[27] See Atlantic Council. 'Transcript: A Conversation with H.E. Anwar Gargash, UAE Minister of State for Foreign Affairs.' August 20, 2020, Online: https://www.atlanticcouncil.org/commentary/transcript/transcript-a-conversation-with-h-e-anwar-gargash-uae-minister-of-state-for-foreign-affairs/ (accessed January 18, 2025).

[28] See Bibbo, Barbara. 'Pope Francis Seeks Dialogue on First Trip to UAE.' *Aljazeera*, February 4, 2019, Online: https://www.aljazeera.com/features/2019/2/4/pope-francis-seeks-dialogue-on-first-trip-to-uae (accessed January 18, 2025).

[29] See Aljazeera. 'Pope Francis to Visit UAE in Historic Trip to the Gulf.' December 6, 2018, Online: https://www.aljazeera.com/news/2018/12/6/pope-francis-to-visit-uae-in-historic-trip-to-the-gulf (accessed January 18, 2025).

UAE retorted with a different exemplar, 'Little Singapore' (Singh 2022, 42). Although Saudi Arabia remains the prize alliance in US calculations, the UAE has profited by the Abraham Accords to pursue an aggressive multilateral economic and military diplomacy that sets the example for its larger, less flexible neighbor.

The career of the exemplary gesture plays out over time across a wide social field that is itself constantly reshaped in shifting and multiplying channels of communication. The Cold War threshold crossing arose in urgent reaction, yet intimate connection, to the horrors of Hitler and the Bomb. Though implicating US presidents and other inarguable global protagonists, threshold crossings depended heavily on the creative labor and commitment of such minor characters as Ceaușescu, Moon, and Gargash. Idealism, opportunism, pragmatism, and cynicism cooperated easily in the production of the genre. In the logic of all networked invention, its uses grew as its user network broadened, and it became both internalized as a mental model and banalized as convenient rhetoric. But the gestural core of exemplarity, which invites the amplification of the cameras, drove the primary trajectory implied in Marx's 'tragedy to farce' metaphor. Thus there is a through line from Nixon's dawning understanding of television's power to Sadat's cultivation of the commentariat to Trump's conflation of leading the world with leading the ratings. The emancipation of spectacle from the lower-level labor of politics entails the proliferation, escalation, and debasement of exemplars. This is the end of the threshold crossing's golden age and probably of modern liberal exemplarity *tout court*, at least in its historic center. As the uptake from Moon and Gargash suggests, however, states on the historic periphery will bear watching, developing important hybrids in their own rise to power. More immediately, alternative traditions have wrested away protagonism in international relations, whether China's post-Confucian state exemplarity (see Zhang, Chapter 6, this volume) or the charismatic authoritarianism whose repertoires continued to circulate in criminal and ludic enclaves of the modern and have now returned to center stage. The outsider exemplarities of nonstate actors – jihadist, progressive, and populist – proliferate, but rarely achieve such global gestures as the 9–11 attacks: their power lies rather in collective action and viral circulation, though they have yet to overcome the mediatic cult of the individual or master the institutional follow-on from performance (see Kverndokk, Chapter 5, and Perea Ozerin, Chapter 8, this volume). Even the stunning revitalization of liberal democratic principle and Western unity in the wake of the Russian invasion of Ukraine depended on an example set at the margins, where no one had expected it (Noyes and Wille, Chapter 1, this volume). For the foreseeable future, it appears that examples will be set from outside or beneath the historic contours of the liberal international order.

References

Bauman, Richard, and Charles L. Briggs. 1990. 'Poetics and Performance as Critical Perspectives on Language and Social Life.' *Annual Review of Anthropology* 19: 59–88.

Berenskoetter, Felix. 2007. 'Friends, There Are No Friends? An Intimate Reframing of the International.' *Millennium: Journal of International Studies* 35: 647–76.

Caldwell, Dan. 2009. 'The Legitimation of the Nixon-Kissinger Grand Design and Grand Strategy.' *Diplomatic History* 33: 633–652.

Cha, Victor, and Katrin Fraser Katz. 2018. 'The Right Way to Coerce North Korea.' *Foreign Affairs* 97 (3): 87–100.

Dayan, Daniel, and Elihu Katz. 1992. *Media Events: The Live Broadcasting of History*. Harvard University Press.

Dayan, Daniel, Elihu Katz, and Pierre Motyl. 1984. 'Television Diplomacy: Sadat in Jerusalem.' In *World Communications: A Handbook*, edited by George Gerbner and Marsha Siefert. Longman.

Evans, Nicholas H.A. 2023. 'Exemplars.' In *The Cambridge Handbook for the Anthropology of Ethics*, edited by James Laidlaw. Cambridge University Press.

Handel, Michael I. 1981. *The Diplomacy of Surprise: Hitler, Nixon, Sadat*. Center for International Affairs, Harvard University.

Hatzivassiliou, Evanthis. 2021. 'Images of the International System and the Cold War in *Star Trek*, 1966–1991.' *Journal of Cold War Studies* 23: 55–88.

Heikal, Muhammad. 1983. *Autumn of Fury: The Assassination of Sadat*. André Deutsch.

Hennessey, Susan, and Benjamin Wittes. 2020. *Unmaking the Presidency: Trump's War on the World's Most Powerful Office*. Farrar, Straus and Giroux.

Kahanoff, Jacqueline. 2011. 'My Brother Ishmael: On the Visit of Anwar Sadat.' In *Mongrels or Marvels: The Levantine Writings of Jacqueline Shohet Kahanoff*, edited by Deborah A. Star and Sasson Somekh. Stanford University Press.

Katz, Elihu, and Tamar Liebes. 2007. '"No More Peace!": How Disaster, Terror, and War Have Upstaged Media Events.' *International Journal of Communication* 1: 157–166.

Kim, Suki. 2018. 'The Dealmaker.' *The New Republic* 249 (11): 34–43.

Koselleck, Reinhart. 1985. *Futures Past: On the Semantics of Historical Time*. MIT Press.

Liebes, Tamar, and Elihu Katz. 1997. 'Staging Peace: Televised Ceremonies of Reconciliation.' *The Communication Review* 2: 235–257.

Marx, Karl. 1852. *Der achtzehnte Brumaire des Louis Bonaparte*. Available from: http://www.mlwerke.de/me/me08/me08_115.htm (accessed June 22, 2022).

Mitchell, Christopher. 2000. *Gestures of Conciliation: Factors Contributing to Successful Olive Branches*. St. Martin's Press.

Moon Jae-in. 2017. 'The Last Divided Nation on This Planet: Germany's Unification Gives Us Hope for Unification.' *Vital Speeches International* 9 (8): 221–225.

Moon Jae-in. 2019. 'The Principles for Resolving Issues Related to the Korean Peninsula Remain Unchanged.' *Vital Speeches of the Day* 85 (11): 301–303.

Moon Jae-in. 2020. 'People Have Now Begun to Talk about the Republic of Korea's Greatness.' *Vital Speeches of the Day* 86 (7): 175–178.

Pechlivanis, Paschalis. 2019. *America and Romania in the Cold War: A Differentiated Détente, 1969–80*. Routledge.

Poniewozik, James. 2019. *Audience of One: Donald Trump, Television, and the Fracturing of America*. Liveright.

Sadat, Anwar el-. 1978. *In Search of Identity*. Harper and Row.

Shorrock, Tim. 2018. 'Historic Korean Summit Sets the Table for Peace – and US Pundits React with Horror.' *The Nation*, 28. May, https://www.thenation.com/article/archive/historic-korean-summit-sets-the-table-for-peace-and-us-pundits-react-with-horror/ (accessed June 22, 2022).

Singh, Michael. 2022. 'Axis of Abraham: Arab-Israeli Normalization Could Remake the Middle East.' *Foreign Affairs* 101 (2): 40–50.

Suri, Jeremi. 2015. 'Henry Kissinger, The Study of History, and the Modern Statesman.' In *The Power of the Past: History and Statecraft*, edited by Hal Brands and Jeremi Suri. Brookings Institution Press.

Wagner-Pacifici, Robin. 2017. *What is an Event?* University of Chicago Press.

Woodward, Bob. 2020. *Rage*. Simon and Schuster.

PART VI

Thinking with Examples

15

Salient Examples in Flawed Reasoning about International Politics

Jack Snyder

Exemplarity, reasoning in a generalizing way from a particularly striking example, is a widespread strategy of empirical and normative inference. People do often reason this way, but should they? Cognitive psychologists might say that exemplarity is a common cognitive bias, or put more charitably, 'a shortcut to rationality' when people are 'thinking fast' (Kahneman 2011).

My field of International Relations has devoted considerable attention to the way political leaders, foreign policy professionals, and the general public draw lessons from salient past events, including their reification as narrative-shaping metaphors. The general conclusion, whether drawn by historians such as Ernest May or political psychologists such as Robert Jervis, is that this common practice is a source of costly mistakes that could be avoided by simple application of a commonsense version of the scientific method (Jervis 1973; May 1973; May and Neustadt 1986). These criticisms of common mistakes in using examples have mainly focused on inferences about factual patterns and causality. I argue that exemplarity as a normative practice in politics and political analysis is likewise problematic.

The editors of our volume have been appropriately careful to avoid endorsing exemplarity as a research strategy or a normative strategy. They document and theorize exemplarity as a social phenomenon but do not necessarily champion it. I want to reinforce that ambivalence and wariness. In this chapter I am particularly addressing what the editors present as the final stage of their stylized process of exemplarity in which salient examples are cited and emulated.

Exemplarity as an empirical strategy

Everyone who bases arguments on evidence reasons from examples, including people who add up their examples into statistical findings. The distinctive contribution of the concept of 'exemplarity,' as I understand it, is that the force of an example comes from its compelling particularity which becomes emblematic of the way things are, the way things should be, or the way a person should be. Through this process a particular example is made general.

In the field of international politics, examples that have been studied in this way are the Munich Crisis of 1938, the Japanese attack on Pearl Harbor, and the Korean and Vietnam Wars. The reification of the first two examples, it is claimed, underpinned hawkish arguments that emphasized the need to show steely resolve to prevent even the smallest Cold War setback and to anticipate the ever-present risk of surprise attack. This mentality justified the militarization of the Cold War and the embroilment of the US in unnecessary foreign wars and tense war-risking crises. The Korean and Vietnamese examples fed a more diverse set of strategic commonplaces, ranging from 'no land wars in Asia' to the 'falling domino theory' and the 'quagmire myth' (in addition to Jervis and May, see Ellsberg 1972, 42–135; Khong 1992).

According to this literature, the use of these examples went astray as a result of oversimplification, indiscriminate application, selection bias, dogmatism, and inductive fallacies. Some of these faults seem baked into the very features that make for compelling examples.

May (1973) stresses the one-dimensional, oversimplified 'lessons' that were drawn from the Munich analogy: totalitarian foes are unappeasable aggressors whose appetites are whetted by concessions and who must be met by unflinching resolve to stand firm. As embodied in the global containment principles of the Truman Administration's NSC-68 defense doctrine, these lessons were indiscriminately applied everywhere. They are still very much with us. As Putin's armies encircled Ukraine on February 13, 2022, Ben Wallace, the UK Defense Minister, told the Sunday London *Times* that 'there is a whiff of Munich in the air from some in the West.'

Jervis combined cognitive psychology and documentary historical research in explaining the selectivity of the examples that dominated thinking and policy. He argued that salient examples emerged because of their easy availability, vividness, and the formative career experiences of their protagonists. Preparing to fight the last war or reliving the last crisis is the norm. These tropes congeal into belief systems, where they are dogmatized by biased evaluations of evidence: information that is consistent with prior beliefs gets internalized as supporting them, even if it is also consistent with contrary interpretations.

Examples are easily reified into commonplaces with general import: Munich and the fall of the French garrison at Dien Bien Phu become the domino theory in which any defeat will snowball into further losses unless met with the utmost resolve to resist. The plot and the 'lesson' become ever more simplified even as its narrative properties, especially its posing a test of character, gain in salience. Given the inherent politicization of this discourse, these uses of examples might be better characterized as the formation of ideology than the result of cognitive bias (Snyder 1991, ch 1 and 7; Krebs 2015).

A more recent case of generalization from a misunderstood example is the role that the humanitarian military intervention in Kosovo played in the promotion of the UN doctrine of the 'Responsibility to Protect.' Updating the norms of international humanitarian intervention to prevent atrocities, R2P recognized the responsibility of the international community to take active measures, including the possibility of military intervention, when the state couldn't or wouldn't provide that protection.

R2P has failed four major tests since its passage in 2005 (Menon 2016). The most consequential was the international intervention in Libya in 2011, which toppled Muammar Ghaddafi's regime and set the stage for an ongoing anarchic civil war, endemic human rights abuse, and the spread of Islamic terrorism to the south. Michael McFaul, the US Ambassador to Moscow, argues that Vladimir Putin blamed his puppet President Dmitry Medvedev for failing to veto the UN Security Council vote authorizing the intervention and for the West's broken promise not to use the humanitarian operation as a cover for regime change. He dates Putin's shift to a strategy writing off cooperation with the West to this episode (McFaul 2018, 217–227). Another test was the UN-authorized military intervention in Côte d'Ivoire's civil war following a stolen election in 2010, which ended in the military defeat of the usurper, but was marred by thousands of casualties, major population displacements, and atrocities perpetrated by the local allies of the international humanitarian force (Mehler 2012). In late 2020, the elected President forcefully installed by the 2011 international intervention announced his candidacy for an unconstitutional third term, coinciding with violent repression of dissent, according to an 'atrocity alert' issued by the Global Centre for the Responsibility to Protect (Global Centre for the Responsibility to Protect 2020). A third test was the failure of European trial balloons lofted for humanitarian military intervention in the Syrian civil war, which were deterred by anticipated vetoes from Russia and possibly China. In the fourth test, the genocide case before the International Court of Justice against the Myanmar military junta's bloody expulsion of the Muslim Rohingya minority provided the occasion for the cringe-inducing testimony of the country's civilian leader, Nobel Peace Prize Winner Aung San Suu Kyi, fending off international accountability.[1]

This dubious track record might have been anticipated if R2P's proponents had had a clearer understanding of the purportedly successful NATO intervention against Serbia in Kosovo in 1999, which was lionized as a model operation reversing the ethnic cleansing of hundreds of thousands of Kosovar Albanians at the cost of zero NATO casualties. What actually happened was that NATO imposed a ceasefire on Serbian counterinsurgency efforts against the Kosovo Liberation Army (KLA) in 1998, freeing the KLA to rearm and ramp up a renewed phase of their military campaign. When Serbia reacted brutally against the KLA and some Albanian civilians, the NATO powers issued an unacceptable ultimatum to the Serbian negotiators at Rambouillet, including the demand that NATO could deploy its forces anywhere in Serbia at any time. The breakdown of talks was followed by NATO air attacks on Belgrade and by Serb President Slobodan Milosevich's desperate decision to violently expel nearly the entire Albanian population from Kosovo. Although some defenders of the NATO strategy claim Milosevic had intended this move this all along, evidence suggests that his preferred strategy was to reestablish Serb control in Kosovo through more limited repressive measures (Posen 2000; Crawford 2001–2002; Lake 2009). With the Kosovo operation as its exemplary model, it is not surprising that R2P has failed to protect human rights.

Why examples are poor guides to understanding and action

Reasoning from an example provides no criterion for evaluating the relevance or probative value of the supposedly exemplary reference point. Exemplarity is an extreme form of reasoning by analogy, where the analogous case is chosen not through a careful assessment of structural similarities between the current situation and its historical reference point but by some pre-established, compelling features of a prevailing example that gets applied indiscriminately. Whatever the question, the answer is to be found in the exemplary intentions of the Founding Fathers, the parables of the New Testament, or Lenin's collected works.

An example is likewise an extreme form of 'selection on the dependent variable.' Used to demonstrate the causes of wars, for instance, it omits not just the wars that might have happened and did not but, but all wars

---

[1] Transcript: Aung San Suu Kyi's speech at the ICJ in full, *Online Burma/Myanmar Library*, December 12, 2019, https://www.burmalibrary.org/en/transcript-aung-san-suu-kyis-speech-at-the-icj-in-full (accessed June 9, 2025).

except one. This is the polar opposite of Karl Popper's notion that testing an argument should proceed not by looking for confirming evidence but by disconfirming outlier examples. The watchword of social science is to study variation, cases that are particularly challenging for the hypothesis under review, cases that are both most similar and most different, not examples (Brady and Collier 2010; Mahoney 2015; Schimmelfennig 2015).

Another questionable feature of reasoning through exemplarity is its overreliance on theory development through induction. In the 1960s, the behavioral revolution in social science brought a wave of highly inductive statistical studies of the causes of war, a brush-clearing exercise designed to check on the empirical correlation of every variable with every other imaginable variable, ranging from alliance relationships to pig iron production. The hope that empirics would lead directly to theoretical understanding didn't pan out, but once the field turned back to more theory-driven research programs, tapping into classical political theories of Kant and Hobbes as well as contemporary theories of rational strategic action, those statistical databases turned out to be useful for testing hypotheses derived logically from more abstract theory. Inductive methods of understanding, whether using statistics or salient examples, work best when filtered through more abstract theory's explicit assumptions and deductions (Waltz 1979, 1–18; de Mesquita et al 1999; Russett and Oneal 2001, ch 1–4). Even exemplary facts don't speak for themselves.

Potentially positive uses of examples

Notwithstanding these qualms about reasoning through examples, it is true that proponents of analytic case studies and small-N comparative methods argue persuasively for the special importance of fully contextualized narrative approaches, especially in the early phases of theory development. They argue that statistical testing is better suited to later stages of research when the theoretical logic and its application to empirical circumstances are better understood. Beginning the sequence with case studies provides a more flexible, wider angle of vision to spot possible causal mechanisms, to more easily identify interactions of strategies and contexts, to understand unexpected results better, and to identify scope conditions of a theory.

Exemplarity, prizing flesh-and-blood details, would seem to be well placed to support this kind of probative process-tracing. It might seem suited for picking out 'poster child' case studies, which are chosen for their clarity in illustrating concretely the basic logical structure and causal mechanisms of a theory. Indeed, International Relations scholars never tire of using World War I to illustrate 'the security dilemma' as a cause of war (Van Evera 1999, ch 7). Philosophers of science know that one of the most important and subtle conceptual moves is deciding how to map the abstract logical structure of a theoretical deduction onto its instantiation as an empirical generalization testable by observations. This requires matching abstract assumptions – in this case about the payoffs expected by the players and about the relative advantages of offensive and defensive military strategies for achieving them – to the known facts of the exemplary case. A good poster case presents an easily understood mechanism that matches the abstract logic to the empirics of the case. However, the exemplarity approach seems more concerned with how the empirical details of the example embody, symbolize, and inspire reality than how they help analyze its mechanisms.

Analytical case studies are not only concerned with ideal-types or representative examples. They are just as concerned with analyzing outliers, hard cases, 'least likely' comparisons, conditional relationships, and limiting scope conditions. Such case studies need to anticipate objections by explaining why reality often deviates from the expected pattern of the poster case. Indeed, most of the hard work of social science research comes in what Imre Lakatos calls the 'protective belt of auxiliary hypotheses' that explain outcomes that don't fit the pattern of easy cases that conform to deductions from hard-core assumptions (Lakatos 1970). The exemplarity approach will be more useful if it devotes more effort to explaining deviation from the exemplary norm.

Overall, exemplarity might be onto something as a description of how people with limited cognitive capacity or a narrative to promote try to depict their world. But as a practice for accurately understanding the world, exemplarity seems to be doing almost everything wrong by accepted standards of scientific inference. As a practice that describes how people take on normative commitments, and as a strategy for promoting normative change, does exemplarity have more to offer?

Exemplarity as a normative strategy

It seems plausible that a vivid, compelling example might play a significant part in promoting normative change, for good or ill. One mechanism for this at the individual level is the role model. A Gandhi or a Martin Luther King can influence others not only through rhetorical persuasion but also by personally embodying normative characteristics for mass emulation. Even fictional exemplars can be role models. Lynn Hunt argues that the oppressed but plucky heroines of 18th-century novels stimulated readers' empathy and admiration in a way that catalyzed the growth of human rights consciousness (Hunt 2007). Likewise, Harriet Beecher Stowe had far more impact promoting the antislavery movement by depicting Eliza's struggles in *Uncle Tom's Cabin* than her prominent father Henry Ward Beecher ever did with his learned sermons.

Another mechanism, which operates at the social level, I will call social proof. This encompasses the ideas of consensus and effectiveness. Some conceptions of exemplarity include the idea that 'everybody does it.' If everybody wears a face mask during a pandemic, that behavior is normative, in the sense of normal. If in addition people believe the community has a low rate of disease transmission because everyone wears a mask, 'is' becomes 'ought.' Wearing a mask becomes the behavior of an exemplary citizen.

Normative exemplars can be used to point out both positive or negative behaviors. Gandhi and King are positive role models; Joseph Kony, the ringleader of the murderous Lord's Resistance Army, was for a time the target of a massive campaign of social media shaming as the ICC-indicted quintessential perpetrator of atrocities. For a time, Myanmar's Aung San Suu Kyi was the Nobel-Peace-Prize-winning exemplar of national resistance to its oppressive military kleptocracy, but after failing to condemn the Burmese junta's genocide of the Rohingya, she became inverted as the exemplar of opportunistic tyranny of the majority. Exemplarity seems to describe pretty well the simplistic normative categorization of her as first heroine and then turncoat, but this tendency doesn't seem to have been very helpful in understanding the political realities in either phase or in devising strategies for dealing with the situation.

Some persuasion efforts seem to favor negative exemplarity; others positive. Recently, Aryeh Neier, the founder of Human Rights Watch, acknowledged that the practice of 'naming and shaming' to make an example of rights violators has been losing some of its force in an era when right-wing, nationalist populists are utterly shameless (Neier 2018). Backlash against progressive shaming efforts on issues such as gay rights and mask wearing has contributed to reactionary political successes in Brazil, Poland, and Iowa (Knut 2020). Nonetheless, Neier concludes that shaming is an indispensable tool for rights promotion. Political scientists' empirical attempts to study the effectiveness of shaming have so far been inconclusive (Hafner-Burton 2008; Murdie and Davis 2012). The bulk of social psychological findings on this form of negative exemplarity, however, suggest that shame and shaming commonly produce some combination of denial, evasion, resentment, anger, and retreat into 'cultures of deviance' (Snyder 2020). Negative exemplarity can be a counterproductive rhetorical style.

Even positive exemplarity can go awry. In inspiring reviews of the first great success of the historical struggle for human rights, Neier and sympathetic scholars of the human rights movement revisit the antislavery movement. Neier portrays the British and American abolitionists as heroes whose relentless energy against the injustice of slavery should serve as the model for today's struggles for human rights (Neier 2012, 33–37). Human rights scholars agree: the abolitionists prefigured contemporary rights activists in their uncompromisingly principled stance, their mobilization of civil society through moral rhetoric, and their tireless use of publicity to shame perpetrators and those who abetted them (Keck and Sikkink 1998, 41–51). In fact, the uncompromising abolitionists were riven by internal divisions, tended to discredit the antislavery movement in the eyes of northern voters, and sometimes contributed to the election of pro-slavery candidates by dividing the antislavery vote. Antislavery's successes were the result of pragmatic coalition-making among groups that had a mix of principled and selfish interests in reining in slavery's excesses, including the success of Lincoln's Republicans with Northern working classes as well as the alliance between British Whigs and religious Non-Conformists (Kaufmann and Pape 1999, 654–657; Snyder 2017). In this case, the attempt of contemporary human rights advocates to project current practices back onto past successes employs the characteristic tropes of heroic exemplarity in a way that uses misleading historical description to support a preferred contemporary prescription.

In this normative and more broadly prescriptive context, it may be useful to be more explicit about the general philosophical viewpoint that I bring to the topic of exemplarity, as the editors and other contributors have in most cases done. As is typical of many or even most empirical scholars of international politics in political science, I have analyzed the consequences of reasoning by example from the standpoint of philosophical pragmatism, consequentialist prudence, and the notion from Weberian responsibility ethics that 'ought implies can' in a specific context (Snyder 2022, 28–31). While these are not the only philosophical reference points that are useful for thinking through the mechanisms and implications of exemplarity, I think the empirical consequences of ideas, rhetorics, and prescriptive examples should be taken into account by any approach to the topic.

Exemplarity as a strategy to persuade and mobilize for normative change loads the dice in favor of the application of invariant principle and against an ethics of circumstantial consequentialism. Reasoning from a single example, especially one that embodies an uncomplicated inspirational or cautionary lesson, leads to overgeneralization, which is the natural terrain of deontology. This is poor terrain for understanding or acting in politics. It happens, but it is most often part of the problem rather than part of the solution.

References

Brady, Henry E., and David Collier. 2010. *Rethinking Social Inquiry: Diverse Tools, Shared Standards*. 2nd ed. Rowman & Littlefield.

Crawford, Timothy W. 2001–2002. 'Pivotal Deterrence and the Kosovo War: Why the Holbrooke Agreement Failed.' *Political Science Quarterly* 116 (4): 499–523.

de Mesquita, Bruce Bueno, James D. Morrow, Randolph M. Siverson, and Alastair Smith. 1999. 'An Institutional Explanation for the Democratic Peace.' *American Political Science Review* 93 (4): 791–807.

Ellsberg, Daniel. 1972. *Papers on the War*. Simon and Schuster.

Global Centre for the Responsibility to Protect. 2020. 'Atrocity Alert No. 227: Côte d'Ivoire, Myanmar (Burma) and Democratic Republic of the Congo,' November 4, 2020.

Hafner-Burton, Emilie. 2008. 'Sticks and Stones: Naming and Shaming the Human Rights Enforcement Problem.' *International Organization* 62 (4): 689–716.

Hunt, Lynn. 2007. *The Origins of Human Rights*. Norton.

Jervis, Robert. 1973. *Perception and Misperception in International Politics*. Princeton University Press.

Jervis, Robert. 2017. *How Statesmen Think: The Psychology of International Politics*. Princeton University Press.

Kahneman, Daniel. 2011. *Thinking, Fast and Slow*. Farrar, Straus and Giroux.

Kaufmann, Chaim, and Robert Pape. 1999. 'Explaining Costly International Moral Action: Britain's Sixty-year Campaign against the Atlantic Slave Trade.' *International Organization* 53 (4): 631–668.

Keck, Margaret, and Kathryn Sikkink. 1998. *Activists Beyond Borders: Advocacy Networks in International Politics*. Cornell University Press.

Khong, Yuen Foong. 1992. *Analogies at War: Korea, Munich, Dien Bien Phu, and the Vietnam Decisions of 1965*. Princeton University Press.

Knut, Pawel. 2020. 'Poland Exit Polls Mean Victory for Homophobic Andrzej Duda.' *Think*, July 13, 2020. https://www.nbcnews.com/think/opinion/poland-exit-polls-mean-victory-homophobic-andrzej-duda-misery-lgbtq-ncna1233643 (accessed June 9, 2025).

Krebs, Ronald R. 2015. *Narrative and the Making of US National Security*. Cambridge University Press.

Lakatos, Imre. 1970. 'Falsification and the Methodology of Scientific Research Programmes.' In *Criticism and the Growth of Knowledge*, edited by Imre Lakatos and Alan Musgrave. Cambridge University Press.

Lake, Daniel R. 2009. 'The Limits of Coercive Airpower: NATO's "Victory" in Kosovo Revisited.' *International Security* 34 (1): 83–112.

Mahoney, James. 2015. 'Process Tracing and Historical Explanation.' *Security Studies* 24 (2): 200–250.

May, Ernest R. 1973. *'Lessons' of the Past: The Use and Misuse of History in American Foreign Policy*. Oxford University Press.

May, Ernest R., and Richard E. Neustadt. 1986. *Thinking in Time: The Uses of History for Decision-Makers*. Free Press.

McFaul, Michael. 2018. *From Cold War to Hot Peace: An American Ambassador in Putin's Russia*. Houghton Mifflin Harcourt.

Mehler, Andreas. 2012. 'From "Protecting Civilians" to "For the Sake of Democracy" (and Back Again): Justifying Intervention in Côte D'Ivoire.' *African Security* 5 (3/4): 199–216.

Menon, Rajan. 2016. *The Conceit of Humanitarian Intervention*. Oxford University Press.

Murdie, Amanda M., and David R. Davis. 2012. 'Shaming and Blaming: Using Events Data to Assess the Impact of Human Rights INGOs.' *International Studies Quarterly* 56 (1): 1–16.

Neier, Aryeh. 2012. *The International Human Rights Movement: A History*. Princeton University Press.

Neier, Aryeh. 2018. '"Naming and Shaming": Still the Human Rights Movement's Best Weapon.' *OpenGlobalRights*, July 11, 2018. https://www.openglobalrights.org/Naming-and-shaming-still-the-human-rights-movements-best-weapon/?lang=English (accessed June 9, 2025).

Posen, Barry. 2000. 'The War for Kosovo: Serbia's Political-Military Strategy.' *International Security* 24 (4): 39–84.

Russett, Bruce, and John Oneal. 2001. *Triangulating Peace: Democracy, Interdependence, and International Organizations*. Norton.

Schimmelfennig, Frank. 2015. 'Efficient Process Tracing: Analyzing the Causal Processes of European Integration.' In *Process Tracing: From Metaphor to Analytic Tool*, edited by Andrew Bennett and Jeffrey Checkel. Cambridge University Press.

Snyder, Jack. 1991. *Myths of Empire: Domestic Politics and International Ambition*. Cornell University Press.

Snyder, Jack. 2017. 'Empowering Rights Through Mass Movements, Religion, and Reform Parties.' In *Human Rights Futures*, edited by Stephen Hopgood, Jack Snyder, and Leslie Vinjamuri. Cambridge University Press.

Snyder, Jack. 2020. 'Backlash against Human Rights Shaming: Emotions in Groups.' *International Theory* 12 (1): 109–132.

Snyder, Jack. 2022. *Human Rights for Pragmatists: Social Power in Modern Times*. Princeton University Press.

Van Evera, Stephen. 1999. *Causes of War: Power and the Roots of Conflict*. Cornell University Press.

Waltz, Kenneth. 1979. *Theory of International Politics*. McGraw-Hill.

16

The Disciplinary Exemplarity of the Concert of Europe

Jennifer Mitzen

Scholars and decision-makers often relate contemporary political decisions to events from the past, treating past events as a locus of knowledge not just about yesterday but also for understanding and confronting present-day political challenges.[1] But it is not always clear exactly how the past informs the present, and different disciplines have different conventions for disciplining knowledge gleaned from historical examples. Speaking truth to power is a key dimension of International Relations' (IR) self-identity as an academic discipline. Many IR scholars seek to 'reach beyond the ivory tower' and 'bridge the gap' between academic and policy, writing in crossover journals such as *Foreign Affairs* and *Foreign Policy* that aim to influence policy practice in some way, often drawing on historical events to ground or deepen their claims (Byman and Kroenig 2016; see also Maliniak et al 2020, 10). This chapter brings an exemplarity lens to the continuing importance of one such political event, the 1815 Congress of Vienna ending the Napoleonic Wars, for debates about international order in the IR discipline and in the discipline-adjacent policy space.

In IR, 1815 is a benchmark date (Buzan and Lawson 2014). The Congress of Vienna inaugurated the Concert of Europe, a 'Long Peace' among great powers rivaled only by the Cold War for its longevity. The Concert stands

---

[1] With many thanks to Dorry Noyes and Tobias Wille for the invitation to be part of this project and for their feedback throughout. Thanks as well to participants in the conference on which this volume is based for the discussions. The chapter benefited from presentations at the International Studies Association (ISA) Annual Conference in April 2021 and March 2022, and at the *Millennium* conference in October 2021. Thanks to Anna Agathangelou and Alex Wendt for comments on previous drafts.

out today because unlike the Cold War, in which war between ideological and geopolitical rivals arguably was held at bay by the prospect of nuclear war, the Concert exemplifies the possibility of avoiding war through purposive, diplomatic action. In 19th-century Europe, a group of former rivals – who had different forms of government and who had just fought an immensely destructive war – worked together through informal yet coordinated, purposive diplomacy, to prevent further great power war. With the decline of the US-led liberal international order and rise of multipolarity, the Concert of Europe case has been picked up on by gap-bridging scholars as a normative lodestar, a model to emulate as a 'new Concert of Powers' for the 21st century (Haass and Kupchan 2021).

IR scholars have focused more on the Concert than the Congress, but all share the premise that the Congress was the triggering event of a Long Peace. As such, interpretations of the Congress are pivotal. Indeed, in the 1990s when Concert scholarship took off in IR, it developed in conversation with diplomatic historians (for example, Schroeder et al 1992; Elman and Elman 1997). But Concert interpretations are now shifting, at least among historians. The 2015 bicentennial of the Congress of Vienna brought a wave of historical scholarship, with many historians challenging prior understandings of the event and the era in ways that call into question key premises and assumptions those IR arguments relied on: levels of analysis thinking; the timelessness of international anarchy; familiar distinctions between public and private, politics and economics; and so on. Some of the knowledge was not particularly surprising: of course, these great powers were mostly empires and not states as we know them today! Of course the Congress required financing! Of course leaders would have known of the revolution in Haiti! Of course women did more than host events and have sex! But it nonetheless raises a question: if the Long Peace rested on mechanisms whose bases are refuted, what is left of the lessons of the Concert for today?

As IR grapples with what it means to be an historical social science (Buzan and Lawson 2015; Buzan, Lawson, and Mitzen 2016), the concept of exemplarity Noyes and Wille develop in this volume suggests a distinct perspective on the relevance of past events for contemporary politics that is not assimilable to either IR social science or history. Like historical events, exemplars stand out for their uniqueness. Exemplarity brings attention to the exceptional more than the representativeness of an event and to the purposive action that produced it. But like social scientific mechanisms, exemplars suggest that 'seeds' of the past circulate politically today, whether contributing to the production of order or spurring change. Exemplarity, however, unlike either social science or history, focuses analytic attention expressly on normativity, homing in on how past events serve as normative guides today. Unique to an exemplarity approach is its focus on what Noyes and Wille call uptake, the capturing of an audience's attention. Uptake is what propels an example forward in time (and potentially to new places). Uptake of an exemplar is never guaranteed; and exemplary action without uptake lacks social effect. Such uptake is tricky to predict: it is an aesthetic and affective process that takes different forms.

In this chapter, I propose that the Concert exemplar has had aesthetic and binding effects on the academic discipline of IR and the discipline-adjacent policy space that make it difficult for IR and debates about international order to absorb the insights from the new Congress histories. That is, the IR discipline has become attached, not to *THE* Concert of Europe, but to one specific Concert of Europe that can serve as a model for pluralistic, consultative great power management today. An exemplarity lens reveals a downside even to normatively desirable examples from the past, in that IR uptake of the Concert exemplar may well be constraining the political imagination, rendering some knowledge unavailable that might bear on the goal of international order.

IR's Concert of Europe and History's Congress of Vienna

In this section I summarize how IR scholars have interpreted the Congress and Concert, which is through the lens of social science theory.[2] Those interpretations were supported empirically by the work of diplomatic historians, but new historical scholarship unseats some of the conventional wisdom that was produced.

The Congress of Vienna was a risky and innovative event, 'the most spectacular peace conference in history' (King 2008, 14). Over 200 European principalities and states were represented, as well as many non-state interest groups (Nicolson 1946, 132–133; Sluga 2017, 1407). Brian Vick points out that it was an unprecedented mixing, symbolically and physically, across class and status (Vick 2014, 12–13). Attendees danced, paraded, and played, but they also talked, in formal diplomatic venues, less formal committee meetings, and at salons and dinner tables, as the self-proclaimed great powers reordered Europe through the Vienna Settlement. This unprecedented and celebratory event was marked with uncertainty: negotiated before Napoleon's final defeat at Waterloo among rival states that had been fighting each other, it was not at all clear that the settlement would hold. It is doubtful that anyone present at Vienna would have guessed that the continent would go without great power war for nearly four decades, much less that scholars 200 years later would be treating their relations as exemplary of a long peace.

---

[2] This section draws on the argument in Mitzen and Rogg (2023).

For IR scholars, the details of the event have mattered little. What matters is the terms of the settlement and the unprecedented great power management it enabled. Indeed, scholars frequently invoke the Concert of Europe as a model for contemporary great power politics. Richard Haas and Charles Kupchan (2021) call for a return to the Concert model: the West is losing ground, illiberalism is on the rise, the system is ripe for great power war. Therefore, the world needs another Concert of Europe. They are not alone in seeing the contemporary vibrancy of the Concert example (for example, Rynning 2015; Lascurettes 2017; Haass 2019; Jung 2023; Rynning 2015; see Popescu et al 2021; Müller and Rauch 2017). The recent flurry of attention echoes similar calls in the 1990s to turn to the Concert as an example for a changing world order (for example, Kupchan and Kupchan 1991, 1995; Zelikow 1992). Then, Robert Jervis argued for the importance of studying the Concert 'both for its intrinsic significance and for its possible relevance in the post-Cold War era' (Schroeder et al 1992, 716). For these scholars, when the prospect of changing great power relations looms large, the Concert model exemplifies a way to stabilize a system in which not all leading states are liberal states, and to do so without the straitjacket of a rules-based organization but rather through a loose system of consultation.

The recent recommendations are rooted in IR debates since the 1990s, which take place in a positivist, social scientific register. The Concert is a common case study of international cooperation in the security domain. Realists, liberals, and constructivists each have advanced explanations for the 19th-century-long peace: brilliant territorial settlement (realist); shared norms and rules (liberal); rational self-interested cooperation (neoliberal institutionalist); transformation of political authority (constructivist). These are very different mechanisms, and there are stakes in privileging one versus another. But what unites scholars in this debate is a commitment to the scientific promise of uncovering the logic and mechanism. The debate is rooted in a model of social causation common among qualitative IR researchers. Knowledge statements about causality in world politics can be constructed and verified. Social events such as war are produced by social mechanisms (Bennett and Elman 2006; Guzzini 2013). Qualitative case study analysis aims to 'discover and validate' causal mechanisms, showing 'how causes interact in the context of a particular case ... to produce an outcome' (Bennett and Elman 2006, 458). Causation is established by 'uncovering traces of a hypothesized causal mechanism within the context of a historical case or cases' (Bennett and Elman 2006, 459). The scholar looks for 'how the accessible evidence matches up with the proposed alternative explanations' (Bennett and Elman 2006, 459).

The role of the historical Concert is as backdrop or site for verifying mechanisms that support or discredit theoretical hypotheses (Lawson 2012, 207; Mackay and LaRoche 2020, 5). To access the historical

Concert, IR scholars have relied on diplomatic historians. The work of contemporary historians, especially the pathbreaking scholarship of Paul Schroeder, fed directly into IR's interpretations. Schroeder's magisterial *Transformation of European Politics* (1994) provided material that supported all of these explanations. All of the IR interpretations rest on an explicit disciplinary consensus. States are the relevant actors; anarchy is the context of their interaction; inter-state war is the fundamental problem; and the European experience is the basis of and generalizable to contemporary global governance. The historical scholarship IR scholars relied on, most of it secondary sources, much of it in English, supported, or at least did not disrupt, that consensus. As such, the many processes and actors that converged at Vienna, not to mention the messy eventfulness of the event, have been 'known' in IR through the prism of seemingly natural objects (Bukovansky and Keene, 2023).

The bicentennial wave of historical scholarship is markedly different. It undermines IR's disciplinary consensus at a deep level. For example, Glenda Sluga (2021) and Beatrice De Graaf (2019, 2020) uncover the presence and power of transnational capital and role of sovereign debt in cementing France's post-war position. Their work demonstrates that the Congress and subsequent peace were politically and financially a networked production of domestic and international, political and economic actors and relations. In other work Sluga (2017, 2021) draws on unconventional sources to elucidate a political agency of women in that time which is not reducible to gender roles, and a new understanding of what counts as diplomacy. She goes further, diagnosing the 'gender work' of sidelining and sexualizing women's political agency as the field of diplomacy consolidated in the 19th century (Sluga 2014). Brian Vick (2014) similarly alters the lens for interpreting the event. He unpacks a wide 'political universe' of multiple locales, diverse actors, and a range of symbols and ceremonies, well beyond the great power leaders sitting at their diplomatic tables. Vick argues that this milieu was 'the very matrix and stimuli' from which ideas central to Concert accomplishments took off.

Moving from the event to the milieu, George Lawson (2019) develops the transnational force of revolution as a threat not so much to individual states as the authority of the state itself. He argues that revolution should be treated as a force of its own rather than a 'second image threat.' Characterizing revolution as 'inter-social' and constituted by 'transboundary entanglements,' Lawson proposes that revolution is aimed not so much at individual states or regimes as it is aimed at 'the international' itself as an overarching structure of oppression (Lawson 2019, 8–9). Finally, Adom Getachew's scholarship (2016) underscores the centrality of colonies and colonial violence for the production of great powerhood. The implication is that avoiding conflict between the great powers of Europe was not an unproblematic accomplishment normatively, in that Europe's peace rested, perhaps relied, on a great deal of violence continuing to be produced elsewhere. All of this scholarship disrupts the very premises of IR's debates – explicit premises such as anarchy, states, and levels of analysis; implicit premises such as the meaning of diplomacy and the separation of politics and economics, public and private.

Some of these insights were uncovered with new archival work; others have been there the whole time. But none of this knowledge has been incorporated into current IR debates about international order. Indeed, Haass and Kupchan acknowledge that a limitation of their Concert model is that it does not incorporate non-state actors, capital and otherwise, all of which now, as opposed to the 19th century, 'have considerable power and need to have seats at the table' (2021, 102). But it is an odd self-criticism in light of the histories summarized earlier, which illuminate the many ways in which non-state actors *were* crucial to the Concert's production of the Long Peace (for example, Vick 2014).

In sum, scholars invoke the Concert example to guide politics today even as Concert historians have unmasked the premises on which it is based. A conversation that in the 1990s was interdisciplinary seems to have fractured. As a result, it is unclear what the fact that the Congress exceeds and unseats IR's interpretation means for its relevance as a model today.

Exemplarity and uptake

Before addressing the question, let me first summarize my understanding of exemplarity as Noyes and Wille have developed it, pulling out especially the aspects that may shed light on the divergence between the new histories and the Concert's relevance.

Exemplarity is a different lens through which to analyze events than social science or history; and it prompts a different kind of knowledge. For social scientists, events can be cases or examples through which to illustrate causal relations and patterns. Social scientists often use the language of mechanisms, positing links between socially correlated phenomena that are objectively verifiable and true across space and time (Guzzini 2013, 535). A mechanism's presence is determined through standardized rules of evidence. Science offers the promise of generalizability, control, and universality. Historians tend to abjure the language of social causation when elucidating events, focusing instead on the particularities that make events unique, including contextualizing them in their social milieu and/or embedding events in larger constellations of social forces.

Noyes and Wille use the social scientific language of mechanism, describing exemplarity as a mechanism of cultural transmission. But the energy of this mechanism is rooted in the historian's valorization of particularity and uniqueness. As they put it, '[t]he affective power of the example … comes from its uniqueness: its life as a salient moment in time (Noyes and Wille, Chapter 1, this volume).' So exemplarity is part social science, and part history. What makes it distinct from each is that exemplarity alone is expressly, overtly normative: 'the example claims to unite what is and what should be' (Noyes and Wille, Chapter 2, this volume). Exemplars[3] are neither samples nor cases – words that suggest empirically verifiable knowledge for practical ends. They are desirable models to be emulated.

Exemplarity highlights agency, that is, 'the ability of specific actors to affect the course of events' (Noyes and Wille, Chapter 1, this volume). A particularly important agency rests with the audience, because without their uptake, the example is not propelled forward but stopped in its tracks. An audience must accept the exemplar and cite, judge, and/or emulate it to propel it forward in society. That acceptance is anything but mechanistic. Noyes and Wille describe the transmission of examples as 'more irregular, less determined, and more episodic' than the transmission of other cultural forms, and posit that exemplarity operates as 'an irregular, point-to-point network, in which relationship and resemblance are claimed across distance and difference' (Noyes and Wille, Chapter 2, this volume).

What makes uptake an unruly moment is that it is not rooted in truth or verification, so there is no assurance that different audiences will receive the exemplar in the same way. Uptake is an aesthetic and affective process, not [or not primarily] an intellectual one. Noyes and Wille unpack uptake in terms of reflective judgment, the active interpreting and relating of the example's particularity to the rules of the social order. In Daase and Wille's words (Chapter 7, this volume), 'Social actors can only "woo" or "court" the consent of others.'

The aesthetic core of the mechanism translates to ambivalent implications for the role of the exemplar in social life. On one hand, through its interpretive openness, by pointing to things worth repeating or striving for, exemplars can make new, previously unthinkable things imaginable for a community, suggesting an emancipatory potential. In Noyes and Wille's words, 'the collective judgment that turns a performance into an example implicates it in some ethos: a valorized way of life with its associated norms' (Noyes and Wille, Chapter 2, this volume). On the other hand, that way of life is not necessarily emancipatory, and exemplars can just as easily valorize and affirm a status quo. Noyes develops a 'dominant exemplarity' logic as a

---

[3] While Noyes and Wille's framework distinguishes between exemplar as doer and example as deed, I will use the word exemplar to refer to IR's uptake of the Concert, because, in contrast to the word 'example,' the word exemplar has connotations of normativity, which is central to my argument.

mechanism of Gramscian cultural hegemony (Noyes 2016, 88–91), where a given exemplar is not associated with 'an empowering or emancipatory exemplarity but one that helps make individuals fit for the world as it is' (Noyes 2016, 90). Along these lines, Zarakol (Chapter 9, this volume) develops exemplarity as a mechanism perpetuating and legitimating hierarchy in an order defined by the ideology of equality.

Concert as exemplar

The Concert circulates through the IR discipline as a case that demonstrates an enduring international political dynamic. But it also can be interpreted as an exemplar – an innovative form of collective agency (Mitzen 2013) that broke through the usual warp and woof of international politics to produce something new. I propose that its exemplarity contributes to the difficulty of absorbing new Congress scholarship into contemporary debates about the Concert and international order.

Concert uptake in the international order debate has been in the register of social science. But like all exemplary uptake, it is not in service of truth and cannot promise objectivity. It is, for its audience, aesthetic, affective, and normative. Each IR citation, each invoking of the Concert as a model for today, therefore does two things. First, it reaffirms the audience's commitment to the power of IR social science to help scholars, potentially decision-makers, make their way in a complex and dangerous world. Second, as it reaffirms science and reassures the audience, it reinscribes a particular understanding of what the Concert was. That is, it reproduces an unspoken consensus that in world politics, states are the relevant actors; anarchy is the context of their interaction; and inter-state war is the fundamental problem. These categories border the event, and a host of things, aspects of the event (processes, people, objects), are rendered invisible. Exemplars orient audiences normatively; they also border, cognitively.

Now, from a social science perspective such borders make sense. The social scientist brackets much of the day-to-day, channeling attention toward some details and away from others to get beneath the noise of everyday politics, to uncover the generalizable, transhistorical mechanisms. Once knowledge begins to cumulate, maintaining the borders of a concept might merely reflect intellectual path dependency, where problems foregrounded early on were built upon by later scholars. But there is no sense of disciplinary dependence on, or culpability in, the borders. Viewed in this way, the order debate is simply a state-centric conversation. The new interpretations of the Congress speak to a different audience: not the mainstream, policy-relevant IR but critical, feminist, non-state-centric, IR.

But the new historical accounts may well illuminate dimensions of the Congress relevant to Concert success which could bear, today, on the goal of international order. Supporting this hunch, Buzan and Lawson (2015, 48, 62–63) have suggested that for IR to function as a discipline, aspects of 19th-century international politics must be suppressed. That is, the discipline is constructed in a way that occludes how dynamics of the 19th century help produce the very war system IR so obsessively focuses on today. This suggests that the Concert's IR borders are reinscribed, and new knowledge kept out, through dynamics of cultural hegemony, which create a positive resistance to bringing certain issues to the fore.

Whatever the cause, whether path dependency or cultural hegemony, the scholar's job is to shine a light on and thematize the new problems that come into focus. But the latter stance implies that change will be exceptionally difficult because the status quo interpretations serve deeply engrained thematic or intellectual interests that will resist movement in ways we may not be consciously aware of. Hegemonic ideology is often understood in cognitive terms, as ideas that naturalize the hierarchies of the social order. But unmasking an ideology can be profoundly disorienting, especially if new knowledge calls into question one's own sense of self as good and moral. In such cases new knowledge might be cognitively resisted. Some scholars have linked societal ignorance more explicitly to the affective or emotional attachment to systems of thought that uphold one's sense of self-worth.

I propose that the Concert exemplar might contribute to making it difficult to absorb new knowledge that could thematize new problems or undermine the framing of old ones. Post-Cold War debates that invoke the Concert are so linked to the production of the long great power peace, which itself is so linked to terror and dread of the *alternative* to great power peace, nuclear annihilation, that it has shut down the ability to see any aspect of the Congress differently. Its exemplarity has produced a *motivated* closing of the mind. There is one story to tell, of great power peace that Europe modeled for the world. To question the assumptions that make the Concert a case of long peace is to question whether long peace is possible.

To that extent, exemplarity is as much a mechanism of bordering knowledge as of ordering our attention, of producing ignorance as much as knowledge. Of course, every time we describe a complicated event we are going to include some things and exclude others – we are engaging in a kind of bordering. But the notion of an 'exemplar' is more than descriptive bordering. It is a bordering laden with affect, where what's inside is particularly admired, or especially repulsive. It seems possible that by being under the spell of the example, the IR discipline produces borders that scholars are attached to without realizing it. The *ordering* of exemplarity is more or less conscious; but the *bordering* of exemplarity is maybe less so.

Conclusion

This chapter has argued that the lens of exemplarity offers a specific take on the way that scholarly and policy communities learn from the past. Sustaining the Concert as a model for international order entails suppressing aspects of its production that may, ironically, bear on the very goals policy makers seek today. Thus, scholars interested in mitigating great power rivalry today may 'bring in' new variables, whether non-state actors, transnational capital, and so on. But what they know for the first time has been there all along. The question is how it has been so successfully held out of mind. An exemplarity lens offers a framework for thinking this through that highlights the affective pull of an example that reaffirms scientific authority, disciplinary cohesion, and the promise of avoiding nuclear war.

From here, two questions emerge. First, what is the role of intentionality in the process of exemplification? The production of Shoah/Holocaust as exemplar was intentional (Alexander 2002; Subotić, Chapter 13, this volume). But exemplarity also could be more of a behind-the-back process, produced through a tyranny of small decisions as the example is amplified and as audiences reflect, and assess, and judge, where a range of different processes in different locales and on different scales combine to produce a condition of 'example.' For instance, in the Concert case, the order and borders of the example stem from processes across several domains: European diplomats using the Congress as a template for later post-war diplomacy; diplomacy becoming consolidated as a male profession, and a sphere of science and reason; IR discipline being born in the 20th century with its agenda of speaking truth to power and the drive to understand the Cold War, and so on. Each individual process then contributes to producing 'borders' of the example, but the role of each in the epistemic closure of the Concert exemplar might be difficult to discern.

Second, now that historians have pulled knowledge of the event from the margins, what will be the impact on disciplinary and policy-focused scholarship about international order? The Concert exemplar demonstrates how exemplarity can be a mechanism of the extant scholarly and perhaps policy order. In line with Perea Ozerin's (Chapter 8) and Zarakol's (Chapter 9) contributions in this volume, the Concert case illustrates how exemplarity can be a mode of transmitting power – here, the ideology of IR as a Western/North American discipline.

But it is not clear this will continue. At the very least, today's conditions of declining hegemony provide a changing context for Concert uptake. In a post-truth, populist period where fact, science, and political elites are distrusted, uptake through scientific conventions may be less authoritative and formal diplomacy less valued. The unruliness of the exemplarity mechanism tells us that undermining scientific uptake is not the same thing as undermining the exemplar itself. Other dimensions of the event may come to the fore as worthy of emulation for the goal of great power peace – informal and private communication as diplomacy, the centrality of transnational capital in the diplomatic process, outsized personalities and negotiating prowess, and so on. This IR benchmark date will certainty continue to order history as an important turning point in international relations; but what will be elevated and emulated is far from clear.

References

Alexander, Jeffrey C. 2002. 'On the Social Construction of Moral Universals: The "Holocaust" from War Crime to Trauma Drama.' *European Journal of Social Theory* 5 (1): 5–85.

Bennett, Andrew, and Colin Elman. 2006. 'Qualitative Research: Recent Developments in Case Study Methods.' *Annual Review of Political Science* 9: 455–476.

Bukovansky, Mlada, and Edward Keene. 2023. 'Modernity and Granularity in History and International Relations.' In *The Oxford Handbook of History and International Relations*, edited by Mlada Bukovansky, Edward Keene, Christian Reus-Smit, and Maja Spanu. Oxford University Press.

Buzan, Barry, and George Lawson. 2014. 'Rethinking Benchmark Dates in International Relations.' *European Journal of International Relations* 20 (2): 437–462.

Buzan, Barry, and George Lawson. 2015. *The Global Transformation: History, Modernity and the Making of International Relations*. Cambridge University Press.

Buzan, Barry, George Lawson, and Jennifer Mitzen. 2016. 'Critical Dialogue: Power in Concert and The Global Transformation.' *Perspectives on Politics* 14 (1): 184–90.

Byman, Daniel, and Matthew Kroenig. 2016. 'Reaching Beyond the Ivory Tower: A How-To Manual.' *Security Studies*, 25 (2): 289–319.

de Graff, Beatrice. 2019. 'Allied Machine: The Conference of Ministers in Paris and the Management of Security, 1815–1818.' In *Securing Europe after Napoleon: 1815 and the New Security Order*, edited by Beatrice de Graaf, Ido de Haan, and Brian Vick. Cambridge University Press.

de Graff, Beatrice. 2020. *Fighting Terror After Napoleon: How Europe Became Secure after 1815*. Cambridge University Press.

Elman, Colin, and Miriam F. Elman. 1997. 'Diplomatic History and International Relations Theory: Respecting Difference and Crossing Boundaries.' *International Security* 22 (1): 5–21.

Getachew, Adom. 2016. 'Universalism After the Post-Colonial Turn: Interpreting the Haitian Revolution.' *Political Theory* 44 (6): 821–845.

Guzzini, Stefano. 2013. 'The Ends of International Relations Theory: Stages of Reflexivity and Modes of Theorizing.' *European Journal of International Relations* 19 (3): 521–541.

Haass, Richard N. 2019. 'How a World Order Ends.' *Foreign Affairs* 98 (1): 22–30.

Haass, Richard N., and Charles A. Kupchan. 2021. 'The New Concert of Powers: How to Prevent Catastrophe and Promote Stability in a Multipolar World.' In *Anchoring the World: International Order in the Twenty-First Century*, edited by Charlsa A. Kupchan and Leslie Vinjamuri. Chatham House & the Council on Foreign Relations.

Jung, Karsten. 2023. 'A New Concert for Europe: Security and Order After the War.' *The Washington Quarterly* 46 (1): 25–43.

King, David. 2008. *Vienna 1814: How the Conquerors of Napoleon Made Love, War, and Peace at the Congress of Vienna*. Crown Publishing.

Kupchan, Charles A., and Clifford A. Kupchan. 1991. 'Concerts, Collective Security, and the Future of Europe.' *International Security* 16 (1): 114–161.

Kupchan, Charles A., and Clifford A. Kupchan. 1995. 'The Promise of Collective Security.' *International Security* 20 (1): 52–61.

Lascurettes, Kyle. 2017. 'The Concert of Europe and Great-Power Governance Today: What can the Order of 19th Century Europe Teach Policymakers About International Order in the 21st Century?' RAND Corporation.

Lawson, George. 2012. 'The Eternal Divide? History and International Relations.' *European Journal of International Relations* 18 (2): 203–226.

Lawson, George. 2019. *Anatomies of Revolution*. Cambridge University Press.

Mackay, Joseph, and Christopher D. LaRoche. 2020. 'Historical Theories of International Relations.' *Oxford Research Encyclopedia, International Studies*. https://doi.org/10.1093/acrefore/9780190846626.013.535 (accessed June 9, 2025).

Maliniak, Daniel, Susan Peterson, Ryan Powers, and Michael J. Tierney, eds. 2020. *Bridging the Theory-Practice Divide in International Relations*. Georgetown University Press.

Mitzen, Jennifer. 2013. *Power in Concert: The Nineteenth Century Origins of Global Governance*. University of Chicago Press.

Mitzen, Jennifer, and Jeff Rogg. 2023. 'The Congress of Vienna in History and IR Theory.' *Oxford Handbook on History and International Relations*, edited by Mlada Bukovansky, Edward Keene, Chris Reus-Smit, and Maja Spanu. Oxford University Press.

Müller, Harald, and Carsten Rauch, eds. 2017. *Great Power Multilateralism and the Prevention of War*. Routledge.

Nicolson, Harold. 1946. *The Congress of Vienna: A Study in Allied Unity, 1812–1822*. Harcourt Brace.

Noyes, Dorothy. 2016. 'Gesturing Toward Utopia: Toward a Theory of Exemplarity.' *NU* 53 (1): 75–95.

Popescu, Nicu, Alan S. Alexandroff, Colin I. Bradford, Richard N. Haass, and Charles A. Kupchan. 2021. 'The Case Against a New Concert of Powers: An Old Remedy Won't Help Today's Troubled Global Order.' *Foreign Affairs*, May 11, 2021.

Rynning, Sten. 2015. 'The False Promise of Continental Concert: Russia, the West and the Necessary Balance of Power.' *International Affairs* 91 (3): 539–552.

Schroeder, Paul W. 1994. *The Transformation of European Politics, 1763–1848*. Clarendon Press.

Schroeder, Paul W., Enno E. Kraehe, Wolf D. Gruner, and Robert Jervis. 1992. 'Forum: Did the Vienna System Rest on a Balance of Power?' *American History Review* 97 (3): 683–735.

Sluga, Glenda. 2014. 'On the Historical Significance of the Presence, and Absence, of Women at the Congress of Vienna, 1814–1815.' *L'Homme* 25 (2): 49–62.

Sluga, Glenda. 2017. 'Who Hold the Balance of the World? Bankers at the Congress of Vienna and the in International History.' *AHR Forum* 122 (5): 1403–1430.

Sluga, Glenda. 2021. *The Invention of International Order: Remaking Europe After Napoleon*. Princeton University Press.

Vick, Brian E. 2014. *The Congress of Vienna: Power and Politics After Napoleon*. Harvard University Press.

Zelikow, Philip. 1992. 'The New Concert of Europe.' *Survival* 34 (2): 12–30.

17

Conclusion: The Fragility and Persistence of Examples

Dorothy Noyes and Tobias Wille

Jack Snyder warns against exemplarity as a regressive habit that obscures our view of historical patterns and limits our ability to deal with daunting new situations. Jennifer Mitzen accepts the inescapability of cardinal examples and sees more dynamic potential within them, showing how they can be revisited and reinterpreted: they can become a sample of a different analytical whole, a case of a different problem, or a model for a different approach. Both would surely argue for a broader range of examples to ground the field of global politics.

This volume does not seek to promote exemplarity as a practical or normative principle for international actors. Nor are we proposing a new paradigm for international theory. Our aim is at once more modest and more complex. We want to highlight exemplarity as a thing in the world, a special kind of thing, in the same way that revolution, deterrence, or corruption are things in the world. Actors recognize these social processes intuitively and are capable of manipulating them; they can be valorized and instrumentalized by leaders, mobilized by revolutionaries and social movements, named and investigated by scholars. We contend that in the modern world exemplarity served as what Raymond Williams (1977, 122) called a residual element of culture: omnipresent as a resource for action, sedimented in vernaculars and institutional jargons, and largely taken for granted, not fully theorized or highlighted in dominant accounts of how the world works.

We write from our historical moment as scholars with professional and emotional investments, however ambivalent, in apparently tottering institutions: the university and the international order of nation-states.

Modern exemplarity seems to be tottering with them. The provision of role models has not brought marginalized populations into secure civic or economic belonging. As this book goes to press, President Joe Biden has presented Liz Cheney and Bennie Thompson, leaders of the Congressional January 6th Select Committee, with the Presidential Citizens Medal for 'exemplary deeds of service' and just days later issued pardons to protect them from being made an example of; Jimmy Carter, his 'exemplary' humility celebrated in every op-ed, has been laid to rest with a full state funeral; simultaneously, a very different set of actors arrives in Washington to smash their legacies. The negative exemplarity of Bashar al-Assad's regime is drawing the global gaze away from current, less consensible, state-led atrocities in the region, while brutality of a similar scale in Sudan is with difficulty kept on the radar. Yet beleaguered liberals still seek points of light, such as the 'spectacular and exemplary reversal' of rape culture effected by the courage of Gisèle Pelicot in stepping to the center of her abusers' trial and making shame change sides.[1] This case provoked talk of a watershed moment, a hopeful discourse more characteristic of the 20th century.

The establishment exemplarity of the liberal West has a well-developed ritual apparatus, with defined roles and narratives to be filled and renewed on a regular cycle. In its mediated public sphere, atypical virtue and energy are amplified in the company of commercial success and pure celebrity. The return on an investment in amplification may be improved by drawing an exemplar from the example: privileging the durable personhood of the actor over the unstable and fleeting act. This shift of focus to the individual also eases citation and emulation for the audience: style and background are more easily appropriated than the difficult exemplary act. Establishment exemplarity is inevitably partisan, celebrating or demonizing the examples that speak to its agenda. It is inevitably myopic, though it will take up outsider examples that are forced upon its notice (and work to assimilate them). It is also omnipresent, endlessly diffused and replicated through broadcast and social media, providing a thin layer of common knowledge among acquaintances, and in this way it is easily transmuted from the sublime to the banal.

Beyond the exemplary center

It is thus unsurprising that, when we convened a conference to bring exemplarity into focus, many participants understood this to mean the amplification, citation, and exhortation to emulation of establishment examples.

---

[1] https://www.lemonde.fr/idees/article/2024/11/28/proces-des-viols-de-mazan-la-lecon-de-justice-de-gisele-pelicot_6417719_3232.html (accessed January 3, 2025).

Thinking from the margins of the liberal order, Ayşe Zarakol describes the resentment of aspiring powers when costly investments in dominant examples failed to earn them a rise in the status hierarchy. Guillaume Wadia echoes this logic at the individual level, demonstrating that the deep socialization of indigenous elites by French colonial officials created true believers who experienced betrayal and alienation when promises were not kept. Jelena Subotić addresses the more disabused response of the eastern countries being 'welcomed home' to Europe after 1989: although a few, like Estonia, became the prize pupils of Europeanness, most accepted conspicuous emulation as the price of inclusion without finding it necessary to transform their own hearts and minds. Such cases support the charge of hypocrisy so generally leveled against the West as exemplary center. It is possible to argue that the example was never a genuine commitment to transmit agency: instead, the originator was elevated as fixed exemplar with others licensed only to imitate, not revise. With this focus on the late history of establishment examples, exemplarity is understandably perceived as a repressive rather than a generative cultural force.

The critique is often justified, but to extrapolate from it to the exemplary process as a whole gives too much credit to the institutional amplifiers, too little to the judgment of even forced emulators. The most potent totalitarian regimes have failed to prevent the ironic uptake of their massified central slogans and rituals. All the more must liberal examples, designed for individualized uptake, surrender their stability. Instability lies beneath even the weighty marble monuments at the center of the agora, for establishment examples had once to be established: they are relics of the competition that brought the present order into being. In the classical world of which Fritz Graf writes, the politics of commemorative statues were lively and engaged a wide public, even if the protagonists had to be assimilated into an 'exemplary template.' In the Cold War, as described by Dorothy Noyes, world leaders strove to outdo one another in producing watershed moments for the cameras. But the transformations announced by the iconic photographs could come undone. Once made, peace can be unmade, and often this is not with a bang but a whimper. The details are tricky; not everyone is on board; the luster comes off the charismatic principals as their fuller personhood is exposed. The amplification process itself dulls examples over time. Once erected, with the motives of controversy receding from memory, most statues and monuments fall into the civic background. They help to normalize dominant assumptions about who acts and what constitutes action, but until a revisionist, in search of a point of entry, singles them out in order to topple their example, they are largely inert. The impetus to emulation falls off when examples saturate landscapes and textbooks. To be sure, this banalization offers other modes of uptake: as Noyes suggests, a historical example can sometimes be reduced to an efficient signaling device.

Examples escape the intentions of even the most powerful originators, for the transmission of form is a transmission of agency. Subotić tells an extraordinary story of the nationalist repurposing of Holocaust commemoration in Eastern Europe, which had such success that populists in the founding countries of the European Union are now emulating the eastern example. Wadia is concerned with the holistic, deep internalization of Enlightenment French personhood by colonized subjects: in this case the imposed example became a powerful resource for both anticolonial critique and national self-creation. Conversely, the metropole is no longer in a position to emulate its own imperial example: instead it has retreated to a belated judgment phase, in bitter collective debate over the legacies of Algeria. Robin de Bruin describes a different post-imperial path: the complex blend of holding on and letting go in the postwar Dutch self-reframing from a benevolent colonial power to a 'guide country' for Europe. Objective possessions could be surrendered; the identity of exemplar could not. Generational transmission is more fully addressed in Kyrre Kverndokk's discussion of Greta Thunberg, whose initial climate campaign was at once a canny appropriation of the exemplary machinery and an inversion of subject positions, in which the supposed beneficiaries of adult care for the future declare themselves compelled to set the example for their negligent elders.

Ying Zhang, for the Chinese public sphere, and Christopher Daase and Tobias Wille, in the context of international politics, demonstrate the importance of particular examples in even the most ritualized and procedural contexts. Zhang shows how collective reflection and judgment at all levels of society converged around the Ming prisoner-exemplars and, later, the exemplars of the COVID-19 pandemic; the explicit norms of a hierarchical order could be located in those who had resisted its immediate authorities. Folk veneration interacted with elite emulation to sustain a style of exemplarity that thereby became not only Confucian but Chinese, not least in its current digital manifestations. Zhang highlights a crucial dimension of the judgment phase: it is not merely cognitive but strongly affective, responding to the corporeal commitment of the initial performance. Surprisingly, Daase and Wille confirm the importance of affect for a seemingly disembodied mode of exemplarity, the justificatory citation of international precedents: 'the conclusion does not compel, it needs to be felt.' While Zhang addresses exemplarity in a context of endemic tension over central power, and Snyder points to the force of emotionally salient examples in crisis decision-making, Daase and Wille emphasize the importance of precedent as a shared 'point of reference' that may win legitimacy for a new intervention in a setting where uncertainty is high and legal consensus has not been achieved. Noyes adds that the awareness of precedent may inform action in more ways than one. A new performance can be energized by an apt citation or the repudiation of a powerful negative example, but it may also take covert example from a precedent too stigmatized to cite: a prior humiliation that must be reversed. Finally, it may simply draw practical guidance from an available model that, made explicit, would pose a distraction.

Our authors also capture uses of exemplarity less visible to actors at the heart of exemplary centers, but vital to the majority relegated to the periphery. Gandhi drew on a range of religious traditions and exemplars to shape his practice of nonviolence; he also built on his own example, as each successful action offered both inspiration and practical guidance for the next. The example of his movement served in turn to inspire and guide civil rights and liberation movements around the world. Ramachandra Guha exemplifies, in every sense, what patient historical research can contribute to the long-term work of judgment and amplification: in contrast to activist appropriation of the deeds and establishment appropriation of the person, the historian brings rounded reflection to both example and exemplar within their context of opportunity. Perea Ozerin takes the story further by looking at how contemporary social movements mine the past and scan the global horizons for useful examples: they are not tethered to their exemplary centers, but can form transnational solidarities that, from mutual emulation, can generate tighter networks of practice.

Finally, Watanabe takes us deeper into the actual work of judgment and emulation, showing what it means to relocate and adapt a model. Her study points to several issues for the study and performance of examples today. First is the partial emancipation of contemporary exemplarity from the high modern centers. The organizational models and design concepts in this Japanese-Chilean relationship draw on a range of traditions and circulate globally, incorporating influences as they go. (It does not come amiss to recall that modernism itself, however universalist in its claims and consolidated by centers of power, was the cosmopolitan creation of exiles and marginals in mutual emulation.) Second is the new humility of the senders, at least some of whom have learned from the failures of high modern projects (Scott 1998) to surrender agency willingly, deliberately leaving projects open to redesign. Third, a new possibility arises as we observe the multiple investments of diverse participants in the process of transmission. Although, in practice, design thinking may allot more agency to metropolitan consultants than to the locals being instructed to shape their own solutions, the recognition of complex agency and iterative process does at least point the way to a less aggressive style of exemplarity. To be sure, the age of the tech bro is ever more deeply invested in singular acts of individual genius, policed by intellectual property law and amplified by hero narratives and celebrity culture. But faith on the ground grows shakier as established exemplars abdicate and new examples fail to generate a stable alternative order. The prestige of public action, which Arendt posited as the highest and properly political realization of the *vita activa* (Arendt 1998 [1958]), is falling off, and a rebalancing toward the humble modes of labor and work may be called for. Accordingly, transnational practitioner communities may set a more immediately useful example for addressing messy global problems than the competitive emulation of highly placed performers.

The future of exemplarity

This brings us to the current moment, in which modern exemplarity seems to be breaking up into multiple cultural processes. Watanabe traces a reflexive, collaborative turn in transnational cooperation with significant grassroots potential. The mainstream of exemplarity in public culture, however, is re-energizing hierarchy, now personalist rather than civilizational or statist in character. This is perhaps surprising, given that the proliferation of technologies, platforms, and content at the turn of the millennium brought in new voices and perspectives, sapping the power of dominant examples and perhaps of examples altogether. Until recently, the English adjective 'performative' was a term of art in speech act theory, denoting an utterance that constitutes an action in itself. In current vernacular usage, to call an action performative is to dismiss it as an empty gesture. In an age of social media, the effortfulness of amplification is radically diminished, and performances are easily proposed as examples. The effortfulness of performance itself comes into question, for visibility can be achieved without committing the body to a dangerous incursion into an occupied arena. Even those performances that risk all to cross a genuine threshold must compete for attention in a saturated climate that limits the energy of collective judgment and the efficacy of citation. Performances are subject to reversal or retraction, and however compelling they may initially be, most of the audience has little scope to verify the corresponding expenditure of self over time. A further complication is the growing power and assertiveness of platforms, committed to maximizing engagement regardless of content and, increasingly, to amplify content that advances the owner's political agenda. Themselves participants in content creation and skilled in the ways of amplification, audiences recognize that events are shaped for them and may be outright falsified. Cynicism towards performance is a natural consequence.

The canniest performers may exploit such cynicism, both to insulate themselves from criticism and to discredit their competitors. Donald Trump grafts this skill onto the authoritarian playbook that stems back at least to Napoleon: first, to exploit the machinery of celebrity; then, once arrived at power, to monopolize exemplarity by taking control of the means of amplification. Trump's efforts along these lines are unlikely to succeed fully, but he has achieved near-ubiquity by other means: the televisual art of driving the ratings. He exploits the ambiguity of the performative through perpetual disruptive gestures, which promise far-reaching consequences and must therefore be covered by the mainstream media, local and global. Frequently reiterated and as frequently reversed, his gestures do not rise to the level of autonomous examples, not even the threshold-crossing of Panmunjom. They do, however, demand 24–7 attention to his personhood and the context in which he operates. America no longer claims to be the indispensable nation, but Trump has made himself the inevitable exemplar.

'The whole world is watching' meant something different in 1968; Arendt's 'space of appearance' has broken up. After the failure of the Soviet example and the betrayals of the liberal one, the transformation of the global mediascape has completed the destruction of the conditions for generalized faith in large-scale examples. But we must finish, as we began, with particulars. A crisis of faith provokes a search for orientation and reassurance, which inevitably falls upon new examples. For individual actors, protagonism seems most easily attained in the digital realm through aesthetic, ethical, and political self-fashioning that draws upon influencer-exemplars. This zone of rapid signaling and response, relatively untethered from ongoing corporeal relationships, tends to flatten competitive emulation into imitation and identification, not only with other individuals but with parties, causes, and leaders. Under these conditions, amplification may precede performance, or even do without it: in a time of generative AI, the presentation of an image before the public has no necessary connection to any event – or indeed to any actual human. Our model, however, identifies exemplarity's foundation in the human: an irreversible act of conduct, a daring commitment of the body, that creates a before and an after. Is exemplarity coming to an end?

More immediately, what does our investigation offer to international theory? All its major strands have grappled in some fashion with the process we have named exemplarity. Channeling Machiavelli, political realists emphasize the process of competitive emulation, in which states and their leaders anxiously monitor the movements of real and aspirational peers in a context of anarchy. To integrate exemplarity with rational calculus here is to acknowledge the role of emotion, and by extension embodiment, long implicit in realist thinking; to recognize the full apparatus of power through which hegemons are made and challenged. In doing so, exemplarity also provides a bridge to the literature on status and recognition (Zarakol 2011; Paul, Larson, and Wohlforth 2014). Realists also have emphasized the importance of political prudence, which they understand with Hans Morgenthau (1954) as situated weighting of the uncertain consequences of political action (Porter 2016; Guzzini 2020; Kumar 2023). Prudent action learns from past examples, but creatively adapts them to new circumstances. A full understanding of the mechanism of exemplarity, its elements and preconditions, not only allows for a more complete theorization of these dynamics, but can also shed light on why they appear to be fracturing in the current political moment. With a growing number of aspiring exemplars, a fractured public sphere, and more decentralized infrastructures of amplification, it is hard to see how competitive emulation can lead to coordinated action, much less guarantee social progress. The same factors undermine a prudent weighting of past examples and replace it with the ungrounded promise of 'unprecedented' successes, be it in peacemaking or asserting the national interest.

Liberalism has long been reckoning with the tensions between performance and practice in the making of the so-called liberal international order. Its proponents recognize that the institutions of the latter could only be built 'after victory' (Ikenberry 2001), that is, after the assertion of power, and then persisted not least because of the economic benefits they provided even in a world 'after hegemony' (Keohane 1984), that is, with US power past its peak. That this order today is in crisis is owed not least to the overconfidence with which both neo-liberal economic reformers and liberal interventionists tried to push their values and institutions on others (Börzel and Zürn 2021). These inherent tensions of liberal exemplarity owe much to the ongoing power of the old examples, set during a moment of vital global sociability and competitive emulation in which a Wordsworth could pay tribute to a Toussaint Louverture.[2] They owe still more to the latter phases of the process, when the institutionalization of the founders impeded the uptake of new examples that is the very motor of liberal progress. To recognize that liberalism was a distributed invention across particulars rather than a diffusion of universals is to honor the examples of those in the colonized parts of the globe who sought to take it up and make it their own. For international theory, the notion of exemplarity adds nuance to existing accounts of the rise and fall of the liberal international order, and provides tools for better understanding how it is currently being both repurposed from within and challenged from without.

For constructivists and practice theorists, each focusing on different scales of social action, exemplarity can both complement and complicate the understanding of what drives social change. With their focus on diffusion and learning, these literatures have a fairly linear understanding of how social forms are transmitted (Finnemore and Sikkink 1998; Checkel 2001; Adler 2008) that has only recently been challenged (Schindler and Wille 2015; Wiener 2018; Zimmermann et al 2023). While norms and practices are different forms than examples, they interact. Established norms inflect the representation and judgment of new performances, while the citation of a different exemplary precedent may challenge the interpretation and application of the norm. The particularities and

---

[2] https://en.wikisource.org/wiki/Poems_(Wordsworth,_1815)/Volume_2/To_Toussaint_L%27Ouverture (accessed January 3, 2025).

frictions of institutional practice can support or undermine the creation of an example. A striking performance can give form and energy to a new direction that may generate a norm or establish a practice, just as the discrediting of reified exemplars can be used to challenge normative orders and everyday practices.

Political actors already know all this, at least intuitively. They operate with the practical understanding of exemplarity that is deep in the modern political habitus. They also exploit freely the cultural rhetorics of exemplarity recognized by their constituents. In a context of global challenges and local distrust, it is advisable for leaders everywhere to gain some distance from their own exemplary lineage and become familiar with the force of other examples. Whether this sends them in new, hybrid directions (as is common with social movement actors) or returns them to their cardinal exemplars, it behooves them to understand the historicity of both individual examples and modern mediated exemplarity: a cycle of rise and decay as well as a durable potential for revival under the right conditions.

In this volume we have sought to illuminate those conditions, especially the social and political contexts in which examples are produced and taken up. Challengers to the current exemplary center, whether rising powers or grassroots activists, are likely to be well aware of these human factors, to say nothing of the post- and non-human agencies interacting with them. As grand public examples become less viable, actors at every level and location may be rediscovering the resource of interpersonal example in their immediate arena. In the meantime, the spectacle continues. We hope that this book will be useful in tracking and assessing the transformations of political performance that underpin it.

References

Adler, Emanuel. 2008. 'The Spread of Security Communities: Communities of Practice, Self-Restraint, and NATO's Post-Cold War Transformation.' *European Journal of International Relations* 14 (2): 195–230.

Arendt, Hannah. 1998 [1958]. *The Human Condition*. 2nd ed. University of Chicago Press.

Börzel, Tanja A., and Michael Zürn. 2021. 'Contestations of the Liberal International Order: From Liberal Multilateralism to Postnational Liberalism.' *International Organization* 75 (2): 282–305.

Checkel, Jeffrey T. 2001. 'Why Comply? Social Learning and European Identity Change.' *International Organization* 55 (3): 553–588.

Finnemore, Martha, and Kathryn Sikkink. 1998. 'International Norm Dynamics and Political Change.' *International Organization* 52 (4): 887–917.

Guzzini, Stefano. 2020. 'Saving Realist Prudence.' In *The Social Construction of State Power: Applying Realist Constructivism*, edited by J. Samuel Barkin. Bristol University Press.

Ikenberry, G. John. 2001. *After Victory: Institutions, Strategic Restraint, and the Rebuilding of Order after Major Wars*. Princeton University Press.

Keohane, Robert O. 1984. *After Hegemony: Cooperation and Discord in the World Political Economy*. Princeton University Press.

Kumar, Manali. 2023. 'Making Decisions under Uncertainty: The Prudent Judgement Approach.' *European Journal of International Security* 8 (1): 109–129.

Morgenthau, Hans J. 1954. *Politics Among Nations: The Struggle for Power and Peace*. 2nd ed. Knopf.

Paul, T. V., Deborah Welch Larson, and William C. Wohlforth, eds. 2014. *Status in World Politics*. Cambridge University Press.

Porter, Patrick. 2016. 'Taking Uncertainty Seriously: Classical Realism and National Security.' *European Journal of International Security* 1 (2): 239–260.

Schindler, Sebastian, and Tobias Wille. 2015. 'Change in and through Practice: Pierre Bourdieu, Vincent Pouliot, and the End of the Cold War.' *International Theory* 7 (2): 330–359.

Scott, James C. 1998. *Seeing Like a State: How Certain Schemes to Improve the Human Condition Have Failed*. Yale University Press.

Wiener, Antje. 2018. *Contestation and Constitution of Norms in Global International Relations*. Cambridge University Press.

Williams, Raymond. 1977. *Marxism and Literature*. Oxford University Press.

Zarakol, Ayşe. 2011. *After Defeat: How the East Learned to Live with the West*. Cambridge University Press.

Zimmermann, Lisbeth, Nicole Deitelhoff, Max Lesch, Antonio Arcudi, and Anton Peez. 2023. *International Norm Disputes: The Link between Contestation and Norm Robustness*. Oxford University Press.

Index

References to figures appear in *italic* type; those in **bold** type refer to tables. References to endnotes show both the page number and the note number (231n3).

9/11 attacks 49, 52, 58

A

Abbas, Ferhat 168–169
abolition of slavery movements 132, 134, 135, 136–137, 269–270
Abraham Accords 237, 248, 254–256, 258
Abray, Jane 134
Abu Dhabi 257
Académie Française 171–172
Adams, John 235
aemulus (rival) 33
affect 10, 26, 30, 41, 84–85, 92, 106–107, 281, 289
African National Congress (ANC) 55
After Defeat (Zarakol) 155
agency 13, 37
Age of Revolutions 129–133
Ahala, C. Servilius 70
Albright, Madeleine 122
Alexander the Great 66
Algeria 164–176
  decolonization 172–174
  destruction of names 169–170
  évolués 167
  First and Second World Wars 168
  French history 170–172
  French language 171
  French *mission civilisatrice* 164–176, 209
  Gauls as ancestors 170, 172
  independence 169
  integration policies 173
  nationalists 167–169
  Young Algerians 167–169
Algerian War of Independence 31, 164, 165, 173
Allison, Graham 9
Alter-Globalization Movement 137
Ambedkar, B. R. 55
American Dream 40–41
American Political Science Association 147
amplification 6, *25*, 27–29, 86, 139

Amrouche, Jean 171
analogies 118, 264, 266
analytical case studies 268
anarchy 147–151
Andrews, C. F. 57
Annan, Kofi 122
Antenor (sculptor) 66
anthropological frameworks 186–188
anti-communist memory resolutions and legislation 222
Antigonos (general under Alexander) 62
anti-nuclear missiles marches 207–208, *207*
antislavery struggles 131–132
Arab League 256
Arab Spring 35–36
Arendt, Hannah 10, 29, 38, 118–119, 290–291, 292
Aristide, Jean-Bertrand 132–133
Aristion (tyrant of Athens) 69
Aristogeiton (Athenian tyrannicide) 60, 61–68
Aristophanes 63
Aristotelian examples (Gelley) 74
Aristotle 38, 67
al-Assad, Bashar 287
Assemblée Nationale, France 174–175
Athens
  democracy 60
  exemplary performance 67–68
  laws 64
  red-figured vases 61–62, 65–66
  Spartan domination 62
  tyrannicides 61–69
  Xerxes conquering 66
Atlantic Council 256–257
audiences 25–26, 74, 279–280
Augustus 70
Aung San Suu Kyi 266, 269

B

Badiou, Alain 186–187
Baksh, Rawwida 137

INDEX

Bandak, Andreas 183, 186
Ban Gu 93–94
Bell, Alexander Graham 40
Berenskoetter, Felix 247n8
Berlin 241, 249–250
Beyen, Johan Willem 212
Biden, Joe 287
Bilge, Sirma 135
Bismarck, Otto von 32, 244
Blackburn, Robin 132
Black feminists 135–137
Black Lives Matter (BLM) 23, 31, 37, 133, 136
Black Power salutes 32
Blair, Eric (George Orwell) 58
Blair, Tony 210
Blinken, Anthony 255
Bolívar, Simón 130–131
'Bombs for Bread' report 203–204
Bonapartism 29
Book of Changes (Sima Qian) 93, 95, 97
Bosma, Martin 213
Bourdieu, Pierre 33
Brandt, Willy 23, 26, 29, 30, 32, 34, 37
Brazil 132
Brown, Gordon 35
Bruin, Robin de 289
Brutus, Lucius 69, 70, 71
Brutus, Marcus 62, 69, 70, 71
Buchenwald concentration camp 225–226
Budapest 224–225, 227
Burke, Kenneth 38–39
Buzan, Barry 281

C

Caesar, Julius 70
Calcutta 54
Caldwell, Dan 239
cameras 244–246, 288
Camp David Accords 32, 240, 255
'cancel culture' 34
'*la caravana escolar de seguridad*' ('*la caravana*') 184–193
Carlos, John 32
Carr, E. H. 152–153
Carter, Jimmy 240, 287
Cato (philosopher) 70
causation 37, 267, 276
Ceauşescu, Nicolae 242
celebrity and exemplarity 15, 40, 97, 246–247, 287, 290–291
  scandals 30–31
Chakrabarty, Dipesh 165
Chancellor, John 243
Cheney, Liz 287
Chen Xiyuan 101
children 180–193
  community-based DRR 190
  disaster preparedness 180–181
  and the future 76
  network of relations 187, 192
  relational and multiscalar 189–190
Children's Memorial, Yad Vashem Holocaust Remembrance Center 227
'the child' trope 74, 75–76, 80, 82, 85
Chile 180–181, 185
China 57, 239, 242, 249
  see also exemplar-prisoners
Chinese exemplarity 92, 103, 107
Chipko movement 52
Christian, Crown Prince of Denmark-Norway 40
Christianity 53–54
Christ's Resurrection (the Event) 186, 187
Chung Eui-young 251
Cicero 69, 70
citations 6, 25, 26, 31–33, 36, 139
civil rights movement 41, 52
Classic of Filial Piety 97
Clichy-sous-Bois, France 175
climate change 76–85
Clinton, Bill 210
Club of Rome 202, 203
Coates, Ben 201
Cohen, Harlan G. 112
Cold War 236–239, 264, 274, 288
Cold War exemplarity 248, 253
Cold War threshold crossing 236, 245, 258
Collins, Patricia Hill 135
'colonization' 170–171
'color revolutions' of 2000–2006 35
Combahee River Collective 136
common law 115, 120n4
communism 218
competitive emulation 238
competitive victimization 223–225
concepts 6–7
Concert of Europe 273–277, 280–281
Confucian ethics 96, 97–98, 100, 107
Confucian exemplarity 91–107
  COVID-19 pandemic 103–107, *104*
  death and suicide 101–103
  emulation through art 95–96
  extraordinary suffering 98–101
  reflexive emulation 92–95, 96–98
  see also exemplar-prisoners
Congress of Angostura 131
Congress of Vienna 26, 132, 273–276, 277
'conquest' events 238, 240–242, *241*
constructivists 114–117, 293
consumer society 172
'coronabonds' 199, 200
Corsín-Jiménez, Alberto 183, 187
Corten, Olivier 110
Costa, António 200
Côte d'Ivoire 265
COVID-19 pandemic 35, 91–92, 103–107, 199–200, 201, 252

297

Crenshaw, Kimberlé 136
Critique of Judgment (Kant) 118
Cronkite, Walter 243
crossing the threshold *see* threshold crossing
The Crying Phoenix (Mingfeng ji) 100
Cuba 128, 132
Cuban Missile Crisis 9
Cullis-Suzuki, Severn 82
Cull, Nicholas J. 200
cultural hegemony (Gramsci) 39
cultural representations 10
cultural transmission 8–11, 13, 23–24, 74
cyborgs 187

D

Daase, Christopher 229–230, 279, 289
Daoism 105
Davis, Angela Y. 134–136
Dayan, Daniel 26, 238, 245
death and exemplarity 101–103
Death to the Tyrants! (Teegarden) 68–69
Debord, Guy 26
'decivilization' 174
deification 97
Delhi 54
Demosthenes 62
deontic normativity 111, 114
    see also normativity
Derrida, Jacques 34, 37
design thinking 180–184
détente 237–240
determinate judgments 118–119
'détournement' (Debord) 26
Dey of Algiers 167
Dien Bien Phu garrison 265
Dijsselbloem, Jeroen 200, 212–213
Diodorus Siculus 62
Dionysius of Halicarnassus 70
disaster preparedness 180–188, 190, 192
disaster risk reduction (DRR) 180, 185, 187, 188, 190
Djebar, Assia 171–172
Djeghloul, Abdelkader 167
La dolce vita (film) 11
domino theory 265
Donnelly, Jack 147
Dorpema, Marc 204
'double enslavement' 135
'double oppression' 135
Dubois, Laurent 130, 131
Duvall, Raymond 37
dynamism 12, 236

E

earthquakes 180, 185, 190
East and Central European states 218, 220, 221–222, 231
    see also named countries

East Asian state building 35
The Economist 252
economy-first doctrines 156
egalitarianism 146
Einstein, Albert 56
Elias, Norbert 154
emancipation 131, 132
'empirical theorizing' (Guzzini) 8
emulation 6, 25, 26, 33–36, 39–40, 107, 139
Environmental Children's Organization 82
Epstein, Lee 112
Eriksen, Anne 74–75
Ernman, Beata 73
eschatological biases 83
ethical perspectives 60
'ethicopolitical cults' 96
Europe
    19th century skepticism 53
    and Dutch identity 212–213
    humanitarian military intervention 265
    self-perceptions 211–212
European Commission (EC) 202
European Common Market 172
European Holocaust Memorial Day 221
European Holocaust memory 219–223
European integration 211–212
European memory practices 34, 221–223
Europeanness 211
European Parliament 221, 222
European Union (EU)
    Dutch scepticism 213
    and East Central Europe 218, 231
    exemplary self-conception 220
    memory divergence 221
    'soft power' 199
European unity 218–219, 228–230
Europe-as-West identity 153
Eurozone debt crisis 200
euthanasia 210
evangelicals 209–210
events 186–187, 190
evolutionary game theory 113
examples
    alternative 41
    compelling 38
    continuum of seriality 183
    exempla (*exemplum*) 6–7
    as models for action 35, 266–267
    positive uses 267–268
    power of 36–41
    precedents 118
    and structural resistance 39
exchanging greetings 11
exemplaire 25
exemplarity 5–13, 41–42, 274–275, 278–280
    behind-the-back processes 282
    bordering knowledge 281
    direct and material 128, 130–131, 134

dominant 279
empirical strategy 264–266
future 12, 78–79, 84–85, 291–294
indirect and immaterial 128, 131, 134
inherent dynamism 236
intentionality of exemplification 282
international theory 11–13
network structure of 6, 12, 19, 24–25, 28, 33, 37–38, 240–243, *241*, 253, 258, 290
iteration 34, 37
normative strategy 268–270
performance 68
political hierarchies 150–151
rhetorical power 38
salience 242
stigma management 154–157
exemplar-prisoners 92
  emulation and veneration 107
  Fan Pang 95–96, 101
  Huang Daozhou 96–98
  Sima Qian 92–96, 98–99, 101, 106
  suicide 101–103
  King Wen of Zhou 92–95, 101
  Yang Jisheng 98–101
  see also China; Confucian exemplarity
exemplars 6, 12, 24, 39, 74, 106, 268, 274, 279
exemplary actions 37, 65, 74, 86
exemplary gestures 10, 258
exemplary normativity 111, 117–120
  see also normativity
'exemplary validity' (Arendt) 119
extremist entrepreneurs 36

F

faith 57
family as analogy for society 81
family time 77–78
Fang Fang 91–92, 103, 105–106
Fan Pang 95–96, 101
Faraday, Michael 56
Feast of Sacrifice 243
felicity conditions 25–27, 36
Fellini, Federico 11
feminist activism 138
feminist legacies 134–137
Ferry, Jules 166
Fick, Carolyn E. 132
Finland 5
Finnemore, Martha 8–9, 115
Fire God *104*, 105
'fire' metaphors 83
First International 134
'Fit for 55' program (EC) 202
Flyvbjerg, Bent 30
Ford, Gerald 205–206
Foreign Affairs journal 273
Foreign Policy journal 273

Fortuyn, Pim 210
Fosse Ardeatine massacre 229
Foucault, Michel 34, 40
France 164–176
  amnesia about Algerian history 172
  Assemblée Nationale 174, 175
  citizenship 167–168
  colonialism bill 2005–158 174–175
  'decivilization' 174
  fall of Dien Bien Phu 265
  and Haiti 132–133
  integration of Algerians 172–173
  'memories and truth commission' 164
  mission civilisatrice 164–176, 209
  revolutionary feminism 134
  riots in *banlieues* 175–176
  Second Empire 236
  superiority of culture 166
  Third Republic 166
Francis, Pope 257
Franco-Prussian War (1871) 166
Frank, André Günder 137
freedom and justice 55–56
free-trade 211–212
French revolution 130, 134, 166
'from tragedy to farce' 235
Fuentes, Marta 137

G

Gaay Fortman, Bas de 203n4, 204, 205
Gandhi, Mohandas K. 49–59, 290
  faith 53
  fast-unto-death 54
  humility 56–58
  non-violence 51
  political practice 58
  reconciliation 55–56
  respect for other religions 53, 58
  self-deprecatory jokes 58–59
  trans-national figure 52
Gao Chaoying 99
Gao Yao (Prison God) 101
Gargash, Anwar 255–258
Gauls 170–171
Geertz, Clifford 26
Gelley, Alexander 74
'gender work' 277
genocide 121, 265
Géricault, Théodore 28
German Death Camp KL Warschau 223–224
Germany 5, 23, 30, 34
gestures 10, 236
'getuigenispolitiek' (testimonial policy) 205, 206
Ghaddafi, Muammar 265
Global Centre for the Responsibility to Protect 265
'God's Funeral' (Hardy) 53

Gogh, Theo van 210
Goldstone, Richard 122
Goli otok, Croatia 225
Gore, Albert (Al Gore) 78, 80
Graaf, Beatrice de 277
Graf, Fritz 288
Gramsci, Antonio 39
Great East Japan earthquake and tsunami (2011) 180
'Greater Holland' 212–213
great men and women making history 37
Great War *see* World War I
Greece 60, 61
  see also Athens
greetings 11
Grimke, Angelina 134–135
'Groeien aan de grens' (Timmermans) 202
Grotius, Hugo 153
The Guardian 4
Guernica 34
Guha, Ramachandra 290
guide country 203–211
'guide land' (Kennedy) 209
Guzzini, Stefano 8

H

Haas, Richard 276
Habermas, Jürgen 173
habitus 9
Haitian revolution 129–133, 133n4, 137–138
'Hall of Tears' (Budapest) 227
Hamas October 7 2023 attacks 257
Haraway, Donna 187
Harcourt, Wendy 137
Hardy, Thomas 53
Hareven, Tamara 77–78
Harmodios (Athenian tyrannicide) 60, 61–68
Hatzivassiliou, Evanthis 239
Havel, Vaclav 52
Hawkins, Darren 115
Heikal, Mohamed 244, 248
Heine, Heinrich 204
Henry IV, Holy Roman Emperor 32
'herbs to the rescue' game (*yerbas al rescate*) 190–191
Herodotus 66–67
heroism 28, 244
Hero of the Crossing *see* al-Sadat, Anwar
hierarchies 145–158
  defining 145
  International Relations (IR) 147–151
  liberal orders 146
  modern international order 151–154
  power and rank 148
  shaping actors 149–150
  stigma coping strategies 154–157
'hierarchy turn' 147–148
'hijacking' (Dayan and Katz) 26

'Himalayan Blunder' (Gandhi) 58
Hinden, Adam 107
Hinduism 53–55
Hippias (tyrant) 66–68
Hirsi Ali, Ayaan 210
historia magister vitae (Koselleck) 236
Historical Museum of Serbia 225
Historical Records (Sima Qian) 92–93
History of the Latter Han (Hou Hanshu) 95
Hobsbawm, Eric 130
Hobson, John M. 153
Hoekstra, Wopke 199, 212–213
Hofer, Alexandra 110
Højer, Lars 183, 186
Hölkeskamp, Karl-Joachim 60
Hollanditis (Laqueur) 208, 213
Holmes, Stephen 33–34
Holm, Isak Winkel 83–84
Holocaust Museum, Rome 229
Holocaust appropriation 223–230
  competitive victimization 223–225
  criminalization of communism 225–228
  myth of European unity 228–230
Holocaust remembrance 218–231
  contested historical memory 219–223
  'cosmopolitan memory' 219–220
  destabilizing effects 222
  discursive prohibitions 32
  'Europeanization' 220
  exemplary appropriation 225–228
  intentionality and exemplification 282
  myth of European unity 228–230
  revisionism 219
  Western mnemonical canon 222–223
hooks, bell (Gloria Watkins) 136
House of European History (Brussels) 228–229
House of Terror museum (Budapest) 226–227
Huang, Chin-Hao, 35
Huang Daozhou 96–98
Huang, Martin W. 94
Huang Tingjian 95–96
humanitarian interventions 121–123, 165, 265
Hungary 224–225, 226–227
Hunt, Lynn 268

I

'I am Malala' petition (Gordon Brown) 35
identity and reputation 35
Ides of March 44 BCE 62
imitatio Christi 7–8
immigration 174
Imperialism 153
'imperial presidency' 248
incompleteness (*fukanzen*) 187, 188
An Inconvenient Truth (Gore) 78

INDEX

Independent International Commission on Kosovo 2000 122
India 51–52, 54–55, 57
Indian National Congress 55
Indians of the Transvaal 49–51
institutional power 39
instrumental normativity 111, 112
  see also normativity
inter-faith dialogues 53–55
Intergovernmental Panel on Climate Change (IPCC) 76, 81, 83
'international cooperation' (*kokusai kyōryoku*) 180–184
International Council of Women (ICW) 134
International Court of Justice 265
International Fellowship of Religions (Sabarmati, 1928) 53
International Holocaust Remembrance Alliance (IHRA) 221
international law 8, 112, 114, 121
International Relations (IR) 8
  anarchy, hierarchy and exemplarity 147–151
  power of precedents 110
  revolutions 129
  speaking truth to power 273
International Studies Association Convention (Toronto, 2019) 13
International Task Force on Holocaust Education, Remembrance and Research 220
international theory 11–13, 292, 293
intersectionality 135–136
In the Name of the People exhibition (Historical Museum of Serbia) 225
Islam 53–55
'Islamization' of Dutch culture 210
Israel 239–240, 243, 254, 257
Italy 39, 200, 229
ius ad bellum (right to wage war) 120
Iza! Kaeru Caravan 184–190

J

James, C. L. R. 133
Jansen, Stef 186–187
Japan 155–157, 180–182, 264
  Ministry of Foreign Affairs (MOFA) 180
Japanese-Chilean relationships 180–181, 290
Japan International Cooperation Agency (JICA) 181
Jean-Charles (survivor of the *Méduse*) 28
Jerusalem 239, 243
Jervis, Robert 263, 264–265, 276
Jewish victimhood 222
Johannesburg, South Africa 49, 52
Judenlager Semlin (Sajmište, Serbia) 226
judgment 6, 25, *25*, 29–31, 290

Judt, Tony 220
Justinian 71

K

Kaepernick, Colin 23, 26, 27–28, 29–30, 32, 34, 37
Kallimachos (Athenian) 61
Kang, David 35
Kant, Immanuel 3, 30, 118
Kapferer, Bruce 186
Kassandros (king of Macedonia) 62
Katz, Elihu 26, 238, 244–245
Keene, Edward 153
Kendi, Ibram X. 133
Kennedy, James 209–210
Kennedy, John F. 238, 242
Kermode, Frank 77
Kier, Elizabet 116, 119
Kim Dae-jung (former President of South Korea) 248–250, 251
Kim Jong-il (former North Korean dictator) 249
Kim Jong Un (North Korean dictator) 235, 245–247, 250, 251
Kim, Suki 247, 251–252
Kimura, Shuhei 180
King, David 275
King, Martin Luther 28, 52
Kinkel, Klaus 121–122
Kissinger, Henry 205–206, 238, 244
Klein, Esther S. 93–94
Kleisthenes (Athenian statesman) 68
KL Warschau concentration camp 223–224
Kniefall (Brandt kneeling) 23, 26, 29, 32, 34, 37
  see also taking a knee
Knight, Jack 112
Knights (Aristophanes) 63
Kok, Wim 210
Konon (Athenian general) 62
Kony, Joseph 269
Korea
  demilitarized zone (DMZ) 247, 248, 250, 252
  North-South détente 250–251
  peace process 249
  see also North Korea; South Korea
Korean War 264
Koselleck, Reinhart 7, 236
Kosovo intervention (1999) 119, 120–123, 265, 266
Kosovo Liberation Army (KLA) 266
Krastev, Ivan 33–34
Kratochwil, Friedrich V. 110
Kritios (sculptor) 61, 65–66
Kuo, Raymond 35
Kupchan, Charles 276
Kushner, Jared 254

Kverndokk, Kyrre 289
Kyzikos, Anatolia 69

L

labor movements 137
Lakatos, Imre 268
Lamian War 64
Langman, Harry 204
Laqueur, Walter Z. 208
Latin America Solidarity Organization (OLAS) 128
Latvia 227
Lawson, George 130, 277, 281
Lazali, Karima 169
'leading by example' 8, 16, 151, 249 *see also* guide country, pilot country
legality and legitimacy 122
legal precedents 112–113, 115, 117
Leosthenes (Athenian general) 64
'Letter in Reply to Ren An' (Sima Qian) 93
Lévi-Strauss, Claude 30
Levy, Daniel 219
Liang Shuguang 104
liberal exemplarity 24n1, 231, 258, 293
liberal international order 146, 151–154, 293
Libya 265
Liebes, Tamar 244
lieux de mémoire 68
Li Ling 93
The Limits to Growth (Meadows) 202, 203
living shrines (Shengci) 105
Li Wenliang 105–106
Li Zhi 102, 103
lone heroes as saviors 238
Long Peace 273–274, 276, 281
'long Sixties' (Netherlands) 206
Lorde, Audre 135, 136
Lord's Resistance Army 269
'love letters' (Kim-Trump letters) 247
Lucan (poet) 70
Lyons, John 82

M

Machiavelli, Niccolò 3, 33, 292
Macron, Emmanuel 5, 80–82, 164, 246
making examples of transgressors 34
Malalas, John 71
Mandela, Nelson 55
Mansholt Committee 203
Mansholt, Sicco 202–203
March, James G. 111–112, 114
'margin-to-center ethic' 136
Marx, Karl 235
massacres 36, 212, 229
Masson-Delmotte, Valérie 76
material power 39
Mattis, James 257–258
May, Ernest R. 263, 264

Ma Yuan cult 98
Mbembe, Achille 165
McFaul, Michael 265
Meadows, Dennis 203
Meadows, Donella H. 202
media amplification 238
media events 237, 244–245
media monopolies 238
Méduse (French frigate) 28
Medvedev, Dmitry 265
Meloni, Giorgia 229
Memorial to the Victims of the German Occupation (Budapest) 224–225
memory appropriation 223
Mercer, Jonathan 116, 119
Merton, Robert 40
#MeToo movement 34
Mexico 39
Middle East peace initiatives 32
Miert, Karel van 208
'militarized agriculture' (Trouillot) 132
Miller, Harry 225
Milosevich, Slobodan 266
Miltiades (Athenian general) 61
Ming dynasty (1368–1644) 92, 102–103
missionary internationalism 212–213
la mission civilisatrice 164–176, 209
 assigning last names 170
 exemplarity 172–176
 negotiating and denying examples 166–169
 trauma 169–172
 see also Algeria; France
Mitzen, Jennifer 30, 286
mnemonic exemplarity 221
Mnuchin, Steven 255
model 25
modern exemplarity 287, 291
modern international order 151–154
modern revolutionary role models 91
modes of exemplary uptake 242, **242**
Moghadam, Valentine M. 134
Mohammed Bin Zayed, Crown Prince 254
Moon Jae-in 248–253, 258
moon landings 237–238, 242
moral exemplars 54, 86, 92, 96, 98, 107, 217, 219
moral integrity 105, 253
Moreno, Jenny 180
Morgenthau, Hans 36–37, 292
mourning space 106–107
Munich Crisis (1938) 264–265
Museum of Occupations (Tallinn, Estonia) 227
Museum of the Occupation of Latvia 227
Museum of Victims of Genocide (Vilnius, Lithuania) 227–228
Musk, Elon 35, 40
Muslims 53–55

INDEX

Mussler, Werner 200
Mussolini 229
Myanmar 265–266, 269

N

Nagata Hirokazu 187, 189
'naming and shaming' 269
naming social phenomena 29
Napoleon 29
'Napoléon le petit' 236
narrative approaches 75, 77
narrow and broad hierarchies 150
Nasser, Gamal Abdel 243
nationalist memorialization 224n3
NATO 5, 121, 204, 266
Natural History (Pliny the Elder) 69
'natural' language 6–7
Nazi Germany 23
Nederlands Dagblad 208
negative exemplars 246, 287
Neier, Aryeh 269
Neo-Confucians (Song dynasty) 93–94
neofascist accelerationism 36
Nero 70
Nesiotes (sculptor) 61, 65–66
Netanyahu, Benjamin 254
Netherlands 199–213
　colonial exploitation 211
　decolonization 205
　elections 2023 213
　and Europe 212–213
　euthanasia 210
　guide country 200–201, 206–207, 208–211
　Hollanditis 213
　internationalist mission 210
　'Islamization' 210
　missionary internationalism 209
　pilot country 203, 212, 213
　post-war politics 208–211
　progressive guide country 213
　progressive politics 202–205
　superior progressive moral stance 205–208
'The Netherlands, Guide Country' report 203
New Labour 210
New York Times 3
New Zealand 35
NFL (National Football League) 23, 27, 34
Nixon in China (Adams) 235
Nixon, Richard 11, 235, 238–239, 239–248
Nobel Peace Prize 251
non-use of force 121
non-violence 51–55, 57–59
'non-Western' states and 'Western' norms 154–155
No One Is Too Small to Make a Difference (Thunberg) 75
Nora, Pierre 63
normative exemplars 269

normative performance 26
normativity 110–124
　constructivists 114
　means and expected outcome 112
　and precedents 110–111, 116–117, 119–120, 123–124
　rationalists 111–112
　see also deontic normativity; exemplary normativity; instrumental normativity
norms 8–9, 115, 118
North Korea 245, 247
　see also Korea
Norway 79–80
nostalgérie (nostalgeria) 173
Noyes, Dorothy 74, 274–275, 278–280, 288, 289
NRC Handelsblad 208

O

Obama, Barack 246, 253
Occitan cultural activists 31
Octavian Augustus 70
October War 1973 239, 243
Olsen, Johan P. 111–112, 114
Olympic Games
　Tokyo (1964) 156
　Mexico City (1968) 32
　Pyongchang (2018) 250
On the Civil War (Lucan) 70
'ontological theorizing' 11
open-ended prototypes 184
oppositional literature 92
Organization of Solidarity with the People of Asia, Africa, and Latin America (OSPAAAL) 128
Orthodox Confucians 101
Orwell, George (Eric Blair) 58
Ory, Pascal 165
Oslo Convention 211
Ottoman Empire 155
'our children' trope 82
'our' possessive pronoun 80–82
outliers in analytical case studies 268
'outsider' actors 154
Ozerin, Perea 27, 35, 282, 290

P

Palestinians 255, 256
Panmunjom Declaration 250–251
Paris Agreement 78, 83
Parks, Rosa 28
participation 182–183
Partido Revolucionario Institucional 39
Partij voor de Vrijheid (PVV) 213
patriarchal model of revolution 134
patronyms 170
'Peace and Prosperity' initiative (Roh Moo-hyun) 248–249

Peisistratid tyranny (Athens) 61, 66
Pelc, Krzysztof J. 114
Pelicot, Gisèle 287
Pence, Mike 250
performances 12
　affective mode 84–85
　amplification 27–29
　détente 239
　disruption 29
　effortfulness 291
　exemplarity 236
　exemplary acts 74–75
　gesture and media coverage 245
　launching cultural object 38
　political actions 240
　preempting interpretation 30
　process model 24–27, *25*
　transmission 236
　before witnesses 26
performances of conduct 5, 25–26, 28, 38
'performative' 291
personal risks 238
'Person of the Century' 56
Pétion, Alexandre 130–131
photographs
　Buchenwald concentration camp 225–226
　and political gestures 244
　watershed moments 288
Picasso 34
Pierrot, Grégory 133
Pijpers, Alfred 208–209
pillarization 209
pilot country 212, 213
Planck, Max 56
Platonic examples (Gelley) 74
Pliny the Elder 69
Plus Arts (NGO, Japan) 185
Poland 223–224
political actions *241*, 242
political actors 294
political controversies 31
political exemplarity 13
Pompeo, Mike 254
Popkin, Jeremy D. 133n4
Popper, Karl 267
popular culture 10, 30–31
popular narrative forms 238
Portugal 200
positive exemplarity 269
post-catastrophic futures 84–85
post-communist Europe 218–219, 222–223
Post, Hans 204
Pouliot, Vincent 115
practice 9, 293
practice theorists 293
precedents 32, 110–124, 289–290
　and analogies 118
　and bad policies 123

common law 115, 120n4
conventional normativity 116
exemplary normativity 117–120
as focal points 114
instrumental normativity 112
intersubjective 119
Kosovo intervention 119, 120–123
normativity 110–111, 116–117, 123–124
overestimating normative weight 123
rationalists 111–114
reasons for action 119–120
situational judgments 119–120
prefiguration 25
preparedness 191–193
prison deities 100–101
Prison God (Gao Yao) 101
procedures 9, 11, 13
Profiles in Courage (Kennedy) 242
Pronk, Jan 205
protests 51–52, 57
prototyping events 181, 183–184, 186–188
public acts and actors 24–27
'public theology' 209–210
Punjab 54
Putin, Vladimir 3, 246, 264, 265

Q

Qaddafi, Moammar 249
Quakers 209–210

R

Rabin, Yitzhak 240
racism 132–137
Rage (Woodward) 245–246
Rand Daily Mail 50
rape culture 287
rationalistm 111–114, 117
Reagan, Ronald 241
realism 292
reconciliation 55–56
'reference groups' (Merton) 40
Reflections on Gandhi (Orwell) 58
reflective judgment 30
reflexive emulation 92–95, 96–98
religious pluralism 53–54
Renaissance 33
representation 9–11, 28
republicanism 8
Republic of Korea *see* South Korea
reputational security 200
Rérolle, Raphaëlle 165
resilience 192–193
resistance 4, 16, 49–51, 57, 60, 127–139, 167, 227–228, 231, 269
'resistance through dialogue' (Djeghloul) 167
Resolution on the Return of Plundered Property to Jewish Communities (EU) 220

'Responsibility to Protect' (R2P) 122, 265, 266
revenge and retribution 54
'reverse colonization' 174
revisionism 155
revolutionary exemplarity 129–133
revolutionary feminism 134
revolutions 35–36, 41, 127–139, 277
rhetorical power 38–39
Rhodes, Cecil 153
rituals 9, 26, 287
Rohingya minorities (Myanmar) 265–266
Roh Moo-hyun 248–249
role models 40, 287
Roller, Matthew 60
Romania 242
Roman Republic 69, 70–71
Roman tyrannicides 62, 69
Rome 60, 229
Roosevelt, Franklin Delano 56
'root paradigms' (Turner) 31
rules 8, 10–11, 13
Russia
  invasion of Ukraine 2022 3–5, 264
  and Serbia 121
Ruys, Tom 110

S

el-Sadat, Anwar 32, 235
  addicted to cameras 244
  assassination 27
  cultivating journalists 243
  'electric shocks' 245
  Feast of Sacrifice 243
  heroic performances 240
  Hero of the Crossing 239, 243, 244
  isolation 240
  October War 1973 243
  and Richard Nixon 248
  visit to Jerusalem 238, 239, 243
same-sex marriage 40
samples 6–7
Sandholtz, Wayne 115, 116
Sarkozy, Nicolas 170
satyagraha (truth force, Gandhi) 51, 52, 55
Saudi Arabia 258
scarcity 244–245
Schauer, Frederick 118
Scheffer, Paul 210
Schelling, Thomas C. 110, 113, 124
Schmelzer, Norbert 204
Schmidt, Brian C. 147
school strike 73–74, 76, 85–86
Schroeder, Paul 277
Scott, James 41
'second marginalization' 136
Segal, Jeffrey A. 112
self-criticism 58

self-interest 112, 152–153
'Self-Narration' (Sima Qian) 93
Seneca Falls Declaration 135
September 9, 1906 protests South Africa 52
September 11 (9/11 attacks) 49, 52, 58
Serbia 121, 226, 266
seriality 183–184
Shakespeare, William 33
Sharman, J. C. 153
Sheldon, Rebekah 76, 79
Shell plc 205
Shilliam, Robbie 130
Shoah *see* Holocaust remembrance
Sikkink, Kathryn 8–9, 115
Sima Qian 92–96, 98–99, 101, 106
single-issue struggles 135
Six Crises (Nixon) 242
Six-Day War (1967) 239, 243
skolia (symposiastic songs) 64–65
slavery 130–132
Sluga, Glenda 277
Smith, Tommie 32
SNP (*Sans Nom Patronymique*) 170
Snyder, Jack 286, 289
social actions 37–38
social change 12
social conventions 116
social hierarchies 151–154
social media 34, 106
social movement actors 31, 32
social movement exemplarity 26–27
social order 13
social proof 269
social sciences 267, 268
solidarity 31, 135–137
Song literati 96
South Africa 40
  Asiatic Registration Act 1906 49–51
  Constitution 55
South Korea 249, 252
  see also Korea
sovereign equality 154
'space of appearance' (Arendt) 292
Spaeth, Harold J. 112
speaking truth to power 273
Der Spiegel 29
spiral model of exemplarity 24–36, *25*
Sputnik 238
Srebrenica massacre (1995) 212
'Standard of Civilization' 16, 153–154, 156
stare decisis 115, 117, 118
Star Trek 239
stigmatization 153, 154, 155–156
Stockholm 73
Stockholm Forum on the Holocaust 2000 220
Stockholm Task Force 221
Stora, Benjamin 164, 172, 176

Stowe, Harriet Beecher 268
Strathern, Marilyn 187
Subotić, Jelena 34, 289
suicide 101–103
'Sunshine Policy' (North and South Korea) 248
superior moral stance 205–208
Surinam 205
Susa 66, 68
'sustainable development' 77
Sutton, Donald 98
Sweden 5, 35, 220
symbolic power 38
Syrian civil war 265
Sznaider, Natan 219

T

Taiwan 97
Takei, George 40
taking a knee 27–28, 29, 34, 37
 see also Kniefall (Brandt kneeling)
Talcahuano, Chile 184–185, 191, 193
Tallinn, Estonia 227
Teegarden, David A. 68–69
De Telegraaf 203
television 243–244
template 14, 17, 31, 36, 40, 42, 61, 67, 71, 222, 228, 282, 288
temporal phenomena 76
'theatre state' (Geertz) 26
Theory of International Politics (Waltz) 147
'Third Way' 210
Third World feminism 136
Thompson, Bennie 287
Thorbecke, Johan Rudolf 211
threshold crossings 238–239, 240–242, 241, 247, 257–258
Thukydides 67
Thunberg, Greta 27, 73–86, 289
 address to Houses of Parliament 2019 76–77, 81
 address to UN Climate Action Summit 2019 82, 84
 affective mode of performance 84–85
 embodied reality 82
 evocation of emotions (fear, panic, rejection of hope) 83–84
 exemplary performance 75
 'fire' metaphor 83
 historical and family time 77–78
 imagining the future 76–77, 79–80, 84–85
 life-scripted narratives 80
 multiscalar 189
 No One Is Too Small to Make a Difference 75
 school strike 73, 85–86
 TED Talk 2018 78
 as a time-traveler 82
 World Economic Forum in 2019 83

Thunder God 104, 105
De Tijd 204–205
Time 77–78
 family 77–78
 historical 77
 individual 77–78
 inversion of normal 14–15
 generational 78
 linear 78
 looped 84
Time Magazine 56
Timmermans, Frans 202
totalitarianism 227–228, 264, 288
Toumi, Samir 170–171
'Tower of Faces' 227
'tragedy to farce' trajectory 248
Transformation of European Politics (Schroeder) 277
transnational collective action 129, 135, 138
transnational feminism 136, 138
transnational social movements (TSM) 134, 136, 137
Transvaal, South Africa 49–51
Trilford, Brittany 82
Troilus and Cressida (Shakespeare) 33
Tromp, Hylke 204
Trouillot, Michel-Rolph 131, 132, 133
Truman Administration 264
Trump, Donald J. 235, 245–248, 251–252, 254, 291–292
Truth, Sojourner 135–136
Tuareg people 170
Tu Fei 102–103
Turkey 155–157
Turner, Victor 31
tyrannicides 60–71
 Athens 61–69
 Rome 69
Tyrant-Slayers statue groups 66
tyrants (tyrannoi) 60–61

U

Ukraine 3–5, 32, 264
Uncle Tom's Cabin (Stowe) 268
unexampled actions ('sanza esempio', Machiavelli) 33, 236
United Arab Emirates (UAE) 254–258
United Kingdom (UK), Aid Strategy (2015) 182
United Nations (UN)
 UN Charter, Article 51 121
 UN Conference on Environment and Development (UNCED, 1992) 82
 UN Conference on Sustainable Development (Rio+20, 2012) 82
 UN Development Program (UNDP) 185
 UN General Assembly (2019) 252
United States Holocaust Memorial Museum 227

United States (US)
  antiracist struggles 133
  civil rights movement 41, 52
  Democratic Party 210
  Department of State 36
  'moonshot' ventures 237–238, 239
  NSC-68 defense doctrine 264
  same-sex marriage 40
  slave and race codes 132
  and Soviet rivalry 237–238
  Supreme Court 112
untouchability 54
upward mobility 151
'user'-driven programing 182
USSR 154
Uyl, Joop den 202, 205–206, *207*

V

vaccinations 40
Veblen, Thorstein 33
veneration 96–98
Verdier, Pierre-Hugues 114, 123
Vergangenheitsbewältigung 219
Verkuyl, Johannes 204
Vick, Brian 275, 277
victimhood and victimization 17, 189, 218–231
Vietnam 35
Vietnam War 264
Villa Torlonia, Rome 229
Vilnius, Lithuania 227–228
violent extremism 36
visual representations 10
Voeten, Erik 114, 123
Vollenhoven, Cornelis van 211
Vorbild 25

W

Wadia, Guillaume 231, 288, 289
Walesa, Lech 52
Wallace, Ben 264
Walters, Barbara 243
Waltz, Kenneth 147
Wang Guangfa 105
Wang Shizhen 99–100
Warsaw Ghetto 23, 223–224
war trophies 68
The Washington Post 4
Watanabe, Chika 30, 231, 290, 291
Watkins, Gloria (bell hooks) 136

Weibo *104*, 106–107
Weimar Republic 31–32
Wellenstein, Edmund 209
Wen of Zhou, King 92–95, 101
'Western World'/'the West' 4–5, 57–58, 152–158, 221–222, 247n8
Wiesel, Elie 225
Wijk, Rob de 201
Wilders, Geert 210
Wille, Tobias 74, 229–230, 274–275, 278–279, 289
Williams, Raymond 8, 286
women 134, 277
women's rights movements 136–137, 138
Woodward, Bob 245–246
World Antislavery Convention 134, 135
World Health Organization 35
World March of Women 137
World Trade Organization 114
World War I 168, 267
World War II 156
Wuhan 91, 105
Wuhan Diary (Fang) 91–92, 103, 105–106

X

Xerxes, Persian king 66, 68

Y

Yang, Ching Kun 96
Yang Jisheng 98–101
Yan Song 98
The Year 2048 (documentary) 79–80
Yoshida doctrine 156
Young, H. Peyton 113
Yugoslav Communist Party 39
Yugoslavia 121

Z

Zarakol, Ayşe 154, 155, 230–231, 280, 282, 288
Zeitenwende (turning point) 5
Zelensky, Volodymyr 3–5, 27, 32
Zhang Jindong 99
Zhang, Ying 289
Zhong Nanshan 103–105, *104*
Zhong Yuan 106–107
Zhou Baohua 106–107
Zhou Enlai 11, 235
Zhu Xi 94

www.ingramcontent.com/pod-product-compliance
Lightning Source LLC
Chambersburg PA
CBHW051528020426
42333CB00016B/1828